Breaking the Chains of Capitalism

Breaking the Chains of Capitalism
An Evolutionary Journey to True Freedom

By

Marco D'Anna

A
True Freedom Technologies
Publication
U.S.A.

First Edition

True Freedom Technologies

Helping accelerate our transition to a predator free society,
for the benefit and unification of all people as equals!

True Freedom Technologies
9003 Leeds RD.
Kansas City, MO. 64129
United States of America
http://www.truefreedomtechnologies.org

ISBN 978-0-9909570-3-4

Dedication

To all of our ancestors throughout our evolutionary development that have suffered and died adapting to the environmental conditions of our evolving predatory social structures as well as all the people that will continue to be lost until our transition to a global predator free society is complete. And to our future descendants, may they live free of predatory conflicts and experience true freedom and universal prosperity as equals.

Part 1
Breaking the first chain of Capitalism

Part 2
Learning the true nature of Capitalism

Part 3
Our predatory past versus our predator free future

Part 4
Breaking the second chain of Capitalism

Part 5
The TFT social economic structure

Charts and illustrations

Preface

My interest in writing this book and starting this project began with a personal challenge to answer a question. I wanted to know what primary factor was responsible for the greatest preventable suffering and death throughout the evolutionary development of our species? My hope was to find an answer to this question and see if I could apply some creative thinking and new technologies to help correct the problem. At first I didn't know if a primary factor or root cause could be found or if it was the result of many smaller factors that needed to be dealt with individually. I knew a root cause would produce many symptoms that could be used to identify the primary factor but to find and correct the problem at the source should remain the ultimate goal. I avoided becoming distracted with superficial solutions because I realized if a primary factor could be identified and corrected at the source all of its many symptoms that individually contribute to our suffering and death would fade away as a result. Much like cutting a massive poison ivy vine at its base. Like a vine that has been killing our tree of life for thousands of years, and preventing our species from reaching our full potential. After identifying the primary factor I was looking for, I needed to shear this information with others and offer a solution to help correct the primary factor at its source. The plan of action outlined in this book is intended to be a comprehensive framework. This framework should be objectively considered with other integrated solutions also capable of supporting a predator free society.

To answer my question above many areas of human development needed to be objectively considered to allow valid conclusions to be formed. I purposely avoided making conclusions based on previously formed opinions and chose to use factual source information where possible to form an out-of-the-box perspective not constrained by conventional thinking. I monitor and deliberately minimize any emotional, cultural or personal influences that may contribute to the conclusions in this book and rely heavily on widely accepted historical, scientific and empirical facts. I wanted the factual data itself to create an image that would become clearer over time as one fact was linked to another. Like making a fact puzzle once the pieces were connected I could stand back and see what the picture revealed. I knew this picture would reveal the worst and the best qualities our species is capable of and even some things I may not want to accept, but the most important thing is that the information would be factually accurate so a viable root cause could be discovered. I also realized denying factual knowledge to perpetuate a conditioned subjective believe could only hinder or prevent the discovery of a root cause and implementing the solutions needed to correct it. Since the primary objective is to reduce preventable suffering and death any subjective belief or reality that justifies and allows the exploitation of the many to serve the interests of the few, will be considered part of the problem to be corrected.

Another motivation for starting this project was the frequent reminder of the preventable loss of life and property by an infrastructure designed to fail under known seasonal conditions and all forms of natural and man-made disasters. I decided to offer for consideration a technical infrastructure capable of providing secure basic survival necessities and energy independence resistant to or unaffected by these conditions. As the picture in my fact puzzle was becoming clearer I could see what was necessary to correct the primary factor and prevent its many symptoms from recurring. A technical infrastructure providing families basic survival necessities at the smart home and community level must be integrated with a new predator free social structure to provide a viable comprehensive solution.

In a way this book describes my own personal intellectual evolutionary development from a child willing to believe in any subjective reality like Santa Claus, into an adult wanting to use factual knowledge to form opinions, make decisions and take actions. It is my hope that readers of this book can use my discoveries in life to help them form stronger objective realities.

Acknowledgment

Of all the many influences and people in my life that led to my desire and ability to create this book special acknowledgment must go to my uncle Robert D'Anna and my mother Jo Ann Greer for playing a crucial role in allowing me the freedom and peace of mind to grow as an individual and maximize my potential contribution to society. It is through their love and patience this book was made possible. I also would like to acknowledge my father Ronald Greer for his influence on my technical curiosity and philosophical imagination.

I feel our forefathers must be acknowledged for their wisdom in giving all Americans citizens the right to free speech, the separation of church and state and the ability to hold free and fair elections. Our forefathers have given "We the people" of America the strongest opportunity for our species to achieve true freedom and lead the world into the next phase of our intellectual evolutionary development.

Special note

If possible this book should be read sequentially from start to finish to provide the best comprehension of the concepts discussed. I have found that the way you present information can be just as important as the knowledge itself when communicating concepts to others. I try to introduce foundational information in the beginning of the book that will allow for a greater understanding of the concepts that follow. Depending on our age and exposure to factual knowledge throughout our lives our perspectives on the concepts in this book will vary widely. Some concepts discussed will seem well known and obvious to some readers while many others will be completely unaware of this knowledge or worse conditioned to reject it without consideration. In an effort to make the concepts in this book easier to understand for the widest possible segment of our population, I try to start with black-and-white examples that are more universally understood and accepted to help readers build a foundation of knowledge making it easier to comprehend the grayer subjects discussed later.

This book is loosely divided into two sections. The first part of the book addresses the primary factor responsible for the greatest preventable suffering and death throughout our evolutionary development including the ongoing tragedies that face our world today, while the second half of the book concentrates on the social and technological solutions to correct the problem. Because our species is rapidly reaching that intellectual tipping point in our evolutionary development where our capitalistic exploitation is becoming known many well-informed authors are describing in detail the disadvantages of living in our advanced predatory social structure. However I also noticed a surprisingly ominous silence and absence of discussion regarding many of the primary concepts in this book. I hope a discussion on these concepts will provide a new perspective allowing people to make an informed decision to help end our predatory social structure and make the peaceful transition to a self-replicating technologically advanced predator free society. And the coolest thing of all is we the people have the power to make this happen right now, so what are we waiting for?

Introduction

A discovery process was made to find the primary factor responsible for the most preventable suffering and death throughout the evolutionary development of our species. This primary factor was identified as our naturally occurring predatory survival instincts encoded in our genetic memory. These survival instincts are reinforced and perpetuated by advanced predatory social economic structures like Capitalism. Our natural adaptation to environmental conditions creates a generational cycle of predatory conflicts and forced competition for survival.

This book describes how our species is undergoing a natural evolutionary transition from creatures still under the control of our predatory instincts into enlightened beings capable of creating technically advanced societies free of social economic competition for survival. It was further discovered that the primary factor was also preventing our natural transition to a predator free society and our species from entering the next phase of our intellectual evolutionary development.

Identifying a root cause is a crucial first step but the real trick is how to eliminate all the symptoms at their source before their corrupting influence can form social behaviors. It was determined that providing the environmental conditions of a predator free society would reverse the detrimental effects of capitalistic poverty while increasing health, education, production and quality of life.

This book offers for consideration an integrated social economic structure and technical solution capable of ending the predatory evolution of our species. The integrated solution in this book describes the creation of an Automated Community Infrastructure capable of supporting a self-replicating technically advanced predator free society. The solution also offers exponential growth of a global network allowing more families to end their predatory competition for survival and start helping others wanting to make the same transition.

Part 1: Breaking the first chain of Capitalism

1. Dream big and dare to fail

When we set out to accomplish great things in life we should first expect to experience some failures along the way. Before I learned this knowledge and could comprehend it's meaning, I allowed my failures to trouble me. As a child in school I had a learning disability that greatly diminished my ability to read, write, spell and solve math problems. As fate would have it, my struggle to compete academically with other children was so emotionally painful I stopped trying. My body may have been in school but my mind was miles away as I excelled to the top of my class at daydreaming. Luckily I wasn't completely devoid of skills or talent and was able to take pride in my artistic and creative abilities. Using the technique of trial and error I failed many times before succeeding at works of art that other children and adults were in awe of. It wasn't until much later in life that I heard this quote by the great explorer Norman Vaughan, he said, "Dream big and dare to fail" it was then that I realized this was the way I had lived my entire adult life. It was a liberating feeling to have such a great man validate with his eloquent words a philosophy that I had aspired to.

How do we define our dreams, successes and failures within the environmental conditions of our predatory social structure? Some religions and philosophies may teach the wisdom of equality and compassion for others. They may explain that the true value or measure of a person's life is not the level of individual power and control they are able to attain over others but instead the contributions they make to society as a whole and its ability to increase the quality of life for all people. However the environmental influences of our predatory social economic structure and the need to compete against one another for our survival define our dreams and how we value other people's lives. By ending our predatory existence and creating the environmental conditions of a predator free society our dreams and motivations can focus on increasing the health and happiness of all people and eliminating the competitive need for individual accumulation of wealth and power. The more we know about how our environmental influences shape our dreams and ambitions the better intellectual control we will have over how many people they will benefit.

Something else I learned along the way is some of the greatest lessons in life can be found by observing nature. Among my first children were a brindle pit bull and a black Labrador. Like many brothers they had different personalities and physical attributes, but the one thing they shared in common was their joy of chasing and retrieving a ball. As they grew to adulthood it became apparent that the intensity and physical ability of my pit bull always seem to allow him to reach the ball before my Labrador. Even though my Labrador was always about a dogs length behind his spirit of competition was still strong. Over the years my Labrador's frustration became more apparent as he never seem to win this competition. What fascinated me most about this observation was how his frustration manifested. My Labrador seemed to accept that he wasn't going to reach the ball first so instead he decided to bite my pit bull's back legs to slow him down and interfere with his success. It wasn't until later in life that I realized this behavior was not unique to dogs. We humans also tend to interfere with the success of others during our competition for survival by telling each other what we can't do or understand, especially when it's something we feel we couldn't do ourselves. Perhaps it's a peculiarity that's universal to all competing life forms but as a validation from another great man this quote by Albert Einstein provided new meaning for me. He said, "Great spirits have always encountered violent opposition from mediocre minds". As I continued my observations of human nature I noticed how true this seems to be.

It is a common misconception that the ability to make intellectual abstract associations between different sources of knowledge must include an understanding of the opinions formed by others that came before us.

It is part of our social conditioning to feel our concepts or conclusions cannot be valid without a formal education that comes from attending an esteemed college and attaining a certification requiring thousands of dollars in student loans. Since our social structure allows intellectual deceptions as a competitive tool to use against others, the actual knowledge becomes less important than the paperwork and degrees employers have been conditioned to value most. To form new and unique solutions to long unresolved problems may requires us to use our imagination and our ability to develop concepts outside the box of conventional thinking. It is true that having a good teacher or mentor that can explain complicated concepts or procedures can greatly accelerate the learning process. However we should never allow the pressures of social conformity, the prejudice of others or their inability to comprehend our concepts, prevent us from offering a positive vision for our future. We would have never achieved controlled flight, put men on the moon or had the audacity to ask, what is the meaning of life, if as a species we did not dream big and dare to fail. Above all we can never allow the excessive greed and lack of compassion from the very few continue to prevent the salvation of the many or the positive evolutionary development of our entire species.

I have a fair understanding of the difficulties involved in accomplishing my dream. As far as dreams go, this one is a whopper. I know the psychological conditioning for many adults will be to strong to allow the consideration of any new factual knowledge or concepts contrary to their subjective beliefs and that it will take future generations to fully accomplish my dream. And that the reallocation of our national wealth and resources will be necessary to accomplish the rapid expansion of a predator free social infrastructure providing the opportunity for all people to experience true freedom and prosperity. I also know the ruling class top predators of Capitalism that benefit most from our predatory social structure will continue to invest billions of dollars to prevent our transition to a predator free society and my dream from coming true. But should I allow all these things to prevent me from trying to accomplish my dream, I think not. I would rather die trying than to die with the knowledge I could have made a positive difference in many lives if only I found the courage and determination

to establish a predator free society is shared among more of the population, a new phase in our intellectual evolutionary development will begin allowing the future of our species to be determined by we the people and not by the elite top predators of Capitalism. As a variation of one of my favorite quotes from a poem by Alfred Lord Tennyson "'Tis better to have loved and lost than never to have loved at all", I feel it is better to have tried and failed than to have never tried at all. So in that spirit I write this book, and attempt to accelerate our intellectual evolutionary transition to a predator free society.

2. Taking control of our decisions and actions

The first step in breaking our chains of Capitalism and achieving true freedom is to understand our decision-making process and how it is used to manipulate our actions. This chain of Capitalism is the most elusive and difficult to break, because it cannot be seen or touched directly and its existence is far easier to deny than to understand and correct. It is the denial of its existence and our inability to understand the underlying principles of how it controls our actions that has allowed its use for thousands of years throughout our predatory social evolution. The stronger our denial is about its existence the greater our overconfidence becomes making us even more vulnerable to this form of intellectual manipulation and exploitation. The architects of Capitalism did not create this chain but instead naturally incorporated it and expanded its use as our predatory social structure became more technologically advanced. It has been a long and tragic journey for our species to finely arrive at this point in our evolutionary development where it is possible to understand and acknowledge the existence of this form of psychological manipulation. Our acceptance of its existence makes it more visible and tangible so we can intellectually analyze and understand the power of its control. In this way we will finally break the bonds of this chain and truly free ourselves of this form of predatory control and manipulation.

To get the best understanding of how our decision-making process works will need to travel back in time to a point in our evolutionary development before our intellectual survival trait made us the dominant species on this planet. For over 99% of our evolutionary development all of our decisions for survival were made without the benefit of knowledge or intelligence. In fact modern day human children deprived of all education or intellectual stimulation will revert back to this point in our evolutionary development. So what is this mysterious force that has dominated our decision-making process throughout our evolutionary development and that we must continue to rely on in the absence of knowledge? The short answer is, our biology or genetics. The longer answer is our hardwired survival instincts encoded in our genetic memory. The actions these survival instincts produce are more like involuntary subconscious reactions to an environmental stimulus than they are intellectual decisions and this is what makes them so attractive for the ruling class top predators of Capitalism to use as a predatory tool for the manipulation and exploitation of their working class prey.

When we encounter strong positive or negative environmental conditions it starts an involuntary biochemical chain reaction in our bodies and more to the point in our minds. These chain reactions are part of our hardwired genetics and help us survive more efficiently in a primitive predatory social structure. These biochemical chain reactions perform their functions well by preparing our bodies for a predatory attack or defense. More commonly referred to as the fight or flight response. The problem is these chemical reactions also inhibit our ability for higher cognitive thought processes like making objective intellectual decisions based on factual knowledge. In other words this process make us dumber and less able to make rational decisions or defend ourselves against intellectual predatory attacks to control our actions. For example when a child in school sees a bully they know wants to do them harm, their bodies involuntarily and subconsciously prepare for a predatory attack and their ability to concentrate on reading, writing and math skills will diminish. Or for example when an employee gets angry with their boss for abusing their position of power they will be less able to perform complex computer skills. Or even when populations of people are systematically deprived of an education, healthcare and basic survival necessities for generations they become less capable of peacefully integrating and contributing to any technically advanced society.

An environmental stimulus offering the potential for food, sex, shelter or economic success triggers our bodies to start creating a feel-good drug. Like artificial feel-good drugs we take for recreation they can also become destructively addictive controlling the decisions we make and the actions we take. In fact our addiction to food and sex is built-in to our genetic memories as two of strongest hardwired survival instincts. Imagine for a moment a species not hardwired to crave food and sex it would starve to death and last one generation before becoming extinct. It's not the actions themselves that we crave its our hardwired genetics rewarding us with a chemical reaction and production of this feel-good drug for doing what is necessary to survive. This process of course happens with non-intelligent creatures as well, just as it did with us for millions of years before we developed our intellectual survival trait. People with food and sex addictions struggle most to control the power of these hardwired survival instincts and the influence they have on our decision-making process.

Have you ever heard the expression "it seemed like a good idea at the time"? This is because the environmental conditions that made it seem like a good idea at the time influenced our decision-making process by triggering a hardwired survival instinct blocking our ability for more rational thought. Later when that environmental condition has less influence and we're allowed to gain more knowledge and intellectual control over our decisions, we often realize that good idea was not so great after all. For example imagine you and a group of friends decided to pick up some beers and go to a remote swimming hole for a day of sun and fun. This swimming hole is known for its natural cliffs that offer some convenient diving platforms for a little added excitement. After a few beers and some peer pressure you decide to jump off a higher cliff to impress your friends. Not realizing jumping off a higher cliff means going deeper in the water you hit the bottom of the swimming hole and break your leg. Even without the alcohol the peer pressure and desire to impress others would still have compromised your decision-making process by triggering a survival instinct to increase your social status, predatory prowess and desire to attract a mate. The alcohol and other drugs can compound the problem because they have a similar effect on our brains by limiting our intellectual ability for rational thought and control over our hardwired instincts.

Just being human makes us vulnerable to our hardwired survival instincts and the control they have to dominate our intellectual survival trait. In a social structure that uses intellectual competition as a primary means for survival it's easy to see how controlling others decision-making process provides the greatest opportunities for manipulation and capitalist exploitation. After all the best forms of predatory exploitation are the ones where the prey is convinced it is in their best interest, is part of an accepted way of life or is completely unaware of the process. The obvious advantage of this type of predatory technique is that the prey can be repeatedly exploited for months, years or even generations until they become intellectually aware of the process used against them. You may think this form of stealth exploitation is unique to only intellectual species like us humans but there are other creatures that have naturally developed this skill as the most efficient means of survival in their predatory social structure. The vampire bat may not have the intelligence to manipulate their own species decision-making process but like us humans their advanced predatory skills allow the stealth exploitation of their prey to continue for many years or even generations. When we allow ourselves to objectively consider the big picture it's pretty humbling to realize that with all of our advanced technologies our intellectual social development has still not evolved beyond using stealth predatory behavior against one another as a means of survival.

Because we humans have developed our intellectual survival trait to a point where we have the tools and technologies to dominate all other species and even alter global environmental conditions we tend to give ourselves far more credit than we deserve. The expression knowing just enough to be dangerous comes to mind. This giant evolutionary leap of technological domination is a little like giving a child a loaded gun to play with before he achieves the intellectual and social maturity to understand it can kill him. After all, our intellectual development is still in its evolutionary infancy as a species, made more evident by our perpetuation of a predatory social structure used by non-intelligent life forms. Collectively our species is far more under the control of our hardwired survival instincts producing involuntary reactions to our environmental conditions than we are able to make informed decisions based on the intellectual consideration of factual knowledge. Especially when we don't have easy access to the factual knowledge we need to develop our intellectual skills and predatory defenses.

Of course our individual intellectual development can swing from one extreme to the other based primarily on the families and environmental conditions we are born into. For example if you are a child born into an isolated lost tribe family without exposure to the last few thousand years of scientific developments. Your intellectual skills may only consist of the best way to blow dart a monkey from a tree, how to build a grass hut that stays drier during a tropical storm or what trees and plants have the best medicinal value. On the other extreme you may have been born into a technologically advanced family of astronauts and engineers with the ambition to be one of the first people to robotically discover life on another planet or moon. Even more interesting is both of these extremes could exist at the same time during our species evolutionary development. It seems apparent that if these children were switched at birth allowing them to adapt to their new environmental conditions their intellectual development, ambitions and perspective on life would also be reversed. This made me wonder what intellectual evolutionary leaps would be possible if only we could provide these advanced environmental conditions for all our people.

We know the decisions we make and the actions we take are a result of two often-competing primary factors. On one hand we have millions of years of survival instincts encoded in our genetic memory that produce involuntary and subconscious reactions to environmental stimulus. On the other hand we have our emerging intellectual survival trait requiring factual knowledge to produce valid decisions giving us better control over our hardwired instincts. I know we all want to feel like we have total and absolute intellectual control over our hardwired predatory and other survival instincts, but let's face it we don't. Even with the knowledge necessary to help intellectually control this process the environmental conditions of our predatory social structure would effectively reverse any progress. This is why it's so imperative that we also break the second chain of Capitalism and provided the environmental conditions of a predator free social structure.

You may be wondering how do we help others to intellectually control their hardwired survival instincts and make an informed decision to end our predatory social structure. The fact is we have already started to correct this social dysfunction by sharing the knowledge necessary to make that informed decision. You have already started yourself by reading this book and making a deliberate decision to have better intellectual control over the actions you take. But perhaps more to the point is how do we use that intellectual control and knowledge of the process to develop predatory defenses minimizing our vulnerability to capitalist exploitation. Once you understand the underlying principles of a predatory social structure and how it requires intellectual competition for survival, the psychological manipulation techniques used for our capitalistic exploitation seem to naturally become more obvious. I guess it's like getting over the learning curve on any subject at first it seems impossibly complicated and then it gets easier and easier until it becomes a commonplace activity of our daily routines. The difference being this subject can allow you to have better control over all your decisions and to better recognize an intellectual predatory attack before damage is done.

What makes us more vulnerable to intellectual predatory attacks and other forms of capitalistic exploitation that manipulate our decision-making process? The short answer is the lack of knowledge necessary to form a good predatory defense. The longer answer is the environmental conditions of a predatory social structure that intentionally limits and distorts the knowledge we need to become aware of our systematic exploitation. I know before the transition to a predator free society is complete there will continue to be many forms of intellectual attacks, but because they all have a common denominator that make them possible the solution for one will be effective on others as well. Acquiring factual knowledge really is the key to formulating effective predatory defenses it's like the difference between stealing candy from a baby and wrestling a fresh kill away from a hungry Tiger. All social levels of human predators from the impoverished street hustlers to the ruling class elite controlling entire counties, know they must prevent their prey from becoming intellectually enlightened to the process used to perpetuate their exploitation. Throughout our predatory social evolution this is how the working class prey have been kept subservient by giving them a limited choice between bad and worse. I guess it's true, factual knowledge really can set you free and more importantly allow an entire species to break their hardwired predatory instincts and take intellectual control of our future.

In addition to limiting our factual knowledge and preventing our natural intellectual evolution. The other common denominator for predatory attacks is to manipulate our decision-making process by provoking a survival trait response limiting our ability for rational thought. It's a very effective two-pronged attack using our biology and lack of knowledge against us as a management tool to efficiently exploit an unsuspecting working class population. I guess the important thing to remember is even though it may seem difficult to intellectually control our hardwired survival instincts and make the evolutionary leap to a predator free society. We are already in the early transitional phase right now. By helping others gain more objective and rational control over their decision-making process we are accelerating our transition to a predator free society one person that time. By the time you're done reading this book you should have all the knowledge necessary to recognize predatory attempts to manipulate your decision-making process. You will understand the importance of forming your opinions based on the objective consideration of factual knowledge instead of an induced emotional response from a hardwired survival instinct.

Remember it's a learning process and it doesn't matter at what level you start only that you understand the importance of the knowledge and use it to help form an objective reality. Even more important is being able to use our intellectual survival trait to evolve out of our predatory past and start forming creative solutions for a predator free future. This evolutionary transition will take place and I feel strongly we are the generation to start accelerating this process. We won't finish the transition to a global predator free society but our ability to take intellectual control of our hardwired instincts and decision-making process will provide the foundational knowledge for generations to expand upon. And it all starts here with you making a single informed decision to end our predatory social structure and work towards creating a predator free future where all people may benefit from our advancing technologies leading to true equality and the unification of our species.

3. A predators high

The thrill of the hunt and the satisfaction of the kill is hardwired into all of us predatory life forms as one of our most basic survival instincts. We've all experienced the feeling of exhilaration, a rush of adrenaline as our heart races and our senses become heightened waiting for that perfect moment to strike our prey as we slowly reach for the refrigerator door. Ok we may have become somewhat domesticated as a species during our transition from stone tipped spears to intercontinental ballistic missiles but far more dangerous to the world. I started wondering how much the thrill of the hunt and our predatory instincts were preventing our transition to a predator free society. And how this process could be used against us as a tool for social manipulation and capitalistic exploitation.

Some people may feel our predatory instincts are too integrated into our genetic memory to ever hope for the formation of a harmonious peaceful society free of war and conflicts. That somehow it's an aspect of human nature that we cannot transcend or ever be able to consider it part of our evolutionary past. This may be true for lower life forms or even for our species if we're prevented from developing our intellectual survival trait and forced to compete against one another for our survival. The good news is both of these social flaws can be corrected allowing us to continue our natural intellectual evolutionary development. I was thinking there must be something else, some mysterious force of nature that if only we understood better would give us the intellectual control we need to break our predatory social structure.

Have you ever wondered why we are naturally compelled to watch a fight or why the violent competition in our sports events holds such a mysterious attraction? Something I found very interesting that represents one of those fact puzzle pieces, that when connected with other pieces allow us to have a much clearer picture of how things work. I learned that our minds are stimulated in the same areas by watching and hearing an activity as they are by doing the activity. This allows us to satisfy our predatory instincts vicariously through the competition of others. If we are going to gain intellectual control over our survival instincts we will need to know the process involved and why we are compelled to spend so much of our money and time satisfying our visual desire for predatory conflicts and violence. Then I remembered another puzzle piece about how our bodies are biochemically rewarded with feel good drugs when we perform activities that are beneficial to our survival. It's a form of hardwired drug addiction built into our genetic memory to help guide our evolutionary development and keep us from becoming extinct.

It seems we must logically conclude, the thrill of the hunt and the satisfaction of a good meal or even our romantic ambitions are all being controlled by subroutines in our genetic code that determines when we get our drug reward and for what activities. Without the intellectual consideration of factual knowledge, this hardwired drug addiction would have full control over our actions. With a good understanding and ability to manipulate this process, a smart human predator could use this knowledge as a competitive tool to subconsciously control and exploit an unsuspecting population out of billions of dollars. What's that worth to a smart capitalist? It's just the kind of thing a top predator of Capitalism would love to use against their working-class prey, and it just happens to be perfectly legal and socially acceptable within our predatory social structure. It may not be acceptable to the working-class masses but what they don't know... can not only hurt them but also continue to exploit their children for generations.

I'm starting to see why our intellectual survival trait is having such a hard time controlling our hardwired instincts. Our entire species has been addicted to this drug since the beginning of our existence, that's a tough habit to break. At least we're getting a better idea what we're dealing with so we can formulate an effective strategy to gain intellectual control of our evolutionary future. No problem is too big when we allow our intellectual survival trait the factual knowledge it needs to find a solution. In fact just by reading this book you're becoming part of the solution. By increasing your knowledge of the process it helps you gain better intellectual control over your hardwired instincts and collectively this brings our entire species one person closer to achieving a predator free society.

I suppose the real challenge would be how to have our proverbial cake and eat it too. In other words we want enough intellectual control of our hardwired instincts to end our predatory social structure, but at the same time maintain the pleasures in life commonly associated with the good feeling we get with a survival response. Even if we didn't need a responsible level of dopamine reward to maintain healthy and productive lives we wouldn't want to limit our pursuit of happiness. As long as it doesn't become destructive it should be considered an area for exploration to increase our quality of life.

I was just realizing there might be a greater opportunity here, instead of using our dopamine response system to perpetuate our predatory activities and prey on unsuspecting working-class consumers, maybe we could reverse the process to promote a peaceful predator free society. It could be used to promote a predator free lifestyle and encourage positive behavior instead of reinforcing predatory instincts. When we gain intellectual control over our drug reward system it can help accelerate the transition of our motivational paradigm from competition and greed to cooperation and compassion. We can use the same power and force of nature responsible for our predatory suffering and death for thousands of years to accelerate our species into a predator free future and the next phase of our evolutionary development. It's the ultimate lemonade from lemons scenario.

4. How our emotions are used against us

Our emotions are a complex and often mysterious force that can involuntarily take control of our conscious thoughts and physical reactions. Even though our emotions can be categorized from pleasurable to tragic they all have a detrimental effect on our intellectual decision-making process. This is because they all biochemically interfere with our intellectual ability to make objective decisions based on the consideration of factual knowledge. Because our emotions are a manifestation of our hardwired survival instincts responding to an environmental influence or the re-stimulation of a past event they should not be considered a weakness but instead more like a natural part of our genetic makeup. Our objective should not be to suppress our emotions but instead to understand the mechanisms involved so we may deliberately and rationally prevent them from being used against us to manipulate our actions and increase our vulnerability to intellectual predatory attacks. The ability to understand our emotions and gain control over our predatory and other hardwired survival instincts will be one of the greatest achievements in our intellectual evolutionary development. Instead of using our intelligence to manipulate other people's emotions as a predatory tool in our capitalistic competition for survival we will be sharing this knowledge to prevent others from becoming prey to this form of attack and control of our actions.

The top predators of Capitalism are well educated and informed about the best psychological manipulation techniques to use on us working class prey. In our free-market predatory social structure that allows the intellectual manipulation and control of others as a competitive tool for increasing profits, these techniques are used to subconsciously and involuntarily trigger an emotional response followed by predictable reactions. This process is well known by ruling class capitalists and is used very effectively to control entire populations unaware of this knowledge and not yet capable of making an informed decision to prevent this form of predatory attack.

Keep in mind this knowledge can be learned by anyone and like all intellectual defense skills they get better with practice and the more we understand the process. After learning these defense skills, instead of being subconsciously manipulated with the emotions of fear, hate, love, greed etc. you will more than likely be consciously amused at their attempt to control your actions. The anger or other emotions you may feel will be less likely to have their intended effect but instead be used to strengthen your resolve in preventing this predatory action from being used on others not yet aware of this manipulation technique. As this knowledge is shared and the processes is known by more working class people this manipulation technique will be rendered ineffective allowing the first chain of Capitalism to be broken, accelerating our transition to a predator free society and the next phase of our intellectual evolutionary development.

Hopefully at this point in the book you're already passed wondering if we live in a predatory social structure. Or whether other humans will use their intellectual skills as a tool to win our capitalistic competition for survival. Or even whether ruling class top predators will use our emotions against us to limit our intellectual defenses and manipulate our decision-making process. I get the feeling that many readers at one extreme are thinking I know this knowledge and already agree so what's the trick to help prevent our emotional manipulation and control of our actions. While at the other extreme many people are still not convinced that there's anything wrong to correct. If you're environmental conditions have been intellectually isolated to a narrow ideology without the exposure to predatory induced suffering and death you may be under the impression that all is well in the world and no changes need to be made. If you're one of the less fortunate working-class masses desperately competing for years to ensure your family's capitalistic survival, you will have a different perspective. And if you have Internet access with knowledge of political affairs then you're probably already sure there's something wrong but just haven't found an effective solution yet. Whether you're at one of the extremes or somewhere in the middle, I will try to provide the knowledge necessary for you to detect an intellectual predatory attack intended to subconsciously manipulate your emotions and help minimize the control these techniques have on our actions.

The good news is there are effective solutions that will limit and eventually prevent our emotional manipulation allowing us to make more objective decision about our future. The bad news is it won't be as easy as flipping a switch or installing an anti-emotional firewall in our brains to prevent intellectual predatory attacks, although that could save a lot of time. The other bad news is the younger members of our species will continue to be susceptible until they learn the predatory defenses necessary and their environmental conditions become completely predator free. Because intellectual and physical predatory attacks increase or decrease based on the level of competition the working-class masses are subjected to, all induced criminal and social dysfunctions should diminish as the transition to a predator free society takes place. But to get things started we need to help each other understand the information necessary to recognize and avoid intellectual predatory attacks designed to manipulate our emotions, control our actions and convince us to give up our wealth and survival resources to the top predators of Capitalism.

Since the best place to start is at the beginning it always helps to go back in time to win the problem or in this case our vulnerability to emotional manipulation got started. At the most fundamental level we know our predatory defenses and other hardwired instincts were encoded in our genetic memory long before we developed our intellectual survival trait or made the first stone tools. Our hardwired instincts and the involuntary emotional responses they provoke were imperative to our survival throughout our evolutionary development. But now we must use our intelligence and objective consideration of this subject to control the processes and limit our vulnerability to this form of predatory attack. I guess the first and most important thing to understand is without the knowledge and intellectual consideration of how this process works we cannot begin to develop the predatory defenses we need to prevent our emotional exploitation or ultimately make the transition to a predator free society. Allowing us working-class little people to get an education and end our predatory domination has taken on a whole new level of importance for me now that I see it is the primary factor preventing our natural intellectual evolutionary development.

It seems once people find out they have been subconsciously manipulated out of their wealth and survival necessities they instinctively want to learn what's necessary to end their exploitation. Don't let the complexity of the subject discourage you or weaken your resolve to take control of your decision-making process and minimize your vulnerability to intellectual predatory attacks. You're probably already well on the way to understanding the fundamentals necessary to help limit your emotional vulnerability and many of the more technical aspects are not necessary to learn unless you want to study the subject further.

Before we move on let's recap the basics of what we've learned so far. Our emotions are a manifestation of our hardwired survival instincts being triggered by an environmental influence altering our decision-making process and the actions we take. In an advanced predatory social structure like ours that allows intellectual deceptions to be used as a competitive tool to increase capitalistic profits, many of these environmental influences are intentionally induced to control our thoughts and actions. The primary reason this psychological manipulation technique is used on we the people is to make us feel emotionally satisfied with our continued exploitation or at least consider our social structure to be the lesser of many evils.

We know just being human makes us vulnerable to this form a predatory attack and the only defense against it is to empower our intellectual survival trait with the factual knowledge it needs to deliberately make an informed decision to end the exploitation process. Now that we have a better understanding of the basic process used to manipulate our emotions and control our actions we should determine our individual vulnerability. This next step will require something we humans tend to have a lot of difficulty with and that is the ability to objectively self analyze, especially what level of emotional interference we contribute to our intellectual decisions. We humans take a lot of pride in our intellectual control even when we have little to no knowledge of the forces dominating our actions. The difficulty being we need at least enough intellectual control over our hardwired instincts and the emotional interference they generate to be honest with ourselves and objectively analyze our decisions and state of mind.

Our emotions should come with a warning label like mind altering pharmaceutical drugs that say, don't make any important decisions while under their influence. Or maybe if all citizens receive a heads-up meter display that superimposed the level of emotional interference versus the intellectual consideration of factual knowledge, more informed decisions could be made. A product like that would effectively end the emotional manipulation of the working-class resource. I should get R&D working on that. We know decisions based on extreme emotions often end in tragedy and a repeated cycle of violence leading to more suffering and death. On the other hand if we allow our intellectual survival trait access to factual knowledge an informed decision can be made avoiding any negative consequences.

Of course this is not to suggest that factual knowledge cannot be used for evil purposes like extracting billions of dollars from an unsuspecting working-class population. Our evolutionary gift of intelligence is a tool much like a hammer it can be used as a weapon for destruction or it can build shelters and provide an increased quality of life. We are hardwired to adapt to whatever social structure or environmental conditions we find ourselves in but when it forces us to use our intelligence against one another for survival, it's no wonder we're having so many social problems.

What if we could create our own personal meter to show the percentage of emotional interference versus intellectual control we have over the decisions we make and actions we take? An external electronic device analyzing brain wave activity may be in our future but for now we need a virtual meter in our heads that doesn't require batteries and can be with us wherever we go. We need a way to objectively analyze our emotional interference for the different decisions we make in life and how our environmental conditions influence that process. It dawned on me, any decision made in the absence of any knowledge would have 0% intellectual contribution and therefore must rely 100% on emotional responses triggered by our hardwired survival instincts. This gives us our first indicator and a way to calibrate our personal meters.

After we humble our egos and achieve the ability to objectively self analyze our decisions and actions we can honestly ask ourselves how much factual knowledge do we actually have about the subjects we are considering. If for instance you have 0% factual knowledge about a subject you will have no valid intellectual control over the decisions you make about it. This will also make you 100% vulnerable to an intellectual predatory attack to manipulate your emotions and control your actions. Another option would be if you reject all intellectual control and allow someone or something else to make the decisions for your life trusting them to protect you from capitalistic predators. On the other hand your factual knowledge about a subject may exceed all other humans currently alive giving you the highest possible intellectual control over the decisions you make. Once we know the extreme limits of our virtual meter we can begin to objectively evaluate the decisions we make to give us some idea how much intellectual control we have over them, and more importantly our vulnerability to emotional manipulation and capitalistic exploitation.

Since our knowledge about a subject is directly proportional to the intellectual control we can contribute to the decisions we make in that area it can be used to accurately determine our personal meters position. Whether your meter is analog with a needle that swings from one extreme to the other or whether it has a digital percentage readout an honest assessment of the knowledge you have in that area will give you the most valid results. Just as your knowledge will vary from subject to subject so will the emotional interference you will contribute to the decisions you make in that area. Sometimes the emotional interference and lack of intellectual control can be as obvious as a drunken bar fight or as subtle as an increased heart rate. Even subtle emotional reactions not outwardly noticeable can adversely affect our higher cognitive functions and intellectual control over decisions. Using these emotional extremes gives us another indicator to track and calibrate our virtual meter to determine what level of intellectual control we have over our decisions and actions.

Using the indicators of intellectual knowledge and emotional reactions, many areas of capitalistic exploitation can be discovered but by adding the third indicator showing the loss of time, money or labor will provide greater accuracy to our overall meter readings. Since time and money both equal a survival resource, the loss of either are considered the same except for wealthier individuals tend to lose more money while the least fortunate among us may only have time and their lives to lose. Our virtual meter has become a Tricorder with three indicators that can, not only analyze our own vulnerability to emotional manipulation but can also be used to determine others. In fact it may be better to use your new Tricorder knowledge on others first. The primary reason being that when we begin to have an emotional reaction it starts to involuntarily and biochemically cloud our objectivity decreasing the accuracy of our Tricorder. The other problem being that we tend to deny our greatest vulnerabilities to maintain our self-esteem and social status among our peers. Being honest with ourselves can be pretty difficult especially when we have little intellectual control over what we choose to believe. Until we get better at recognizing and minimizing our own emotional interference and achieve more objective control over our decisions and actions the observation of others can help our learning process.

Testing others for their vulnerability to predatory attacks uses the same indicators needed to evaluate our own. You need to approach it somewhat scientifically and find a willing test subject that will answer some questions and preferably lets you analyze their physical response like heart rate while you observe behavioral adjustments indicating an emotional reaction. Attempts to avoid the subject and repeated interruptions to increase your emotional interference and disrupt the analytical process would indicate a reaction. If talking about a subject takes a conversation from calm and rational to emotionally out of control that would strongly indicate the potential for predatory exploitation in that area. For example the subjects of politics and religion seem to provoke an involuntary emotional response in many people. It's no coincidence these two subjects have provided the greatest opportunities for exploitation of the less educated working class people throughout our social predatory development.

One of the most important things in doing a scientific study is to get unaltered non-biased factual data to analyze or else your conclusions will not be as valid. It may be difficult to get factual data from your test subjects because once they know it's a test that will alter their behavior and make the results less accurate. Depending on how well you know your friend or family test subject you may be able to do a stealth analysis to get more accurate results. A double-blind test where you and your subject are unaware of the process would give the most valid and non-biased results but would require more elaborate preparations. We can use our imaginations and find creative ways to get valid data from our test subjects while also learning to monitor and minimize our own emotional interference to different subjects. But the objective will still be the same, to find the level of factual knowledge, emotional interference by their response and money or time lost for all of the most important subjects in an individual's life.

Because all three indicators of your Tricorder tend to vary from subject to subject we can use those variations to create simple profiles. We can then analyze these profiles combining all three indicators for an overall assessment regarding our predatory vulnerability and intellectual control of different subjects. When analyzing profiles there are a few rules of thumb to keep in mind. The higher the factual knowledge reading is about a subject the better. By factual knowledge I mean scientifically verifiable not something someone told you that they heard from someone else or information that is part of a subjective belief that got started thousands of years ago.

A high level of factual knowledge about a subject allows for greater intellectual control over our hardwired survival instincts and the ability to formulate effective predatory defenses. Low factual knowledge reading for a subject means a high vulnerability to intellectual predatory attacks and capitalistic exploitation. The lower the emotional reaction/interference

Future Tricorder/Smart phone app showing our vulnerability to emotional manipulation and capitalistic exploitation

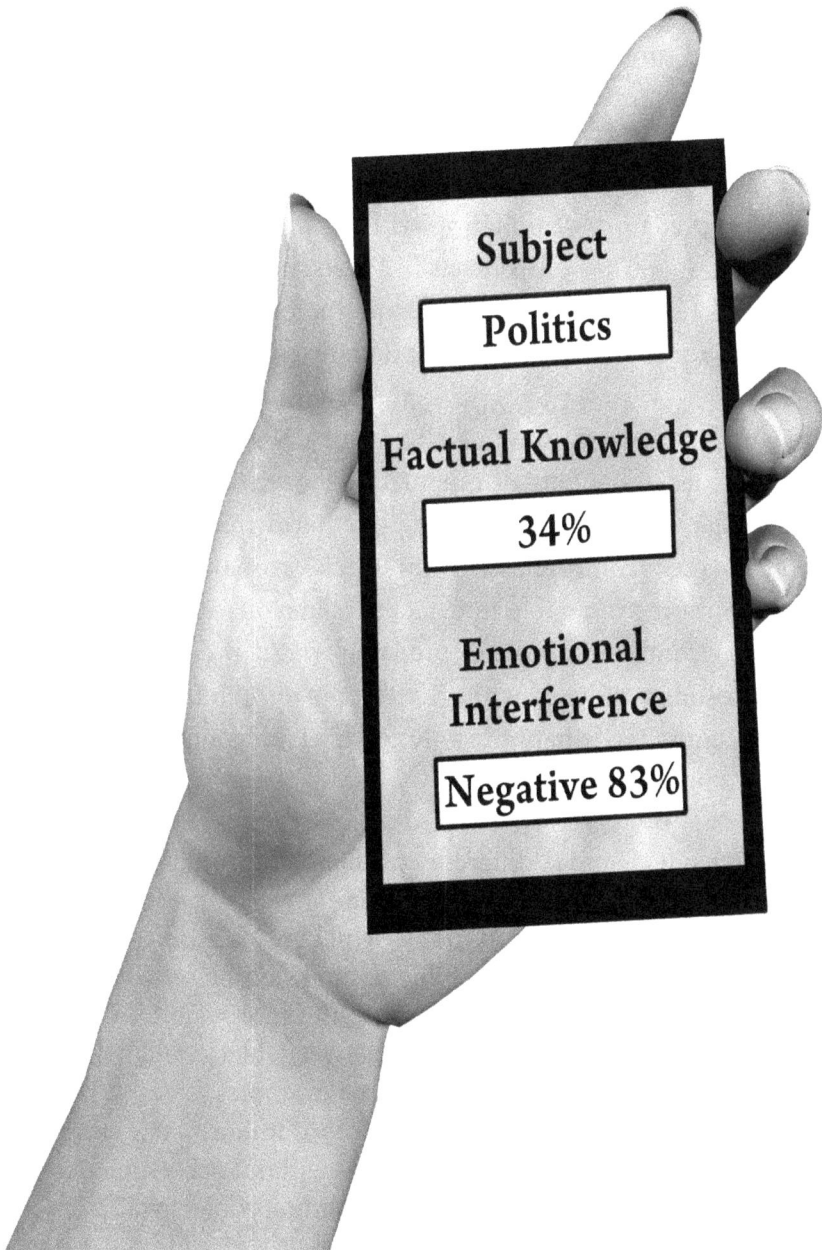

reading is about a subject the better. Low emotional readings about a subject would indicate less interference and greater intellectual control. High emotional reactions about a subject provide greater opportunities for manipulation of the decision-making process and the actions people take.

The last rule of thumb to keep in mind when analyzing profiles is in regards to the third indicator of lost time and money or if you prefer labor and wealth. Since time is often considered money anyway, they will be combined to represent one survival necessity and measured as a percentage of household income. The subjects that produce the greatest negative flow of time and money have the greatest potential for capitalistic exploitation. There can be no predatory exploitation without the negative flow of labor and or wealth from you to someone else. These have always been the two primary survival resources targeted for exploitation by opportunistic top predator looking for low information emotionally compromised prey.

Also if that negative flow of labor and or wealth is to wealthier individuals as a necessary part of our predatory existence, it induces the emotions of anger and fear by triggering our hardwired instinct for self-preservation further compromising our decision-making process and making us even more vulnerable to capitalistic exploitation. Just the kind of psychological conditioning a top predator would prefer to have their working-class resource induced with. That's a powerful form of control but it's all about to come to its natural evolutionary end as our species makes the transition to predator free society.

Let's consider some different profiles and analyze them for vulnerability to predatory attacks and intellectual versus emotional control of our decision-making process. At first we will consider some extreme but generalized profiles with no specific subject. It always helps to understand the extremes of a subject before considering the more subtle differences. Much like it's easier to see the contrast between black and white than between different shades of gray. The extreme examples for each indicator are represented by 0% to 100% for each subject of interest. An example of 0% factual knowledge would be any individual without access to education or perhaps a young person just not familiar with that subject yet.

100% factual knowledge about a subject would be like the top 10 most knowledgeable people in the world at any given point in our evolutionary development. 0% emotional interference would be a very difficult state of mind for an individual to achieve like a deep meditation with no environmental influences to trigger a hardwired survival instinct. 100% positive or negative emotional interference would indicate a complete loss of intellectual control over mind and body. Like a nervous breakdown or the effects of the Jerusalem syndrome would be a good example. 0% loss of time and or money on every subject is practically impossible to achieve in a predatory social structure that requires one or both to survive. 100% lost available time and money on a single subject is also practically impossible even among the most isolated monks in a distant monastery or cult followers dedicating their lives to a new God.

Extreme profile one, subject genetic.
Level of factual knowledge about the subject: 0%
Level of emotional association with subject: 100% positive or negative
Percentage of lost time/money survival necessity: 100%

If this extreme profile were possible it would indicate 100% vulnerability to an intellectual predatory attack intended to manipulate our emotions and control our actions for capitalistic exploitation. It would also indicate 0% intellectual control over any decisions made or actions taken involving this subject leaving only our hardwired survival instincts or the beliefs of others to determine our future.

Extreme profile two, subject generic.
Level of factual knowledge about the subject: 100%
Level of emotional association with subject: 0% neutral
Percentage of lost time/money survival necessity: 0%

If possible this extreme profile would indicate the lowest possible vulnerability to an intellectual predatory attack and no possibility for unknown capitalistic exploitation on this subject. It would also indicate the highest possible intellectual control over our decision-making process producing the most valid conclusions for this subject.

Subject selection for profile analysis can be done in several ways. You can start with the largest loss of time/money survival necessity in your lifestyle or the highest level of emotional association you have with different subjects. You can select one of the more commonly used survival instinct triggers of food, sex, prejudice, self-preservation or direct drug addictions like cigarettes, pharmaceuticals and alcohol. Try to objectively determine if you have any special vulnerability to these subjects. Keep in mind our objective should be to find and analyze subjects in our lives where we are vulnerable to intellectual predatory attacks and attempts to manipulate our emotions for capitalistic exploitation. We want to gain maximum intellectual control over our decision-making process especially with the most important subjects regarding our safety and family's future. These may seem like baby steps on an individual level but the collective intellectual enlightenment of our species will change the world and accelerate our transition to a global predator free society.

There are so many different ways to intellectually and physically exploit other people for profit and with an advanced predatory social structure like Capitalism it can be hard to select a subject to profile or know where to begin. Assuming our primary objective is to reduce preventable suffering and death among our species it seems the logical place to start is with the subjects or products responsible for the greatest contribution. To reduce any external or internal threat to our people and national security we must first gather some factual knowledge to find the primary cause then use our intellectual survival trait to minimize any emotional interference, only then we can formulate a more viable solution.

The World Health Organization and Center for disease control estimates the use of tobacco products are responsible for nearly 6 million deaths worldwide and around 480,000 just in the United States. You may think an addictive drug product responsible for millions of deaths per year would certainly be illegal and the factories run by some evil underground network of criminals. Even if we combine the deaths from all the illegal

American Deaths Put Into Perspective

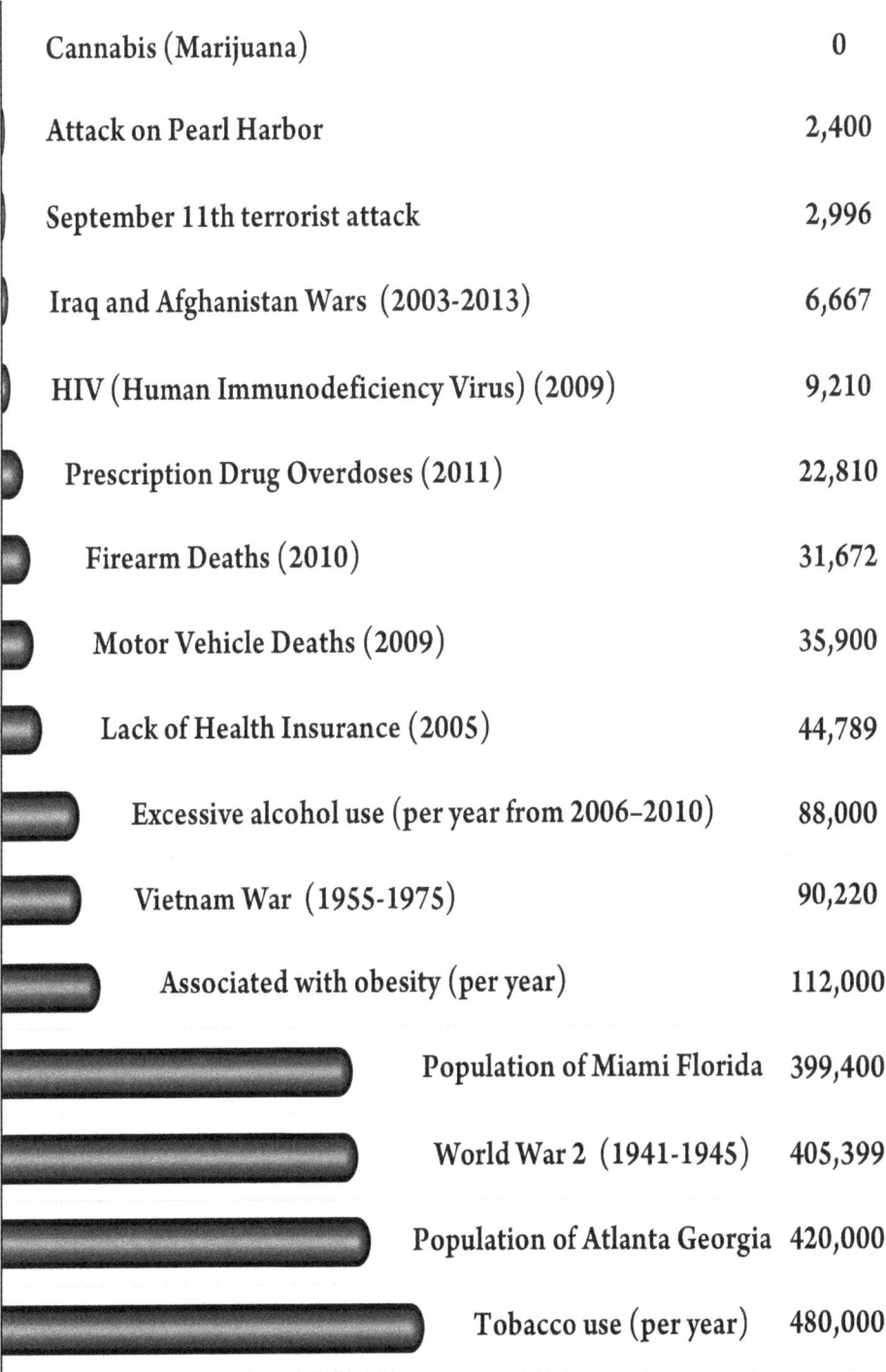

Cannabis (Marijuana)	0
Attack on Pearl Harbor	2,400
September 11th terrorist attack	2,996
Iraq and Afghanistan Wars (2003-2013)	6,667
HIV (Human Immunodeficiency Virus) (2009)	9,210
Prescription Drug Overdoses (2011)	22,810
Firearm Deaths (2010)	31,672
Motor Vehicle Deaths (2009)	35,900
Lack of Health Insurance (2005)	44,789
Excessive alcohol use (per year from 2006–2010)	88,000
Vietnam War (1955-1975)	90,220
Associated with obesity (per year)	112,000
Population of Miami Florida	399,400
World War 2 (1941-1945)	405,399
Population of Atlanta Georgia	420,000
Tobacco use (per year)	480,000

Source: The National Center for Health Statistics (NCHS), United States Centers for Disease Control and Prevention (CDC), National Center for Biotechnology Information (NCBI), United States Department of Defense, United States Census Bureau, Prepared by True Freedom Technologies (TFT)

drugs it only amounts to a very small percentage of the deaths legally allowed under Capitalism for profit. Yet the CEOs of these companies are not hunted down like the head of a drug cartel but instead considered highly successful businessman functioning within the legitimized predatory social economic structure of free-market Capitalism. And I used to think our laws were created to protect we the people not make our exploitation more efficient and profitable for top predators.

To consider 6 million deaths per year to be an acceptable cost of doing business underscores the destructive power of Capitalism and how the social conditioning of our predatory social structure alters our moral values. Drug products that produce strong addictive dependencies manipulate our hardwired biochemical reward system directly and don't need to trigger a survival instinct with an environmental stimulus. The physical dependency to the drug will take control of our decision-making process producing the desired action within a subject/customer, which is to buy more of the product.

Subject profile: the addictive drug product tobacco
Level of factual knowledge about the subject: 20%
Level of emotional association with subject: positive 75% to negative 90%
Percentage of time/money survival necessity: .7% ($323 annually for an average US family)

This profile represents a typical tobacco consumer with a high vulnerability for predatory attack and drug manipulation of their decision-making process. In the more educated countries tobacco customers understand consuming this product is putting their health at risk however once the physical addiction takes hold this chain of Capitalism becomes much more difficult to break. The 20% factual knowledge represents what they know about this subject's dangers suppressed by the emotional interference of the drug addiction.

A positive 75% to negative 90% emotional association is directly related to the level of the addictive drug in the blood stream and the satisfaction or despair it creates. It's the perfect carrot and stick control mechanism to provide the pleasure or pain necessary to manipulate our actions and make us feel emotionally satisfied giving up our wealth. This addictive drug product supercharges our natural pleasure and pain Biosystems hardwired into our genetic memory that are instrumental in shaping the evolutionary development of our species. Except now they're being artificially induced into our social development as a control mechanism to increase the profits for the ruling class few, again at the expense of the working class many, also known as We The People in the United States of America and around the world.

The .7% time/money survival necessity reflects only the amount of money spent on tobacco products by an average American household and not the time away from work and family to satisfy the addiction or any of the transportation costs and lost time acquiring the drug. People with lower incomes and higher addiction levels will clearly suffer more economically from both buying more product and higher healthcare costs. It seems this capitalistic activity is designed to produce high profits for the tobacco and health care industries, create large tax revenues for the ruling class elite to distribute as they see fit, while devastating the working-class people's lives and their ability to keep our country strong and productive.

When I first became aware of how many American citizens are legally allowed to suffer and die to increase capitalistic profits for the few, I had to ask myself even if this preventable epic tragedy could be justified morally, why would this threat to our national security be allowed? What could be more important than the health and safety of our citizens and the future prosperity of our country? Is the need to exploit the working class resource and transfer national wealth to the ruling class elite so important our entire species must suffer the loss of millions?

Exploiting a working-class resource with an addictive drug is one of the more obvious capitalistic opportunities our predatory social structure offers for those wealthy enough to invest in lawmakers willing to legitimized the sale and distribution of these products. The pharmaceutical and alcohol industries all do their best to stay competitive and get the largest consumer market possible for their addictive drugs. Again resulting in far more legitimized suffering and death for capitalistic profits than all the illegal drugs deaths combined. Yet we still waste billions of our tax dollars on the so-called war on drugs. As my fact puzzle became clearer, I was starting to see something vary wrong with this picture.

Most products sold in free-market Capitalism don't get to use a drug addiction to ensure repeat customers. Instead they must manipulate our less rewarding hardwired addictions to food, sex or another survival instinct by providing an environmental stimulus that will produce an emotional response compelling us to buy their products. Because we are conditioned to accept our predatory social structure and the need to compete against one another to buy our survival necessities many opportunities for capitalistic exploitation are used to extract the maximum amount of wealth from the working class resource. We are also conditioned to use our intelligence as a competitive tool to find new and creative ways to exploit the less informed and emotionally compromised members of our society.

By triggering our hardwired addiction to food we are easily convinced to buy and eat more than we need. I don't think the CEOs of food industries want Americans to over eat creating an epidemic of obesity and economic crisis for our national healthcare system. They're just doing what's necessary to stay competitive in our free-market capitalistic social structure. Everyone wants their food products to look its best in advertisements and entice people to buy as much as possible even if it's known to be an unhealthy choice leading to obesity among their customers. Of course after the application of every possible psychological manipulation technique to subconsciously control our decision-making process and compel us to buy their product, we then get to use our freedom of choice and do exactly what they want. Well maybe not exactly what they want, or the epidemic of obesity would be even worse and the food and health care industries would dominate the throne of Capitalism and rule the world.

It occurred to me that we can use the rate of increased obesity as an indicator showing how well we Americans are able to resist the manipulation techniques used to trigger our hardwired addiction to food and the emotional satisfaction it provides. We humans try to use our intellectual survival trait to override our hardwired addictions but it can be difficult when they are targeted for predatory attack and capitalistic exploitation. In addition to fighting our hardwired addiction to food we humans are genetically predisposed to store excess caloric energy when not needed for daily survival. It was and still is a useful autonomic survival trait for populations with unstable food supplies and the potential for mini famines. Even though the least successful capitalistic competitors in this country often go without food and other basic survival necessities most Americans are not likely to suffer famine conditions. And the more sedentary our social structure becomes the more excess energy we store as fat.

It's interesting how one industry makes a profit accelerating our epidemic of obesity spawning whole new diet and weight loss corporations offering the solution for a price. The tobacco and alcohol industries seem to do the same thing by making a profit creating the problem allowing others to make money providing a solution. With free-market Capitalism the problem and solution industry can even be part of the same multinational corporation. It seems like a good business decision to maximize profits and better manage the entire exploitation process. And like a capitalistic dream come true it can all be made perfectly legal in a predatory social structure. This reminds me of the expression "they got us coming and going".

The more I think about it the real winner seems to be our healthcare industry. All three top causes of death in America collectively create a windfall of additional customers for the healthcare industry that would otherwise live healthier and more productive lives. With emergency room healthcare costing thousands of dollars per hour this industry can make huge profits from a working-class resource desperate to survive.

It's ironic how our strength and success as a nation has created one of the greatest threats to our future. We Americans are very fortunate compared to most people in the world. For those capitalistic competitors that can afford the American dream our country truly is the land of plenty. Our access to high calorie food, our genetic predisposition to store excess calories and our predatory social structure that allows the psychological manipulation of the working-class resource have all collectively created the environmental conditions accelerating our epidemic of obesity. Any process, system or form of exploitation that makes the working-class people of a country less healthy and productive weekends that nation and its ability to stay competitive in a global capitalistic marketplace. Our capitalistic need to stay competitive with one another is destroying our nation from the inside out by preying on the very working-class people that make us strong. Remember it's we the people that make this nation strong, not the top predators that prey on us as a resource for capitalistic exploitation.

Let's consider what a subject profile would look like for our hardwired genetic addiction to food. The profiles factual knowledge indicator is not on the subject of food itself but more so on our hardwired addiction to it and how it is used to get us to buy and eat more than we need. The profile focus should always be on how much intellectual control we have over the decisions we make about the subject and how much our emotions are being subconsciously manipulated for capitalistic exploitation. As well as how much of our time/money survival necessity we are compelled, conditioned or forced to give up to stay competitive and or just survive within our advanced predatory social structure.

Subject profile: hardwired genetic addiction to food
Level of factual knowledge about the subject: 10%
Level of emotional association with subject: positive 80% to negative 90%
Percentage of time/money survival necessity: 12% ($6,133 annually for an average US family)

This profile would represent a working-class individual with an average education competing for their survival within our predatory social structure. The low 10% level of factual knowledge does not reflect what they know about food, it's preparation or nutritional value. But instead how well they understand the process controlling our desire to buy and eat more food than we need and how to prevent it from being used against us as a manipulation technique for capitalistic exploitation.

As with the addictive drug products, our emotional association will rise and fall but instead of the active ingredient concentration in our bloodstream controlling our actions it will be the degree of hunger we feel that will modify our behavior. If we have just had an emotionally satisfying meal followed by our hardwired dopamine response biochemically rewarding us for doing what's necessary to survive, then our emotional association would be around 80 % positive. If on the other hand we have been stranded on a desert island for days our hunger could drive our emotions well over 90% to the negative side and make us obsessed with finding and eating food. The amount of time and money we spend acquiring a sufficient level of nutritious food as well as all the extra unhealthy stuff we don't need to buy or eat would include trips to the grocery store and eating out. The money part of this survival necessity would equal about 12% of an average US family income. The percent of time/money survival necessity will vary depending on size of the family and overall income.

The third most prevalent actual cause of death in the United States is the addictive drug product alcohol or more accurately it's over consumption. This over consumption of alcohol produces two distinct results within our predatory social structure, just a few successful capitalists will make billions of dollars in profit annually and around 88,000 American working-class citizens will die. A few ruling class elite may consider this a necessary cost of doing business and staying competitive within the social economic structure of free-market Capitalism while many thousands of working-class citizens must suffer the consequences for their capitalistic success.

Even though alcohol products do not come close to producing the number of predatory deaths caused by tobacco or obesity it uses the primary motivational triggers from each product. Alcohol is kind of a hybrid product using addictive drug properties like found in tobacco and it triggers the emotional satisfaction our bodies naturally produce when consuming food or drink. The level of addiction to alcohol may be weaker than tobacco but the physical side effects produce a loss of hand eye coordination leading to a higher incidence of accidental deaths. Also unlike tobacco it does add calories to our diet, inches to our waistline and hours more to our workouts to prevent obesity.

Another drawback keeping this product from being a better capitalistic success is the more it's consumed the less intellectual and physical control people have over their professional and family activities leading to a direct breakdown in any social structure. It's a rather remarkable achievement to condition a population of people to pay for our own chemically induced suppression of our intellectual predatory defenses increasing our vulnerability to multiple forms of capitalistic exploitation.

Subject profile: the addictive drug/ product alcohol
Level of factual knowledge about the subject: 10%
Level of emotional association with subject: positive 60% to negative 80%
Percentage of time/money survival necessity: .9% ($457 annually for an average US family)

This profile seems typical for a recreational alcoholic consumer from America except for the 80% negative emotional association would indicate the withdrawal symptoms from an addicted user. The 10% level of factual knowledge does not reflect the history, composition or manufacturing of alcoholic beverages but instead what effects this product has on our decision-making process and how vulnerable it makes us to capitalistic exploitation. The emotional association swing from positive to negative indicates the classic reward and punishment motivation and manipulation technique produced from an addictive drug product.

We feel the positive emotional reinforcement or high from buying and using the addictive drug. Without the drug we feel the negative motivation from the physical and mental withdrawals urging us to repeat the process trying to maintain that elusive level of euphoria. This reminds me of an expression I heard Sinbad the sailor share with one of his wayward shipments that found himself in an oasis of abundant pleasures. He said to him "If the pleasure remains does it remain a pleasure"? It was one of those questions that seemed to have hidden meaning for me, a riddle that I needed to solve. Consider this, can there be light without the darkness, can the sensation of pleasure exist without first knowing its absence? If a pleasure remains it will become the norm and lose its allure.

Each one of these causes of death in the United States is in some way directly or indirectly related to our predatory social structure and capitalistic competition for survival. Each cause of death is another symptom of the overall disease damaging our nation's health and limiting the intellectual evolutionary development of our species. The Centers for Disease Control and Prevention have declared tobacco use the leading cause of preventable death. I found there was a more fundamental reason making the tobacco industry the deadliest symptom contributing to our preventable suffering and death. It wasn't convincing enough just knowing this level of exploitation and damage to our country was perfectly legal and acceptable under Capitalism. I needed to know how this could be allowed within an educated modern society with a functioning democracy and constitution intended to protect we the people from this kind of exploitation for profit. I started to realize all the other forms of predatory exploitation must also be symptoms of a much older and more fundamental problem.

The more obvious predatory techniques for capitalistic exploitation like drug-induced addiction or triggering a hardwired survival instinct for food or sex are fairly easy to recognize and understand. However there is a more mysterious form of predatory manipulation and control so powerful it can induce mental dysfunctions leading to acts of homicidal violence and suicide. You may wonder what form of evil could have such power over the decisions we make and ultimately the direction in which our species evolves. I had to know the answer because I knew it would help me find the primary factor and root cause responsible for the most preventable suffering and death throughout our evolutionary development. Like other forms of predatory attack, it also seeks to minimize and eliminate any intellectual defenses by creating environmental conditions without the factual knowledge necessary to realize their exploitation. The emotion of love is used to create an option between the warm and fuzzy feeling of its embrace and the cold uncertainty of its absence.

Instead of using an addictive drug to directly manipulate our hardwired reward/punishment control system love is used as a substitute for the strong emotional satisfaction or despair it can produce. I wondered, if our emotions are a manifestation of our hardwired survival instincts subconsciously manipulating or actions into doing what's best to ensure our survival, then what purpose do the feelings of love and sympathy for others serve? The emotions of lust and love can be attributed to a survival instinct related to reproduction and a stronger bond among family members would be a beneficial survival trait for natural selection to choose. It's easy to see the survival disadvantage for a broken family unit unable to show compassion or love for one another and perhaps more to the point share knowledge on how to prevent predatory attacks. Individuals that are physically and or mentally weekend by their environmental conditions become the easiest prey within a predatory social structure. Even modern family units torn apart and stressed out by our capitalistic competition for survival become more vulnerable to all forms of legal and illegal predatory attacks. It's like when many of our abandoned or runaway children becoming prey to street predators looking to improve their social economic status and win the capitalistic game they were conditioned to play.

It seems logical that the emotions of love and sympathy are rooted in a survival instinct that favors a strong family unit and or tribal group. We naturally feel emotionally satisfied among trusted family members or within our tribal group just as we can feel negative emotions when isolated as an individual among strangers. It seems we have a genetic predisposition to subconsciously classify people inside and outside our tribal group as friend or foe. This genetic predisposition to produce subconscious prejudicial decisions based on the emotional interference generated by a hardwired survival instinct can be corrected by the conditioning of a predator free social structure. But instead this hardwired survival instinct is targeted for manipulation using positive and negative emotional triggers to produce predictable behavior and induce conflicts. It's an ancient "divide and conquer" strategy used as a management tool to distract a working-class population from discovering the true source of their exploitation.

This manipulation technique can be 100% effective on an unsuspecting population deprived of factual knowledge and emotionally compromised by competing against one another for their survival. This technique has been well known among the top predators of our species for thousands of years and is still widely successful as a fundamental form of predatory exploitation. To explain how this predatory technique works I'd like to start with an extreme example for easier recognition of the process.

You may have wondered what would possess a seemingly normal person into joining a cult where their leader is universally considered to be their new God. They love and honor their new God/cult leaders with the same level of devotion many other gods have received back through time. We know the believers in cult leaders are sincere because of their willingness to commit acts of self-mutilation, homicide and mass suicides. Of course we the people in America are far too educated to ever be vulnerable to this form of predatory attack that manipulates our emotions and decision-making process into believing something that crazy, right? You may want to finish this book before you answer that question.

It would seem rather obvious that if a group of people has been convinced that their leader is a God, some form of psychological manipulation and predatory exploitation is taking place. The cult leader taking the social position of an almighty top predator and all their many followers become the prey. I guess there are some cult leaders that have made themselves into a benevolent God that truly want the best for their little people instead of a vengeful God that demands total obedience and human sacrifices. It seems like only the more extreme religious leaders get caught after doing things like using their follower's children as sex slaves or convincing their believers to commit mass suicide. . It's easy to recognize the extreme effects of this manipulation technique but the more subtle effects can go unnoticed and become socially acceptable daily ritual.

We can learn a lot about human nature by understanding the process that makes people vulnerable to believing a cult leader is a God and why serving their predatory interests seems like an acceptable way of life. There may be a genetic component created from thousands of years of artificial selection making us more susceptible to this form of predatory attack and manipulation of our emotions. However it seems the environmental conditioning of intellectual isolation and emotional instability is the dominant factor making us vulnerable to believing any charismatic predatory cult leader can be a God.

Subject profile: generic religious cult
Level of factual knowledge about the subject: 5%
Level of emotional association with subject: positive 90% to negative 90%
Percentage of time/money survival necessity: 100%

The 5% factual knowledge does not reflect how much this person knows about their particular religion or the storyline their cult leader uses to make themselves into a God. It does reflect their knowledge about cult psychology, induced subjective realities and how to prevent their vulnerability to this form of predatory attack.

The positive 90% emotional association reflects the level of love and devotion they feel for their cult leader God as is customary with highly devoted followers of any religion. Just as devout followers of major religions are often willing to give their lives to serve their God, so too are the believers in smaller cult religions. Once we understand what makes a person willing to kill and die for a God we can begin to stop the bloodshed that has shaped our social development for thousands of years. The 100% time/money survival necessity reflects a total vow of poverty and physical devotion to their new top predator God. If religious cult leaders can condition their followers to allow their families suffering and death they could certainly convinced them to give up their wealth and dedicate their lives to serving their interests.

Now that we've considered a few symptoms of our predatory social structure and how they are used to manipulate our emotions and control our actions, let's objectively consider our overall capitalistic society and how it naturally creates these advanced forms of exploitation. We humans tend to focus too much on the obvious symptoms of a problem that we can relate to and understand better than the complexities of the overall structure that created them. It also seems to be human nature, to blame individuals or groups of people for our systematic exploitation and not the overall environmental conditions that produced the predatory activity. Identifying our predatory social structure as the underlying systemic problem has proven to be difficult so far but this is changing as our factual knowledge of the subject increases and the conditioning to accept our exploitation becomes less effective.

It's easier if you think of our capitalistic social structure as a movie script where our world governments are the stage and all the people are actors playing the roles we were born into. For the most part we stick to our scripts and simply adapt to whatever role or environmental conditions we were subjected to throughout our formative years. A few of us are fortunate enough to be born into or achieve capitalistic royalty and assume the role and social status of a top predator, while the overwhelming majority of our species naturally become the working-class prey. Our emotional feelings may want to believe our capitalistic social structure serves all people equally and our national heroines and heroes all live happily ever after enjoying the American dream. And that our intellectual consideration of the subject would realize a predatory based societies that forces competition for survival will never be fair for the least fortunate competitors. It's time we the people become the directors of our future movie and not just the actors following a script to repeat our roles as working-class prey. We've always had the power to unite as a people and achieve true freedom and prosperity within a predator free social structure, now we have the knowledge and technology to make this transition a reality. We will become an unstoppable force achieving a peaceful transition to the next phase of our intellectual evolutionary development.

Subject profile: our capitalistic social structure
Level of factual knowledge about the subject: 5%
Level of emotional association with subject: positive 30% to negative 80%
Percentage of time/money survival necessity: 100%

The 5% factual knowledge about this subject reflects an average US citizens understanding of how our government and social economic structure works to serve or exploit we the people. As with all subjects big or small the less factual knowledge we have, the more vulnerable we become to intellectual predatory attacks and capitalistic exploitation. The 30% positive emotional association reflects a working-class families ability to successfully pay the bills and maintain their survival necessities for another month. The 80% negative emotional association reflects working-class families struggling to pay for their necessities and not become one of the many American citizens that don't survive our capitalistic competition.

As with any predatory social structure the higher up on the food chain you are the more you tend to like the system that put you there and therefore tend to have a high positive emotional association as long as profits are up or the paychecks keep coming. Likewise if you're one of the working-class prey conditioned to compete against other people for your survival and the privilege to serve the wealthy elite you'd probably be less enthusiastic about our predatory social structure.

The 100% time/money survival necessity is intended to reflect an average between the people fortunate enough to have a family income that exceeds their capitalistic survival necessities and the families that fall far short of affording the housing, transportation, food and health care costs needed to buy the American dream. The efficiency of our predatory social structure has forced many working-class families into debt or in other words running a perpetual negative balance on their time/money survival necessity for this subject. This social structure forces the least fortunate of our citizens to sacrifice the time they could be spending building strong family bonds instead they're competing for their capitalistic survival and satisfying their employers lust for higher profits. When families are forced into debt it often means compromising a survival necessity, increased stress, higher health-care costs, less productivity and prosperity for our entire country.

It's always been one of the more difficult challenges for the ruling class top predators to manage their working-class resource in a way that maximizes their exploitation while still giving them the illusion of prosperity. It's a delicate balance between patients and greed. A smart top predator would be patient and allow the working-class resource to retain some of the wealth they generate. They would also know a healthier and happier workforce will create greater future returns on their capitalistic investment. A greedy top predator more under the control of their predatory instinct and or induced subjective reality may only consider the present day profits they can make and disregard any future consequences for the working-class resource. Of all the suffering and death the symptoms of our predatory social structure can bring this may be the most dangerous and destructive. To jeopardize our global climate and the future of our species to increase the wealth and power of a few kings of Capitalism illustrates what an intellectual species is capable of just before they make the evolutionary transition to predator free society.

A person living in a predator free social structure will be fully educated about the concepts surrounding their philosophy. A primary objective of this philosophy is to eliminate the intellectual isolation of the working-class resource allowing them to understand their future social structure options. The rate, at which people break the first chain of Capitalism by using their objective reality to make an informed decision will be greater than the rate at which the second chain is broken by expanding the technical infrastructure capable of supporting a predator free society. Because the transition to a predator free society may represent the largest paradigm shift our species has made during our intellectual evolutionary development it can be difficult to predict a subject profile to analyze and compare with our current capitalistic social structure.

Subject profile: a predator free social structure
Level of factual knowledge about the subject: 90%
Level of emotional association with subject: positive 80% to negative 10%
Percentage of time/money survival necessity: 0% to 60%

The 90% factual knowledge about this subject would reflect an individual familiar with the concepts in this book and with a high degree of intellectual control over their hardwired instincts and decision-making process. This individual will have already broken the first chain of Capitalism gaining objective control over their reality minimizing their vulnerability to all forms of intellectual predatory attacks. The 80% positive emotional association with this subject would represent an individual experiencing true freedom without the need for predatory competition against other members in their community.

Even though a high positive or negative emotional association with a subject would traditionally be considered a predatory weakness and target for capitalistic exploitation, the individual's knowledge of the process would render this technique less effective. A positive emotional association with this subject may also come from the knowledge that their contribution of labor and creative skills will be part of a comprehensive solution to increase the equality and prosperity for all people, instead of helping to accelerate our predatory exploitation.

The 10% negative emotional association with this subject may reflect the burden that often comes with new knowledge. Realizing all the preventable suffering and death in our past and feeling a profound sadness about our inability to correct this social evolutionary dysfunction before many more are lost. It may also reflect a sense of predatory withdrawal left over from millions of years of evolutionary development. We will need to create some non-predatory recreational substitutes to satisfy our hardwired addictions because exploiting other people will no longer be necessary for our survival or considered an acceptable social activity.

The intellectually stimulating environmental conditions of a technically advanced society may provide some anxious moments at first until people become more acclimated and comfortable with their surroundings. There will also be unexpected challenges working out social and technical inefficiencies especially for the first prototype Automated Community Infrastructure. These challenges may induce some stressful moments leading to negative emotions. However a well-designed infrastructure with pre-tested modular components as well as automated community and smart home systems should minimize any unexpected challenges.

The percentage of time/money survival necessity is based on an individual already living in a predator free social structure. All of the 0% to 60% would be only time not money contributed to the overall community and its primary purpose would be the expansion of the predator free society and its network infrastructure. All basic survival necessities and many luxuries are integrated directly into the predator free Smart home and community infrastructure. The time wasted making money to buy housing, transportation, food etc. within a capitalistic social structure, will now be available to benefit the entire community and help others receive the same opportunity.

The 0% time contribution would be an individual that was too young, injured, ill or elderly. The 60% time contribution would be someone that enjoyed what they are doing so much it was considered part of their recreation time. A conventional workday would consist of eight hours sleep, eight hours recreation and eight hours at work or contributing to the community. Preferably we would get at least 50% of our awake time for family and recreation and 50% work/contribution however these lines will become blurred as the traditional perception of these activities evolve. For example teaching our children would normally be considered part of our family time but it also contributes to the overall society by increasing the collective knowledge of the community.

Some people like myself may enjoy the technical challenge of designing and automating the production of new products or troubleshooting some system malfunction like a mystery to be solved. I would be making my contribution to the community by doing what I like to do and knowing my efforts will be helping others to make the transition just makes it that much more rewarding. This is the kind of intrinsic social motivation possible within a predator free society that values cooperation and compassion for others over competition and predatory conquests.

Because buying things has become an accepted part of our survival, the act of shopping can trigger a hardwired instinct and a pleasurable emotional response. The opposite is also true for individuals unable to pay for their basic necessities by producing a negative emotional response driving them to become more aggressive to ensure their capitalistic survival. The more fortunate or successful capitalistic competitors may consume so much they overdose on their hardwired reward system and often start to feel deprived if not able to live the lifestyle they have become accustomed to.

Repeated exposure to our predatory social structure for generations has conditioned us to be good consumers and capitalistic opportunists by manipulating our hardwired dopamine reward/punishment mechanism used for natural evolutionary development. With the right knowledge, technology and control of government legislation a working-class population can be conditioned to feel emotionally satisfied with their exploitation and consider it an accepted social ritual associated with achieving the American dream and capitalistic success.

It seems even though our intelligence has made our predatory existence more technologically advanced, the working-class prey must still suffer and die so the ruling class top predators can increase their individual power and wealth. Demonstrating how far we have come yet how little we have learned. It's easy to see who's been losing this class warfare since the beginning of our existence. Begging the question, why have the working-class people continued to allow their exploitation for thousands of years during our social evolutionary development? They must not have realized the ability to end their predatory exploitation was always within their power of numbers and how to use our intellectual survival trait to initiate this evolutionary transition. An understandable excuse for the ancestors of our primitive past but not for a socially enlightened well educated modern day population.

The emotional manipulation of other competitors as a technique to increase profits has been an accepted social practice long before Capitalism began to dominate our predatory development. This subconscious and involuntary technique is a strong form of conditioning also known in this book as the invisible first chain of Capitalism. Because this control technique deals directly with our decision-making process it infiltrates all areas of our society from the simplest products we buy to how we elect the leaders of our countries and ultimately the evolutionary progress of our species.

It is imperative that we understand and break these invisible bonds that manipulate the decisions we make and the actions we take to allow our species to end our predatory social structure and make the transition to predator free society. This form of manipulation will first be broken by individuals that understand this process best and are able to use their intellectual survival trait to override their hardwired survival instincts and the different forms of environmental conditioning that trigger our emotional responses. These individuals will then help others to understand the process until a critical mass is reached allowing for the accelerated transition to a predator free society and the next phase of our intellectual evolutionary development.

By accepting the existence of these emotional manipulation techniques and by reading this book to learn how they are used to control our actions you will become one of the first individuals to break this chain of Capitalism and help others to understand this process. Understanding the process in theory is a crucial first step, but of course intellectually overriding our hardwired instincts and environmental conditioning will be far more difficult in practice. Our hardwired instincts were encoded in our genetic memory over millions of years and our environmental conditioning started creating strong neural pathways from the beginning of our lives so we shouldn't expect overnight results or a quick solution to this problem. In fact our human physiology will always limit our ability to have full intellectual control over the subjects we consider or repel predatory attacks to manipulate our emotions. However by understanding the process we will be far more capable of recognizing attempts to manipulate our emotions for capitalistic exploitation. Our lack of knowledge and experience in life will no longer be a target for predatory attack.

As our knowledge and accelerated education to prevent our emotional manipulation reaches a tipping point and predator free societies become more prevalent, this form a predatory attack will eventually lose its effectiveness. With most forms of capitalistic and predatory exploitation just becoming aware of the techniques used against us will allow us to make an informed decision to end the process.

Predatory attacks to trigger our hardwired survival instincts and manipulate our decision-making process into feeling emotionally satisfied with our capitalistic exploitation will continue until the working-class resources of the world unite with a common goal of universal salvation for all people as equals. In other words hundreds of thousands of working-class prey (American citizens) will continue to suffer and die every year so that a very few ruling class top predators of Capitalism can live in excessive opulence. See anything wrong with this picture? The fact that many people don't, even after suffering from its effects shows the power this manipulation technique has to condition a working-class population into accepting their exploitation. Of all the symptoms that are created by our advanced predatory social structure, using our intelligence to deceive and manipulate others peoples emotions and behaviors for the purpose of mass exploitation is one of the most destructive to our evolutionary development.

I can imagine what life would be like for a child growing up in a predator free society. There will be no competition for individual survival only cooperation for the greater good of the entire community. The goal in not to be smarter than everyone else in order to increase our social and monetary status but instead to help other kids reach their full potential. There will be no need or desire to manipulate other people's emotions for capitalistic profits. All the negative symptoms of a predatory social structure will be removed allowing children to grow up free of the burden that has stunted our species intellectual evolutionary development since its beginning. What's hard to imagine is how much the transition to the environmental conditions of a predator free social structure will accelerate the intellectual development of our species? Let's find out.

5. Induced subjective realities, free our minds, free our future

Induced subjective realities are the most effective form of long-term psychological manipulation. The use of induced subjective realities to condition less informed people into making decisions based on their emotional feelings developed quite naturally. It was found to be an effective competitive tool in our evolving predatory social structures. This form of psychological conditioning has been effectively used against all people, all over the world for thousands of years throughout our intellectual evolutionary development. Its true power lies in its ability to convince parents to induce their own children creating a self-perpetuating form of exploitation that can continue for generations.

For the top human predators of our past this form of intellectual exploitation was far easier than using threats of violence, brutality and public executions. The objective was to motivate their working-class peasants to pay taxes, make crop donations and give up their children to be used in wars and or servants to their God like rulers. This new way of controlling populations was almost too good to be true, the top human predators could still exploit their working-class peasants but now they were willing and even emotionally satisfied to give up their wealth and lives to serve their self ordained ruling class leaders. This early form of patriotism and devotion to serve wealthy rulers as gods created a subjective reality that

that has altered the intellectual development of our species into accepting the technologically advanced predatory social structures of our modern day societies.

Understanding how induced subjective realities work, as a predatory tool for exploitation will give us the intellectual power necessary to override this manipulation technique and its ability to control our thoughts and actions. We humans live in two types of realities, one being subjective and the other being objective. The control of our decision-making process will shift from one reality to the other depending on our intellectual knowledge of the subject and the effectiveness of the induced subjective belief we were conditioned with primarily throughout our childhood. To get a better understanding between the two types of realities a simple definition breakdown will be a good place to start.

Objective: Not influenced by personal feelings, interpretations, or prejudice; based on facts, unbiased, as in an objective opinion.

Subjective: Existing in the mind, placing excessive emphasis on one's own moods, attitudes, opinions, etc., unduly egocentric.

Reality: the state or quality of being real, real things, facts, or events taken as a whole.

The first thing you may notice is that the words objective and reality seem to have a lot in common. They both deal with things that are real, based on facts and not influenced by personal feelings or prejudice. However the words subjective and reality are such opposites that the term "subjective reality" would qualify as an oxymoron. You may already be realizing what kind of reality you would prefer to control your decision-making process and the actions you take.

A person functioning with an objective reality will want true and factual information to form a valid decision, especially in areas regarding their survival necessities and the safety of their family. People functioning with an objective reality have greater intellectual control over their hardwired survival instincts and ultimately over any emotional interference to their decision-making process. An individual using an objective reality to analyze the communications they receive from others will be far less vulnerable to intellectual predatory attacks to control their actions.

A person functioning with a subjective reality will not require factual information or anything real to form opinions, make decisions and ultimately take actions even regarding matters of life and death. This type of reality suppresses our intellectual survival trait and allows our decision-making process to be dominated by our emotions and hardwired survival instincts. Most ruling class top predators of our past and present understand this process well and use this knowledge to target individuals with subjective realities as easy prey for intellectual predatory exploitation.

Induced subjective realities are primarily used on children and un-educated young adults willing to give up their money, labor or lives for something that is not real or factual. Once an individual becomes educated and intellectually aware that the subjective belief is false and perhaps intentionally designed to deceive them. The power this psychological manipulation technique has to control their actions will be neutralized and rendered ineffective. Better-educated individuals and older adults that have already formed an objective reality based on factual knowledge are far less susceptible to this form of predatory attack.

It's human nature to feel like we're in total intellectual control over the decisions we make and the actions we take, perhaps it's an internal mechanism to protect our self-esteem. Acknowledging our human vulnerabilities can be so difficult for some people they would prefer to continue a life of predatory servitude and illusionary bliss, then finding the courage to intellectually break the control of their subjective realities and create a better future for their children. Because the most effective subjective realities are designed to self perpetuate for generations by getting parents to induce their own children, breaking through the denial can be too emotionally painful for many older adults to accept. It will be the younger members of our families not yet fully conditioned and induced with a subjective reality that will evolve beyond their intellectual isolation and find the knowledge necessary to finally break the generational cycle of subjective beliefs. Only then will they find true freedom and salvation from the most difficult to break form of psychological manipulation our species has ever been subjected to.

Before you start feeling like you would never be vulnerable to an induced subjective reality, you should know it's not a matter of strength of character or intellectual fortitude but instead a naturally occurring human vulnerability encoded in our genetic memory that makes us all susceptible to this form of predatory manipulation. In fact most of us were and many of us still are under the control of some form of subjective belief.

One of the simplest ways to explain an induced subjective reality is our belief in Santa Claus when we were young. As children many of us were traditionally conditioned by our parents to believe in the subjective reality of Santa Claus. This is a subjective belief that involves a central character Santa Claus and an elaborate storyline all of which does not exist in the real world. A child with no understanding of what's real or false can be easily induced with any imaginable subjective reality. But at some point during their childhood the factual knowledge of Santa Claus becomes great enough to overcome the conditioning of their subjective reality. This is also the point in our lives when our reality regarding the existence of Santa Claus switches from subjective to objective.

The tradition of inducing a subjective reality about Santa Claus seems innocent enough after all our children find out the truth before they become adults and start living their lives based on a false belief. However consider for a moment what would happen if we never found out our subjective reality about Santa Claus was false and all the adults around us were also absolutely sure this storyline was factually true. We would all become adults absolutely convinced this myth was true and live out our lives in a subjective reality that included Santa Claus as a real person. As adults with the absolute belief that our realities were true we would naturally condition our children with the same storyline creating an entire culture where the subjective reality of Santa Claus was accepted as fact. The fact that no one had ever really seen him crash-land his sleigh and reindeer's on someone's roof or squeeze down a chimney could be explained away in an effort to maintain the emotional satisfaction this subjective reality provided.

Now consider that it was an accepted part of this subjective belief to give some of our labor, time and wealth to Santa Claus by way of just a few of his special elves. All the good people of the community loved their Santa so much they created great statues and monuments to him where his special elves could live. Even though these few special elves were really just people in long robes and golden adornments they assured their believers that their continued donations would be rewarded. They would receive many presents and a life of luxury after they die and passed on to the North Pole where they would live with their beloved Santa forever. The very fortunate few elves helped their followers to learn what was necessary to serve their beloved Santa and how to teach their children what roles they will play within their collective subjective reality.

After many generations the people of the community began to suffer at an increasing rate while the few special elves and their families continued to enjoy a life of luxury with the accumulated wealth and resources they had received from their faithful followers. Some of the kind and generous people started to doubt their beloved Santa and wanted to keep more of their wealth to help relieve they're suffering. A few of the smarter elves decided to create a government with laws to force the nonbelievers to give up their wealth or suffer an even worse fate for denying the existence of Santa Claus. For many more generations, these laws were accepted by the majority of the good people still willing to suffer and sacrifice their lives for the belief that one-day they would die and be with their beloved Santa forever.

One day many of the kindhearted people started to learn that the few wealthy elves that had been living in luxury from their donations had really been deceiving them for generations. A few well-educated elves knew

Santa wasn't real but kept the truth from the good people so they could keep getting their donations of wealth, labor and time. Eventually all the people including the believers and nonbelievers alike used their new knowledge to unit and totally break their subjective reality about Santa Claus. They convinced all the wealthy elves that the future prosperity and survival of the whole community was more important than the individual accumulation of wealth and power by the very few, and of course, they all lived happily ever after.

If only our adult subjective realities were as easy to break as our childhood belief that Santa Claus is a real person. The good people of our worldwide community are also becoming aware of their induced subjective realities, helping to accelerate our transition to a predator free society. The ruling class elves of Capitalism can no longer prevent the knowledge of our exploitation from reaching the people of our global community. Just as a child outgrows their need for comforting fantasies and must eventually rely on their factual knowledge of the real world to make valid decisions about their adult survival, the intellectual evolutionary development of our species will also make this transition.

The social dysfunctions of prejudice, racism and bigotry are all good examples of the detrimental effects of an induced subjective reality. There may be a hardwired survival instinct encoded in our genetic memory to fear people that look or act differently than we do but the primary cause of these social dysfunctions are environmentally induced throughout our childhood. Any imaginable prejudice can be artificially induced into a child throughout their formative years and become an integral part of their adult subjective reality. The repeated and prolonged environmental conditioning to fear people that are different from us, form well-worn neural pathways that can be difficult to redirect even with the application of new factual knowledge contrary to their established beliefs. Like other induced subjective realities these social dysfunctions tend to be passed down for generations and become part of a regional, religious and or cultural belief.

One of the most insidious aspects of an induced subjective reality is their ability to get people to reject any factual knowledge that may end their exploitation. Because of this I will start with a black-and-white example that the majority of people will easily recognize as being some form of psychological manipulation. Of all the creative and bizarre subjective realities people were conditioned to believe in throughout our intellectual development, a more modern religious group called "Heaven's Gate" led by Marshall Applewhite should provide an obvious example to learn from. As with most cult religions, there is a central charismatic leader seeing a vision and or hearing a voice giving them the storyline to preach to their followers.

The storyline of this particular startup religion was elaborate and included elements of modern science fiction and widely accepted Christian doctrine. As with many of these new cult religions their leader claimed to be directly related to Jesus giving him instant recognition and respect among many believers of that religion. You see it makes it easier to start a new religion if you can convince your followers that you are somehow related to one of the larger established religious icons in the world. It's interesting how cult leaders use name recognition to deceive and attract more believers like capitalistic corporations due to attract more customers. It seems to be part of an overall acceptance to our predatory social structure and our willingness to use our intelligence against one another to increase our economic status.

It is true that many neo-religious leaders are fully aware they are deceiving their followers for the purpose of capitalistic exploitation however many of them are also under the control of their own subjective reality. This can lead to self-fulfilling apocalyptic prophecies where not only all of the believers die but also the cult leader like the tragedies at Jonestown led by Jim Jones and Waco led by David Koresh. As an extreme example of how much control subjective realities can have over an individual's actions, Applewhite and his male followers underwent voluntary castration. To any modern educated man or woman functioning with an objective reality this would seem like obvious insanity. However I understand castration was and still is considered a traditional way of pursuing religious and spiritual goals by avoiding natural pleasures. As it turns out the voluntary mutilation by Applewhite and his male followers was just a prelude to the ultimate tragedy produced by this subjective reality, that being the suicide death of 39 believers in this new religion.

Of all the psychological manipulation techniques used on people throughout our history to subconsciously control our decision-making process, the absolute most effective over time is the induced subjective reality. A subjective reality about any semi-believable storyline may be induced into people willing to base their decisions on the way they feel things are instead of the way things really are. Any individual that relies on their emotional feelings to determine reality instead of objective factual knowledge is more than likely already under the control of a subjective belief. People relying on their subjective reality to make decisions regarding wealth and politics are targeted by top predators as human prey primed for capitalistic exploitation.

This form of psychological manipulation is so effective that seemingly average people in our society will be willing to take another person's life or give up their own live or even the lives of their children to maintain the illusion of their subjective reality. A form of manipulation and control that can override our hardwired biological imperative to survive and protect the lives of our children is a powerful tool for mass exploitation. In a social economic structure that legitimizes the use of predatory attacks as a competitive tool for capitalistic success. Individuals willing to abandon their intellectual survival trait for the comfort of a false subjective reality are the low hanging fruit for the human predators of our world today. It's like wearing a sign saying I'm an easy target prey on me, I'll believe in anything.

Once a subjective reality is established it can be so strong it will prevent even the most well intended attempts at basic communication about the subject. Even when the objective of the conversation is to simply convey the most basic established facts well known for thousands of years. An individual will emotionally rejected the communication to preserve their subjective belief and prevent any intellectual progress. This rejection of factual knowledge not only prevents positive communication and

and intellectual progress but the environmental condition often triggers a defensive hardwired instinct and biochemical reaction like the flight or fight response. This biochemical reaction interferes with our higher cognitive thought processes further diminishing our ability to have positive communications and make intellectual progress. This form of mental de-evolution not only prevents intellectual progress but this primitive emotional response can often turn violent or even fatal.

The same Tricorder techniques we use to determine our vulnerability to intellectual predatory attacks and emotional manipulations can also be used to identify subjects where we may be under the control of the subjective reality. Induced subjective realities can only be effective on people unable or unwilling to acquire and understand the knowledge necessary to realize the subjective reality is false. In other words once we learn how we are being preyed upon for profit we simply make an informed decision to end the process. This is how the first chain of Capitalism will be broken. This is also why the first Tricorder indicator of knowledge about the subject is so important in evaluating our vulnerability to different forms of capitalistic exploitation.

Keep in mind like non-intelligent species human predators also target any weakness in their prey. And when their prey is billions of working class humans all over the world our greatest weakness is our inability to develop intellectual predatory defenses. Interesting how many of our ruling class leaders in government are diminishing access to public schools even suggesting eliminating the Department of Education even though they are fully aware of the damage it is doing to our country's ability to stay competitive in our capitalistic competition with other countries. If nothing else I hope this book will give readers a whole new perspective on the importance of education.

When a subjective reality is induced, as a predatory technique for long-term even generational exploitation, hardwired survival instincts must be triggered to manipulate our biochemical reward and punishment behavior modification system. As with most intellectual predatory techniques the ones that subconsciously manipulate our decisions and actions are preferred especially for long-term exploitation. In other words they don't want their prey to find out they're being exploited so their profits can continue for generations.

To create the environmental and social conditions where the prey feels emotionally satisfied in giving up their wealth, labor, survival necessities or lives is the objective of an induced subjective reality. The more effective subjective realities also induce an element of pain for noncompliance this allows for greater control over their human prey and the ability to exploit a greater segment of the population. Using the virtual Tricorder to determine the level of emotional association with subjects in your life may help identify areas where you will be vulnerable to, or under the control of subjective belief.

The last Tricorder indicator of time/money survival necessity, where time is an individual's waking hours dedicated to the subject and money would be the percentage of household income spent on the subject, could also help identify areas of potential exploitation using a subjective reality. The ultimate goal of inducing a subjective reality into a population is to facilitate the efficient transfer of wealth and labor from the working-class masses to the ruling class elite. This exploitation can take many forms from primitive human slavery requiring all labor, to our highly sophisticated socially engineered modern societies extracting just wealth or better yet both providing even more control over a working-class resource.

It may be difficult to identify the most effective subjective realities, as they have become an accepted aspect of our predatory social structures and cultural beliefs. The physical and intellectual competition of our modern societies can make it hard to distinguish between legitimized forms of exploitation and ones that are criminalized. The one thing is becoming more obvious, the socially engineered inequality of our societies favors higher profits for the ruling class top predators of Capitalism over the preventable suffering and death of we the people. It's definitely time we correct this social dysfunction and provide a new predator free paradigm for our future.

To understand how induced subjective realities are used for capitalistic exploitation on an individual, national and global scale will be a crucial part of the factual knowledge needed for us to make an informed decision to end the process. If we are to learn the lessons of our past to provide a better future for our species it will also help to understand how subjective realities have altered the development of our evolutionary process. If we are able to just momentarily break the conditioning of our predatory social structure and subjective realities we can imagine what our world would be like if as a species we made the transition to a global predator free society 100 or even 1000 years ago.

I imagine a world of wonder and joy where we use our collective intelligence and creative skills to solve global problems and unify our species. A world where the use of induce subjective realities and all forms of psychological manipulation for predatory domination and capitalistic exploitation are not needed for survival or even considered acceptable within an intellectually enlightened society. The top predators of our past and present may have prevented our evolutionary transition to a predator free society so far but as explained throughout this book that's all about to change. We will break the control of our subjective realities and make an objective decision to end our predatory social structure and provide true freedom and prosperity for the future of our species.

6. Collective Stockholm syndrome, defending the top predators

The Stockholm syndrome is a phenomena known to affect the decision-making process of people being held against their will and dependent on their captors for survival. Some of these people will begin to sympathize and even defend their captor's point of view. These environmental conditions create a subjective reality where the absence of abuse is interpreted as an act of kindness, and this begins to take control of the victims mind. This well documented phenomenon can take over an individual's decision-making process in as little as six days. After just six days of this form of environmental conditioning some individuals were willing to risk bodily harm in preventing their captor's apprehension and later refuse to testify against them. The Stockholm syndrome is a powerful example of how our environmental conditions can trigger a survival instinct that affects our decision-making process making our managed exploitation seem like an act of kindness to be thankful for. How weird is that?

Two disturbing conclusions about Stockholm syndrome are, the subjective reality can produces acts of violence and the conditioning has lasting effects even after one exposure of just days. Another consideration is only about 27% of hostage victims show evidence of Stockholm syndrome. I had to ask myself why are some people so easily conditioned to accept their exploitation, defend their abusers and even commit violent acts on their behalf, while the other 73% are not affected. If over a quarter of our population is vulnerable to this form of conditioning, the only thing they need to trigger this syndrome is the environmental conditions that create it. Now we need to ask ourselves, do those environmental conditions exist within our current predatory social structure?

I can't remember how many times I heard working-class people say, "they feel trapped" in our current social economic system with minimal prospects for upward mobility. Another common expression used to describe surviving our capitalistic competition is "barely keeping our heads above water" also statements like "I have no choice" if I don't work this hard I will lose everything. Many working-class families are just one lay off or healthcare issue away from bankruptcy and loss of their survival necessities. It seems the cost of the American dream is kept equal to or just more than most hard-working families can make. Interesting how it works that way, is this a miraculous coincidence that has continued for generations or good management skills by our ruling class masters? The American working-class people are clearly being made to work harder and accept less, but does this establish the first environmental condition necessary to trigger the Stockholm syndrome?

When I was a young boy I thought if people in Africa were starving and dying in poverty why didn't they just move to America then they could have a life as nice as mine. Our worlds are so small when we're young. As I got older I noticed a similarity between the countries of the world and the different areas of the United States. There are some areas of the United States allowed to decline into abject poverty while other areas proudly display excessive opulence. That's one of the first things that didn't feel right. What kind of social system would allow such inequality where the few have the power and control over the many? Being so young my fact puzzle was still small and unclear but it was already becoming obvious something was wrong with this picture.

What keeps a coal miner in the South risking their health and life when they could just drive to Wall Street get a safe cushy desk job as a hedge fund manager making billions? It may be they feel they can't afford the education necessary or it could be their family is counting on their monthly income and to take a chance at a better life is too big a risk in a competitive society where there is always someone even more desperate ready to take their place. For whatever reason working class people do feel trapped in an economic social structure that treats them like a resource for exploitation. The first environmental condition of feeling trapped is created by the highly efficient and technologically advanced predatory social economic structure of free-market Capitalism.

How about the second environmental condition needed to induce the Stockholm syndrome, now we must ask ourselves, does our social structure make us dependent upon it for our survival? Our entire social economic structure and the distribution network for our basic survival necessities seem to be carefully constructed to more efficiently manage a working-class population. Some people may feel we have the most technologically advanced infrastructure for the distribution of our survival necessities and the best social economic structure to allow we the people the greatest opportunity to reach our fullest potential and the highest quality of life possible. I did, once upon a time. If only it were true, we could all be enjoying prosperous lives where our creative skills are not wasted on physical and intellectual competitions for basic survival necessities and the needs of the many are not subject to the predatory desires of the ruling class few.

I had assumed the objective was to find the most efficient way to create and distribute basic survival necessities to all communities to maintain the health and prosperity for the entire population. I noticed our current distribution system requires family members to drive often miles from their homes to buy food at centralized outlets. When any thing prevents us from reaching those stores or the food outlets from receiving the goods we depend on for our survival, there could be mass starvation across our entire country. After objectively considering this system my first thought was, this is a terrible design, what were the architects thinking?

Then I started to realize the architects of our capitalistic social structure couldn't be that incompetent, so their design objectives must be for something more important than creating a stable supply line and keeping our populations from starving to death during national disasters. From a top predators point of view making heavy capitalistic investments in government to socially engineer our society for maximum future profits only makes good business sense. After all controlling a working-class population by manipulating their survival necessities is a well-known strategy used in predatory social structures throughout our evolutionary development.

There are levels of existence we the people are willing to accept in order to survive within our predatory social structure. They seem to have a direct correlation with our social economic status. For example the most fortunate capitalistic competitors may plan their survival in intervals of years, while many middle-class citizens may live month-to-month even less fortunate people may have a day-to-day existence. Keeping the working-class resource on the shortest leash possible does provide better control for the top predators of Capitalism. However it also keeps the populations emotionally frustrated and more concerned with their individual survival than any creative contributions to their country or global community.

The second condition needed to induce a Stockholm syndrome is created by the social engineering of our society forcing the working-class population to become highly dependent upon our ruling class top predators for our basic survival necessities. There are even control mechanisms capable of dialing up or down the suffering and death experienced by the working-class population providing that absence of abuse that get interpreted as acts of kindness within the subjective reality of a Stockholm syndrome victim.

We now know our predatory social structure produces both environmental conditions necessary to induce a collective Stockholm syndrome within a population. We also know that approximately 27% of our population is susceptible to the control of an induced Stockholm syndrome when exposed to these environmental conditions for just days. And that this form of conditioning forces our decision-making process to be dominated by our survival instincts and emotional responses increasing our vulnerability to intellectual predatory attacks and all forms of capitalistic exploitation.

This raises some interesting questions. If just days of this form of conditioning can induce a subjective reality where emotional acts of violence to protect a predatory captor seem acceptable, what would years or even generations of exposure due to an unsuspecting population? Is over a quarter of our population really vulnerable to the influence of a collective Stockholm syndrome and will they feel compelled to defend the very ruling class top predators responsible for their capitalistic exploitation?

The obvious concern becomes whether or not the control of this subjective reality will cause this segment of the population to resist the transition to a predator free society and therefore further delay our intellectual evolutionary development as a species. Also many top predators more concerned with maintaining their capitalistic domination over their working-class resources will continue to prey on and manipulate this segment of the population into preventing their own salvation. Wow, there are so many things to consider, but have no fear, because the factual knowledge necessary to break the control of the Stockholm syndrome and other forms of subconscious manipulation of our actions will become widely available for objective consideration, all leading to an informed decision to end the exploitation process.

I wondered how such a large percentage of our population could be so susceptible to this form of subjective reality and manipulation of their actions. Then I remembered the very unnatural process of artificial selection performed by the ruling class top predators for thousands of years during the evolutionary development of our predatory social structure. The earliest top predators were not intellectually capable of understanding the concept of artificial selection. However their lust for predatory dominance inherently resulted in the death of anyone with the courage to oppose them, leaving only the most submissive people willing to accept their exploitation to replenish the working-class population. This process has altered the intellectual evolutionary development of our species for thousands of years and created a modern day population more willing to accept our predatory existence and our social status as working-class prey.

After understanding the nature and effectiveness of this artificial selection process it seems the percentage of the population susceptible to a collective Stockholm syndrome would be higher. I feel the reason for this may be our species is reaching a point in our intellectual evolutionary development where our collective realities are becoming more objective and the subjective beliefs of the past will no longer be considered adequate to guide our future. In other words our species is starting to accept the reality that Santa Claus is not real and that we need to start counting on one another and not the illusions of our subjective realities to solve our global problems. What an interesting time we live in, we are watching our species grow up like a child learning about their world and the power they have to control their future.

7. Breaking the subjective reality to serve Gods and Governments

As a young boy just starting to learn about our world I went to Bible school a few times with my neighborhood playmates as another game to play but even then what I was being taught raised more questions than provided answers. One of the first things that confused me was there were so many religions and different Gods that people believed in, but like most young children I thought adults had all the answers and that they were never wrong.

Then I learned something scary, the adults of different religions were all absolutely certain their God was the only one that was real and that any adult or child that believed in a different God would burn in hell for all eternity or some other horrible fate. On the other hand if I chose the right God and religion to believe in I would never die and live in heaven forever. No pressure. After getting over my initial concern I got to thinking, most of these adults had to be wrong no matter which God was real. And that if some of the adults were wrong maybe they all were wrong and none of their Gods were real.

I wondered why gods would cause such suffering and death for the people that didn't want to believe in them. Okay maybe I was overly skeptical for a child but something about that didn't feel right. I also wondered why any God would hate the children in Africa so much they would allow them to starve to death even before they were old enough to decide what God and religion to believe in. Would the God that made them suffer in life now make them suffer for eternity after death and what could these children have done to deserve such torment? Why are a few children born into great wealth and luxury while so many others are destined to suffer and die? Did some God make things this way?

These seemed like important questions that no adult could answer only that if I made the wrong choice it would mean the difference between going to heaven or hell and that I just needed to trust them and their God to guide my decisions and actions for me. Even as a child I didn't like the idea of letting other people control my life especially some person I couldn't see or touch. I had already broken my subjective reality about Santa Claus and I was learning how to form decisions based on the objective consideration of factual knowledge and not what I was told to believe. I knew I didn't have all the answers but I wanted the chance to learn for myself then choose how I wanted to live my life and not be rushed into an emotional decision with threats of eternal pain and suffering.

As I grew older I became interested in history and wanted to find out why there were so many different Gods and religions throughout our intellectual evolutionary development. I learned that long before the more modern religions of Christianity and Islam there were the ancient Gods and Goddesses. Our ancient ancestors were even more certain their Gods were real than people today believe in their more recent religions. If a person of our ancient world was struck by lightning they obviously angered Zeus or when a ship was lost at sea the vengeance of Poseidon was responsible.

I had to know where did all these gods go, why were they replaced with newer religions and perhaps even more important, where did they come from in the first place. As I learned about these ancient gods and the people that believed in them, the one thing that troubled me most was their willingness to kill and die for them. Not only did the ancient people of faith devote their lives to their gods but they would also fight wars to kill off all the people that wanted to believe in any other god but theirs.

Ancient wars were won or lost on the power of the gods their warriors believed in. After all the people that believed in the weaker gods were massacred only the religions with the largest armies and the best weapons were left to continue our evolutionary development. My first question about where all of the ancient gods went was becoming clear, they died along with the people that believed in them. Some of the earliest ancient gods were so completely erased from history their names and the people that believed in them will never be known. The best part about these ancient gods and religions not existing anymore is that no more people will be conditioned to suffer, kill or die to serve them. No more wars, religious genocides, human sacrifices or apocalyptic prophecies will continue in their names.

The worst part is after thousands of years all the weaker gods and their believers have been killed off and replaced by the stronger more powerful gods and the people they blessed with larger armies and more advanced weapons. This must be one of those mysterious ways that God's work but with a more objective consideration it seems like a form of "survival of the fittest" as the evolutionary development of our species finds new ways to use our intellectual survival trait as a predatory tool against one another.

We now know that during thousands of years of our evolutionary development ancient Gods, religions and the people that believed in them were mostly massacred and replaced by the people believing in the newer Gods and religions, but I still wanted to know where did these Gods come from in the first place. If our ancient Gods cease to exist at the very point in time when there was no one left to believe in them and no writings or artifacts remain that bear their names. Then it stands to reason that the very first God came into existence exactly when the first human was able to contemplate their existence and believe they were real. As the origination and progression of human intelligence is well documented we can safely say the first God came into existence just after our species developed this survival trait and with it the ability to imagine or more accurately to form abstract concepts from more basic knowledge fragments. This is also approximately the point in our evolutionary development when we quite naturally began to use our intelligence against one another as a predatory tool for survival.

To get a better understanding how the first God came into existence we will need to travel back in time to a point when our intellectual survival trait was just emerging and about to become one of the most significant evolutionary development this planet has ever seen. Imagine for a moment you are the first one of our ancient ancestors to break our primordial fear of fire and capture its power of light and heat. As your firelight shined bright into the dark moonless night it would attract other primitive humans like moths to a flame. To our primitive ancestors with little to no intelligence yet, a fire burning in a distant cave at night would be similar to having a modern human see a UFO parked on the side of a mountain.

The curiosity would be overwhelming for our primitive ancestors all wanting to see this light in the night that never seems to die. Cold and curious humans would come from miles away to be in awe of your ability to control this wondrous power of light and its soothing comfort of warmth. Our pre-fire early ancestors that had only known darkness and bitter cold nights since the beginning of our existence would naturally consider an individual with this kind of power to be some kind of supernatural human or God. It seems logical that in this way the concept of the first God/human hybrids were created. The very first occurrence of an induced subjective reality being used as a predatory tool for exploitation probably happened when one of our early ancestors accidentally noticed the power it had to manipulate and control other peoples thoughts and actions.

Like magic tricks to a child, the knowledge and intellect developed by some humans seemed like acts of supernatural powers to the young and uneducated masses. These supernatural acts were not only awe-inspiring ways to get instant admiration and devotion from their followers but they also had practical applications to increase the quality of life for the community. These people were natural leaders and became the first warlords, kings and top predators of our ancient world. At some point in our evolutionary development the top human predators of our ancient world began to realize their ability to manage and manipulate the future of an entire working-class population. As fathers ruled their nuclear families the ruling class leaders were considered the patriarchs of their entire extended village.

The parent-child relationship dynamics transferred into cults where the ruling class leaders made themselves godlike fathers to their working-class children. Just like fathers in a nuclear family, the ruling class parents would demand absolute obedience and devotion from their working-class children. The accepted use of fear and the threat of violence to condition children in nuclear families naturally transferred as a control technique to ensure the obedience of entire communities. The practice of nuclear families requiring their children to labor and support the family also evolved into entire kingdoms being forced to labor to serve their Godlike Kings. In this way the natural formation of the first intellectually assisted predatory social structures were created negatively impacting the evolutionary development of our species.

It's easy to see how the earliest humans were naturally induced with a subjective reality that their ruling class leaders were Gods worthy of killing and dying for. Thousands of years ago there wasn't a lot of factual knowledge going around for the working-class peasants to form an objective reality and make an informed decision to end their exploitation. Our entire species including the more knowledgeable top predators were still almost entirely under the control of their hardwired survival instincts and emotional reactions to environmental influences.

Then I started to realize this ancient form of subjective reality and predatory exploitation is still used very successfully on modern day humans even after thousands of years of intellectual evolutionary development. Modern day religious cults all over the world still have godlike leaders with followers under the control of some apocalyptic subjective reality that commonly include the suffering and death of nonbelievers. Lucky for us not many of these modern day religious leaders acquire enough wealth and power to carry out their apocalyptic subjective realities on the general public and tend to be isolated to just the suffering and death of their believers. You may wonder how could this ancient form of intellectual predatory control still be so effective at manipulating the decisions and actions of modern-day humans like us.

The simple answer is the same environmental conditions needed to induce this kind of subjective reality that existed thousands of years ago, also exist today. However, far fewer modern day adults living in countries with access to education are susceptible to this form of predatory manipulation. Young adults induced with a subjective reality throughout their childhood are now breaking its control as they become increasingly exposed to factual knowledge. There are two primary factors at play here, the environmental conditions that an individual, group or population are exposed to and the biological condition of the subject or subjects to be induced with a subjective reality.

The biological condition needed to efficiently induce this form of subjective reality would require an individual with little to no intellectual knowledge of the exploitation process or the psychological manipulation technique they will be subjected to. An individual or population physically and emotionally stressed out and weakened by a social structure requiring primitive predatory or advanced capitalistic competition for survival would be preferred. And of course any individual or group of people conditioned to reject factual knowledge and take actions based on their emotional feelings will be targeted for long-term generational exploitation. You see from a top predators point of view they would like the largest percentage of the working-class population to defend their exploitation aided by the collective Stockholm syndrome and reject any factual knowledge that could help the victims end the process.

Have you ever wondered why the subjects of politics and religion seem to provoke some of the strongest emotional reactions during conversations? What is it about these two subjects that will often drive two otherwise rational adults to lose all intellectual control over their hardwired instincts causing them to regress back to the a more primitive in our development? Individuals seem to develop their emotional interference and loss of intellectual control involuntarily and subconsciously just after an opposing opinion about one of these subjects is mentioned. This would seem to indicate a hardwired survival response encoded in our genetic memory is reacting to an environmental condition or stimulus, which in this case is a discussion on politics and/or religion. In other words it's more of a hardwired reaction than an intellectual decision to have an emotional response to these subjects.

The strongest hardwired survival traits deal with predatory attacks and defenses, life and death struggles throughout our evolutionary development. They provoke the strongest emotional reactions for manipulating the working-class resource and inducing subjective realities to serve gods and governments. I wanted to know what life and death struggles throughout our evolutionary development were so powerful they could encode our genetic memory into having such a strong emotional reaction to any opposing views on the subjects of politics and religion.

From the earliest times when our species first started using our intelligence against one another as a predatory tool for survival, ruling class top predator warlords and Kings were both God and government all rolled into one almighty authority. There was no concept of human rights, no protesting the level of exploitation they were subject to, no democracy or free speech just public humiliation, torture and death for anyone denying the subjective reality that their king was indeed an almighty God. Being the God and head of government gave the top predator Kings of our past two of the most important and powerful tools to psychologically manipulate and manage their working-class peasants and slaves into excepting their predatory existence as their best chance at surviving.

Forcing the peasants and slaves to labor and pay taxes to their government/King was a socially accepted form of exploitation much like it is today but instead of tax evaders going to for-profit jails, a person would more likely become that day's entertainment at their public torture and execution. The combination of thousands of years of artificial selection by killing off all the nonbelievers unwilling to accept either the religious or patriotic subjective reality of their top predator God Kings, and the atrocities witnessed by the surviving population must have been of such intensity and duration to encode our genetic memory for an involuntary emotional response sensitive to these two subjects. The subjects of religion and politics evolved an association with the survival trait of self-preservation provoking the emotions of fear and anger.

The fear of gods mysteriously destroying lives, causing earthquakes, floods and all forms of natural disasters was a collective subjective reality all people were traditionally induced with throughout their childhood like some modern-day societies do with Santa Claus and his magical powers. The difference being our ancient ancestors lived their entire lives believing the subjective reality that their top predator kings really were gods, again just like the believers in a modern day religious cult are conditioned to feel about their leaders. Finding the common denominator between ancient and modern subjective realities helps identify the problem and possible solutions to prevent this form of intellectual predatory exploitation.

To maintain a patriotic subjective reality to serve governments and top predator kings over generations was much more difficult than subjective realities to serve Gods that can take any form our imaginations can conceive of. As God Kings grew older and died the illusion of their subjective reality cannot be maintained. However Gods that have no physical form and do not exist in reality can live on for generations as a control mechanism. Or at least until the induced population reaches a level of intellectual awareness capable of understanding the nature of their exploitation and makes an informed decision to end the process. In addition to accepting and understanding the factual knowledge necessary to break the control of our subjective realities to serve Gods and governments, is the courage to change generations of tradition responsible for the countless loss of lives. We must find the courage to acknowledge and correct the mistakes of our past to help end our current preventable suffering and death and create a more harmonious and prosperous future for our species.

As mentioned throughout this book it was a natural evolutionary process for our species to use our developing intellectual survival trait to create technologically advanced social structures based on our hardwired predatory instincts. After all it's the only playbook we had to work with for millions of years before we developed intelligence. Our biological evolutionary development may be difficult to track back through time because of the scarcity of human fossils. But before our intellectual evolutionary development began our species progressed much like all the other non-intelligent creatures on this planet. However our intellectual development is a complicated survival trait to track and analyze through time.

Our primary obstacle seems to be an inability to objectively self analyze either our personal development throughout our lives or the intellectual evolutionary progress of our species. Even the way we measure that intellectual progress is evolving, along with our evolutionary development and understanding of this process. You can imagine the paradoxical difficulty this would present a species using a developing intellectual skill to analyze the evolution of that very survival instinct.

As far as we know we are the first species to take this evolutionary journey and even though it's been a bumpy ride using our predatory instincts to guide our social development. We will learn from our mistakes as a species and accelerate our transition to a predator free society. These concepts are important to consider and as you learn more they will all begin to connect like a giant virtual puzzle giving you a much clearer perspective of the big picture.

As I became more interested in the evolutionary progress of our predatory social structures and the many religious and patriotic subjective realities that were used to exploit their working-class people, I noticed what seems to be an early form of free-market Capitalism taking place. With free-market Capitalism as with all forms of predatory social structures there is fierce and often violent competition for survival. Of course unlike all the other species on our planet we humans get to use our evolving intelligence as the most effective tool in our predatory competition against one another.

A good capitalistic entrepreneur could create a new product to help make our competition for survival a little easier providing some emotional satisfaction to their customers. But why go through the trouble of making and selling things when you can just provide emotional satisfaction directly. The satisfaction of a subjective belief is a mental escape from the objective reality of our predatory social structure and the many negative symptoms it creates. I guess one of the biggest advantages of using induced subjective realities to extract wealth from a working-class resource is that they can provide different levels of emotional satisfaction much like an addictive drug would but without the need to produce, distribute and sell a product.

No need to invest millions of dollars in politicians to legitimize the exploitation process like with an addictive drug product. In fact the right to induce or be controlled by a subjective reality to serve gods and governments is guaranteed by the Constitution, which legitimizes this form of intellectual predatory attack on we the people and more to the point it is severely hindering our transition to a predator free society.

If a population is unaware of and emotionally satisfied with their exploitation they will not know there's a problem to correct and continue to live out their subjective realities in blissful ignorance with minimal intellectual control over their future. If the required level of competition is high enough the working-class population will not even have the time to consider their exploitation or if our advanced predatory social structure is the future they want for their children. Even the oldest tricks work well on a population unfamiliar with the tactic. How can we build better intellectual defenses against this form of predatory attack when we're unaware of the advanced tactics used against us? We learn, adapt and prevail.

From the earliest induced subjective realities of our ancient past to the most advanced capitalistic exploitation techniques used today the objective stays the same to convince or condition people to willingly give up their wealth/survival resources as an accepted part of their predatory survival. It never has mattered whether the people get anything of real survival value in return as long as they feel emotionally satisfied with the exploitation process. The trick is to keep enough healthy workers alive to continue or even expand the exploitation network of working-class prey to increase profits for the ruling class top predators. That's the power of a subjective reality, just the illusion of prosperity, freedom or salvation from an oppressive social structure is all some people need to kill and die for their God or government.

The working-class populations of the world will never achieve true freedom and prosperity within a predatory social structure. This is why it is so critical that we break our subjective realities giving us the opportunity to accept the factual knowledge we need to finally put an end to our predatory existence. And the best part is, it's within our power to do so right now. Imagine an event as large as accelerating the intellectual evolutionary development of our species starting with something as simple as individuals making informed decisions based on factual knowledge. Now imagine millions of individuals making an informed collective decision to unify our species ending our need for predatory survival techniques conditioning the working-class resource into giving up their wealth and time.

With free-market Capitalism like any predatory social structure the objective is to destroy the competition and accumulate the greatest percentage of available wealth and global resources. The logical progression of this process would result in a single dominant multinational corporation that every human in the world must depend upon for their survival, giving them ultimate control over our species evolutionary development and what level of predatory exploitation we the people will be subjected to. This form of free-market cannibalization and consolidation of the many smaller businesses into a single giant multinational corporation is often referred to as the Wal-Mart effect. The Wal-Mart effect is a highly predictable consequence for any predatory social structure that allows their top predators to dictate the evolutionary development for the majority of the species designated as working-class prey.

Our ruling class leaders were aware of this manifestation of our predatory social structure for decades, but instead of doing what was right for we the people they instinctually chose to capitalize on the opportunity and create the most profitable and efficient system for mass exploitation this world has ever seen. It's just like a primitive predatory social structure where the few big fish use their size and power to dominate, exploit and consume all the many smaller, weaker less fortunate ones. As I write this book I can't help but reflect on how our species has misused its gift of intelligence to evolve a capitalistic network capable of global exploitation of the working-class resource instead of making the evolutionary leap to predator free society where all people can prosper and live as equals. We the working-class people of the world are about to make that evolutionary leap and use our collective intelligence to end our exploitation and take control of our future.

As I learned more about all the ancient Gods that people believed in, I noticed the same capitalistic/predatory manifestation of the Wal-Mart effect being used to eliminate the smaller less popular Gods from the competition to gain control over the minds and souls of potential believers. Before the more modern Gods instructed their followers that they would not tolerate the belief in any other Gods, they at least seemed to accept each other's existence. In capitalistic terms it may be similar to a new grocery store convincing its customers they will go to heaven and live forever as long as they only shop at their store but if they go to any of the competitions stores their souls will burn in hell for eternity.

These things may seem silly to many modern people today but during the ancient times everyone was under the control of a similar subjective reality like a group of young children that haven't gained the factual knowledge necessary to break their illusion about the existence of Santa Claus. It seems likely this was one of the first forms of free-market competition for profit using the socially accepted belief in Gods and a good religious subjective reality to win over the hearts and souls of the unsuspecting working-class masses. After their hearts and souls were won over or more accurately the induced subjective reality had taken full control over their decisions and actions, they quite naturally wanted to please their new God with offerings of wealth and survival resources.

One of my favorite historical figures is Hero or Heron of Alexandria (Heron Alexandrinus) also known as Michanikos (the machine man). Heron was an extraordinarily creative individual doing design engineering and mathematics during the first century A.D. in Alexandria Roman Egypt. Among his many accomplishments is the first wind-powered machine and the first recorded steam engine. There are moments in time where some individuals have the power to dramatically change the evolutionary development for our entire species. Heron died at 60 but if he was able to live perhaps just another 10 years longer he may have made the critical connection linking the power of his steam engine to a mechanical output shaft, starting the Industrial Revolution in the first century A.D.

How would the course of our evolutionary development have changed if our intellectual acceleration began in the first century A.D.? I believe our accelerated industrial development would have led to advanced communication technologies over 1000 years ago. The ability to utilize global communication technologies would have accelerated our intellectual evolutionary development into creating the first technologically advanced predator free societies hundreds of years ago. And the world as we currently know it would be completely different, perhaps even beyond our ability to imagine or comprehend.

Heron's technical wizardry was available for those wealthy enough to afford it. Not surprisingly some of the wealthiest individuals were the priests collecting all the donations for the stronger more popular Gods. Just like today the more wealth and power a person or God can accumulate the greater their ability to manipulate our predatory social structure to their advantage. When a subjective reality is induced to serve a God it usually includes some ritual offering that requires the believers to give up some of their wealth or survival necessities. One of these rituals required the believers of the more successful Gods to buy holy water blessed by the priests.

As it turned out the wealthy priests had a little inconvenience that was perfectly suited for Heron's problem-solving skills. Their God became so popular and their believers so numerous that blessing each one's water individually while also collecting all their money became too burdensome of a task for such few priests. The wealthy priests may have also been practicing a common capitalistic tactic to invest excess wealth to create a gimmick or some source of entertainment to attract customers/believers. This was one of those moments in time when there was a need for a new technology coming together with an individual capable of creating it.

One of the most fascinating parts of this story is that it was the very inspiration for the creation of the first known vending machine. I'd love to know if this concept originated with Heron and he approached the priests with a way to save them time and increase their profits or if they came to him knowing his reputation of using technical wizardry to solve complex problems. Heron's creative skills were far ahead of his time but then the priests with their excessive wealth also had access to the rare luxury of higher education. If only we could witness that moment in time.

I was just realizing, Heron's vending machine also marks a very important turning point in our evolutionary development, where the combination of an induced subjective reality and our evolving technology has created the first form of automated exploitation of the working class people. Have you ever wondered how income inequality got started? The separation between the few wealthy top predators and the many working-class prey began to grow as their exploitation process became more efficiently automated. It may not have been called Capitalism but these priests acted as any good CEO of one of the Fortune 5 top income corporations of the ancient world would have done to increase profits. They would quite logically hire the smartest people they could find to help automate the exploitation process of their working-class customers.

The problem was their believers were use to getting some personal acknowledgment for faithfully giving up their wealth and they may lose that crucial emotional satisfaction they get for following the control of their subjective reality. So it was decided the utility value of this holy water dispensing machine should be combined with some form of entertainment value to presumably reinforce the emotional satisfaction needed to maintain the subjective reality. It may be hard to imagine but even the smallest things we take for granted today would be unbelievably fascinating and entertaining to the people of the ancient world.

Heron's holy water vending machine is thought to look like an ornate flowerpot with a pedestal on the bottom and a slot on the top where coins would drop onto a flat plate connected to a lever. The lever was connected to a water valve that would open using the extra weight of a coin on the plate. As the holy water was dispensed the plate would continue to tip down until the coin slid off at which point a counterweight would return the mechanism to its original position closing the valve. In this way a consistent pre-measured amount of holy water could be delivered for each deposited coin of uniform weight.

As you can imagine, the people of the ancient world must have been mystified as to how this could be possible after all this was the first time anyone had seen this kind of technology. Many assumed there was a tiny person inside but there really wasn't enough room for that, others may have thought it was some form of magic but most people were conditioned to believe all things unexplained were simply the work of Gods playing tricks on us mere mortals and flaunting their power to control our lives. As a tribute to Heron of Alexandria I plan on reproducing many of his creations to be put on educational display for members and visitors to the first Automated Community Infrastructure.

I admire Heron's ability to combine the utility, entertainment and artistic value within one product or work of art. Unfortunately the use of his creative skills to automate the exploitation of thousands put our species on a negative evolutionary path. Well-educated top predators began to catch on and see the opportunities this combination of psychological manipulation and technical automation offered them to more efficiently manage and exploit their working-class resource.

In Heron's defense he was also forced to adapt to the dynamics of his own predatory social structure and the influence of the subjective realities of his time feeling compelled to do whatever was necessary to survive and acquire the resources to carry on his work. I know our forced competition for survival and predatory existence was a naturally occurring evolutionary process. But somewhere along the way some ruling class top predators must have figured out how things work and started having discussions on the best ways to secure their predatory dominance over their working-class resource.

Not long after Heron's automated holy water dispenser began turning a profit some top predators drunk on their excessive wealth, predatory success and probably some temple brewed alcohol started to formulate a diabolical plan. Some ruling class top predators started to realize if they could convince believers to automatically give up their wealth to serve a God maybe they could also get them to pay for all of their basic survival necessities as part of a patriotic ritual to serve a government, also controlled by them.

Maybe a social structure could be engineered requiring the working-class population to compete against one another to acquire enough wealth to buy their basic survival necessities from the top predators. But then they would also need to be induced with a subjective reality to provide some emotional satisfaction to make their exploitation seemed like an acceptable quality of life. This way the ruling class few can make a profit off of both their religious and patriotic subjective realities maximizing the useful output of their working-class resource. What a Eureka moment it must have been for the first top predators when they realized the power these predatory techniques had to control and manipulate the future of their working-class prey. Do you think this is how Capitalism got started?

The more I learn the better I can imagine some of the conversations that must have taken place as our ruling class top predators of the past realized the awesome power they had to control the evolutionary development of our species. My question now is how long have they known and was our intellectual and social development intentionally prevented from making the transition to a predator free society just to maintain the predatory domination of a few ruling class top predators? No... they wouldn't do that, would they? This will be an interesting subject for further study but since our transition to a predator free society has already begun to accelerate I would prefer to concentrate on the social and technical solutions for the future. However until more people are able to break their subjective realities and make an objective decision to end our predatory social structure, we must continue the educational phase of the transition.

Another machine created by Heron is believed to be the first automated door opener. This device also commissioned by wealthy priests would mysteriously open Temple doors after a fire was made at the altar of that God. Heron cleverly used the heat from the fire to increase the air pressure in a sealed chamber with water at the bottom. As the pressure increased the water was pushed out into another container. As this container filled up with water it pulled down on a rope wrapped around spindles that were connected to the door hinges. The process would reverse when the fire went out causing the doors to close again. Even though the automated temple doors were far more difficult to create and install than the holy water dispenser it didn't seem to have an obvious way to collect the believer's wealth. Now if a coin drop mechanism would have opened the Temple doors giving the believers access to the giant marble and gold likeness of their God with some automated sound effects for a more comprehensive show/miracle, that would make more sense than having them start a fire to get inside. I have a feeling this may have been one of Heron's next improvements to his temple door design.

To have the very first automated door opener designed by one of the greatest inventors of his time must have been a considerable investment that only the most successful businesses could afford. It seems inducing subjective realities requiring people to give up their wealth to please a God was one of if not the best way to extract money from a working-class population. It's difficult to say whether forced taxes or the pleasure of an induced response to please Gods extracted more wealth from our ancient ancestors, because the priests, kings, Gods and government were often the same people or person living in the same lavish Temple or Palace.

Even though the priests of the more popular Gods were able to accumulate excessive wealth, like any smart modern day capitalist they would want to invest in the future to acquire more customers, an even greater profits. Without any obvious ways of extracting wealth from their believers like the holy water vending machine that took their money directly how would this large automated temple door investment bring in more customers and convince them to willingly give up what little money and resources they needed for their own survival and that of their families?

The simple answer is it made their God stronger than all the smaller weaker Gods not capable of performing miracles. All ancient people were induced from childhood with a subjective reality to fear and respect Gods especially the more powerful vengeful ones known to kill us mere mortals for their amusement. It seems the term God-fearing people got started thousands of years ago as that emotion proved to be one of the best tools for predatory manipulation and social engineering. As I was considering the free market competition between the ancient Gods and their priests to secure the largest temples and percentage of the working-class resources wealth, it reminded me a lot of modern-day car dealerships and their salespeople trying to accomplish essentially the same goals.

The name recognition and emotional satisfaction people associate with a car brand would represent the God. A luxury sports car worth over $100,000 would represent a more powerful feel good God/emotional response than a rusted out pickup truck that smokes. The dealership represents the Temple where the God and their priests live. And the salespeople would clearly represent the priests that live and work in the Temple both trying to attract as many customers/believers as possible willing to give up their wealth. Just like the more successful dealerships may have accumulated enough wealth to invest in some new gimmick like a searchlight or inflatable giant people to attract more customers. Temple priests would also use emerging technologies to give their believers the emotional satisfaction and sense of security that their God was truly more powerful than all the others and thus would protect them from all the real and imaginary threats inherent in their more primitive predatory social structures.

The flashier Gods with the most impressive miracles and temples drew the largest crowds, created the strongest emotional responses for better memory recall and word-of-mouth advertising. Thousands of years ago there weren't many entertainment options besides the occasional public humiliation, torture and executions used to condition the population into submission, allowing the collective Stockholm syndrome to have greater influence over the social evolutionary development of our species. The Temple miracles and priests trying to convince potential believers to give up their wealth was one of the best shows in town.

Some may wonder why it's important to understand the ancient Gods and the people that believed in them. After all we have newer Gods now and religious beliefs that explain how the ancient Gods were not real. And how our ancestors were clearly under some form of mass delusion because nobody really believes in the ancient Gods anymore and they certainly wouldn't kill or die to serve them as in the past when these Gods were still real. One of the reasons it's so important to understand our ancestors and their beliefs is because they are to us as we will be to our descendants. Our descendants will have learned the transition to a predator free society eliminated the need to use induced subjective realities as a predatory tool for capitalistic exploitation. However, until then there will continue to be new religions and Gods to kill and die for.

As another example how absolutely certain our ancestors were about the Gods they believed in and what level of control their subjective realities had over their lives, can be better understood by a quick review of the Seven Wonders of the ancient World. Keep in mind these were some of the greatest feats of architectural engineering ever created, they were icons of excessive opulence, wealth and power. These wonders were unimaginable to the peasants of the ancient world. A little like an American child born in the ghettos growing up in poverty with only a limited knowledge of the world seeing their US Capitol building in person for the first time. That's the kind of thing that creates a memorable emotional experience of humbling insignificance in the face of great power.

Three of the seven ancient wonders were constructed to honor and serve full Gods that only existed in a non-corporeal form like the statue of Zeus at Olympia, the temple for Artemis, and the Colossus of Rhodes that was created in the likeness of the sun God Helios. One of the seven ancient wonders, the great Pyramids of Giza, was built for one person (Khufu) who was believed to be a God. And surprisingly two of them seemed to have been built for love. One of these two ancient wonders, the tomb of Mausolus was built for the love of a husband/brother King Mausolus. It was however adorned with many statues of Gods and Goddesses. It is said that King Mausolus forcibly imposed many hardships on his people and even practiced creative forms of wealth extraction like imposing a tax for having longhair. This is a good 560 BC example of a predatory abuse of power to manipulate a working class resource much like a modern-day politician uses their position in government to increase their personal wealth and income potential. These early forms of predatory social structures helped generations of ruling class top predators evolve the best ways to exploit their working class resource and get them to willingly comply with their managed exploitation. Artemisia, the wife of King Mausolus created this wonder of the ancient world using the great wealth acquired from predatory conquests and taxing their working-class people.

Of the seven ancient wonders my personal favorite is the hanging Gardens of Babylon, they seem to be the result of a true love story. King Nebuchadnezzar created the hanging gardens of Babylon for his ailing wife Amytis. It was said to be because she missed the gardens of her native land of Medo-Persia. Thousands of working class peasants labored for many years to create this great wonder of the ancient world, all to ease the suffering of one very special person. The last of the seven ancient wonders, the lighthouse of Alexandria was the only one that had a practical application like the safety of shipping and commerce.

It's important to understand the evolution of different religions, how they start and why they end. Thousands of years before our modern religions started their own evolutionary branch, stories of the ancient Gods and their many heroic exploits were the stuff of bedtime stories for all the peasant children throughout the land. Providing what appears to be a clear example of a self-perpetuating subjective belief that continues into adulthood and then becomes a social reality. Imagine if we lived in a world where all the people that read comic books as a child grew up to be adults in a society where those heroes and villains were considered real people. This may seem silly to an educated present day individual functioning with an objective reality but our illiterate ancestors working with their hardwired survival instincts and emotional reactions would kill or die while following their subjective beliefs.

As old as these ancient Gods were compared to our modern religions, there were even older Gods that our Neolithic (Stone Age) ancestors believed in. Many of the oldest Gods and the people that believed in them will never be known but lucky for us new technologies have helped

World religions by percentage of population, (2013)

Date of formation or origination by founder

B.C. ▬▬▬▬▬   A.D. ▬▬▬▬▬

Religion	Date	Percentage
Baha'I	1852 A.D.	.11%
Jewish	2000 B.C.	.22%
Sikh	1469 A.D.	.35%
Anglican	10 A.D.	1.26%
Atheists	500 B.C.	2.01%
Orthodox	10 A.D.	3.96%
Protestant	10 A.D.	6.15%
Buddhist	500 B.C.	6.77%
Non-religious	500 B.C.	9.66%
Other religions	10,000 B.C.	10.95%
Hindu	2000 B.C.	13.80%
Roman Catholic	10 A.D.	16.85%
Muslim	610 A.D.	22.74%

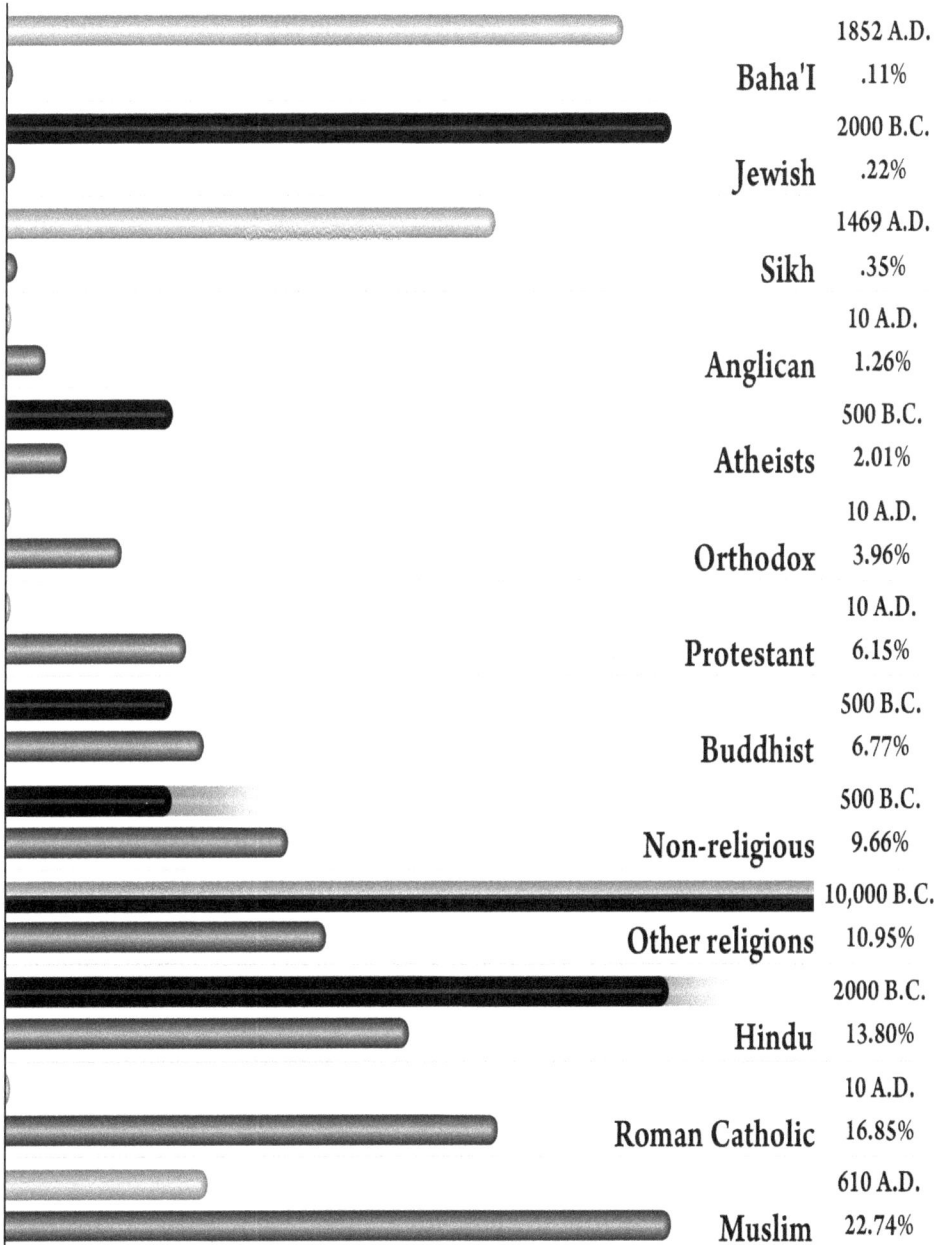

Source: The CIA World factbook, Prepared by True Freedom Technologies

discover what is believed to be the oldest Temple used for religious rituals. Göbekli Tepe is a Neolithic structure created by some of our Stone Age ancestors around 12,000 years ago in what is now modern day southeastern Turkey. Fortunately Göbekli Tepe was intentionally buried protecting its secrets from thousands of years of Mother Nature's wrath and human development, much like fossils are protected in layers of sediment and rock.

Each new ancient discovery like Göbekli Tepe helps fill in the missing pieces of our evolutionary development as well as the progression of our religious beliefs. Before Göbekli Tepe it was thought that our species developed farming and settlements before religions and the belief in Gods. It didn't seem like our earlier hunter-gatherer lifestyle would allow for enough leisure time form complex subjective realities such as a religion or even contemplate the existence of Gods. It now appears the belief in Gods and the need to honor them with temples came before our more practical evolutionary developments like basic farming, secure communities and a better quality of life for our people. I'm starting to see why this mindset is still so prevalent in our modern societies. It may be difficult to intellectually override 12,000 years of social conditioning but now that we know how the process works nothing can stop our evolutionary progress towards achieving true freedom and prosperity for our species.

There is a general consensus that just a few elite ruling class religious leaders were in charge of the construction and ritual activities carried out at this Neolithic temple. These religious leaders may be the very first priestly caste in the evolution of our species. This may be the very place where the concept of organized religion was born starting its own parallel track of evolutionary development. All the Gods in every religion ever conceived of for the next 12,000 years owe their existence to the priests at Göbekli Tepe or perhaps even earlier ones that will never be known. This is a key piece for anyone's fact puzzle, allowing his or her big picture to becomes much clearer.

The stone carvings on the temples pillars seem to indicate this was a time when our ancestors realized how our intellectual survival trait distinguishes us from other creatures, and with this distinction of superiority and predatory dominance, the first egocentric mindsets were created. Sure we were genetically encoded from the beginning for predatory competition but now we're beginning to use our intelligence and form abstract strategies to more efficiently exploit our environmental resources and one another.

Göbekli Tepe may also be where the very first subjective reality to serve a God, priests and ruling class top predators was intentionally induced into other people for the purpose of social exploitation. It seems natural that the first God's were related to the animals, land, water, fire and all of the environmental elements that we depended upon for our survival. As our intellectual survival trait became more dominant and our understanding of our environmental conditions grew exponentially, new Gods and religions started to branch out like limbs on a tree.

The first problem with the evolutionary expansion of new Gods and religions is they are dependent upon their priest's ability to induce a subjective reality sufficient enough to help expand their customer base and acquire more believers. Before the evolution of advanced communication technologies, people were deprived of the factual knowledge they needed to form objective realities, so inducing an uneducated population with a subjective belief became a socially accepted way of life. If all global transportation and communication technologies were to fail and the intellectual enlightenment of our species were to be prevented by some natural or man-made catastrophic event, the use of predatory subjective realities could continue indefinitely. Or at least until we once again reach that tipping point in our intellectual evolutionary development, when our social exploitation and planned inequality is no longer tolerated by a working-class resource.

The second problem with creating new Gods and religions to believe in is that the evolutionary process is inherently predatory like our free-market capitalistic competition for survival. Over time the Gods and their believers seem to settle on this battle cry of intolerance "There can be only one" no other Gods or even the belief in other Gods will be tolerated. As the newer Gods and the people that collected wealth for them got smarter they started to realize the advantage of this basic capitalistic strategy, eliminate the competition, consolidate the customer base, limit profits and power to just a few ruling class top predators thus allowing for more dominant control over the marketplace of available believers.

Inducing subjective realities that include the religious genocide of any believers in other Gods was an effective means of eliminating the competition and consolidating the available wealth among a few ruling class priests, warlords and kings. Using a subjective religious belief to justify the massacre of entire populations, plunder their wealth and force the surviving women and children into slavery has become unacceptable as our intellectual survival trait gains control over our hardwired predatory instincts. This form of intellectual manipulation is rapidly losing its effectiveness within modern-day societies that allow their people free access to high quality public education.

Can you imagine just a few multinational corporations using their power and wealth to convince a global working-class resource to literally eliminate the competition and any of their fellow consumers that still wanted to buy a different product? Or convincing a modern-day consumer the only way they will end their earthly suffering and receive eternal pleasures in heaven is to exclusively buy their product. On the other hand if we decided to buy another product and give our wealth to another corporation, our mortal lives would be filled with torment and our souls would burn in hell for eternity.

As crazy as this may sound to individuals familiar with this psychological manipulation technique, millions of our young people and uninformed adults are still vulnerable to this form of predatory attack. And with a religious subjective reality we don't even get a tangible product for giving up our wealth, just the emotional satisfaction that our God will love and protect us forever. At least with a subjective reality to serve a capitalistic government there's a chance of winning the lottery or even becoming a ruling class top predator. It's not like capitalists take a vow of poverty and dedicate their lives towards easing the suffering and death created by our predatory social structure, although creating the illusion of compassion will help maintain the subjective reality among the uninformed masses.

Unlike the extinction of a species from the process of natural selection all of the weaker and more vulnerable Gods, priests and their believers could be targeted and eliminated using the process of artificial selection aided by our advanced intellectual survival trait and predatory skills. Because early God Kings were also the supreme government authority they could simply make it a law that anyone that opposed their Godliness would be accused of blasphemy and publicly executed as an example to others. Once our species started using our predatory instincts to artificially select, which members of our species would live or die depending on the God or King they believed in, the effects of natural selection on our species development began to be dominated by the process of artificial selection. For at least the last 12,000 years the ruling class top predators have used their positions of power to shape the religious and social development of our species. The use of artificial selection to control a species evolutionary development can be as innocent as producing the perfect shade of lavender rose or as sinister as the social engineering and psychological condition of a global working-class resource.

The ability of top predator kings and priests to manipulate and alter our intellectual evolutionary development has given them better psychological control over the majority of our species. The first top predator kings were unaware of the process of artificial selection, only that if they killed off all the nonbelievers that dared to challenge their divinity and domination, the only people left to have children were the ones most willing to accept their induced subjective reality. Even though these ruling class Kings were not Gods or even the children of Gods, their uneducated working class people were so well conditioned they would kill or die to serve them.

An easy way to understand this concept is to study the social dynamics in a modern day religious cult. There are many empirical examples to study where the Godlike cult leader was able to induce a subjective reality so strong their followers would kill their own children or commit mass suicide. Their absolute faith in their Godlike leaders is equal to the control their subjective reality has over the decisions they make and actions they take. Again, individuals willing to give up their intellectual survival trait for the illusion of a subjective reality make themselves easy prey for predatory human attacks and all forms of capitalistic exploitation.

Ruling class top predator Kings naturally began to use subjective realities to serve Gods and governments as a tool to manage and exploit their working-class prey. Over the years I have become more interested in our evolutionary development. I realized the better we understand our past the more effective we can be at analyzing and finding solutions to present day problems. My particular interest is with any natural or artificial evolutionary process that may have contributed to our past and present preventable suffering and death also any areas where our intelligence was used to manipulate our hardwired predatory instincts creating social structures designed for systematic exploitation.

Of the many events throughout our social development where ruling class top predators used their power of artificial selection to manipulate and shape our future the following seems to be one of the most influential in determining our current demographics of religious beliefs. In the fourth century 313 A.D. the Roman emperors Constantine and Licinius decided to tolerate the Christian religion allowing it to compete with others.   Then just 67 years later in 380 A.D. the Emperor Theodosius declared Christianity to be the supreme religion and the state church of the Roman Empire. When the top predator of the greatest empire on earth decides which God and religion the people must believe in, it effectively ends the free-market competition for the immortal souls and the immense wealth of all the Roman citizens, peasants and slaves under their rule.

Imagine the president of the United States declaring all capitalistic people must now eat at and give their money to only one government owned restaurant where they control the profits. Keep in mind even more than today convincing people to give up their money for the protection and love of a God was big business and one of the best ways to extract wealth from a working-class resource. Oh yes… it's good to be Emperor, with the power to consolidate all of the wealth generated from every religious subjective reality and the ability to eliminate the competition preventing opposing philosophies among future believers. This chain of events may have heavily influenced the evolution of religious subjective realities for our species, but from an objective point of view we must admit it was a masterful act of strategic predatory domination. Something modern-day capitalists can only dream of.

By reducing the number of Gods people could believe in to just one, it did eliminate much of the suffering and death created by religious competitions. It also prevented the priests of other Gods from inducing their subjective realities on an unsuspecting public already fully conditioned to give up their wealth as part of a commonly accepted ritualistic behavior. The wealth and resources that was distributed among the many is now being consolidated among even fewer more powerful top predators, further increasing the gap between the working-class population and the ruling class elite. People under the control of a modern religious subjective reality should realize a good God wouldn't want them to be exploited for profit. If some God, alien or whatever was telling me the many must suffer and die so that my chosen few can live as Kings, I would tell him no thanks Mr. God, I may only be a mere mortal but even I know that's not right. And since I have your attention, you should also know I will not kill or die to serve you.

Thousands of years of artificial selection have increased our current population's vulnerability to predatory exploitation. And even though this form of social engineering has encoded our genetic memory and hardwired us to accept our predatory domination, the application of factual knowledge within the environmental conditions of a predator free society should override these limitations within one or two generations. This may seem like a long time but not when you consider this manipulation technique has dominated our species intellectual evolutionary development for thousands of years. That's a big deal, and in general, big things that take a long time to get this bad, likewise take a long time to get better.

The real threat preventing our transition to a predator free society will most likely be the top predators of Capitalism continuing to use their power and wealth to maintain our current predatory social structure. When this interference can be better controlled and eventually eliminated the transition to a predator free society can accelerate exponentially making our tragic evolutionary past and present a subject for study as we move into a more enlightened phase of our intellectual development.

The subjective reality of a terrorist may be difficult to imagine with only a superficial understanding of the subject, but with a closer examination it may start to feel familiar.
Many people wonder what would make a person become a terrorist willing to inflict such suffering and death on others and then take their own lives. Before we objectively consider this question it's important to keep in mind throughout history the difference between a mass murder and a courageous hero is determined by what side of the conflict a person is born into or perhaps more accurately what religious and or patriotic subjective reality they were induced with throughout their lives.

Even the founding fathers of our United States were considered revolutionary troublemakers to the British Empire. Gaining our independence from the British Empire was a rare example of the many working-class prey rising up for equality and prevailing over their ruling class top predators. If it can happen once... It gets easier the smarter and more united we become as a species, all the way up to the point when our transition to a global predator free society is complete and predatory conflicts for survival will be a thing of the past.

To truly understand someone's motives for wanting to commit mass homicide and end their life we would need to live their life and experience the years of psychological conditioning used to create a subjective reality where killing other people is an acceptable form of conflict resolution. Also keep in mind, adapting to a predatory social structure naturally induces us with a subjective reality that considers the suffering and death of others a socially acceptable consequence of our competition for survival. Accepting the deaths of our prey and other competitors has been hardwired into our genetic memory from the beginning of our existence. However, as formidable as our genetic programming is at controlling our thoughts and actions the fast adaptation of our intellectual survival trait will take control of this evolutionary process accelerating our transition to a predator free society.

When we consider how terrible the enemy is and want to understand their motivations, we should first realize we are like opposite sides of the same coin each induced with a subjective reality that our God and country holds the moral high ground. Our Gods and countries are used to induce us with the moral superiority and subjective reality that the massacre of nonbelievers and enemies of the state are religiously justified and legally sanctioned. On the other hand, as long as we are forced to adapt to a predatory social structure we must devote national wealth and resources to defend against other governments and ideologies around the world with similar ambitions of global capitalistic and religious domination.

Having said that, our actions and motivations seem to fall into two major categories, the biological and the intellectual. For example the biological motivation to find food when we're hungry or shelter when we're cold. Our hardwired survival instincts can motivate us to perform desperate acts of violence especially when forced to compete against one another within a predatory social structure. We know biology controls the motivations and actions of all life forced into predatory competition for their survival. Defects in our biological development from industrial waste or other environmental contaminants can also produce erratic and seemingly unexplainable acts of violence as well as other social dysfunctions.

Because we humans have naturally accepted the use of our intelligence as a predatory tool to use against others in our capitalistic competition for survival we must also consider how it influences our other actions and motivations. If a competing predator learns of a way to convince others to kill or die to serve them or a God the last thing they would want is to give up their predatory dominance by allowing their prey to become intellectually aware of their exploitation. Inducing a subjective reality to reject factual knowledge has worked well for top predators that need their working-class prey to willingly kill or die to maintain their predatory dominance and illusion of absolute power. After the intellectual control of an induced subjective reality is established convincing a believer to kill or give up their life to serve their God, government or predatory masters can be as simple as issuing an order.

Of course in our more civilized modern predatory societies the suffering and death of millions for profit can be legitimized with the stroke of the pen. Why is the death of millions of our people considered acceptable in the pursuit of capitalistic domination and excessive wealth, while the death of one individual during a low-level predatory conflict for survival is considered a crime worthy of a legal execution? See anything wrong with this picture? I have to keep asking myself as obvious as this problem is why haven't we the people used our democracy and power in numbers to correct it and move in to the next phase of our intellectual evolutionary development. Then I realized the power of induced subjective realities and how we must break their control before we can end our predatory exploitation and make social progress towards intellectual enlightenment.

The objective reality I have developed so far would consider anyone willing to commit mass homicide to serve a God is under the complete control of his or her religious subjective reality. We must assume a person willing to commit mass homicide, genocide and suicide for a God or government is unaware of the factual knowledge necessary to prevent this form of predatory exploitation. And how, the predatory control of their actions will accelerate its destructive effects, by exacerbating the conflict increasing preventable suffering and death. Without the knowledge to prevent their exploitation an individual will naturally rely on our hardwired survival instincts and emotional reactions to environmental influences to form their decisions and determine their actions. Even from a casual observation it seems like a practical way to de-evolve an individual, population or species preventing them from using their intellectual survival trait to form predatory defenses and prevent their exploitation.

Another example of how induced religious subjective realities directly interfere with our mental health is a phenomenon known as the Jerusalem syndrome. This condition occurs with people of faith when traveling to the great city of Jerusalem and is not specific to any one religion. The individuals affected become emotionally overwhelmed knowing that they are in the very place where their God or son of their God lived, died, and ascended to heaven. The one thing these people have in common is a strong belief in their God's existence and an inability to control their emotions or actions with factual knowledge and objective reasoning.

The symptoms of the Jerusalem syndrome may range from simple conversations with their God, visions/hallucinations up to full-blown psychotic episodes with a complete loss of any objective reality. Most of the people afflicted with this syndrome were not previously diagnosed with psychotic symptoms leaving their religious experience as the common denominator. However the people affected by this disorder must have been more susceptible to being controlled by their subjective reality than a more casual believer. Because the overwhelming emotions responsible for this syndrome affect the brain much like that of a drug overdose, the treatment to bring these individuals back to a mental state where they can function in society is similar.

The Jerusalem syndrome has become so common with people of faith that special wards have been created to specifically deal with this disorder. Without prior conditioning to induce a religious subjective reality this form of mental disorder would not occur, and our intellectual survival trait could maintain objective control over our decisions and actions.

As another example of how devastating a subjective reality can be on a population is the 1994 genocide in Rwanda resulting in the deaths of over 800,000 men, women and children during a 100 day period of time. To help put this into perspective, that would be equivalent to having the entire population of San Francisco getting massacred with machetes in a little over three months. It's almost beyond imagination, we naturally want to block it out as something so horrible it can't be real, but when we allow that to happen we cannot learn from this tragedy and help prevent a similar event. The best way to honor those lost in predatory conflicts is to learn from the tragedy and prevent others from needlessly losing their lives while

while under the control of a similar subjective reality.

Our objective should be to understand the underlying cause that perpetuates these predatory conflicts and eliminate the conditions that created it, thus preventing the formation of the primary factor responsible for our avoidable suffering and death. Other predatory conflicts around the world share similar pre-genocide environmental conditions with populations also under the control of their own subjective realities. They must gain the factual knowledge necessary to break their subjective realities and end the predatory control of any present or future top predator wishing to use them as a resource for exploitation.

It's interesting to note that the genocide in Rwanda was not motivated by religious subjective realities which are known to produce a similar loss of intellectual control, greater vulnerability to predatory manipulation and irrational acts of homicidal violence. Rwanda's population is about 93% Christian and 5% Muslim. Many of the priests died defending the Tutsi population while other priests helped the Hutus with their genocide. Even among people sharing the same religious subjective reality the control of their ethnic beliefs was stronger. In order for subjective realities to control the actions of individuals or a population into acts of genocidal violence, the initial conditioning must break down all the commonalities we share as people and exaggerate the insignificant differences into a perceived threat. This perceived threat, may have no basis in fact or exist in reality, but that is the essence of subjective realities and why the deaths they produce are so senseless.

The shared commonality of genetic makeup and religious beliefs were defeated by the lack of intellectual predatory defenses and top predators willing to kill their own working-class resource to increase their personal wealth and power. When the subjective reality of ethnic superiority wouldn't work on the more educated and older Hutus they were forced to participate in the genocide or publicly tortured to death as an example to others. What makes a population of people revert back to the same old primitive predatory manipulation techniques used for thousands of years?

They were simply adapting to the environmental conditions of their predatory social structure and subjective realities just as our ancient ancestors did.

In a way the conflict between the Hutus and Tutsis started long before these two people even met. It's natural for all people to develop a sense of pride in their ethnic, cultural or national backgrounds. It appears a naturally occurring subjective reality starts to develop a sense of moral superiority and self-righteousness. This seems to be especially true among the more powerful and technically advanced cultures relative to the other contemporary populations. As the subjective reality of ethnic superiority grows all other ethnic groups by default must become inferior diminishing their value as real people. To induce a subjective reality strong enough to condition a population into committing genocide, victims would need to be convinced that the people on the opposing side of the conflict are less than human and therefore their deaths are of no consequence.

Of course with most conflicts both sides are equally convinced they hold the moral high ground and that only their atrocities are justified. Neither side realizing they're both being controlled by a common enemy we are now able to join together and defeat eliminating the need for all predatory conflicts. But we're learning fast as a species and soon that common enemy will no longer prevent us from reaching the next phase of our intellectual evolutionary development. That being the formation and exponential expansion of a global predator free society.

It is primarily for people of faith that I write this book. I realized more than any other segment of our population they have been targeted for their willingness to make decisions and take actions based on their subjective reality. Again induced subjective realities are a powerful form of psychological manipulation used for predatory exploitation and they should not be taken lightly. They are capable of causing a victim to kill others and or themselves for the belief in something that is not real. All of our ancestors for thousands of years were artificially selected into a population most willing to accept the belief in any patriotic or religious subjective reality being induced by the ruling class top predator Kings and priests.

There have been so many Gods that have come and gone throughout our intellectual evolutionary development but people of faith keep adapting to their new God's and religions with the same willingness to kill or die for their convictions. Again the reason for this is our hardwired survival instincts, and the environmental conditions necessary to produce this form of predatory control have remained relatively unchanged for thousands of years only the names of the Gods and the people that kill and die for them have change.

It should be acknowledged that most religions preach peace, tolerance and harmony at least among their own believers and sometimes this even extends into tolerating the belief in other Gods, cultures, rituals etc. It is also true people of faith throughout our evolutionary development have relieved much suffering and death among the weakest and most vulnerable segments of our populations. Their convictions and belief in their Gods compelled them to put their lives in harms way to help others in need. Many priests and people of faith made the ultimate sacrifice to follow their convictions to help others knowing their death would guarantee eternal life in the loving presence of their God.

Using subjective realities to manipulate people into doing the right thing may have been necessary in the past but now we will use our intelligence to make informed decisions based on factual knowledge not creative forms of predatory deception. We won't need the threat of hell or the promise of heaven just and objective understanding of the right thing to do for the benefit of the many and not just the few.

It should also be acknowledged that not all of the money and natural resources collected for Gods went into building great marble monuments and lavish cathedrals or to increase the wealth and power of the top predator priests and kings. As needed some of that wealth was and still is used to feed, cloth and house the least fortunate among us and to induce the subjective reality of their religious beliefs. We humans can be condition to believe in any subjective reality especially when the alternative is starving to death or dying from exposure. Also we are most vulnerable when we are weakened and from lack of basic survival necessities and mentally stressed out from years of predatory competition.

Our natural ability to adapt to any environmental conditions or social structure makes us all naturally vulnerable to the influence and control of an induced subjective reality especially during the formative years of our childhood. It's important to remember there is no dishonor to have fallen victim to a subjective reality these are things outside our sphere of control at such an early stage in our individual development. It's only after the isolation of childhood that many of us seek or otherwise become aware of the factual knowledge necessary to break our subjective realities and end the exploitation process.

Because subjective realities are passed down for generations, the belief in them may have been responsible for the suffering and death of many of our ancestors willing to die for their God and religious convictions. The emotional conflicts this presents for our parents and grandparents may prevent them from accepting any factual knowledge contrary to the subjective reality they have been induced with for their entire lives. Younger generations with exposure to modern science and technology will naturally start to develop objective realities strong enough to break the control of any ancient religious beliefs they were induced with during their childhood

I feel it's worth mentioning from time to time that my primary objective is to reduce suffering and death by helping to end our predatory evolution that has dominated our evolutionary development since the beginning of our existence and to accelerate our peaceful transition to a predator free society. It only seems logical to correct the root cause at its source and allow its many symptoms to fade away, but in order to accomplish that goal we need to reach that critical tipping point in our intellectual evolutionary development where our collective realities become more objective and our predatory social structure will no longer be acceptable.

However, in order for us to reach that critical tipping point in our evolutionary development where our intellectual survival trait overrides our hardwired predatory instincts. We must help others get access to the factual knowledge they need to break their subjective realities and end their capitalistic exploitation. It is for this reason I cannot avoid the subjects of religion and politics since they have proven to be major contributors to our preventable suffering and death and the most effective tools used by top predators throughout our social evolution to control and manipulate us working-class prey.

If we're really serious about reducing the preventable suffering and death of our species and advancing our intellectual evolutionary development, we will need to address the most serious obstacles directly without delay. Avoiding the problem is not a good strategy for finding a solution but as obvious as this may seem, it's exactly what we have been doing. No wonder big changes are so difficult. I may just be one of the little people but I am not willing to wait for a subjective illusion or our ruling class leaders to end our capitalistic competition for survival and accelerate our transition to a predator free society. And the coolest part of all is we don't need them anyway, not really because the true power behind any nation flows from its working-class people. We just need to learn that we possess this power and how to use it to make an efficient and peaceful transition to a predator free society and a level of true freedom and prosperity like most of us can barely imagine.

8. Let's play God... or Aliens

If it's good to be king, it's better to be God. For many of the ruling class top predators of our past just being an almighty King was not good enough. Their egos and subjective realities needed them to be Gods, children of Gods or any other deified symbol of authority they could get their uneducated working-class subjects and slaves to believe in. After all what makes a God? These Godlike kings did have the power of life and death over all of their people and they both knew it. They directly determined what level of freedom or exploitation their working-class people would suffer under their rule. And perhaps most importantly they determine the intellectual evolutionary development of our species.

As another example of how the working-class masses around the world are breaking their subjective realities and making an evolutionary transition to a more intellectual decision-making process, is we don't believe our ruling class top predators are Gods anymore or even the children of Gods. No leader would ever suggest such a silly thing in a modern society for fear of being labeled mentally unstable with delusions of deified grandeur. We've come a long way as a species however, claiming the most popular God wants you to rule over others still seems acceptable to some people as a legitimate means for achieving power and control over them. Most of us know now our ruling class leaders and top predators of our world today are really just regular people like us but with nicer clothes, better educations and maybe more money than God.

It is a philosophical belief and considered scientifically valid that if Gods were real entities they would only be a more technically and socially advanced life forms not a supernatural humanoid with a long white beard wearing robes and sandals. Giving our Gods and alien visitors human characteristics seems like a clear attempt to create some commonality for us to relate to. After all it would be a little difficult relating to a life form that we cannot see, hear or touch and only exists in a dimension we can't comprehend yet. It's human nature to form subjective realities around the way we want things to be and disregard any rational explanation contrary to that believe.

The actual physical form, if any, of an advanced alien species capable of being like Gods to us, is most likely beyond our ability to intellectually comprehend at this stage of our evolutionary development. On a relative scale it would be like our house cats trying to imagine the diversity of life in our oceans or thinking most fish probably look like them. And if cats were intelligent enough to create their own Gods or contemplate alien life forms, I feel certain they would have soft fur, claws and purred when they were happy.

An advanced alien species capable of manipulating the life-cycle of stars and the creation of organic life within a solar system would certainly seem like Gods to us, as we would seem like Gods to our bacterial cultures in a lab. It seems for a life form to be considered Godlike or not is relative to their level of intellectual and technological development compared to other species. Even within the same species as seen in our own history. The more technologically advanced humans were perceived as Gods among the less advanced cultures they encountered.

Taking this concept to its logical conclusion we are already both Gods to many life forms as well as possible participants within some grand conception beyond our ability to comprehend. There are over 500 different life forms living within and on our bodies. We are, a self-contained mobile universe where trillions of individual entities live out their lives unable to comprehend the greater multi-verse they are a part of. It is logical to assume we too are part of a multi-verse where we are the microbes on our planet living out our lives unaware that we are part of a much larger living system.

Why would any self-respecting intellectually advanced extraterrestrial life forms want to start diplomatic relations with an evolving creature not yet capable of fully comprehending or controlling their hardwired predatory instincts? Or still uses their emerging intelligence to systematically exploit their environment and prey on one another instead of working together for the benefit and survival of their entire species? I can't think of a good reason.

Imagine a rocket scientist giving up their pursuit in advanced technologies to travel to a remote section of Africa to start diplomatic relations with several warring ant colonies or trying to teach them the survival benefits of cooperation over competition. It's hard to be humble or to put our existence into perspective when we have the Godlike power of life and death over all other creatures on our planet. This is just another phase in our evolutionary development we must transcend to become a more socially mature intellectual enlightened species worthy of contact by any advanced extraterrestrial life form that may be watching.

Even if Godlike aliens played a role in creating our solar system and a planet like Earth capable of supporting intelligent life it's up to us now. If they have been following our evolutionary progress they clearly don't mind allowing millions of us to die during our intellectual development to a predator free society. Even worse they seem to be willing to allow millions more of us to die before our transition is complete. Then again maybe the whole point of the experiment is to determine how long it takes an intelligent life form to understand and gain control of their hardwired predatory instincts and make the evolutionary leap to a predator free society.

Maybe we're unknowing participants in a galactic bet among advanced extraterrestrial on how many people will die in predatory conflicts before we reach that critical point in our intellectual evolution when our social exploitation will no longer be acceptable. I don't know about you but I'm not willing to wait for any Gods or aliens to fix our problems and judging on how they've handled things so far I wouldn't want them planning our future either. Trust me, were far better off using our advanced intellectual survival trait to solve our global problems than relying on a subjective reality about Gods or aliens. We need to have intellectual control of our future to provide true freedom and prosperity to all people as equals.

We humans have been playing God for thousands of years on our own species and others without the knowledge of how this would affect our biological and intellectual evolutionary development. The effects of artificial selection by top predators of our species over a period of thousands of years has shaped our subjective realities into considering our predatory social structure is an acceptable way of life. Far more than Gods, Aliens or even natural selection the ruling class top predators throughout our evolutionary development are responsible for our current social structure and its systematic exploitation of the working class resource, also known as we the people. Our species would have developed in ways difficult to imagine if not for thousands of years the predatory inspired artificial selection. This is exactly what we're about to fix as we make the transition to a predator free society and the next phase of our intellectual evolutionary development.

At some point during our evolution top predators begin to realize how the process of artificial selection works. Advanced social engineering techniques were developed to more efficiently exploit and condition the working class resource. The separation between the few elite top predators and the many working class prey was about to get wider by design. Consolidating wealth and power among the very few by the managed exploitation of the many is a natural consequence of any predatory social structure especially the most technologically advanced ones like Capitalism. Using our intellectual survival trait as a predatory tool against one another has never been so good for the top predators of our species.

The top predators of our world today are definitely not Gods, and probably aren't aliens, but having the power to control the intellectual evolutionary development of our species must make some of them feel like Gods. The top predators of our past may have been following their natural predatory instincts and embracing their elite social status. However, most of the top predators of our modern world are too well educated to use the excuse of ignorance, and if they didn't already know they soon will, allowing them to make an objective decision what role they would like to play in our transition. It's not just for equal rights and prosperity for our country but instead a more fundamental solution and evolutionary milestone for the intellectual development of our entire species.

Another way we humans are playing God with our own evolutionary development is with our ability to understand and manipulate our own genetic code. This is a huge milestone in the intellectual progress of our species, it's a little like one of our computers growing up to become self-aware and learning how to rewrite its own software. It's also interesting how the binary code of just ones and zeros are used to create many computer applications where our biological code is made up of four nucleotide chemicals and is used to create many different forms of life like us. Even more interesting is how little subroutines of genetic code are reused in different applications to perform similar tasks.

On one hand it would be easy to conclude that an advanced life form would have the ability to program a self-replicating biological system much like we write computer code. However, if one of them did design our self replicating system it seems to have naturally developed as part of a much larger experiment with little to no interference since single celled life forms got started on this planet. The fossil records clearly show the progression of life on earth starting out with the simplest of creatures eventually developing into the most complex life form we know, and now we're learning how to rewrite our own genetic code and intellectually control our predatory instincts. Yeah, I'd say we've come a long way, but this isn't the end of our journey or the pinnacle of our evolutionary success, in a way it's just the beginning. This is when things start to get interesting. It's a lot like a child growing up and learning there is a whole world of wonders to experience and feeling that newfound freedom that comes from knowing they get to control their own future now.

Once we gain the ability to alter, correct and redesign our own genetic code we will be able to prevent many diseases, increase our sensory perceptions to different environmental conditions and even extend the human life cycle indefinitely. Under the predatory social economic structure of Capitalism these life-extending advanced technologies tend to only be available for the more successful competitors. Life extending technologies should be just as available to the working class many as they are to the ruling class few. As long as there is a distinction between the two classes there will be unacceptable inequality and conflicts to correct this symptom. The things that should be considered a human right for all become a privilege for the fortunate few under Capitalism.

No social structure or ruling class leader should have the power to play God and damage the future of our species in the pursuit of their individual predatory ambitions. Keeping advanced technologies proprietary until a capitalistic strategy can be formulated to extract the maximum amount of profit from the working class resource is just one of the symptoms of a predatory social structure that will be corrected with the transition to a predator free society. Even though our ruling class leaders unknowingly played God for thousands of years severely slowing down our intellectual evolutionary development, we are now about to very intentionally eliminate those barriers and make up for lost time.

I am interested in doing research and development in the area of 3-D bioprinters that are capable of printing out replacement organs, missing limbs, new skin etc. It seems this technology will be very beneficial in the future for extending our overall life-cycle especially in combination with minimally invasive robotic surgery. Taking this technology to its logical conclusion it will be possible to print out or grow an entire new body in which our existing brains can be transplanted into. As long as our fragile neural pathways can successfully interface with the new biotech support systems, the possibilities could be limitless. This technology will eventually give us the Godlike power of immortality at least from natural causes and greatly reduce the likelihood of an accidental death.

Our brains, with their ability to learn and comprehend the complexities of our existence, are the ultimate feat of bioengineering whatever the processes was that created us. Like any complicated system, parts should be capable of being upgraded as new technologies and materials become available. All of our body parts will eventually fall into this category except for the one organ that holds the very essence of who we are, all the memories of our past and the experiences of our future will be contained within our brains. All of our other body parts seem to provide the support systems our brains need to perform our survival tasks.

In addition to our achievements in bioengineering and genetic research we are also advancing the quality of life for our species with creative combinations of new materials and technologies. Our biological and technical achievements towards longevity seem to be advancing on parallel tracks both competing for greater relevance as our species evolves towards immortality. Both systems have advantages and disadvantages for performing the tasks in life we need for survival or want for recreation.

I suppose the design challenge would be to create a hybrid system using the best of both technologies while minimizing their disadvantages. The final organ, body part or entire hybrid system must perform as well if not much better than the organic original. Even more challenging will be how to make these subsystems compact and reliable enough to supply and or synthesize what our brains require to be healthy and happy. If I could play God with my own short-term evolutionary development I would definitely want wings and maybe gills but I'm just not sure if they should be organic, synthetic or some combination of both technologies.

Imagine for a moment some individuals genetic memory could have evolved to not only subconsciously aid in their survival but consciously record events of their past lives. Then consider that these genetic memories can only be realized at a point in their lives when they reach a level of maturity capable of comprehending the wisdom they provide. How would these individuals be perceived? In a world of fear and ignorance conditioned to destroy anyone or anything that is different, should they stay silent and wait for things to change or should they take a chance to share their knowledge. What would you do? If you knew the evolutionary progression of our predatory social structure was leading to a mass extinction for our species would you stay silent or would you risk everything not knowing if you would ever get another chance in a future life? Just imagine… what would you do?

All of the negative social dysfunctions that were commonly accepted throughout our predatory evolution must now be left behind, like childhood toys we've outgrown. At one time these toys were our whole world but now we know they were only building blocks for us to learn from. It seems all intellectual species must complete this rite of passage as part of their natural evolutionary development to a predator free society. It would always be more difficult for the first species that developed intelligence on a planet or moon, perhaps that's why it took us so long to finally get to this point in our evolutionary development. Imagine for a moment how our evolutionary development would be different if we were not the first species to develop intelligence on this planet (at least that we know of). If we had a benevolent mentor species to help guide and accelerate our intellectual development with an emphasis on social compassion and technical cooperation we may have reached this critical evolutionary milestone over 1 million years ago.

I guess some species have to learn the slow and hard way to become a kind of intellectual pioneers for their planet, but the good news is, we have finally made it. We finally reached that point in our evolutionary development where the peaceful transition to a predator free society can take place. After the transition we will look back with sadness and regret that so many had to suffer and die as we struggled to understand and gain control of our hardwired predatory instincts. We honor the fallen best by learning the lessons of our past and present, accelerating our transition to a predator free society and creating a better future for our entire species. These things are within our power right now. Once the burden of predatory competition and its many forms of psychological manipulation are removed from our social structure, our intellectual evolutionary development will be accelerated as people network their special talents and creative skills into a global problem-solving machine. At least this seems like a logical conclusion. What do you think?

9. Changing human nature

Over the years I have heard a lot of discussions about how human nature is some kind of immutable mystical force beyond our ability to comprehend or change. Like the predatory social structure that has dominated our species evolutionary development since the beginning of our existence it's something we must accept as a law of nature. I don't think so. Not only can human nature and our predatory social structure be changed but they have both been in transition for thousands of years.

Our human nature has been making the transition from a non-intelligent creature functioning entirely on hardwired survival instincts and primitive reactions to environmental conditions, to an enlightened species capable of using factual knowledge and objective reasoning to take control of our evolutionary development. As we rely more on our intellectual survival trait and less on our primitive hardwired instincts an inevitable transition to a predator free society will occur as our growing populations become increasingly aware of their capitalistic exploitation and the solutions necessary to end this process.

If we define human nature as the hardwired survival instincts encoded in our genetic memory, we'd be right to assume this might be a difficult thing to change. But we won't let a little challenge like that interfere with our efforts to find a solution and achieve true freedom. If we look at the overall evolutionary development of our species we can see a lot of intellectual progress has been made since the days when human sacrifices were socially acceptable and top predators ruled their kingdoms as Gods. Our intellectual evolution has grown out of that primitive predatory past into a more technically advanced modern day society where the capitalistic exploitation of millions has become a socially accepted standard for success. Even though the level of sophistication used by top predators to manipulate and manage the working class resource was more primitive in the past it can no way compare to the increased suffering and death allowed for profit in our current capitalistic society. You may be thinking, well that's no improvement in our human nature especially if your progress is measured by our ability to show compassion to others and intellectually control our hardwired instincts for predatory competition.

Of all the technical achievements our species has made throughout our evolutionary development, how is it we're still unable to eliminate the most destructive aspects of our human nature from plaguing our modern societies? It seemed a little odd when I thought about how technically advanced our species has become yet how little progress we have made toward controlling our own human nature and creating societies where people are truly free from predatory competitions for survival, (Like the non-intelligent life forms must still do). If allowed to develop naturally our technical progress and social enlightenment should evolve at relatively the same pace unless something is accelerating one while simultaneously suppressing the other.

Could there be some forces at play powerful enough to socially engineer the development of our species? Yes, and there's only one species that we know of smart enough to socially engineer our evolutionary development, in other words we're suppressing the enlightenment of our own human nature. Primarily by the thousands of years of artificial selection and environmental conditioning by top predators to better manage their working class resources and by limiting the education necessary to break our subjective realities and make an informed decision as to what aspects of our human nature we want to keep or reject.

We know how to bring out the very worst aspects of our human nature the ones that make us disregard or even promote the suffering and death of others. We would simply create the environmental conditions where people must compete against one another for limited survival necessities within restricted territorial boundaries, then just let our hardwired predatory instincts take control of our thoughts and actions. The reason the positive attributes of our human nature and social enlightenment hasn't kept pace with our technology is because, the negative environmental conditions of predatory competition is controlling our social development. However, all of that is about to change as we reach that critical tipping point in our intellectual evolutionary development when we reject our predatory past and make the natural transition to our predator free future.

Just as we know how to bring out the worst in human nature and make it an integral part of our social structure, we also know how to reverse this effect promoting the more compassionate and constructive attributes our species is capable of. It seems logical to assume if doing one extreme makes things worse then doing the other extreme might make things better. Going from the environmental conditions of predatory competition for capitalistic survival to a predator free society is the extreme social transition we need to bring out the best qualities of our human nature.

10. What is love?

Love is a nebulous thing intangible to the touch but with the power to control our lives. It can be the source of our greatest joy while the loss of it can cause our deepest despair. Love seems to be one of the most misunderstood emotions with one of the greatest influences over our thoughts and actions. Like other emotions triggered by our hardwired survival instincts love plays a crucial role in our ability to survive a predatory social structure. Of the many hardwired instincts encoded in our genetic memory our desire to love one another and build mutually beneficial relationships must be the extreme polar opposite of our need to prey on each other and win our predatory competition for survival. This may explain why there are so many conflicts integrating the subjects of survival and love.

Our predatory social structure suppresses our natural desire to love one another by triggering our hardwired instinct for self-preservation. After objectively considering this concept I started to realize once the environmental conditions of predatory competition for survival are removed from our social structure the hardwired instinct to love one another and show compassion to others will be allowed to flourish setting new humanitarian standards for the future of our species. Wow, I kind of like that idea. And the coolest thing is, we the people have the power to make this happen.

When I think of love it often reminds me of a little song I used to sing to my son at bedtime. This little song called The Nature Boy written by George Alexander Aberle, known as eden ahbez and made more popular by Nat King Cole, is a short story about a strange enchanted boy that travels the world in search of great knowledge. He traveled great distances over land and sea searching for the wisdom to unlock the secrets of life, happiness and prosperity for all people. Knowing that the greatest of knowledge can come from the least likely of sources, the nature boy would listen to all people from the poorest outcasts to the wealthiest of kings.

During his travels and search for knowledge the nature boy became very wise and eventually found that the most important thing that we could ever learn, was just to love and be loved in return. You may wonder as I did why this lesson would be so hard for us humans to learn. And then I realized, it's not that we can't or don't want to learn this lesson, it's that our predatory social structure is teaching us the wrong thing. That if we show love and compassion to others, our acts of kindness will be considered a weakness, making us the preferred prey for capitalist predators looking for any intellectual vulnerability. We humans need to change the lesson we're teaching our people but in order for it to be put into practice we must end our predatory competition for survival and accelerate our intellectual evolutionary transition to a predator free society.

Part 2 - Learning the true nature of Capitalism

1. The evolution of an intelligent species

All over the world and back through time our species has been asking the same question, why must the many suffer and die so that the fortunate few can live like kings? This was one of those questions I really wanted an answer to. I wondered what force of nature could prevent the majority of our species from using their strength in numbers to end their exploitation and take control of their future. It is true we've had many revolutions throughout our social development as a result of poor management skills among the ruling class elite to effectively manipulate their working-class resource, leading to excessive suffering, increased awareness of their exploitation and demands for equality. Sound familiar? It's not the fact that we little people raise up for equality from time to time that interested me most. It's how for most of our social evolution we were convinced by ruling class top predators to give up our true freedom and prosperity. To accept our social status as working-class prey, like it is the natural order of things, something so fundamental to our existence it cannot be changed.

To best illustrate how our hardwired genetic memory and our environmental conditions influence the direction in which our species evolves and why our predatory social structure seems like an acceptable way of life. We will need to travel back in time to a point in our biological development when our genetic structure and social interactions began to take form. It is important to understand the natural progression from the way we were in the beginning to the way we are now. And how we must evolve further in order to be considered a true intellectually enlightened species.

We are about to become the first known life form to deliberately advance their social evolution into a predator free society. How cool is that? You've heard the expression "this is an opportunity of a lifetime". This would be for our entire existence. It's the opportunity to advance our intellectual and social evolution in ways we could only dream of before. We must open our minds to objectively consider the true origins of our past so we may better understand how to successfully plan for the future survival of our species.

From the time multi-celled life forms got started on this planet there has been a predator/prey relationship between them. We developing life forms didn't make these rules but as players in this game we all had to live and die by them. The main goal of this game is to stay alive long enough to reproduce. New players will evolve into prominence along the way while many others will become extinct with the only record of their existence being literally written in stone for us to read in their fossilized remains. The staying alive part of the game proved to be quite challenging. A successful life form would need an edge perhaps a physical adaptation or new survival trait allowing them to become a better predator or develop a better predatory defense.

A competing life form must be a good predator and have good predatory defenses just to stay in the game and not become extinct. A successful player in this game needed a way to pass on their predatory and other survival traits to the next generation of their species. This process needs to produce nearly exact reproductions of the parent life form with all of the key survival traits and physical adaptations fully intact. The ability to pass on our predatory instincts and other survival traits became one of the most important survival traits of all. The better a life form was at passing on their predatory instincts the better their chances were to stay in the game.

Our DNA is the mechanism for recording and passing on all of our physical adaptations and survival instincts. Within our DNA is a special code, a set of instructions to reproduce behavioral survival traits. These behavioral survival traits are stored in our genetic memory and are responsible for involuntary reactions to certain environmental stimulus. For a life form to stay in the game it needed to have hardwired immediate reactions to any sensory inputs detecting the presence of a predator. The slower reacting players would get eaten first, not get a chance to reproduce and simply become another extinct species.

This game has been in play for over a billion years on our planet and the current survivors are undoubtedly the best of the best. We surviving life forms had to be the best in several competing categories like, hardwired reactions to avoid predators. This process of having our bodies involuntarily controlled by hardwired survival instincts encoded in our genetic memory has served all of us surviving life forms well by keeping us in the game.

Since this game began there seemed to be a natural balance to things. Some life forms were more successful than others but all the players were still confined to a basic set of rules. Then something different happened around 2.5 million years ago when the first stone tools were being made and a new survival trait was emerging. Intelligence! This is the point in our species development when the evolution of our intelligence was born. Like a child just starting to learn about the world around them our species was still completely under the control of our hardwired survival instincts with only a sparkle of intelligence in our eyes. The introduction of intelligence as a survival trait proved to be a real game changer now just one species has evolve the power to not only dominate and destroy all the other players but also the ability to reset the game for the entire planet.

It seems one of the best advantages this new survival trait has is its ability for rapid changes to environmental conditions compared to the much slower biological evolutionary process non-intellectual species are restricted to. Another big advantage is when the concept of past, present and future began to take form allowing us to make the association that the past affects the present and the present affects the future. The ability to plan predatory attacks and defenses in advance gave the most intellectually evolved humans a supreme tactical advantage over all non-or less intellectual players in the game. At the same time we started using our new intellectual survival trait to dominate and control all other species we quite naturally started using it on one another with the same predictable results. A young or uneducated person without the time or ability to develop any intellectual defenses will be just as vulnerable to predatory attacks as any non-intelligent species, even more so if conditioned to be subservient and trust other humans without question.

The roots of slavery go much farther back than recorded history. It seems likely the naturally occurring patriarchal social structure in a nuclear family made women and children the first slaves. Not surprisingly this behavior and form of human regression can still be seen today in countries with primitive predatory social structures. The first organized large-scale slavery probably happen once two groups of humans started to develop independently from one another. One group was fortunate enough to evolve in an area with abundant natural resources of freshwater, food and secure shelter. The other group, suffered through some natural disasters, experienced high levels of stress for generations and suffer from health issues related to poor nutrition and repeated exposure to seasonal changes in weather. The fortunate group of humans having better access to all of the their basic necessities used their good health and extra time to develop their intellectual survival trait and build better weapons for predatory attacks. With consideration to our known evolutionary conflicts, as soon as the healthier more intellectually evolved humans became aware of the weaker group they would be compelled to attack them, steal all of their possessions and kill or enslave all of their people.

Captured humans from less intellectually evolved cultures were treated like livestock and considered to be subhuman which made their abuse and exploitation acceptable to their new masters. It's important to understand at this early point in our intellectual evolutionary development the action of exploiting a weaker group of people, as prey is more of a hardwired predatory instinct than an objective decision to be cruel to other humans. If the conditions had been reversed and the less fortunate group of people were lucky enough to have abundant basic survival necessities, good health and more stress-free leisure time to develop new weapons and greater intelligence, they would have become the predatory masters instead.

For millions of years all the players in our evolutionary game for survival were restricted to the rules of natural selection. Only the environmental influences of nature, biological adaptations and the occasional radioactive mutation could alter the evolutionary development of a species or give one life form a predatory advantage over another.

However, now that we have developed enough intelligence to be capable of manipulating the evolutionary development of our species it has introduced the unpredictable and dangerous element of artificial selection into the game. Instead of random acts of nature and other forms of natural environmental influences affecting our progress, now just a few ruling class top predators can artificially alter the evolutionary development of other humans to satisfy their hardwired predatory instincts for domination and control.

Mother nature has always been very efficient at eliminating the small, weak and slow members of a species allowing only the most capable to reproduce. Now that top human predators control the evolutionary development of our species their selection process for elimination centers on any of their working-class humans unable to supply sufficient levels of labor and or profit. The weak and slow still die from restricted basic survival necessities but now any individuals intelligent enough to understand and disagree with their exploitation and publicly denounce their systematic oppression would be targeted for personal extinction. You know, the troublemakers, like Jesus was to the Romans. After thousands of years restricting the intellectual development of the working-class masses and eliminating the strongest leaders most capable of ending our predatory social structure, it's no wonder so many people are still willing to accept their exploitation under Capitalism.

If Godlike super aliens created the rules of this evolutionary game and have been observing our progress as some kind of cosmic experiment, it seems they would have to know the introduction of intelligence and eventually artificial selection onto the playing field would change everything. Giving the deadliest top predators on this planet the ability to control the evolutionary development of other humans as their working-class prey could only lead to more efficient exploitation and increased suffering and death among the least fortunate members of the population. Or maybe the experiment is to determine how long it will take for us to control our predatory instincts and make the transition to a predator free society.

For thousands of years top human predators accelerated their intellectual evolutionary development with the latest techniques on how to manage and exploit their working-class prey. The working-class people were not allowed an education or the ability to develop any intellectual predatory defenses. The intellectual gap between the few well-educated top human predators and their many uneducated working-class prey became much larger and more defined as each class of people settled into their respective roles.

Following the same predator/prey game book that was hardwired into our genetic memory we quite naturally created social structures, societies and laws to legitimize the systematic exploitation of the working class people. It was and still is widely accepted among the ruling class elite that the working-class little people only need enough of an education to perform their labor skills, anymore and they would risk their intellectual advantage and predatory domination. Without the intellectual knowledge of how they were being manipulated the exploitation of the working class people became an accepted way of life and a profitable source of income for their more educated ruling class master.

The ability of working-class people to communicate with the written word and compare levels of exploitation by their rulers started a process of growing intellectual awareness. This awareness is accelerating as our species relies more on factual knowledge and less on predatory instincts to form our decisions. Throughout our social development top human predators continued their efforts to prevent their working-class prey from evolving intellectually by burning books, using torture and public executions as examples of what to expect for anyone defying the beliefs or laws of the established religion or government authority. Any knowledge allowed beyond their labor skills would be a carefully crafted subjective reality to get their working-class resource to enthusiastically except their exploitation as some form of patriotic or religious duty.

This was a time when the majority of our species intellectual development was still in its early infancy, and just like a child without the knowledge to determine what is real or illusion, shadows on the wall can become demons in the night. With little to no predatory defenses the working-class populations were easily induced with subjective realities where supernatural humans, Gods and dark magic controlled every aspect of their lives and the world they lived in. Not so surprising the induced subjective realities always seem to require the transfer of wealth, labor and resources from the many working-class prey to the very few ruling class top predators.

All forms of natural disasters, disease, starvation, etc. were the result of angry Gods, demons or sorcerers that didn't get the proper offerings from the people that suffered and died. Whole cultures and new religions were created to capitalize on the lack of intellectual predatory defenses among the uneducated working-class masses. The majority of the working-class people were conditioned to love, fear and sacrifice their lives so ruling class God/Kings and their families could live in ivory towers of marble and gold.

Between our natural predatory evolution, the top predators artificial selection to eliminate the troublemakers and the induced subjective realities to condition the population into compliance, the exploitation of the working-class prey appeared to have no end in sight. So many years went by and it seemed the people had accepted their level of exploitation as the best quality of life they could hope for. The power top human predators have to prevent the intellectual evolutionary development of their working-class people and the awareness of their exploitation has finally reached a tipping point as advanced technologies are increasing world literacy. With the increased availability of knowledge throughout the world our ability to use our intellectual survival trait to make informed decisions to end our exploitation will accelerate.

Our understanding of how our hardwired survival instincts have dominated our social development will help increase the intellectual control we have over the decisions we make leading to the true salvation of our species. All of the suffering and death attributed to millions of years of forced competition for survival within a predatory social structure will come to its natural evolutionary end as our species makes the transition to a predator free society.

The efforts by top human predators to maintain their social economic control will create many conflicts and the potential for violence. But unlike the evolutionary process that allowed their predatory domination for millions of years this new phase of our intellectual evolution will be under intelligent control by we the people, with a primary objective of achieving true freedom and prosperity for all our people as equals. Thousands of years of predatory manipulation and exploitation of the working-class people is coming to an end. The true freedom and prosperity possible within a predator free social structure is within our grasp. This will be the point in our intellectual evolutionary development that we can look back on and say this was the time when everything changed. The new motivational paradigm of cooperation for the benefit of the entire community began to heal the psychological and physical wounds from generations of forced competition for survival and systematic exploitation.

I can only imagine the things possible in our future predator free societies where the entire infrastructure and social objectives are designed to provide the greatest opportunity for individuals to develop their creative talents and skills. Hoarding technical advancements to gain personal wealth and power over others will be replaced with a desire to share knowledge and contribute to the overall success of the entire community. The need to exploit and compete against other people for our survival will never prevent our intellectual evolutionary development again. This is an exciting time to be alive, but what will we do with this opportunity?

2. Adapting to our predatory social structure, or not

One of the most fundamental requirements of all successful life forms is their ability to adapt to changing environmental conditions. Without the ability to adapt to seasonal conditions and the occasional natural disaster a species would become extinct. Our ability to physically or biologically adapt to changing environmental conditions is one of our hardwired mechanisms to aid in our survival. When we get goose bumps or shiver this is our hardwired involuntary response to cold environmental conditions just like sweating is too hot conditions. Bodybuilding is an environmental influence that tricks our bodies into thinking we need larger muscles in order to survive more efficiently. The opposite effect can also be observed where adapting to conditions without physical exercise will result in muscle atrophy.

Our bodies are the most amazing biological machines because of their ability to subconsciously regulate our body systems, self-repair smaller injuries, use a flexible fuel source, adapt to changing environments and self-replicate down to the finest details. All these things happen in the background without our control allowing us to use our big brains on more important things like rocket surgery and brain science. It's much like how our computers run small subroutines in the background allowing them to function so we can concentrate on using the main applications.

We must be mindful of the involuntary and subconscious changes our bodies make while adapting to the environmental conditions of a predatory social structure. Without the knowledge of how this process works we will not be able to intellectually override our hardwired instincts and our predatory competition for survival would continue like it has throughout our evolutionary past. Luckily, us working-class masses around the world are becoming educated at an increasingly accelerated rate and part of the factual knowledge we will be receiving is how to deal with predatory exploitation techniques and how to eliminate them from the predator free social structures of our future.

Even better, there is a solution that corrects all of the symptoms created by our predatory social structure before they get a chance to contribute to our preventable suffering and death and continue to limit the intellectual evolutionary development of our species. Providing the concepts and technical knowledge necessary to implement this solution is the objective of this book and the reason for establishing the nonprofit organization True Freedom Technologies.

Besides our ability to adapt biologically we humans can also adapt intellectually to changing environmental conditions. Our ability to intellectually adapt to different environmental conditions or social structures is also a hardwired survival trait encoded in our genetic memory that produces involuntary and subconscious reactions to aid in our survival. The dynamics behind the Stockholm syndrome are a good example of this process. We seem to have two forms of intellectual adaptation, one of them is an involuntary natural process that is often manipulated to induce subjective realities and the other is more of an objective process based on factual information. In short, allowing human predators to manipulate and control our natural intellectual adaptation is the problem and using our objective decision-making process to override and prevent our systematic exploitation is the solution.

When we are denied an education and access to factual knowledge we are unable to adapt and prevent our predatory exploitation, again this is well known by many top predators and is used to perpetuate a subjective reality that benefits the ruling class few at the expense of the working class many. It seems there are three phases of our intellectual evolutionary development. Before we evolved our intellectual survival trait, the long evolutionary journey to acquire enough intelligence to break the control of our hardwired instincts and the phase we are about to accelerate into, a predator free social structure designed to provide true freedom and prosperity for all people as equals.

It is by accelerating into this last phase of our evolutionary process we will finally break the control of our induced subjective realities and abandon the notion there is a way to provide equality in a predatory social structure like Capitalism. We can understand the need for non-intelligent creatures to continue their predatory existence after all their less-developed brains must rely entirely on their hardwired instincts and involuntary reactions to environmental conditions to ensure their survival. However, as our intelligence continues to evolve these primitive survival techniques will no longer be tolerated or allowed to perpetuate the preventable suffering and deaths of our species.

Some people feel our savage nature can never be tamed and we are destined to kill each other off until the extinction of our species. You can take a human out of its predatory social structure but you can't take the predatory instincts out of the human, kind of thing. Sure there will always be some people nostalgic for the thrill of the hunt and the emotional satisfaction of the kill but even these things can be satisfied with advanced competitions of body and mind. We may not be able to reprogram our hardwired predatory instincts out of our genetic memory yet but we can do the next best thing by removing the environmental conditions that require their use for survival.

Sure I know we have been genetically hardwired to accept our predatory instincts since the beginning of our existence and artificially conditioned with induced subjective realities throughout our social development, but should we let that stop us? I think not! Maybe before we had the knowledge of how to end our predatory social structure and take control of our future, but certainly not now. We will find the courage to use our new knowledge and achieve true freedom and prosperity for all people as part of the natural adaptation process and intellectual evolutionary development of our species. Our objective should be to accelerate this natural process to minimize the suffering and death of our people until a global predator free society can be established.

Not only can we neutralize our hardwired predatory instinct and break the control of our subjective realities but it can be done in as little as one generation. Intrigued? ? To be able to neutralize the source of the greatest human suffering and death throughout our evolutionary development would give us the advantage we need to fully accelerate our transition to a predator free society. The strategy to implement this solution is fairly simple, understand the biological and environmental influences that create and make the problem worse and reverse the process, or better yet prevented it from starting in the first place.

To better illustrate this solution we will need to objectively consider the genetic and environmental influences on two different children and how adapting to these conditions can determine their ability to compete for their survival and reach their full creative and intellectual potential. We will use the environmental conditions of two extreme opposite social structures to better illustrate the differences between them.

Child (A) will be raised in our current advanced predatory social structure and child (B) will be raised within an equally advanced predator free society. Keep in mind the overall objective for each social structure is quite different with respect to how we the people are considered. One is designed to manage the working class resource and perpetuate an efficient flow of wealth to the elite ruling class top predators of Capitalism, while the other is designed to provide true freedom and prosperity for all people as equals. They are pretty much extreme opposites, so making an objective decision about which social structure we would want for our children, country and the future of our species should be fairly simple. It will no doubt be easier for most of us to relate to our existing predatory social structure than it will be to imagine the environmental conditions of a predator free society, so I will do my best to describe the wonders and advantages that await us.

Even though the earliest years of a child's development can be sheltered from the detrimental effects of a predatory social structure their parent's competition for survival will diminish their ability to provide a healthy, compassionate and intellectually stimulating, environmental conditions for their child. If we consider that the parents of child (A) have suffered the most extreme environmental conditions within our current

A step up from the most extreme conditions would be parents still living but barely surviving the detrimental effects of our capitalistic competition. Dealing with the symptoms of stress-related health issues, domestic violence, mental instability, desperate acts for survival etc. all while being responsible for the safety of their newborn, child (A).

Contrary to popular patriotic and religiously induced subjective realities, all children are not created equal within a predatory social structure. The biological disadvantages for child (A) will have started long before he or she was born and would continue to compound as they are forced to adapt to the environmental conditions of a dysfunctional family, community and national social structure. The least fortunate of our young capitalistic competitors like child (A) will have physical and mental disadvantages from birth limiting their ability to compete against other children for their social status and future economic survival. By having the misfortune of being born into the extreme environmental conditions of an advanced predatory society, the biological disadvantages of child (A) will now severely limit their ability to acquire knowledge. This intellectual skill is needed for capitalistic competition against other children fortunate enough to be healthy having received all of their basic survival necessities.

Because we humans use our intellectual survival trait as our primary competitive tool against others, child (A) would naturally turn to their primitive hardwired instincts for survival. Their predatory instincts for survival would be intact but their intellectual ability to control them will have been prevented by the environmental conditions of our predatory social structure, too often resulting in desperate and senseless acts of violence. This is another symptom that contributes to our preventable suffering and death that will be corrected with the transition to a predator free society.

Once child (A) becomes part of our capitalistic competition for survival and enters the ranks of the working class prey their systematic exploitation will become an accepted part of their subjective reality. It's not that the suffering and death created by our predatory social structure is not real, only child (A)'s conditioned believe that our exploitation is an acceptable way of life or that we the people are powerless to change it. An abusive family/street life and years of predatory competition has conditioned child (A) to have an utter disregard for life or any compassion for others. Child (A) will have a lot of difficulty making social bonds, personal commitments or developing the good communication skills needed to acquire and keep a job.

The frustration and mental exhaustion of predatory competition can lead to apathy, homicide and ultimately suicide. The high incident of excess stress, mental instability, homicidal and suicidal tendencies, are all predictable result of forced adaptation to any predatory social structure. Especially for an intellectual species becoming aware of their exploitation while longing for true freedom. This would also be especially true for the more technically advanced predatory societies where the top predators have mismanaged their working class resource by extracting too much wealth leading to increased suffering and death among the least fortunate competitors.

Many Americans are all too familiar with the detrimental effects of our predatory social economic system. While many of our more successful competitors are just now becoming aware to what extent we the people will be willing to suffer to serve the interests of the ruling class top predators of Capitalism. Less known is the underlying fundamental elements responsible for creating our predatory social structure or how to eliminate the preventable suffering and death this process produces. Also not well understood is the critical damage it has done to the intellectual evolutionary development of our species.

We humans have spent our entire existence adapting to our evolving predatory social structures each one more technically advanced than the last. However, now that our collective intelligence will no longer tolerate our systematic exploitation we will now enter the next phase of our evolutionary development. During this transition more and more of our children will be adapting to the environmental conditions of a predator free

free society which brings us to our second child in this sociological comparison.

Just as child (A) naturally adapts to their predatory social structure, child (B) will likewise adapt to their predator free society including all of the advanced technologies integrated into their Automated Community Infrastructures. As the physical and mental disadvantages for child (A) began before they were born, the advantages for child (B) will also begin with the health and social security of their mother. If the parents of child (B) are fortunate enough to be raised within a predator free society their physical and mental health would have been monitored as an integrated feature of their smart home and community infrastructure. For parents making the transition to a predator free society it would be preferred that they were pre-acclimated with strong objective realities capable of breaking their pre-existing subjective beliefs and the ability to intellectually control their hardwired survival instincts. The better this can be accomplished, the more favorable the environmental conditions will be for their first generation predator free child (B).

The health and happiness of the family unit before, during and after a child's birth plays a critical role in their psychological development and ability to adapt to the environmental conditions of any social structure. The joy of innocence and the wonders of life will continue for child (B) beyond the sheltered environment of their nuclear family into their predator free community. When we teach our children to share their toys and show compassion to others they will be able to put those lessons into practice throughout their adult life instead of abandoning those principles as they are forced to adapt to society based on greed and the individual accumulation of wealth and power.

During the transition process predator free communities will be similar to islands of tranquility and rational thought within a sea of capitalistic exploitation and psychological deceptions for profit. Because some parts of these communities are designed to have public access allowing visitors to compare the philosophy and social structure of a predator free society with their current capitalistic competition for survival, child (B)'s exposure to the outside world can be introduced in a more controlled manner. Very much like getting a vaccination and allowing our bodies and minds to build immunities and a strong resistance to deadly virus.

The philosophical and technical education of child (B) will be accelerated by the objective realities of their parents and predator free community minimizing the detrimental effects of any predatory exposure they will encounter. Their vulnerability to intellectual attacks attempting to trigger one of their hardwired survival instincts and manipulate their emotions will diminish with age and a better understanding of the process. The influence of a subjective reality and its ability to control the thoughts and actions of child (B) should be almost completely eliminated as they learn to use modern factual knowledge to form their opinions and not rely on ancient beliefs and deceptive illusions to determine their future. His or her body and mind will be free of these destructive predatory manipulation techniques allowing them to concentrate their creative skills on the more important things in life like eliminating the suffering and death of our people and accelerating the intellectual evolutionary development of our species.

You may still be wondering how do we neutralize our hardwired instincts and break the control of our subjective realities within one generation allowing for the peaceful transition to a predator free society. The first thing to keep in mind is that this transitional process will not happen all over the world within one generation. Having said that, the self-replicating social system and technical infrastructure of the predator free society offered for consideration in this book is designed to exceed exponential growth. The limiting factor will not be a technical one because the creative skills, global wealth and resources currently exist to break the second chain of Capitalism.

The difficulty will lie in breaking the first chain of Capitalism and the conditioning that our predatory exploitation is an acceptable way of life. Equally difficult or perhaps even more so will be breaking our subjective realities to serve Gods, kings and governments as well as allowing these things to determine our future. Once the first chain of Capitalism is broken the exponential growth of a predator free society can proceed with little resistance.

For this transition to take place within a single generation the environmental conditions of a predator free society must be created with minimal to no detrimental influences of our past predatory social structure. We know if children are isolated from factual knowledge they can be induced with any subjective reality imaginable. This is because of our hardwired ability to intellectually adapt to whatever environmental conditions or social structure we find ourselves born into. This amazing ability is both one of our greatest strengths as well as our greatest weakness, at least until we learn how to control it.

When our ability to adapt is used against us as a tool for predatory exploitation, it will continue to increase the suffering and death of millions. However, if this burden were removed our intellectual development would naturally accelerate as we the people adapt to the environmental conditions of a predator free social structure. Our first generation predator free child would simply adapt to their new environmental conditions providing them with the factual knowledge necessary to create and maintain an objective reality and strong predatory defenses against any form of capitalistic exploitation. This will create the social conditions necessary for the first generation predator free children to flourish forming the foundation for an accelerated global transition.

3. Capitalism, the ultimate achievement of our predatory evolution

Like most, born and raised, red-blooded, corn fed American children I was conditioned by our society to be the fiercest capitalistic competitor possible. I learned early in life the extreme inequality between the many families living in working-class poverty and the extremely fortunate few living a life of excessive opulence. My social conditioning was very clear and effective, I needed to make a lot of money as fast as possible to win this game and become what my society considered to be a success. My predatory instincts didn't seem to be satisfied with just surviving I wanted to become the capitalistic king of the world. Okay, maybe the conditioning worked a little too well but I was still young and I think big.

The one thing I kept struggling with is that I didn't want to harm anyone else to achieve my success. It seemed no matter what occupation I chose my good fortune would have to be someone else's misfortune. Sure it feels good to be stronger, faster, smarter, or whatever but when that competition is for our survival the losers aren't just sad they lost, their quality of life is compromised and that really bugged me. I kept wondering why must some loose so others may win. I guess in a way my personal evolutionary development had reached a point where my intellectual survival trait was starting to take control over my hardwired predatory instincts. I started to realize my empathy, sympathy and compassion for others was going to interfere with my plans for capitalistic domination of the world.

After finally coming to the conclusion that I was not going to be able to have my cake and eat it too I decided to start a business and make a product where I had little to no competition. At this point in my life I felt certain my destiny was to be a great artist creating works of art that would make the Fabergé eggs seem like costume jewelry. My only problem was I didn't have the Czar of Russia supplying me with gold, gems and as many jewelers as needed. I heard being an artist would be a difficult way to survive but living below the poverty line with no academic achievements to speak of, getting into a prestigious college and becoming a rocket brain surgeon astronaut wasn't very likely. So I decided to design and hand make chains and clasps in silver and gold.

I eventually created a state-of-the-art website that allowed customers to design bracelets and necklaces online with the photo and custom price updating in real time. Pushbutton gemstone clasps, bimetal and trimetal gold color chain designs, diameter and length were all options to allow for over a 1000 variations of unique works of art. I had created a unique market niche that very few jewelers seemed interested in even trying to do. It seems there is far more profit in setting diamonds in cast rings than making handmade chains one link at a time. My capitalistic venture was challenging and rewarding but still not profitable enough for me to be considered a successful competitor and afford those things normally associated with the American dream.

I offer my life experiences to show I was not always anti-capitalistic, in fact before I tried to determine what the primary factor responsible for our preventable suffering and death was, I had no idea the social economic structure of Capitalism was going to be identified as the ultimate achievement of our predatory evolution. I hadn't even identified our hardwired predatory instincts and forced competition for survival as the root cause until just a year or so before I wrote this book.

I may have been conditioned to be the best capitalistic competitor possible but I could not let that interfere with my objective to identify the root cause, so that the problem could be corrected at the source eliminating the many symptoms that contribute to our preventable suffering and death. I guess in some ways my capitalistic conditioning wasn't effective enough or I would have rejected any factual knowledge identifying my beloved social structure as the problem to correct and continued my life of blissful ignorance. I'm glad this was not to be, I would rather be burdened with the truth and the challenge to do something about it than to live out my life oblivious to the knowledge I could have made a difference.

Over the years there have been many opinions formed about the destructive nature of the social economic structure of Capitalism. Part of our social conditioning is to accept our capitalistic exploitation and reject any factual knowledge from sources that don't share our political or religious subjective reality, ethnic background, cultural beliefs, etc. However, there are some historical figures so well known and respected for their intelligence and accomplishments that their words demand consideration even among the most resistant individuals determined to accept their exploitation as an inevitable part of life. The following quote is by one of my historical heroes. Albert Einstein explained, why Socialism? In 1949.

"I am convinced there is only one way to eliminate the grave evils of Capitalism, namely through the establishment of a socialist economy, accompanied by an educational system which would be oriented toward social goals. In such an economy, the means of production are owned by society itself and are utilized in a planned fashion. A planned economy, which adjusts production to the needs of the community, would distribute the work to be done among all those able to work and would guarantee a livelihood to every man, woman, and child. The education of the individual, in addition to promoting his own innate abilities, would attempt to develop in him a sense of responsibility for his fellow-men in place of the glorification of power and success in our present society."

I completely agree! It's hard to express the sense of satisfaction I felt when finding out one of my greatest heroes not only shared my dream to eliminate the grave evils of Capitalism but also formulated a solution with the same corrections to our social structure. What's most interesting to me is that even though I've admired Einstein's thinking for years I was unaware of his views on Capitalism until after the concepts and solutions in this book were fully formed. I've always found it fascinating how people living in different times and places in the world with completely different life experiences can arrive at the same conclusions when they objectively consider the base elements of the problem.

As mentioned in my preface I wanted my analysis to be based on the elements of the problem and not on the opinions of others. Especially from someone I respect so much that it might affect my objectivity and ability to form valid independent conclusions. It's always important to verify your information sources especially the ones we are conditioned to trust without question. Try to build a consensus from independent, non-bias factual information sources and never give up your intellectual survival trait for the illusion of an induced subjective reality.

An objective consideration of the information in this book will allow many people to break their first chain of Capitalism, that being the invisible and somewhat mysterious force that manipulates our decision-making process into feeling a sense of satisfaction with our managed exploitation. Once the first chain is broken and we the people become aware we have the power to peacefully end our predatory competition for survival. Breaking the second chain of Capitalism will become more of a logistical matter of reallocating national wealth and resources.

You know what's really cool... Einstein's solution to eliminate the grave evils of Capitalism may not have been possible in 1949 but in just 64 years of accelerated intellectual evolution we have developed the communication, construction and manufacturing technologies necessary to break our subjective realities and finally end the predatory social structure that has dominated our species since the beginning of our existence. I can't think of any greater intellectual or social achievement for the evolutionary development of our species.

It kind of makes me feel sorry for all the non-intelligent species forced to continue their existence in a predatory social structure competing against one another for their survival. However, the good news is once we stop systematically preying on our own species, the exploitation of other animals and natural resources will not be as necessary for our survival or rewarded with excessive power and wealth. We will finally be able to focus on the things that matter most like reducing the preventable suffering and death of our species. And providing a self-replicating infrastructure and social system capable of supporting a predator free society. At least this seems like a good place to start.

The definition or term "to capitalize on" does have some different financial meanings but the ones that best represents our predatory social structure are "to take advantage of, to exploit, to profit by, or to utilize" The more I was learning about how our capitalistic social structure works, the more questions I needed to have answered. Like, why do our laws value profits for the wealthy elite more than the health, safety and prosperity of its citizens? Why are so many working-class people allowed to suffer and die so the ruling class elite can live like kings? How could so many of us working-class people allow our exploitation and be convinced to serve the ruling class elite? Why is our social economic structure intentionally constructed so that, the working-class people's basic survival necessities are tightly controlled by the most powerful members of our society. How can a government for the people become so corrupted as to devolve into their instrument of exploitation? Who does it benefit most to create a fragile supply line infrastructure dependent upon foreign oil instead of naturally abundant and domestically available secure sources of energy? If we don't learn enough facts to ask intelligent questions, we will never find the answers we need to become aware of our exploitation and collectively evolve into a predator free society.

For many years now I've been painfully watching and hearing the working class people crying out for a social economic system that cares more about their suffering and death than it does about corporate profits and multimillion dollar executive salaries for our ruling class elite. The social economic system of Capitalism has become a model for the most efficient way to manipulate and manage a working-class resource, while still allowing the maximum amount of wealth, labor and natural resources to be extracted and systematically transferred to its ruling class elite. Capitalism's efficiency as the most advanced predatory social structure flows from its ability to psychologically condition its working-class resource into accepting our exploitation. It allows our ruling class top predators to use their wealth and power to buy our government, make our laws and control our basic survival necessities.

More than non-intellectual creatures within their naturally occurring predatory social structure, our human top predators are willing to sacrifice as many of us working-class prey as necessary to maintain their dominance, control and high profit margins. Even as technologically advanced as our species has become, our elite top predators are still able to maintain their dominance and control over us working class prey by using our socially accepted intellectual competition for survival as a tool for exploitation. They use their knowledge to formulate advanced psychological manipulation techniques to control our decision-making process making our exploitation seem like the best economic social structure to provide future prosperity for our families and country.

Many people are just now waking up from their American dream, to learn we've been systematically deceived and exploited by the ruling class elite top predators of Capitalism. We've been conditioned all our lives to feel proud of our country's freedoms and the opportunities it provides for us common working-class people.

In fact we do have more freedom and opportunities than working class people living in other countries under a single dictatorship, with no democracy at all. Or for example a country that maintains a more primitive predatory social structure by suppressing its peoples right to vote removing their ability to determine their future. Or perhaps the top predators of a country may diminish or prevent their people from acquiring an education and the knowledge of their exploitation. Or the ruling class leaders of a more primitive government may deny health care to their people just to increase their own individual wealth and power. A more primitive country would eliminate environmental protections maintaining the health and safety of its citizens giving complete control to for-profit corporate entities focused on resource exploitation. A country fully controlled by its top predators may eliminate some human rights or regulations created to minimize the suffering and death of its working-class citizens. A primitive predatory social structure would provide absolutely no shared prosperity generated from their country's national resources. Is this starting to sound familiar, maybe in some primitive oppressive country but not in the greatest most powerful country on earth, not in the land of the free?

We Americans can and should be very thankful all of these things that should be considered basic human rights have not been completely capitalized on yet and made into a privilege that only the more fortunate and wealthy competitors can receive. We can and should be thankful that we have the right to free speech and that we generally have the opportunity to peacefully assemble and protest our exploitation by the ruling class top predators of Capitalism. We should also be very thankful that we try to have a separation between church and state so godlike egocentric leaders with apocalyptic visions of the future are not able to completely manipulate and control what God we must believe in. Just remember, "in God we trust", or at least in the large amounts of American currency that this quote is printed on. Some may wonder, of all the Gods of our past and present, which one is this quote referring to. Well that would be whatever God and religion you believe in of course so you can feel the emotional satisfaction that comes from knowing your government and God are literally on the same page. A kind of marriage made in heaven. Like a good fortune cookie or the Mystics and Oracles of the past, it's better to let the subject fill in the blanks to whatever makes them feel more comfortable, after all we want happy citizens or perhaps more accurately emotionally satisfied working class prey.

If we the people of America only consider the effectiveness of our social economic structure to provide equality and prosperity for our working-class populations in relative terms to other countries, it could provide us with a feeling of complacency and stifle our visions to create a better future. We can simultaneously be thankful for the freedoms we fought and died to receive while still acknowledging we have a long way to go. We the people of America must build upon the freedoms we have achieved and use that leverage to fight for the least fortunate competitors in our own country and around the world.

The strongest and most fortunate among us must use all of our creative skills and technical resources to fight for those that have been beaten down and weakened by our predatory competition for survival. Because we the working-class people around the world are conditioned to compete against one another for survival there is an inherent lack of compassion and motivation to help others. Just understanding this fatal flaw in our evolutionary development on an individual basis is not good enough as long as top predators around the world control the social structure and laws we must live and die by to maintain their predatory domination.

Working class people around the world are starting to compare notes. They're asking each other how bad is your abuse? Like victims of the Stockholm syndrome, people with the least abuse naturally feel their country is being kind to them and that their lives and social structure is the best they can hope for. Worse yet many people are convinced that our pride for our country equals the blind acceptance of our exploitation and anything less should be considered anti-American or unpatriotic. The mechanisms used to manipulate collective Stockholm syndrome victims within a social structure seems to be quite effective on some working class people susceptible to this form of control. The true measure of a country's success should not depend on the ability of its ruling class elite to manage their working-class resource into producing the maximum GDP (Gross Domestic Product) and tax revenues. But instead it's ability to provide a social economic system with the highest level of health, education and standard of living for all of its citizens as a human right and not a privilege to compete for.

As the most influential country in the world we the people of America have an obligation to break the control of our predatory social structure first and proudly set an example for all to see. We must show with our actions what we truly stand for and stop our efforts at global domination through psychological manipulation and capitalistic exploitation. I feel it's better to be respected for our ability to help others than to be feared and known for our destructive power. We've got a lot of work to do if we are going to show the world with our actions that we are capable of correcting our own mistakes and leading our species into the next phase of our intellectual evolutionary development. I feel were up for the challenge and this is the perfect time in our evolutionary development for this transition to take place.

The tragic effects of forcing people to compete against one for their survival may be intellectually obvious to many modern-day humans educated to understand this process. So how were the working-class people around the world forced and or convinced to accept their exploitation since the beginning of our social evolutionary development? Because the acceptance of our predatory social structure started long before our intellectual survival trait gave us the ability to form societies, the cause must originate from our hardwired instincts encoded in our genetic memory. In fact all life forms are genetically encoded to accept or at least adapt to a predatory social structure to survive. After millions of years of relying on our predatory instincts for survival, how is an enlightened species going to make the transition to intellectual control of their decision-making process and the formation of a predator free society? With some difficulty to be sure, but again this transition seems inevitable as part of the natural evolutionary process for any intellectual species.

The creation of Capitalism is a natural culmination of thousands of years of predatory social structures each one more technologically advanced than the last but all with the same objective of more efficient management and exploitation of the working class population by its elite ruling class top predators. As my fact puzzle started to reveal Capitalism as the most technologically advanced predatory social structure ever created it became very clear this was not a system I want to make more efficient. If during my research I discovered that the social economic structure of Capitalism only needed a few minor or even major corrections to provide equality and prosperity for the majority of the population, I may have devoted my life like many others towards making those changes. However, this is not the case, not even close. It is true that after countless deaths we have achieved a lesser or perhaps more sophisticated and acceptable level of exploitation but true freedom and prosperity will never be achieved by us working-class prey as long as we are forced to compete against one another for our survival.

The core principle of Capitalism that requires our intellectual competition against one another for our survival is responsible for accelerating a potentially fatal deviation in our evolutionary development. By allowing the environmental conditions that promote intellectual predatory attacks as the standard for human survival, we are altering the evolutionary development of our species into creating super predators with super egos all looking for the best way to prey on one another and rule the world. In fact we've been on this evolutionary path since we started to develop our intellectual survival trait and it naturally became our best tool for predatory attacks and defenses. If we continue down this evolutionary path of using our intellectual survival trait as a predatory tool and allowing top predators to dominate and control our global resources, the exploitation of us working class prey will increase as well as the level of suffering and death experienced by the general populations of our species.

The chains of Capitalism may be a metaphorical reference but their ability to prevent the equality and prosperity of us working-class people is very real. These chains consist of psychological manipulation techniques to subconsciously and involuntarily control our decision-making process and a social system with technical infrastructure designed to produce complete dependence for all of our basic survival necessities. Now that we have become fully dependent on Capitalism a profit can be made on every one of our survival necessities and emotional desires. It's a little like having a short choke collar on a dog that gets beat by the same person who feeds them, the dog dreams of freedom while the master desperately tries to maintain dominance and control with the emotion of fear and environmental reinforcement of pain.

The more aggressive predators or winners of our capitalistic competition have realized they don't need to wait for a profitable crisis to come along where people are forced to pay what ever it takes to survive. It's far easier to manipulate an entire society into requiring their product as a basic survival necessity needed for competition. The greater the crisis and threat to our survival the larger amount of money people are willing to pay to stay competitive and survive. When this psychological manipulation technique works well us working class prey are even emotionally satisfied with our continued exploitation and feel we are living the American dream.

Imagine for a moment some top human predators of Capitalism discover a global resource to exploit and it has the potential to make them billions of dollars. The only problem is there's no demand for this product and it will contaminate our air, water and food supplies needed for a healthy and productive working class population. Keep in mind a controlled level of suffering and death among the working-class resource, has long been an acceptable consequence among the ruling class elite in order to maintain their predatory dominance. Creating a global demand for a resource no one wants, or more specifically to socially engineer a society to require a product for its survival is no easy task. Even when our ruling class top predators in government are eager to receive millions of dollars to promote the transition and they're working class prey are already primed for exploitation.

The real trick is how to create an infrastructure where working class people would need this product to survive, or at least to become a functioning competitive member of this new social economic structure. Whole industries would need to be created to consume and supply this new product to an expanding working-class resource.

Ruling class top predators in government would need to be paid millions of dollars to use their positions of power to cut or create red tape allowing their masters direct access to their working-class resource. They'll also need to subvert our democracy by inducing subjective realities that will effectively manipulate the uninformed voters into allowing the contamination of their food, air and water, severely compromising the health of their children and the future of our nation.

As our need and desire for this global resource grows it would create a social economic condition similar in function to the chemical dependency of an addictive drug. Where the withdrawal pains can be used as a control mechanism to increase or decrease our nation's level of productivity and the suffering and death experienced by the working-class resource. Once the infrastructure is complete entire societies would require this product for their survival and the top predators of Capitalism will have a whole new way to control their global working-class resource. Making that choke collar on the dog that gets beat even shorter and giving our ruling class masters much greater control over our lives and the future evolutionary development of our species.

A smart capitalistic social engineer would also realize the greatest inefficiency for the use of their product would provide them the highest profit margins. If the proper capitalistic investments were made to buy key lawmakers in government, a society could be created that legally and legitimately wastes more energy than it's forced to consume. Imagine that, creating a social infrastructure that forces the working-class resource to compete against one another just to pay for a product they waste over half of. It's a capitalistic dream come true for the top human predators creating an economic trap and ecological nightmare for the working-class prey that will continue for generations. Feeling that choke collar yet?

This form of mass manipulation and exploitation of a global working-class resource is what makes Capitalism the most advanced predatory social structure this world has ever known. Some people without the knowledge to make an informed decision and or fully under the control of an induced subjective reality may think this story is a figment of my wild imagination used to illustrate an unrealistic concept. While others with an objective and historical understanding of how our capitalistic social structure works will recognize this product is fossil fuels and this scenario is the society we currently live in.

Some people may also feel this was a natural evolution of our technology in an honest and innocent attempt to provide a higher quality of life for our global populations. It's true our intellectual development and creative skills were far less developed at that time but honest and innocent, not a chance. If our ruling class top predators objective was to provide equality and prosperity for their working-class resource, we would currently be living in a vibrant green predator free society fully fueled by carbon neutral and naturally abundant alternative energy sources. Things would be quite different now if not for the moral motivation of greed and allowing our hardwired survival instincts to guide our evolutionary development into advanced predatory social structures.

It can also be debated that our natural escalation of predatory competition between nations for world domination and control of global resources demanded the use of high-energy fuel sources in a desperate effort for self-preservation. And without the industrial capacity to mass-produce weapons of war Hitler's Third Reich would have started their 1000 year domination of the world. The farther back we go into our intellectual evolutionary past the truer it is that people and even countries must defend themselves against more primitive predatory attacks and blatant forms of aggression. It's also true that even as far as some countries have evolved towards providing more freedom and equality for their people many leaders around the world if given the power to do so, would force their neighboring states under their dictatorial rule. This threat is still very real and predictable given the unnecessary escalation of our predatory social structures and willingness to accept the exploitation of others for profit. This is why the countries with the most power and influence must lead the way into the next phase of our intellectual evolutionary development and accelerate our transition to a global predator free society.

I am reminded of a life experience that helped me form my objective reality about the grave evils of Capitalism. In a way the concepts that I learned during this experience was like connecting a few key pieces to my fact puzzle, allowing me to see the big picture much more clearly. I attended a pretty affluent health club for a while where I had the opportunity to rub shoulders and observe the wealthier social class mindset and how some of them consider other Americans in our country. During our wait for the next game a conversation began about a current gas shortage crisis that was causing millions of Americans great hardships trying to reach their employment locations. Families living in working-class poverty were already struggling to pay for their basic survival necessities so when the lines started forming and the inevitable price gouging began, their suffering got worse.

It wasn't just the least fortunate working-class Americans that suffered the small businesses that hired these individuals were feeling the pain too. Now multiply that by millions of small and large businesses across our country, and then our entire nation will feel the pain by lowering our ability to compete within the global economic structure of free-market Capitalism. Again we have allowed the ruling class few to control the survival necessities of the working-class many. This is an evolutionary and strategic mistake that will be corrected as we the people become more aware of our systematic exploitation and make an informed decision to end the process.

As our conversation continued it seemed we all agreed that the suffering among the people in our country was real although perhaps not experienced by all present. What really opened my eyes was what I heard next by one of my distinguished gentleman athletic competitors. He explained that this gas crisis was the best thing that happened to him in years, how it was making him rich and that he hoped it would never end. I started to wonder how could the suffering of the American people and the crippling of our nation's ability to function make someone so happy and rich. He further explained to us how he had bought a lot of stock in the very oil companies that were also making billions of dollars off of this crisis.

While some of the gentlemen may have been speed dialing their stockbrokers my fact puzzle was becoming clear as the true nature of Capitalism was being revealed. I felt privileged to hear such blatant honesty. Normally this is only done when in the company of other wealthy capitalists that share a common disregard for fellow Americans in their pursuit for higher profits and elevated social status. Much like the 47% comment made by Mitt Romney during a private presidential fund raising event revealing a rare glimpse of objective reality for our nation to observe. I know our intellectual enlightenment is a learning process however, it's moments like this that really help accelerate the process, even for those least likely to accept the truth.

I started to realize we have a social structure that allows a few ruling class top predators to control the levers of power that decide whether we have a gas crisis or not. If that's not bad enough they're also the same top predators that stand to make the highest profits by capitalizing on the low supply and high demand. As one of the "we the people" in our Constitution and one of the 99% of working-class Americans, this is a terrible social structure for us, it gives a few wealthy top predators the power to control our lives and use us as a resource for exploitation. How could we allow things to get this bad? The good news is this colossal evolutionary mess has a relatively simple solution. As the chains of Capitalism are broken, the environmental conditions of the predator free society will naturally diminish all negative social dysfunctions while we make the transition into the next phase of our intellectual evolutionary development. It's going to be amazing.

Say for example some smart capitalistic competitors realize there is a plant that if commercialized and sold to the public would produce a strong physical and psychological addiction. Any predatory capitalist looking for the best way to exploit the working-class resource would instantly realize the unfair advantage an addictive drug would have within our free-market capitalistic system. Even though high levels of suffering and death among the working-class resource has long been accepted within a predatory social structure, legitimizing the sale of an addictive drug product to unsuspecting young consumers all over the world would be challenging. The real trick would be how to induce a subjective reality within the working-class resource making them feel this addictive drug should be legally acceptable and highly desirable while other competing addictive drugs should remain illegal and considered evil. Making this capitalistic deception even more challenging is the drug to be made legal will result in the death of millions every year, while all the drugs that are to be made illegal will only kill thousands or in some cases may even be medically beneficial. This would seem like a hard sell to a well-educated population.

Some people may feel that our children and young adults are too well educated to fall for a capitalistic deception like this. The numbers of people that consider this statement to be true are quickly diminishing as they themselves are dying from the use of this product. Also as the natural intellectual evolution of our species is making us more aware of the psychological and physical manipulation techniques used against us.

The first thing to keep in mind is that our children and young adults are targeted because they have not had the time to develop intellectual defenses against the many forms of capitalistic exploitation that have become an accepted part of our predatory social structure. Also it is well known at least among better-educated capitalistic predators that once our youngest working-class prey are addicted to this legitimized drug they will be physically and psychologically compelled to buy and consume this product until their premature death. The most insidious and effective aspect of this product is the same thing that makes a more successful parasites in that it doesn't kill its host right away but instead takes many years allowing the infestation to spread also helping to create the illusion of innocence.

Their working-class prey could be legally deceived and psychologically manipulated into buying and consuming this product with a subconscious positive emotional association indicating its use would make them real men, sexier women, more successful, or increase their social status etc. After multimillion-dollar payoffs to elite ruling class legislators in our government to legitimize this drug for legal use and sale to our young adults, the result would be the predictable and preventable death of hundreds of thousands of our fellow Americans every year. Because free-market Capitalism is globally accepted in many countries, millions of annual deaths worldwide are legally allowed to increase corporate profits and executive salaries. The suffering and death of all these working-class people in other countries around the world is also considered an acceptable consequence of free-market Capitalism.

One of the best strategies for capitalistic exploitation is to prevent the education of the working-class resource through legislation until a large majority of the population becomes physically addicted and economically dependent on the sale and production of a product. Then use freedom of choice to manipulate the people into defending their own exploitation. If the working-class resource in a country is able to break this cycle and become educated to their exploitation a multinational corporation can simply sell this addictive product to other countries with better control over their population. Tragically the true nature of our predatory social structure and the advanced psychological manipulation techniques used against us will not be learned soon enough to prevent the suffering and death of millions each year. If you have been reading this book sequentially or if your life experiences have allowed you to form an objective reality and the ability to break the conditioning of our predatory social structure you will know that this product is tobacco or more specifically its commercialization in the form of cigarettes.

Say for instance I'm a newly minted well-educated young entrepreneur looking for the best/most profitable product to produce and sell within our capitalistic free-market predatory social structure. Having done my homework and through careful observation, I would have noticed some of the largest most profitable corporations are allowed the highest levels of suffering and death among the working-class resource, also known as we the people or 99% of most populations. Even though I have not yet attained the high levels of wealth and power associated with top predators or the ability to make the capitalistic investments in government necessary to create and alter laws or manipulate social structures to my favor. I will still realize that certain levels of suffering and death will be allowed from the consumption or use of my product. It's not the unavoidable or unexpected accidental injuries associated with our natural development of a new technology I need to be concerned with. It's the preventable suffering and death that must be regulated to maximize profits while minimize public awareness and limiting any governmental interference to both.

As a well-educated young entrepreneur eager for capitalistic competition, I will know my social structure has legitimized the use of advanced predatory tactics as the primary means for achieving success. My capitalistic free-market conditioning will have taught me how to develop my intellectual survival trait into a competitive weapon to use against others too young or inexperienced to form predatory defenses.

Even though we have long been hardwired and environmentally conditioned to accept the suffering and death of any prey within our predatory social structure. As a predatory capitalist, I must still be careful not to be too obvious because the working-class resource is rapidly becoming more educated and aware of their systematic exploitation. Creating and legitimizing an addictive drug to ensure a good repeat business may be becoming too obvious among the more educated countries. However, that old trick won't be necessary to guarantee high profits because we working-class prey are already born addicted to several hardwired requirements for survival.

Knowing that the psychological manipulation and or use of my intellectual survival trait as a predatory tool against an unsuspecting population has become the new standard for achieve capitalistic success, I would want to create a product that subconsciously triggers as many of those hardwired addictions as possible. This way the illusion of free will is maintained and a sense of emotional satisfaction can be achieved and associated with the purchase and use of my product. And most consumers will be completely unaware of the process, but hey... what they don't know won't hurt them, right?

If my objective is to take full advantage of our predatory social structure and achieve capitalistic domination over a global working-class resource, and if my evil mastermind top predator training has prepared me with all of the state-of-the-art psychological manipulation techniques. Then I will find many opportunities to use my new creative skills to deceive the misfortunate many and become one of the privileged few. Any moral convictions or sense of fair play I may have been taught during my youth must become a distant memory as the art of capitalistic deception becomes my accepted reality and new standard for survival within our technologically advanced predatory social structure.

My hardwired predatory instinct to accept the suffering and death of the working-class prey must be embraced if I am to achieve capitalistic domination and the social status of top predator. During my higher education it may have become apparent that forcing the working-class resource to compete against one another for their survival is, for a lack of a better expression, the "root of all evils". And that it has set our species on an evolutionary path of accelerated destruction and death, but without a comprehensive solution to correct such a monumental problem the path of least resistance becomes my course of action to achieve social and economic domination.

I have decided to use one of the strongest hardwired survival addictions, our need for food as the primary trigger to subconsciously motivate my customers with a secondary trigger suggesting the potential for greater success, better social status and more sex. My capitalistic masterpiece will be a collection of specific molecules designed to stimulate the senses in a predictable manor, altering the decision-making process, resulting in the desired action of buying and consuming my product. Preferably without any conscious thought or intellectual consideration from my faithful customers. I want the wealth of my working-class prey/consumers acquire from forced competition to flow like water from the many of them to the one of me. I want this transfer of wealth to feel as natural as breathing air or being born into a social structure that requires it for their survival.

Of course my new product should resemble something wholesome and natural to complete the illusion and satisfy our visual sensory inputs. The molecular recipe for my food product will begin with the most universally accepted legally abused addictive drug in the world. It may not have the motivational power of nicotine, alcohol, cocaine or heroin but its ability to be legally marketed to the youngest of consumers with the free will to give up their wealth makes it an excellent choice to include in my masterpiece of capitalistic confection. In addition to caffeine, I will include another one of my personal favorites chocolate. Or at least an advanced synthesized chocolate like molecule that will trigger a strong subconscious response capable of attracting the largest demographic of consumers. I want to keep my molecular recipe simple using some of the least expensive and widely available fillers to create the proper texture, look and taste. Knowing we humans are hardwired to desire high calorie foods as an involuntary survival instinct and wanting to provide that rich creamy taste, animal and or vegetable fat molecules will be added to the recipe.

Of course the more successful capitalistic food products created for the American working-class resource, must include the three silent assassins of bleached white flour, sugar and salt. It seems people feel more comfortable eating foods that provide the illusion of purity at the expense of proper nutrition. Or perhaps more accurately we're conditioned to desire it in order to extract higher profits from the working-class resource while providing less nutritional value. I feel if educated and allowed the choice most people would not choose a lifestyle that would result in a premature and preventable death for their selves, their children and genetic descendants. Especially once they realize they're premature suffering and death was a socially induced set of circumstances to facilitate the excessive accumulation of wealth and power by a few ruling class top predators of Capitalism. To complete the illusion of capitalistic perfection my food products should include some colorful dyes to reproduce demographically oriented patriotic and religious symbols consumers will have a favorable emotional reaction with and a strong subconscious desire to buy.

I will need a very catchy name for my new line of capitalistic confections, something that will stick in the minds of all consumers like glue. Perhaps I will use some form of advanced psychological manipulation to formulate one of those jingles people can't seem to get out of their heads. I want it to be the first thing they think of the morning and something they dream about at night. Of course it still needs to maintain the illusion of free choice and personal selection or the consumers may identify the deception. A nice catchy name like, "Sweet capitalistic delights" the American super treat of the future!   With advertisements explaining, nine out of ten nutritionists recommend Sweet Capitalistic Delights as the only food necessary for a full and balanced diet. Why go through the unnecessary time and hassle buying all those other foods when you can enjoy the convenience of just a few dozen Sweet capitalistic delights per day. There's no need for all that messy preparation, extensive cleanups or lingering food orders, Sweet Capitalistic Delights will eliminate all these problems with just one convenient product.

Your children will love the delicious creamy taste of Sweet Capitalistic Delights as they build strong healthy bodies in 14 different ways. All hard-working families deserve the luxury and convenience of Sweet Capitalistic Delights so you too can experience a life of excessive pleasures where all your needs and emotional desires can be satisfied with one delicious bite after another. It's like having all the wholesome goodness of the American dream rolled up into one delicious treat of capitalistic perfection. What more could any red-blooded God-fearing consumer want? Now remember this amazing product will sell out fast so be sure to hurry and purchase as many Sweet Capitalistic Delights as you can afford before supplies run out and you miss your chance at experiencing the American dream. Are you feeling an uncontrollable desire to run out and buy a box of Sweet Capitalistic Delights yet? Oh well, I've been told I'm not a very good salesman, something about being too honest.

One of the things Capitalism seems to excel at is not only can huge profits be made creating the problems but also equally large amounts of power and wealth can be generated providing the solutions. For each one of the capitalistic for-profit corporations that contribute to our preventable suffering and death, there is one industry that directly benefits from the devastation they create. It's not the many working-class individuals making these corporations profitable that benefit most from their labor but instead they're CEOs, executive officers and shareholders wealthy enough to own their stock. It is well known among populations that are allowed or have demanded an education from their ruling class leaders that, we the working-class people of the world need to have our basic survival necessities met, like shelter, clean water, nutritious food, etc. to maintain productive and healthy lives. Perhaps less well known is that the success and prosperity of any country within our global struggle for capitalistic domination depends on the health and productivity of its working-class citizens and not the excessive accumulation of wealth and power by their ruling class top predators.

Our for-profit healthcare industry currently extracts over $2.5 trillion from we the people per year and a large percentage of this income is a direct result of preventable capitalistic exploitation of the American working-class resource. The for-profit healthcare industry like all other corporations competing for their capitalistic survival, must value the excessive accumulation of wealth and power for a few top predators over the health and prosperity of the many working-class prey. The fact that our capitalistic leaders have created a predatory social structure that legitimizes preventable forms of suffering and death for profit is bad enough. However, when psychological manipulation techniques are allowed to be used on an unsuspecting public turning our freedom of choice into a legitimate way of getting us to willingly pay to create our own national health care crisis, that's going too far. And even more to the point this form of capitalistic exploitation is becoming increasingly obvious as more working-class people break their subjective realities to serve the ruling class elite. In the true spirit of Capitalism, we the people can not only be conditioned to induce our own preventable health care crisis but we also quite naturally will give up our life savings in an effort to extend our lives. After all, the American working-class resource provides the wealthiest target for capitalistic exploitation, getting us coming and going is just a smart business decision within a free-market predatory social structure.

One of the tricks Capitalism uses to make us working-class prey dependent upon our own exploitation is to tie our survival to the profits and greed of Wall Street. Say for example you are a middle-class American citizen successful enough to invest in the stock market. Free-market Capitalism has taught us to invest our hard earned money in the most successful stocks available so we may make the largest profits for our investments. Because Capitalism like any predatory social economic structure requires competition for survival the largest and most successful companies must value profits over all other considerations if they want to avoid becoming extinct in this highly competitive marketplace. In order to stay competitive and provide the highest profit margins for their shareholders the corporation you have invested your life savings in has been using your money to lobby some key senators into deregulating the environmental protection laws known to protect American citizens against birth defects and cancer. Not surprisingly the corporation you are relying on to make you rich and provide a better future for your children left this information out of their advertising brochures.

Tragically you find your grandchild happens to be one of the thousands of unfortunate children being born in the very part of our country the corporation you invested in decided to contaminate in order to increase your profits. Of course if you knew your grandchild would suffer and die to increase the profits you were going to use to help them have a better future you would not have provided that company the money they needed to pay off the lawmakers willing to deregulate the environmental protections used to prevent their birth defect.

If you feel the previous scenario could not be possible in a country as progressive and enlightened as the USA, or any other based on a capitalistic social structure. You may be under the influence of a subjective reality using greed to manipulate your decision-making process into denying available factual knowledge.

An objective reality allowing for a factual consideration of how Capitalism works may have avoided this tragedy not only for your child but thousands of others with parents too poor to invest in the stock market. It seems Gods and Capitalism have something in common, they both work in mysterious ways. The technologically advanced social economic structure of Capitalism can also produce thousands of mysterious unexplained deaths just like Gods.

For thousands of years the deaths of our ancestors were often unexplained mysteries attributed to angry Gods and demons until science was able to explain the real causes. Our natural intellectual evolutionary development will also reveal our capitalistic exploitation and forced competition for survival within a predatory social structure to be the primary factor responsible for countless preventable tragedies. Once the mystery is gone and the root cause identified, it will be corrected allowing for a smooth evolutionary transition to a predator free society.

The following is a chain of events for an all to common venture capitalistic investment. A Corporation built by generations of hard-working Americans has expanded over the years to employ thousands of working-class citizens. Although, recently the dynamics of globalization has brought countries with slave labor wages in direct competition with the higher paid American workforce. The American-made Corporation is now on the verge of bankruptcy barely able to pay the wages for the thousands of families that have become dependent on them for their basic survival necessities. Desperate for a solution a decision was made to give some venture capitalists control of the company in an attempt to prevent bankruptcy and return the corporation to a profitable status.

In the beginning a quick return on capital investment is desired, a third of the workforce will be cut from middle management and the remaining employees must assume their responsibilities while taking a slight reduction in pay or benefits or both. Later new automation technology has allowed removing the unnecessary expense of wages and healthcare benefits for half of the remaining workforce. The workers willing to take the lowest wages and least benefits for the highest skilled labor are allowed to remain in order to operate and maintain the automated equipment and of course to perform any tasks still needing to be done by human hands.

To complete the capitalistic investment and provide maximum profit for a few top predators, the remaining employees are instructed their final job will be to train their overseas replacements before the entire production facility is transferred offshore. This will allow a few venture capitalists to maximize their investment using a more manageable and desperate to survive working-class resource. It's nothing personal, a top predator of Capitalism must remain focused, competitive and often indifferent to the consequences of their actions. However, those consequences are becoming too well known among the many for the few to continue denying their existence.

What's really amazing is some people that still have their jobs can be conditioned to believe this is in our country's best interest, and that the top predators that are exploiting our fellow citizens are just good and honest businessmen following their American dream. These are the moral values our predatory social structure conditions us to find acceptable. When we hear about the hundreds of thousands of Americans that are losing their competition for capitalistic survival we feel a sense of satisfaction knowing that at least for now we still have homes to live in, food to eat, health care when we get sick or injured and some form of public education for our children. We may feel so lucky as to tolerate abuse by our employers, increased hours, less pay and no workers rights or safety regulations. But at least our heads are still above water unlike many of our less fortunate working-class American competitors that have already drowned during their struggle for capitalistic survival.

Because we have been conditioned to accept a capitalistic social structure that values the individual accumulation of wealth and power over the health and safety of its citizens, it changes our reality and the way we look at things. It's commonly accepted that the primary objective in our capitalistic game for survival is to acquire more wealth, power and global resources compared to everyone else. Most of us will not have the opportunity to become the supreme capitalistic ruler of the world but we will naturally want to improve our survival conditions relative to other competitors. For this reason we naturally reward our most valued citizens with wealth, power and elevated social status.

Average U.S. family expenditures for 2009

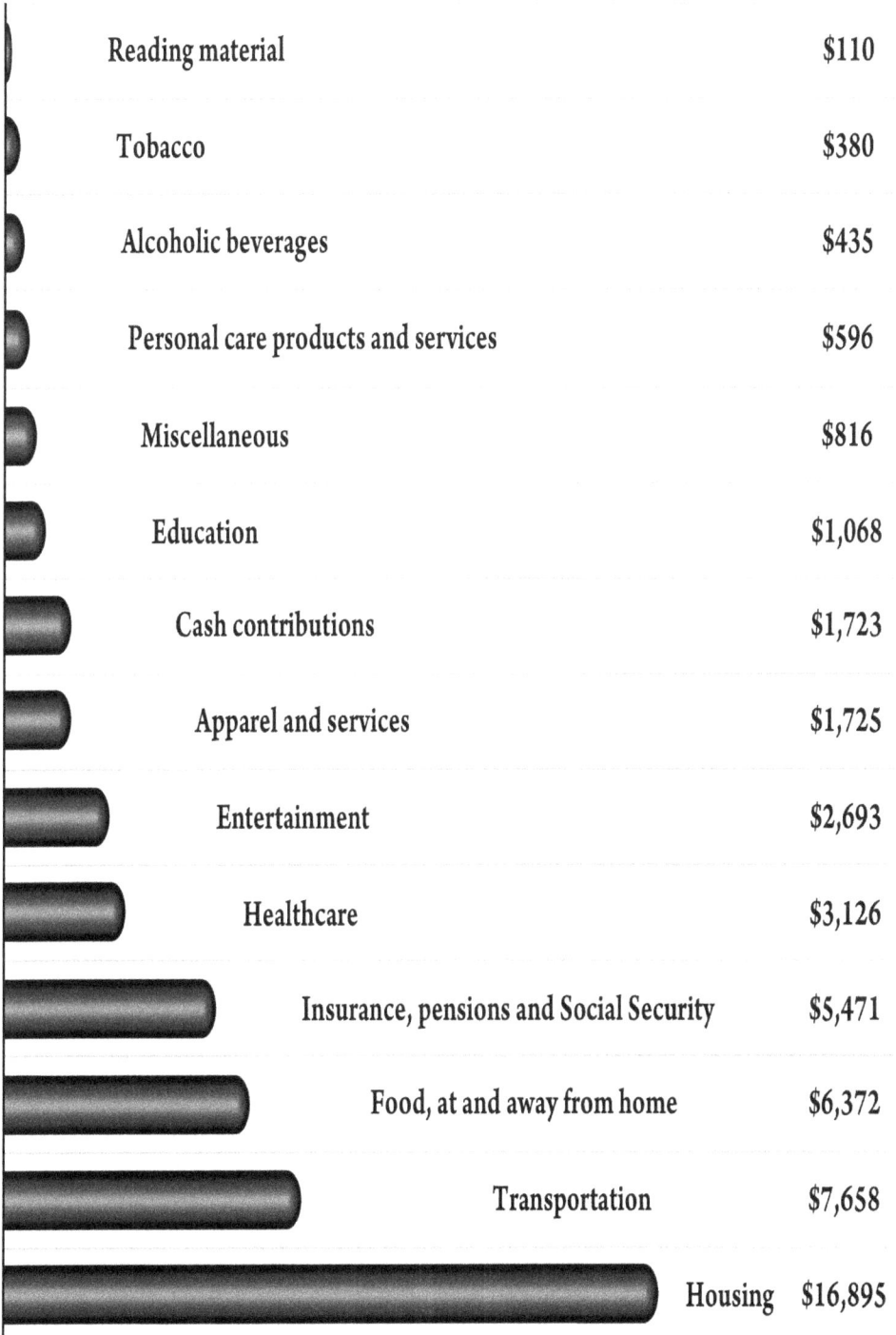

Reading material	$110
Tobacco	$380
Alcoholic beverages	$435
Personal care products and services	$596
Miscellaneous	$816
Education	$1,068
Cash contributions	$1,723
Apparel and services	$1,725
Entertainment	$2,693
Healthcare	$3,126
Insurance, pensions and Social Security	$5,471
Food, at and away from home	$6,372
Transportation	$7,658
Housing	$16,895

Source: U.S. Census Bureau,
Prepared by True Freedom Technologies

Annual expenditures total $49,068

I got to thinking if anyone deserves elevated social status and multimillion-dollar salaries it would be the people that risk their lives to help others and keep our country safe from foreign or domestic threats and not the top predators that use their wealth, power and influence in government to find the best ways to manipulate and exploit a global working class resource. Our priorities are completely backwards, with a socially induced motivational paradigm like that it's no wonder we're evolving super predators willing to allow millions of us working class pray, to suffer and die in order to achieve their capitalistic conquests. We live in a socially engineered society and technical infrastructure designed to extract the maximum amount of profit from We the People without actually killing the golden goose. We are made to work and pay for every one of our basic survival necessities from water to food and shelter. On top of that the maximum amount of taxes are extracted from the segment of our population with the least power and representation over our capitalistically controlled government and funneled to the ruling class top predators with the greatest influence over their legislative colleagues and servants.

Some people may still be surprised to realize how much control any ruling class top predators would have over their working-class population. However, once they are allowed to use their wealth and power to socially engineer our society and create laws we the people must conform to, it's not so hard to see. Imagine getting together with a few million of your closest buddies for a friendly competition where everyone must compete against one another for their survival. The only catch is just a few of you get to create the rules of the game making it absolutely certain they would always win while everyone else loses. Our intellectual ability to objectively recognize the absurdity of this scenario would lead us to reject the rules of this game while our hardwired survival instincts and the conditioning of our predatory social structure would continue to make our exploitation seem like an acceptable way of life. Compared to many other countries the American working-class resource is allowed to retain much of the wealth we generate giving us the option to pay more for all of our basic survival necessities, competitive products and recreational luxuries.

There are so many ways to legally exploit a working-class resource within a free-market predatory social structure I could write books on the subject for years but for now I will just concentrate on the ones that result in the most preventable suffering and death. Many skilled authors are writing numerous books on this subject helping us to break our subjective realities to serve the top predators of our species. The majority of us working class prey may have been slow to catch on but the grave evils of Capitalism were clearly known by many of the more educated and gifted members of our species, made evident by Albert Einstein's remarks on this subject as early as 1949.

As explained throughout this book our species has finally reached a critical tipping point in our intellectual evolutionary development where the working-class prey of our world will increasingly demand the end of our predatory social structure and the transition to a predator free society. The social economic structure of free-market Capitalism has become both the ultimate achievement of our predatory evolution as well as the inspiration needed to allow the majority of our educated global populations to become aware of their exploitation, thus accelerating our species transition to the next phase of our intellectual evolutionary development. My only regret is that it did not happen soon enough to prevent the millions of lives that have been and will continue to be lost as a result of our delay.

4. Politics, the illusion of respectability and the epitome of corruption

As young Americans we learn in school our political system and government is there to serve and protect we the people allowing us to be a more powerful and productive nation. That our Constitution and democracy would ensure our elected officials always place our safety and economic prosperity above their own political or personal interests. We learn how the three branches of our government all work together in bureaucratic harmony to provide us with the fairest and most efficient social economic system possible. And how our political transparency of public officials and free speech would prevent any corruption, and alert us voters so our democracy could function properly and remove them from office before any harm could be done to our citizens and country. We also learn how we have two major political parties to provide the checks and balances necessary to prevent any special interest from exerting undue influence on our governing system or subvert our democratic process. That all US citizens can feel confident with the knowledge that our political system and the social economic structure it produces will provide the highest level of freedom, equality and prosperity for all Americans.

Like children naturally expecting our parents would want us to succeed and prosper we start out believing that our political system and government is designed to create a social structure that will allow us to achieve the highest quality of life and greatest contribution to our society. We want to believe that our elected officials would never betray our trust or intentionally do anything to cause us pain and suffering. As we grow older and become working-class members of our capitalistic competition for survival, we learn our country doesn't seem to love all of its children equally. For many of us this may be too emotionally painful to accept and far easier to deny. Like finding out the subjective reality about Santa Claus was just a comforting childhood deception and the truth is armies of grinches are in control of our political system, government and social economic structure. We must try to give these grinches a heart before all the working-class people wake up from their American dream to find our nation has been transformed into a third world country.

There are many good definitions to explain the activities of politics. The title of this section may not be an accepted definition you will find in any dictionary but many people that understand the true nature of politics would agree that it might be the most accurate. An accepted definition explains that politics is in essence an often-dishonest competition between interest groups or individuals for power and control of government. Politics is the system that allows the perpetuation of Capitalism as the most advanced predatory social structure ever created. Our political system allows the wealthiest of the ruling class top predators to control our government and laws with the objective of exploiting the largest amount of profits from the American working class resource.

In an unregulated free market capitalistic system that values excessive profits for the few over the suffering and death of the many, the best return for a ruling class investor is political candidates willing to serve their interests in our government. In our current political system elected officials must serve two masters to gain their position of power and influence. On one hand they must be willing to serve the wealthiest ruling class individuals and corporations that control our government or risk their wrath, and on the other hand they must convince enough working-class voters that they will serve their interests first in order to maintain the illusion of a fully functioning democracy.

An individual becoming a politician is similar to a waiter getting a job at a fine restaurant. Ruling class individuals and corporations play the role of the restaurant owner while the working-class voters are the many customers they serve. Before a waiter can show their customers how well they will be served they must first convince the restaurant owners they will be a good capitalistic investment to increase their profits. The difference being that the working-class customers can barely afford their meals and only tip in pennies while the restaurant owner pays their wages and decide whether they get to keep their job. Our political system is intentionally constructed to require potential candidates to raise millions of dollars to secure a public position that only pays less than a couple hundred thousand a year. How's your fact puzzle coming along, see anything wrong with this picture yet?

Many of our congressional candidates are already millionaires before they seek the position of a trusted public servant. It would be like a millionaire seeking a minimum wage job that allows them to pick lottery numbers and leak information to their friends so they all can make millions more during their service and after they quit. It's not so much the salary or even the fame of being a political celebrity that attracts them it's the position of power that gives them a seat at the table of the most lucrative and corrupt game ever played. Every multinational corporation wants the largest piece of the American working class resource and every smart high-level politician knows they'll have to go through them to get it. That's the kind of power that corrupts.

For working class Americans to receive any social economic relief to their suffering we must rely on our two major political parties of Democrats and Republicans to work together and solve the problems that face our country. The decline of America's economic and moral standing domestically and around the world is a result of their lack of success in that regard. Their ideological points of view have been well stated for many years and the distinctions between the two parties are becoming better known among the politically educated individuals in our country. Far more reliable than their publicly stated objectives are their actions, the bills they sponsor and votes they cast resulting in the laws all Americans are required to obey. The Democrats stated allegiance is with that of the working-class masses and the Republicans stated allegiance is with the ruling class elite. However they both share the same dilemma of serving two masters to attain their positions of power and trust among the working-class voters and their ruling class campaign contributors.

Many politicians say the lack of progress to achieve their stated objectives to be part of our political checks and balances and or the balance of power between the many undereducated working-class voters and the few well educated super wealthy ruling class elite. Even though our democracy and constitution would suggest we the people have the power to control our society, the working-class segment of our population is suffering and dying at an increasing rate while the most fortunate ruling class capitalists are continuing to attain larger portions of our national resources and wealth. This is a natural and highly predictable result of an advanced predatory social structure that promotes the individual accumulation of wealth and power over the suffering and death of its many working-class people.

Many people with knowledge of how our political system works have asked this question for years, how is it that Democrats always seem to repeatedly snatch defeat from the jaws of victory? Especially when considering the majority of voters overwhelmingly support their stated objectives to increase the social economic prosperity of their working-class constituents. If the balance of power between the many working-class voters and the few ruling class elite is equal, why is the suffering and death of the majority of our population continuing to rise while the top predators of Capitalism are making record profits? Even individuals not familiar with our political system or the nature of our predatory social structure are becoming aware of their exploitation as they see more of their friends and families lose their jobs, homes, family structure and quality of life.

We see our democratic champions laughing and playing golf with their Republican colleagues all celebrating their success to maintain their positions of power while the American dream continues to slip away for the majority of our population. It's starting to look like a good cop bad cop type of deception to perpetrate a divide and conquer strategy keeping both ideologies competing against one another. While the real culprits go largely unnoticed and continue exploiting trillions of dollars from the American working class resource. As long as the balance of power is perceived to be equal, this form of advanced intellectual predatory exploitation will continue to distract Democrats and Republicans voters alike while trillions of dollars are extracted from our country and added to we the people's national debt. For individuals functioning with an objective reality the empirical facts are undeniable who the winners and losers are of our capitalistic competition for survival.

If Democrats are the good cops than the Republicans are definitely the bad cops. Their ideologies and allegiance to serve the ruling class elite is not even being denied as in the past when talking to the public. However, private comments revealing whom they serve have matched the way they have voted on legislation for many years. One such well-documented statement revealing their true masters occurred in 1994 after the Clinton's national health care plan was defeated. If passed this national health care plan would have accomplished two things it would have reduce the suffering and death of millions of working-class Americans while limiting billions in profits for some of the largest ruling class top predators that control our government. This well-documented statement by Republican Bob Packwood "We've killed health care reform…now we've got to make sure our fingerprints are not on it" revealed the true nature of how our political system works to create our advanced predatory social structure. Knowing that Americans were beginning to become aware of their capitalistic exploitation and the political corruption within our government, the last thing the Republicans wanted is for working-class voters to know their increased suffering and death was the result of a unified decision by their elected officials to increase profits for their ruling class masters and colleagues.

For many Americans willing to consider the facts objectively, the ability of the ruling class elite to use their wealth and influence in government to subvert our democracy is becoming clearer. Any legislator not willing to take campaign contributions for their vote would be targeted and defeated by a well constructed advertising campaign designed to psychologically manipulate voters into making emotional decisions based on their induced subjective realities. Even the good cop Democrats learned a painful lesson that if they don't serve their ruling class masters they too will lose their positions of power and influence. Both political party ideologies were force aside to serve the higher master of Capitalism or suffer the certainty of falling prey to our advanced predatory social structure. This was a defining moment for my understanding of politics that demonstrated the delicate balance between deceiving the voters with a comforting subjective belief and serving the ruling class capitalists that control our government and political system.

As a major concept mentioned throughout this book it is imperative that we the people not only become aware of our capitalistic exploitation and the techniques used to accomplish it but most importantly the best way to end this process allowing our species to make the transition to a predator free society. The well educated ruling class elite that uses their knowledge as a predatory tool, are fully aware of this and are using their control of government to legislate laws to prevent it. They use their control of government to funnel trillions of taxpayer money to them and then use their political allies to convince the working-class people there's not enough money to provide them with an education, safer environment, health care etc. This form of deception works best on the segment of our population willing to allow a subjective reality to form their decisions and control their actions. The top predators of Capitalism target working-class voters willing to make decisions based on their emotional feelings and not their intellectual knowledge of the subject. I've always despised bullies that use their size, strength or knowledge to manipulate others, this form of capitalistic exploitation to deceive millions into giving up their basic survival necessities is a primary obstacle to be corrected before our species can end our predatory social structure and advance to the next phase of our intellectual evolutionary development.

Because induced subjective realities require the rejection of factual knowledge to maintain their illusion of truth, the working-class voters most under their control will be the last to accept and understand the process used to manipulate them. What may be intellectually obvious to individuals functioning with an objective reality will be likewise emotionally and even violently rejected by individuals under the control of a subjective reality. All working-class voters concerned about our children's future and the survival of our species must ask themselves, is my political party trying to force an emotional decision from me or are they trying to give me the knowledge necessary to form an objective opinion? One of our two major political parties openly rejects science and use of knowledge to help their voters reach objective conclusions to determine what is true and what is false.

One political party more than the other fully embraces the use of religious subjective realities as a form of manipulation and control of their working-class voters. Their ruling class masters using well-paid consultants explore to what extent they can manipulate the working-class voters without becoming too obvious or breaking any laws they were unable to eliminate. If you don't already know which party this is then you are either new to the dynamics of our political system or may be under the control of an induced subjective reality that is designed to produce your denial. This should not be considered a weakness but instead a universal human vulnerability that predatory humans use as a tool for exploitation. It is human nature to be susceptible to this form of psychological manipulation and even though it is allowed in our capitalistic social structure, factual knowledge and a good understanding of the process used against us will prevent this predatory action from determining our political decisions.

The complexity of our government's bureaucracy seems to be intentionally designed to prevent it's understanding by average working-class citizens much like the words in legal documents that can only be understood by lawyers trained to decipher this language. This intentional complexity makes it difficult for working-class voters to get the knowledge necessary to make informed decisions. Without an intellectual understanding of how our government and political system works we must rely on our emotional feelings and subjective realities to determine if our elected officials have our best interest in mind.

The ruling class top predators pay lobbyists and lawyers millions of dollars to write the legislation for our elected officials to vote into law. The ultimate objective for capitalistic investors is to buy influence over all three branches of government at the same time allowing them the highest level of wealth transfer from the American working class resource/tax payers to the ruling class elite. This would create an economic collapse by destroying the vary people that make our country strong and productive.

When the elite capitalistic predators are allowed to gain the greatest control of our government their working-class prey will encounter the highest levels of suffering and death. Trillions of dollars that could be used to increase the quality of life and economic prosperity of the working-class people as well as decrease the national debt is diverted to the wealthiest segment of our population. Giving tax cuts to billionaires, initiating wars that favor wealthy oil and weapons manufacturers, deregulation of environmental health and workers safety standards, will all predictably lead to better domination of the working-class people, giving rise to the evolution of capitalistic super predators.

When the exploitation of the American working class resource reaches a limit of certain economic collapse, a global panic will require more money to be extracted to bail out the very deregulated financial corporations that created the problem. Making the American and world economy dependent on these companies designed to be too big to fail is one of the ways Capitalism became the most advanced predatory social structure ever created. The reasons behind the suffering and death of us working-class people within a capitalistic social structure is becoming more obvious as the level of education increases among the general public allowing objective opinions to be formed as to the nature of our exploitation.

All politicians need to say what voters want to hear to gain their positions of power and influence, and a few of them are actually sincere about providing we the people a better standard of living. Politicians also know, that of the American people that do actually vote in elections only a small percentage of them are aware of the legislation they submit, block and or pass into law. It also true that many of our politicians start out with the intention to deceive the public in order to get into office and work closely with their ruling class masters, friends and colleagues to more efficiently exploit the working class resource. Others may start out with the best of intentions and find the pressures to serve the ruling class top predators are too high to resist if they want to keep their positions of power and influence.

Among the Democrats and Independents it may be difficult to determine whether their words match their actions. As with any politician the only true way to determine whether they serve the ruling class elite or the working-class majority is a careful examination of the legislation they pass or intentionally destroy. Even though the Democratic Party has long been the champions of the working-class majority, individual elected officials are still human, as far as we know, and therefore susceptible to the corrupt influence of our advanced predatory social structure. Among the Republican politicians their public comments are beginning to match many years of legislation and social engineering that has created the most sophisticated and widespread opportunities for capitalistic exploitation of the working class resource.

Comments and actions made by the Republican leadership need to be objectively considered to understand their true agenda and why our country and its working-class people will continue to suffer and die under our current political system. It has been made public that the Republicans number one priority is to regain political control of the executive branch of our government and not for instance help rebuild our country from the economic devastation created by their last administration. The Republican Minority leader in the Senate, Mitch McConnell publicly announced, "The single most important thing we want to achieve is for President Obama to be a one-term president."

The subjective reality that our top Republican legislators care more about their working-class constituents than returning control of our country to the ruling class elite is beginning to turn objective as more Americans are becoming educated and aware of their true intentions. Another action taken by Republicans must also be intellectually considered without emotional interference to understand their true objectives. All 42 Republican Senators united in a pledge to block all legislation until the Bush tax cuts were extended for the wealthiest ruling class elite. Even an attempt to compromise by the Democrats to just exclude the wealthiest billionaires and millionaires was adamantly denied. Among the legislation blocked was Health-care benefits for 9/11 responders, START (Strategic arms reduction Treaty), extension of unemployment benefits and don't ask don't tell. The ruling class Republicans willingness to increase the financial suffering of US citizens that risk their lives to help others, allow our country's security and freedom to be threatened. And to prevent American working-class people from receiving basic survival necessities and prevent equality for men and women serving in the armed forces, all confirms a known allegiance with their ruling class masters and colleagues. This process is now becoming more obvious than ever before as our education and communication technologies increase.

Other comments made by Republicans must be objectively considered to reveal their true level of compassion for the American working-class people. Some Republicans openly admit their willingness to allow our country to default on its national debt, again resulting in greater suffering for the poor and working-class members of our society. Like any national crisis the weakest and most vulnerable of our working-class people would suffer the most while the ruling class billionaires and millionaires would go largely unaffected. These Republican politicians willing to allow this crisis would certainly feel differently if they personally felt the pain and suffering of going without basic survival necessities. Likewise the justification for wars would not be as enthusiastically fabricated if the ruling class oil and arms investors would be the ones to suffer and die instead of making billions in profits.

The ability of our Republican leaders and ruling class top predators to emotionally disassociate themselves from their working-class prey is a natural result of adapting to their social status within our capitalistic society. Again, this lack of compassion is part of our hardwired instincts to accept the suffering and death of our prey as a consequence of survival within a predatory social structure. We must use our intellectual survival trait to break this predatory instinct and its ability to control the evolutionary development of our species.

The recent willingness of the Republican Party to publicly admit their allegiance to the ruling class top predators of Capitalism seems like political suicide when considering they need independent voters to win a general election. Also considering the changing demographics of our country, our species accelerated intellectual evolution and the growing awareness of our systematic exploitation by the ruling class elite. It would seem to be a fatal error in their attempt to gain the trust of the independent working-class voters. Possible explanations are that they feel more confident than ever with the Supreme Court decision of citizens united that allows unlimited and undisclosed money to subvert our democracy. Knowing this will allow for greater investments in high-powered television campaigns to psychological manipulate the public with induced subjective beliefs about how much better their lives will be under their leadership. Or perhaps more effective is their ability to trigger the negative emotions of fear and hate then associate them with their Democratic opponents to manipulate the decision-making process of the independent voters needed to swing the election in their favor. It could also be they know the use of these intellectual predatory manipulation techniques have worked well in the past to secure the last eight years of Republican domination of government. And even though this led to the great recession and near global economic collapse, many unaffected voters will still feel emotionally satisfied with their leadership.

Another effective strategy our Republican leaders seem to be employing is to prevent any legislation that would provide economic recovery for our country or anything that might be considered a success for our Democratic president. Republican elected officials have already publicly admitted with their words and proven with their actions they are willing to allow our country and the working-class people to suffer for political leverage against the Democrats in order to achieve their objectives. Again, the escalation of our economic crisis will not as adversely affect the elite politicians or their ruling class masters and may even provide some additional capitalistic opportunities to further control and exploit the American working-class resource. As long as a large segment of our population remains unaware of their true objectives, this strategy will continue to be quite effective.

The top predatory corporations of Capitalism were set up to make record profits yet refuse to use their trillions of accumulated wealth and power to provide jobs for the many that have suffered or help repair our country's economic devastation created during their control of our government. The only real uncertainty they are concerned about is their ability to manipulate the working-class people into electing another Republican president and creating a government that will allow greater control over our environmental, financial and consumer protections. Even if they are never again able to convince a majority of working-class voters to give them control over all three branches of our government and create another global economic crisis, the trillions they have already exploited will allow them to better socially engineer our predatory social structure. Getting the working-class resource to pay for their own social engineering and more efficient exploitation is one of the more insidious aspects of how Capitalism works.

There are so many ways for the few ruling class top predators of Capitalism to use their control of politics and government to systematically and legally exploit the working class populations of the world that the documentation revealing these events is becoming overwhelming. So many honest and dedicated people have devoted their lives to breaking through the institutionalized bureaucratic barriers to uncover countless forms of capitalistic exploitation. One of the difficulties of identifying and eliminating these threats to our society is that these systems for exploitation are made into socially acceptable forms of intellectual competition to increase profits for the wealthy elite. Its just free-market Capitalism functioning as it was designed, nothing for us little people to be concerned about.

It's becoming so blatantly obvious how corrupt our political system is within our predatory social structure that I would like to leave explaining the grave evils of Capitalism to others and spend all of my time implementing the solutions to correct the problem. However, in an effort to provide a more comprehensive book explaining the problems and the solutions, I will include a few of the more offensive forms of psychological manipulation, abuses of power and blatant disregard for human suffering and death. I must also remind myself that even though I am ready to move on to the solutions and make the many symptoms of our predatory social structure a subject of historical study. A large segment of our working-class population have not received the factual information necessary for them to break their subjective realities and make an informed decision to end our capitalistic exploitation. It is natural that some will learn before others but I feel the best way to accelerate the awareness of our capitalistic exploitation is to create prototype community infrastructures capable of supporting a predator free society allowing all people to evaluate the clear distinction between both social structures and the quality of life they offer.

I would like to start with one of the biggest political deceptions that we the people were willing to believe would be in our best interests, it is called the trickle-down theory or trickle-down economics. The notion that we the people give the top predators of Capitalism even more of the wealth and power we generate than they already systematically exploit from us in hopes that they will feel sorry for us little people and throw us a bone, borders on mass insanity. Like most forms of induce subjective realities for predatory exploitation, they attempt to condition the uninformed masses to make decisions and take actions based on the illusions generated by their emotional feelings, which are easily manipulated. When done correctly victims will violently defend their subjective reality as valid and be emotionally satisfied with their continued exploitation. Using our intelligence for legitimized exploitation of an uninformed working-class resource may be acceptable in a predatory social structure like Capitalism, but I see it as an advanced form of bullying like a more knowledgeable or older child stealing candy from their younger sibling that hasn't learned any defense strategies yet.

Over the years I have noticed an accelerated awareness by the working-class people as to their capitalistic exploitation and not only in America but all over the world in areas that are allowed an education and have access to modern communication technologies. The long accepted corruption in politics and the predatory social structure of Capitalism are starting to receive increased resistance. This corruption of our society is becoming so obvious that many people are bravely going public to expose a system of exploitation that has been protected and allowed to continue for generations. I feel these individuals have reached a level of personal evolutionary development where their intellectual survival trait and accumulated factual knowledge has started to take control over their hardwired predatory instincts and induced subjective realities. They are no longer willing to allow the few to use their influence and power to deceive the many into blindly accepting their exploitation. The number of individuals making this transition is naturally increasing as our species collectively relies more on our intelligence and objective realities than our hardwired predatory instincts and subjective conditioning to serve the ruling class elite.

One such individual willing to brave the criticisms from peers is a conservative columnist by the name of David Frum. David summed things up quite well with one statement as he explained, "the Republicans have been fleeced, exploited and lied to by a conservative entertainment complex". Even though this has been widely known for years among people that follow politics, I must commend all individuals willing to bravely speak the truth in public and risk reprisal or retaliation by top predators hoping their working-class prey will never become aware of their systematic exploitation. I daresay it's not just Republicans that have been fleeced, exploited and lied to, but instead all working-class people struggling to attain that elusive American dream within a highly advanced predatory social structure. However, the Republican segment of our population seems to be far more willing to reject factual knowledge for the illusion of a subjective reality like trickle-down economics and the belief that our ruling class top predators care more about us little people than the billions of dollars they would receive from our continued exploitation.

It seems most of the corruption in politics is specifically designed to subvert our democracy and increase the ability for the top predators of Capitalism to fleece and exploit the working-class resource while simultaneously attempting to prevent us from becoming intellectually aware of the process. For generations while our country was young and less educated, it used to be so easy to use all the dirty tricks of politics to deceive us working class people however, those days are quickly coming to an end. "Citizens United", or more accurately "Corporations United" may have been successful at returning a higher level of government control to the ruling class top predators of Capitalism if not for our country becoming more educated and aware of these political tactics to subvert our democracy. This Supreme Court decision was such an overreach of conservative appointed power that there is a concerted effort to return control of our democracy to we the people and away from wealthy corporations as our Constitution intended.

I believe our forefathers understood the corrupting influence of power and the need to prevent the largest corporations and top predators of our world from controlling our political system, our state and federal governments and the laws we the people must survive during our pursuit of happiness. I'm sure our forefathers had no idea how our Constitution would be twisted and manipulated to serve the capitalistic greed of the ruling class elite. Our forefathers were certainly no Angels and with the social conditioning of their time it seems rather amazing they could remain so objective while trying to create a society not controlled by wealth and power.

Even though our social structure has reached the epitome of capitalistic greed and predatory domination, I'd like to think our forefathers would be proud that we the people have also reached a point in our national evolution where we are finally capable of creating the first technically advanced predator free society. Like a well-educated young farmer showing a grandparent the advantages of modern day combine technologies over the ox drawn wooden plow that they used during their youth. As our national intellectual evolution eventually broke the very real chains of slavery providing a higher level of freedom and equality for we the people, so too will we break the chains of Capitalism and achieve true freedom within a predator free society. Now that's something to be proud of.

One of the better known dirty tricks of politics or perhaps more to the point, ways to abuse power to serve the ruling class elite, is known by the name gerrymandering. Don't feel intellectually deprived if you have never heard of gerrymandering before, it's one of those things the top predators just assume we didn't become aware of, but that's not working so well for them now days. We little people keep getting smarter and then we start telling each other what we've learned at the exponential rate possible by modern communication technologies, and before you know it, that dog won't hunt anymore. Once we learn how the exploitation technique works we simply use our intellectual survival trait to create predatory defenses so we won't be susceptible to that form of attack. Well at least it's simple in theory however, in practice acquiring the factual knowledge necessary to end the detrimental effects of gerrymandering will much more difficult. Preventing our ruling class leaders from deceiving us to gain their positions of power and control of our country will be a whole lot easier once we unite as a people and make the collective decision to end this form of exploitation, allowing for a functioning democracy to better represent our citizens needs.

In short the objective of gerrymandering is to ensure political victory by systematically redrawing districts to exclude people that wouldn't vote for them. Whether they are Republican or Democratic candidates running for office it would give them an unfair advantage if 90% of the voters in their districts were known to be of their political party. When public servants use their position of power to redraw districts for the strategic purpose of subverting our democracy and guaranteeing victory for the candidates of their political party, that's considered gerrymandering. With the proper capitalistic investments ruling class top predators can use their power and wealth to install many political servants in our government to create or prevent laws that will aid or hinder the efficient exploitation of their working-class resource also known as we the people.

Now that ruling class Republicans have accurately calculated their future loss of the popular vote among almost every other demographic except for white, wealthy older men, they have wisely decided to use other political tactics to achieve and maintain control of our government and laws. Because these laws determine what level of predatory exploitation the working-class resource will be subjected to and who gets the majority of the profit, top predators of Capitalism will do almost anything to control these positions of power and influence. What's interesting is all these different forms of intellectual deception tend to work best when the prey does not find out that they're being manipulated and used as political pawns to give the Kings of Capitalism better control over our government. I'm not sure if it's a predator high-induced lapse of judgment or a deep unexplained desire to be honest to the public but the Republican State leadership committee seemed quite proud of themselves for successfully using gerrymandering to secure a 33 seat Republican margin in the 113th United States Congress, even though the Democratic candidates received over 1 million more votes. I was slow to catch on at first but now I'm learning how a democracy works within an advanced predatory social structure like Capitalism.

Keep in mind these political deceptions may be mind-boggling and new to us, but for the evil masterminds of capitalistic politics, this stuff is just another day at the office. Imagine a think tank of highly educated top human predators in thousand dollar suits using all their collective intellectual skills to find the best ways to exploit the working-class resource while staying within the legal limits allowed for by our predatory social structure and political system. You've got to admit it takes a lot of skill to pull together a coalition of political players in key positions of government and different fields of science like demographic psychology, statistical probability forecasting, and a number of other hard to pronounce occupations. Seriously, it's probably at least 10 times more complicated than anything the majority of us Americans can imagine. It's not just the challenge and recognition for creating a capitalistic masterpiece of intellectual deception that motivates these individuals, it's also the huge amounts of money that we are conditioned to idolize. This is how Capitalism forces us to abuse our gift of intelligence. What a waste of creative skills.

Another well-known way to use political power and public trust to subvert our democracy is voter suppression. During the 2012 presidential election the liberals and progressives were all complaining about

Republicans intentionally using voter suppression techniques known to diminish the Democratic vote. The Republicans responded by saying things like, we are only trying to protect the integrity of the voting system and would never do anything to subvert our democratic electoral process so that our candidate for president may have an unfair advantage. It's almost un-American to suggest such a well dressed and respected public servants would even consider doing such a thing.

Sometimes people get so caught up in their subjective realities they can start to feel everyone must share their belief or maybe they just didn't get the memo what they should and should not admit to the public. In what must have been a shocking and rewarding, I told you so moment for the liberals and progressives, Mike Turzai a Republican legislator in Pennsylvania. Made what seems to be a classic Kinsley gaffe when he was proudly announcing a list of accomplishments at a partisan political event. He said "voter ID which is going to allow Gov. Romney to win the state of Pennsylvania, done!" It's interesting how the Republicans said they needed this new voter ID law to prevent fraud and corruption, now we know it was like trusting the fox to protect the henhouse.

Republican governors and election officials in key swing states that may have easily determined the outcome of the 2012 presidency of the United States, started to enact such obvious forms of voter suppression even nonpolitical working-class citizens began to notice. It's like they just didn't care what us working-class voters think anymore, they had the power to create or eliminate laws and there was nothing we little people could do about it. Even when federal laws are broken and our constitutional rights are violated they knew it would be worth it to get their candidate in control of our government. If they could just get the timing right the election might be over before a federal court could rule on the unconstitutionality of their political deceptions or the voters became aware they were being manipulated. These kinds of political deceptions may have gone largely unnoticed in the past and would have been quite effective on an uninformed public. However, in what seems to be a clear indication of our recently accelerated intellectual evolution, we the people not only noticed we were being manipulated but became even more determined than ever to exercise our right to vote and have some small control over what level of capitalistic exploitation we will be subjected to.

Even though our elected Congress is intended to rule by majority allowing the will of the people to influence our legislation the political party in the minority is given a parliamentary procedure called the filibuster to delay or prevent laws from passing. I may be kind of new to politics, but in combination with gerrymandering, this seems like a good way to subvert our democracy and prevent any legislative progress that doesn't get the top predators of Capitalism what they want. The filibuster rule like every other bureaucratic lever of power has been corrupted and used as a tool to prevent laws that may interfere with the efficient transfer of wealth from the working class many to the ruling class few. For the filibuster to be used as a political tool to help perpetuate or enhance the exploitation of we the people is a highly predictable manifestation of an advanced predatory social structure like free-market Capitalism. I keep getting reminded that our predatory social structure is creating the very corruption we are fighting so hard to defeat, while the easier solution is to prevent it from starting by changing our environmental conditions and correcting the problem at its source.

It's also true that a filibuster can be used by the minority in state governments to prevent the abuse of power by a ruling class majority. Sometimes the majority can feel their power and ability to deceive the public is so great they can use political tricks to pass laws in the night when nobody will notice that their constitutional and human rights are being diminished. A filibuster can expose this trick by giving the public time to consider the laws they must conform to. I suppose it comes down to our ability to understand the issues and to know what political tricks are being used to serve the ruling class few or protect the working-class many.

Most of us Americans are aware of the two recent wars in Iraq and Afghanistan. Fewer Americans know about the reallocation of our tax revenues to favor the super wealthy and the deregulation of our too big to fail financial institutions all leading to the most devastating economic collapse since the Great Depression. Some people may feel this was a result of extreme incompetence at the executive level in combination with the inherent greed and corruption that is a natural manifestation of our predatory competition for survival. While others may feel there were too many years of well-calculated and deliberate actions for our leaders not to be fully aware of the increased suffering and death that would result from their decisions. Also the timing of the economic collapse seemed overly suspicious right at the end of eight years of Republican executive control of our government before leaving in disgrace and turning over a devastated country to a Democratic administration.

From an evil ruling class political mastermind point of view this would be an excellent plan to extract the maximum amount of wealth from an unsuspecting working class resource and then blame the Democratic administration during the following years when the general population would experience the most pain and suffering. Then the increased national stress could be used to help build negative subjective realities that can be directed towards the current administration. If the small segment of our population that actually determines elections were susceptible to these subjective realities it could return control of our state and federal governments back to the Republicans. If only they could keep us little people from finding out how these things work.

It can be difficult to determine if some of our political leaders just lack the proper management skills to keep their working class resource emotionally satisfied with their increased level of capitalistic exploitation. Or whether they're just following their predatory instincts to accumulate more power and wealth and keep us working class pray dependent upon our ruling class masters. Either way their efforts are failing to keep we the people unaware of the factual knowledge we need to make an informed decision to end our predatory social structure and follow our natural intellectual evolution to a predator free society. We're not there yet, but we're learning fast.

Because the Social Security act and Medicare needed to get through both the House of Representatives and Senate before getting signed into law by the executive office, I was curious how these two humanitarian acts of compassion for we the people could be allowed by our developing predatory social structure. As it turns out, not every wealthy capitalist or their assets in congress wanted social security or Medicare to become law. It seems many of our lawmakers in government at the time were okay with letting our elderly citizens that made our country great suffer and die in the streets like a third world country living under some dictatorship. Ironically many of these public officials would not have attained their position of power, if not for some of the very people they were willing to deny human rights. As disgraceful as this is, this lack of compassion would be an expected symptom of a predatory social structure. I wanted to find out if there was any distinction between the Republicans and Democrats on the vision they had for we the people and the future of our country.

The Social Security act of 1935 passed Congress with 344 Democrats voting yes and 16 no votes, where 97 Congressional Republicans voted yes with 19 no votes. After the overwhelming Democratic support in Congress, it was also a Democratic president Franklin D. Roosevelt that finally signed the Social Security act into law proving to working-class Americans and the rest of the world this is what our country stands for. Defining our two major political parties even more than Social Security was when Medicare became the law of the land in 1965. When Medicare was being considered for Americans older than 65 and younger people with disabilities there were 294 Congressional Democrats that voted yes and 55 no, where 83 Republicans voted yes and 85 no. Again with overwhelming Democratic support in Congress, it was again a Democratic president Lyndon B. Johnson that signed Medicare into law. Because these two laws reduced the suffering and death of millions of Americans allowing them to have children, it's clear many of our current citizens owe their very existence to these Democratic leaders and presidents that fought to give we the people basic human rights.

Our country has clearly made progress at providing basic humanitarian acts of compassion for we the people and accomplishing that most elusive of objectives, making our predatory social structure fairer for us working-class prey. Whether they are truly acts of compassion or brilliant management skills by top predators that know the importance of keeping their working-class resource emotionally satisfied, it's still a win for us American people by increasing our quality of life and reducing our preventable suffering and death. The next logical step in our social evolution at providing we the people a higher standard of freedom, prosperity and longevity is to allow all of our citizens to receive universal health care as a human right and not another opportunity for capitalistic exploitation.

My conditioning while growing up in America always gave me the impression our country was on the cutting edge of not only developing technologies but also our pursuit of freedom, equality and justice for all. And when compared to many other countries with more primitive predatory social structures, America certainly provides a higher quality of life for our capitalistic competitor that are successful enough to afford it. Knowing how beneficial universal healthcare would be for any working-class people and the advantage this would bring by increasing a country's productivity, I started to wonder what's taking us so long. It's not like this is a rocket brain surgery. Maybe our political leaders knew the advantage that universal healthcare would bring to our people and country but just couldn't figure out a way to make it happen on a national level. Of course any program or system within a predatory social structure that deals with large transfers of taxpayers wealth is subject to corruption at the highest levels no matter how noble the cause. In fact some form of capitalistic exploitation may need to be designed into the program before it can be used on the working-class resource. I was a little surprised to learn many countries were far ahead of the U.S. at providing some form of universal health care for their citizens.

I learned about the UDHR (Universal Declaration of Human Rights) that was adopted by the United Nations General assembly way back in 1948. The 25th article in the UDHR is the "right to health" and it states:

(1)   "Everyone has the right to a standard of living adequate for the health and well-being of himself and of his family, including food, clothing, housing and medical care and necessary social services, and the right to security in the event of unemployment, sickness, disability, widowhood, old age or other lack of livelihood in circumstances beyond his control."

(2)   "Motherhood and childhood are entitled to special care and assistance. All children, whether born in or out of wedlock, shall enjoy the same social protection."

All things considered It's not like our ruling class leaders didn't have enough time since 1948 to figure out a practical way to provide universal healthcare for we the people, so something else must be preventing our country progress towards human rights.

Adopting the UDHR seems to be a significant milestone in our species intellectual evolutionary development towards a predator free society by making a global acknowledgment among countries that all people are inherently entitled to basic human rights. Or in other words the ruling class top predators of the world should not blatantly abuse and exploit their working-class resource for profit and then let them die. 48 United Nations members voted to adopt the declaration and 0 voted against it with eight abstentions for national leaders too cowardly and or corrupt to make a stand on human rights. However, just voting to adopt the declaration at the United Nations doesn't mean a country will ratify (formally approve and make legally binding) all 30 articles providing these human rights for their working-class populations. It's like when a politician makes a big public speech with their words about national pride and a better standard of living for their constituents, and then quietly continues their efforts to exploit the working class resource with their actions, knowing most of their little people will not notice the deception, and probably vote for them again.

Because the United States is currently the wealthiest, most powerful and influential country in the world that often makes big public speeches about human rights, equality and freedom for all. Other nations expect us to be leaders with our actions and not resort to the all too common political deceptions with our words. However, the working-class people of the world are becoming too educated to accept the political deceptions of the past and are beginning to make objective decisions based on factual knowledge as to what level of capitalistic exploitation they feel is acceptable in their country. This is how it starts.

Many other countries around the world that have better control over their top predators have decided to not only adopt the UDHR publicly but also provide a moral example by ratifying them in some form of national legislation. Again, I had to ask myself, how could a country as great as America with all our wealth, resources and power to guide the intellectual evolutionary development of our species, not be far ahead of other countries by providing functional societies that have fully ratified all articles under the UDHR to provide basic human rights to our citizens?

Since adopting the UDHR way back in 1948, our leaders have had access to the intellectual and creative skills necessary to create a social structure that embodies all the human rights called for in this declaration. It seems America could have and should have been leading by example on human rights for at least the last 50 years. I can't help but to think how much closer we would be to achieving a predator free society if we truly embraced the spirit of the UDHR instead of finding better ways to capitalize on our need for survival necessities. I am proposing that we not only make up for those lost 50 years, but that we also take a giant leap into the future beyond the obstruction of partisan politics and the need for capitalistic exploitation. We should start creating predator free societies where our survival necessities are technically integrated into our infrastructures and considered a human right for all people. Why wait for the future when we can do it right now and save millions of lives in the process. I'm tired of waiting for others to act, how about you?

America's evolutionary struggle for human rights does have many smaller victories for we the people as well as the more significant achievements of Social Security and Medicare. We have also publicly declared to the world we are in agreement with the UDHR and that all people should have the right to health, but I still wanted to know what is it about our political system and predatory control of government that has prevented us from providing universal healthcare for our people. After their victories to achieve Social Security and Medicare it seems the Democrats were at it again trying to expand human rights for we the people when the Clinton health care plan otherwise known as the American health security act of 1993 tried to provide universal healthcare for all American citizens and control the cost of our health care system. It seems expanding human rights for the working-class prey within an advanced predatory social structure and government controlled by capitalistic greed, would be too difficult of a task during that period of our countries evolution.

Most working class people during that time were much less familiar than they are today with the cause of our preventable suffering and death or how to use our democracy to expand our human rights and limit our capitalistic exploitation.   Without the factual knowledge necessary to identify and counteract psychological manipulation techniques used to control our decision-making process the working-class people were easy prey. Keep in mind what may seem like futuristic science fiction to some people are for others just routine capitalistic exploitation techniques used to increase profits. It's all perfectly legal and business a usual in our predatory social structure. Manipulating the decision-making process of the working-class resource isn't so difficult when you have direct access to their brains via their visual and audio inputs. Many Americans may not have good access to public education or healthcare but if there's any way possible they will have a TV that serves as a digital to biological interface and network connection into every human being on the planet, or at least the more fortunate ones.

You may feel our TVs main function is to condition us into being impulsive consumers. An advertising tool used by those corporations wealthy enough to inundate our brains with commercials that also include some entertainment content to draw our attention like a moth to a flame, and you'd be right. However, once you have direct access to the brains of a working-class resource and their social structure allows the manipulation of their decision-making process, it only makes good business sense to take full capitalistic advantage of their infrastructure investment to induce subjective realities and political preferences. I remember life was so much simpler before I learned this stuff and decided to do something about it, but to deny this knowledge now would make me feel like an ostrich sticking my head in the sand, which they really don't do by the way. They may have really small brains but even ostriches aren't that dumb.

Not only do wealthy corporations have direct access to our brains helping us make political and legislative decisions based on our emotional feelings about a person or subject. They have of course invested heavily in members of Congress to prevent or pass any laws that could interfere or accelerate the efficient flow of wealth from the working class many to the ruling class few. If someone wanted to find the real reason why we the people of the United States have not achieved a level of human rights consistent with the UDHR during the last 65 years, we only need to direct our attention to the corporations that stand to lose the most profit.

An individual functioning with an objective reality conditioned by a predator free society could easily identify which corporations and their congressional conspirators were preventing we the people from achieving a higher level of human rights, so corrections could be made. Isn't this what our forefathers intended to happen, isn't this the whole idea behind our constitution? They certainly didn't intend for we the people to be used as a resource for capitalistic exploitation by the ruling class elite. In fact isn't that exactly what they were trying to prevent? How far we have strayed, but the good news is we the people are about to find out that we have the ultimate power to control our future, not the ruling class top predators as we were conditioned to believe.

An individual functioning with an objective reality conditioned by a predator free society could easily identify which corporations and their congressional conspirators were preventing we the people from achieving a higher level of human rights, so corrections could be made. Isn't this what our forefathers intended to happen, isn't this the whole idea behind our constitution? They certainly didn't intend for we the people to be used as a resource for capitalistic exploitation by the ruling class elite. In fact, isn't that exactly what they were trying to prevent? How far we have strayed, but the good news is we the people are about to find out that we have the ultimate power to control our future, not the ruling class top predators as we were conditioned to believe.

The political and social dynamics surrounding the Clinton health care plan and its attempt to provide we the people with a higher degree of human rights is well documented. This historical event provides an excellent example how free-market Capitalism and our predatory social structure work together to benefit the ruling class few at the expense of the suffering and death of the working-class many. Our health care system has long provided some of the best medical care money can buy, but in the true spirit of predatory Capitalism hundreds of billions of our taxpayer dollars are being systematically diverted into waste fraud and abuse otherwise known as profits for large corporations that control our government.

The trade-off between allowing we the people to have an increased level of human rights, better health, advanced education, more prosperity etc. and the excessive accumulation of wealth and power by a few ruling class top predators has been well known for decades. You may still be wondering, as I did, how could we the people allow our systematic exploitation to continue for so long. The primary reason is we are genetically hardwired and environmentally conditioned to accept our predatory social structure as an inevitable part of life. Our capitalistic competition for survival is unnecessarily extending our naturally occurring predatory social structure for the sole purpose of benefiting the fortunate few at the expense of evolving true freedom and prosperity for our entire species.

For anyone still undecided what the primary difference is between the Democrat and Republican political parties, it should be noted that the healthcare insurance, pharmaceutical and other industries worked very hard with the Republican leaders in Congress. Investing millions to defeat the Clinton health care plan and prevent we the people from achieving the level of human rights more consistent with the UDHR that our country publicly committed to over 65 years ago. While some Democrats in Congress fought for a higher level of human rights others sought a compromise that the healthcare corporations and Republicans may accept. With the healthcare corporations and Republicans standing firm with their objective and the Democrats fragmented a filibuster proof majority was not possible, so the bill was defeated as millions of Americans continued to go without health insurance.

Knowing the baby boomers were getting older, the induced epidemic of obesity would continue and of course all the tobacco smokers in America, there is a lot of profit to be made from a wealthy population so willing to accept their exploitation. I keep wondering how much suffering and death it will take before the people say enough. It seems the real art of Capitalism is to get the working-class prey to pay for their own exploitation and then feel emotionally satisfied that they have made the right decision. This is how Capitalism has become the most successful form of evil designed to convert human lives into profit.

If we fast-forward past the dark years of our Republican President George W. Bush's administration, where capitalistic greed and corporate domination of government was allowed to devastate our country and create a global economic crisis for the working-class people around world. We come to the next real attempt at some form of universal health care capable of increasing the basic human rights of we the people. Here again, it appears to be one of those bleeding heart liberal progressive Democrat that had the audacity to think he may actually be successful where others have failed. It's like they just can't help themselves from trying to make Capitalism fair for the working-class prey, they refuse to accept how our predatory social structure works to manipulate government and maintain control over we the people.

As it turns out things were different this time, we little people have been accelerating our intellectual evolutionary development and we are becoming increasingly aware of our capitalistic exploitation. Political deceptions may still be allowed by our predatory social structure but the better we understand how these techniques work the quicker we can render them ineffective, break our subjective realities and return national power to we the people as originally intended in our Constitution. This may seem like a radical concept to some people, but if we stand back and look at the big picture it becomes a natural progression of our intellectual evolutionary development on our way to achieving a predator free society. Once we better understand this transition we can focus on accelerating the process and minimizing the suffering and death inherent in the predatory social structures of our past and present.

The Democratic do-gooder above is of course President Barack Obama and his attempt at increasing our human rights was called The Patient Protection and Affordable Care Act otherwise known as Obamacare. As with the Clinton administrations attempt at health care reform the political battle lines were predictable. Wealthy corporations and their Republican asset in government got concerned about losing hundreds of billions in annual profits they worked so hard to create with a health care system designed to be a masterpiece of capitalistic deception to fleece the American working-class resource. This time they spent hundreds of million more on carefully constructed TV ads to create a negative emotional response to associate with Obamacare. You may still feel as I did, that it was just some form of honest incompetence or lack of intellectual skills at the highest levels that keeps our health care system so inefficient at providing a level of service equal to the trillions of tax dollars it receives.

Then I learned in addition to artificially inflating our national health care crisis by legitimizing products like cigarettes and accelerating our epidemic of obesity. Some of the same corporations and their congressional assets are also fighting hard to protect over $700 billion per year in waste, fraud and capitalistic abuse of power. And at the same time our Republican leaders that represent these corporations are telling us working-class prey our government doesn't have enough money to provide basic human rights for we the people. My fact puzzle just got a lot clearer. Just imagine how much suffering and death could be prevented if we the people were allowed to keep those hundreds of billions of dollars. Or for instance how many technically advanced community infrastructures could be created accelerating our transition to a national and eventually global predator free society. What amazing progress our species will make once this burden is removed.

Have you ever noticed our Republican leaders suggest government bureaucracy is responsible for limiting their ability to provide a higher level of prosperity for the American people? However, when it comes to writing new corporate tax loopholes, deregulating financial industries, limiting environmental protections, or laws to promote gender inequality, our government works like a well-oiled machine. As more Americans suffer and die, the more apparent it will become that we are being lied to, fleece and exploited by individuals trying to maintain our advanced predatory social structure.

We were told trickle-down economics was the best solution to provide a higher quality of life for us working-class Americans and if we only trust our government officials and allow trillions of our tax dollars to be diverted to our ruling class elite everything would work out just fine. On the other hand if we use any of our own tax dollars to provide better health care for our people it would certainly be the end of the American dream for our entire country. Here are just a few of the things in Obamacare that we are being told would destroy our country, as if increased health and human rights for we the people was a bad thing and not part of what made our nation so successful.

1. Insurers are prohibited from dropping policyholders when they get sick.
2. Insurers are prohibited from imposing lifetime dollar limits on essential benefits, like hospital stays, in new policies issued.
3. Enhanced methods of fraud detection are implemented.
4. Insurers are prohibited from discriminating against or charging higher rates for any individual based on gender or pre-existing medical conditions.
5. Insurers must spend 80% (for individual or small group insurers) or 85% (for large group insurers) of premium dollars on health costs and claims, leaving only 20% or 15% respectively for administrative costs and profits, subject to various waivers and exemptions.
6. All new plans must cover certain preventive services such as mammograms and colonoscopies without charging a deductible, co-pay or coinsurance.

While Obamacare is a huge victory in our ongoing battle to provide a higher level of human rights for we the people, some healthcare corporations and their congressional assets in government were able to prevent the "public option". This public option would have removed the incentive and opportunity for capitalistic exploitation by providing a level of competition top predator could not meet without sacrificing hundreds of billions of dollars per year. It can be difficult to imagine what an incredibly sweet deal it is to fleece hundreds of billions of dollars from the American working-class resource as part of an accepted socially engineered aspect of our predatory social structure. It can be equally as difficult to imagine what an incredibly bad deal it is for us working-class prey, it not only robs us of the wealth and resources we need to provide full human rights and prosperity for all Americans, but it actually limits our natural intellectual evolutionary development to a predator free society.

We must form objective realities and make the collective decision to end our predatory social structure before more permanent damage is done. We've always had the power to do this, but didn't know how to use it until now.

It also seems important to consider if the public option was allowed to become an integral part of our predatory social structure it would then be subject to the same corrupt influence that has diminished our public education system. Then both our human rights for education and health would be under the control of ruling class top predators and used as levers of power to manage their working-class resource. Pay no attention to those top predators behind the curtain. You can trust the giant talking heads on your television, after all they seem like your only chance to achieve the American dream and live happily ever after. And if you're not satisfied with the way things are now just remember, they could be a lot worse like death panels and pulling the plug on your grandma worse. So show some American spirit, work harder for less pay, don't complain and be happy with what you get. I think the real problem here is that these levers of power are in the wrong hands. I don't trust the giant heads anymore they're thunderous voices and scary words seem more like an illusion now trying to get me to accept my predatory exploitation under free-market Capitalism. Our species is becoming too intellectually advanced to accept this level of exploitation. Can't steal candy from this baby anymore.

The one thing about Obamacare that healthcare corporations and Republicans must really appreciate is to have our government mandate by law that most Americans become customers to for-profit organizations competing for their capitalistic survival. After all this was originally their concept and vision for we the people. Forcing people to compete against one another for our survival necessities is bad enough but this seems to create another thing to fight over and more opportunities for capitalistic exploitation. However, one of the Obamacare objectives is to reallocate some of the hundreds of billions of dollars that are being diverted to top predators back into providing healthcare as it was intended to do.

In addition, limiting the amount of capitalistic exploitation health insurance providers are allowed to subject we the people to will also provide more revenues to reduce the suffering and death of the American working-class resource.   After the implementation of Obamacare the solvency of Medicare will be extended 9 to 10 years longer and the federal budget will be reduced by over $100 billion during the next decade. Don't expect the Republicans to give up fighting for the healthcare corporations, while filibustering all attempts to rebuild our economy and give President Obama a political victory. Instead they've been busy spending our tax-payer dollars voting to repeal and eliminate Obamacare 48 times so far, and still counting.

As if the systematic exploitation inherent in our predatory social structure wasn't bad enough.   Some of the wealthiest multinational corporations use their power and influence in government to manipulate our laws to allow them to avoid paying their fair share of taxes and then on top of that, get we the people to pay them in subsidies. It's easy to understand the frustration for all the individuals trying to make Capitalism fair for us working class prey, when our laws have been manipulated for generations to create a socially engineered masterpiece for predatory exploitation. Sure our societies have been socially engineered to make us little people dependent upon large corporations for our basic survival necessities giving them the levers of power to ratchet up or down the suffering and death experience by the American people, but it doesn't mean things have to stay that way, not anymore.

Many countries are rapidly becoming intellectually enlightened to our systematic exploitation and are attempting to make our international laws provide more equality for the working class prey of the world. Even though the working-class populations of the world do have the ultimate power to end our predatory social structures, attempting to work within the laws created by top predators to provide equality has been largely ineffective. It is a great thing that our intellectual evolution has finally reached the point that we are becoming aware of our predatory exploitation, but without the real option of a predator free society as an alternative our progress will be too slow for millions of our least fortunate competitors.

It is estimated that our American treasury loses about $90 billion per year from corporate tax loopholes. Where that money could be used to reduce the suffering and death of we the people instead of increasing the power and wealth of some of our most fortunate top predators of Capitalism. I was surprised to find out that much of the inequality we are suffering today started over 50 years ago under the moderate Republican President Dwight D. Eisenhower. He used his power and influence to rewrite our tax laws to favor the wealthiest top predator multinational corporations. It seems Eisenhower and his advisers wanted to encourage US multinational corporations to build factories and higher workers in other countries by not requiring them to pay US income tax on any reinvested profits. Over the years US corporations naturally took full advantage of our corrupt political system to manipulate and expand these international tax loopholes to increase corporate profits.

I started to realize what this old law/tax loophole for multinational corporations means for the average working class American citizen. We the working-class people of America are actually paying the wealthiest corporations to close manufacturing facilities we need to survive and move them to other countries where slave labor is an acceptable form of exploitation. And then, their profits can be kept away from our United States treasury. This would seem to be one of those foundational elements that helped socially engineer our modern day social construct. These deliberate acts weaken our people's ability to survive and our country's ability to compete globally. I had to ask myself, why hasn't this been considered a threat to our national security? Is this the new standard for exploitation our top predators hope we will accept? Is this the kind of leadership we offer the world? This $90 billion in tax loopholes may be a small amount compared to the hundreds of billions of dollars exploited from our healthcare system but it still represents one of the symptoms of our predatory social structure and how it contributes to our overall preventable suffering and death.

We need to reverse our priorities as a country, and then lead by example. Imperialistic Capitalism and the predatory domination of the world may seem like the only game in town, but it just seems that way.

There are far more important pursuits in life, philosophical and technical breakthroughs that our entire species may benefit from, for our top predators to waste any more time or creative skills on the individual accumulation of wealth and power. It's a learning process for all of us.

It's not that these tax loopholes and the billions in lost revenue had not been noticed and efforts to correct this law have not been made, but the predatory corruption of our political system and government has continued to prevent progress or any equality for us working class prey. As it turns out quite a few of our leaders in Congress cosponsored a bill to correct Eisenhower's 50-year-old tax loophole for wealthy corporations, allowing billions of dollars in new revenue to help reduce the suffering and death of the American working class people. The bill to be considered by Congress was called the "Bring jobs home, act" and it proposed:

(1) Giving corporations a 20% tax credit on any expenses for relocating businesses located outside the United States back to America. Providing we the people more jobs, prosperity and helping to relieve some of the economic devastation created by the great recession.

(2) Eliminating tax deductions for selling out their fellow Americans, increasing poverty, weakening our country and relocating a US business outside the United States.

I may be paraphrasing the bill just a little but you can find the exact text online. A simpler way to look at it is, this proposed law offered tax incentives to create American jobs, and eliminated the tax incentives for outsourcing American jobs.

Even though individuals living in other countries working in slave labor conditions have a much higher-level of exploitation by their ruling class top predators, most Americans would rather see these jobs stay in the United States helping millions of our citizens rise above the poverty line. The top predators of Capitalism that manipulate our political system wouldn't mind allowing the 20% tax credit to become law, although it's doubtful they would ever use it unless of course it could increased profits. However the second half of the bill proposed cuts to the very heart of their ability to control our government. It would threaten years of social engineering and billions of dollars in capitalistic investments to continue their predatory domination. The masterminds of Capitalism would be adamantly opposed to giving up any of their control of government so we little people may have a higher quality of life.

A casual political observer may easily get the impression this bill would be a bipartisan issue for all American politicians whether they be Republicans, Democrats or independents. After years of political observations, I'm kind of sad to admit it's not so surprising anymore that an all American law like this capable of reducing the suffering and death of we the people would be highly partisan. It seems this bill had 15 Democratic cosponsors, with 50 total Democrats and 4 Republicans voting to allow this bill to precede into law, and 0 Democrats trying to prevent it. The not so shocking thing about this bill for people that follow politics is that 42 Republican senators voted to prevent this bill from becoming a law, then used the filibuster to prevent its passage. Wow, and some people still wonder why Republicans are getting a bad name and becoming known as the party of, by and for the super wealthy ruling class top predators of Capitalism. People are going to start noticing these things. Who needs smoke-filled back rooms when our exploitation is legitimized as just another function of our government conducting its business to serve and protect we the people. And they got us paying them to increase our exploitation. As evil as Capitalisms is, one must admire the sheer scope of the deception and the social engineering required to control entire populations. Luckily we're growing out of this ugly phase of our evolutionary development and this deception will come to its natural end.

Some of our ruling class political leaders intentionally display an appearance of respectability as part of an illusion, but the power and control they have over their working class resource can create Godlike super egos that justify corruption on the grandest of scales. We feel proud of our ability of our ability to catch street predators forced into capitalistic survival while the political architects of our predatory social structure receive millions in profits from their ruling class masters. What form of conditioning and intellectual isolation could make this seem acceptable? Are induced subjective realities really that effective? Yes.

You may have heard of the budget sequestration also known as, the sequester. A name given to a mindless across-the-board cut to federal spending intended to be a backup plan that nobody wanted to use. It would only be necessary just in case the Democrats and Republicans couldn't come to a compromise on the best way to spend our money and manage our predatory social structure. Surprise, there was no compromise, our divided government and partisan politics is not turning out to be that shining example of bureaucratic harmony that we learned about in school. Is this why our elected lawmakers get the big bucks? I think I want my money back. Maybe we can still return this government and get a new one based on a predator free society. Do you think it's still under warranty, someone check the Constitution... I think it is.

This sequester starting in 2013 is scheduled to extract around $85 billion per year from the federal budget. Billions that helped provide education and health programs for millions of the least fortunate Americans living in capitalistic poverty will end. Things that we Americans use to consider part of being a citizen of this great nation are being rapidly diminished. The part of the American dream that makes us feel our country cares more about we the people than serving the top predators of Capitalism is fading from memory and being replaced with the objective reality that things need to change.

Without intelligent direction or purpose the sequester had the potential to effect the wealthiest ruling class few in our country but as with all austerity measures the people that will suffer the most are the least fortunate of our fellow Americans living in working-class poverty. The majority of Democrats were warning about the detrimental effects this sequester would have on the middle and low income working class

Americans families, while most Republicans were okay with the across-the-board cuts except for they wanted to protect the corporations supplying the Department of Defense. Some of the Republicans even began to think of the sequester as a good thing, considering it an effective way to cut waste from the budget something they wanted to do anyway.

Then something interesting happened that helps us learn just how our government works. The detrimental effects of the sequester started to show up throughout our society causing inconveniences for some of our most fortunate citizens, while threatening the survival and very existence of many of our least fortunate Americans. Our country was starting to feel the pain but it was being evenly distributed, or at least what passes for equality in our current predatory social structure. So everyone was doing their fair share to serve God and country knowing that their sacrifice was for the greater good. Then one of the sequester consequences became so intolerable that it demanded immediate Congressional action to fix. Did Congress finally realize in a great country like America we couldn't allow the preventable suffering and death of our citizens just so wealthy capitalists could continue to exploit billions of dollars from we the people? Maybe they were concerned about their public image or being perceived as heartless ruling class elitists deceiving the public for profit.

It wasn't humanitarian relief helping Americans survive their economic hardships brought on by the great recession that demanded our elected officials immediate attention, it was delays in air travel, or more specifically it was an inconvenience they and other wealthy capitalists would need to experience personally. I thought they might shut down the government again until this terrible threat to national security was resolved. All of a sudden picking and choosing what parts of the sequester stay and what parts must go became a top priority. Any illusion of shared sacrifice and equality went right out the window. Some Democrats were hoping to use this inconvenience on the wealthy to force Republicans into refunding humanitarian programs for Americans suffering in poverty, this effort failed as the Republicans claimed victory. Without the now common use of the filibuster by Republicans to block economic progress, eliminating this single inconvenience became one of the fastest moving bipartisan legislations during President Obama's administration. It seems Congress wanted to fix this terrible problem before they caught their next flights home. I guess bureaucratic harmony and rapid bipartisan progress in government is possible, but only to prevent any inconveniences for our ruling class elite, and not to prevent the suffering and death of our least fortunate American citizens. This is how our government serves and protects we the people.

So it was decided the least fortunate working-class citizens would just need to tighten their belts a little more and pull themselves up by their bootstraps if they want to continue their capitalistic competition for survival and chance to achieve that elusive American dream. When a large segment of the population is living on the edge of survival, giving them that extra push will predictably result in a breakdown of social order. If someone wanted to destroy a society from within or get a nation to self-destruct with internal conflicts this would be an effective strategy. Forcing a working-class resource into desperate acts of survival where our predatory instincts take control over our intellectual desire for peace and harmony is just asking for trouble. Especially when dealing with the most heavily armed civilian population in the entire world. The last thing we would want to do is increase the collective mental instability of our nation and the level of predatory competition needed for survival. It seems our ruling class masterminds of Capitalism must realize the damage this is doing to our country, so what's their endgame?

These negative environmental conditions would produce many preventable mental and physical disorders eventually leading to a breakdown of society and widespread anarchy. Why would anyone want to put our country on that road? Who would benefit from such a thing? Are our top predators getting too greedy or have they just lost their ability to maintain the subjective reality that makes us feel like our capitalistic exploitation is the best form of life we can hope for. I think we're just getting too smart, the old political tricks are losing their effectiveness. The top predators of our world must have seen this coming too and also realized there's nothing they can do to stop it. That doesn't mean they can't delay our natural

U.S. Federal Tax Receipts, in $Billions (2011)

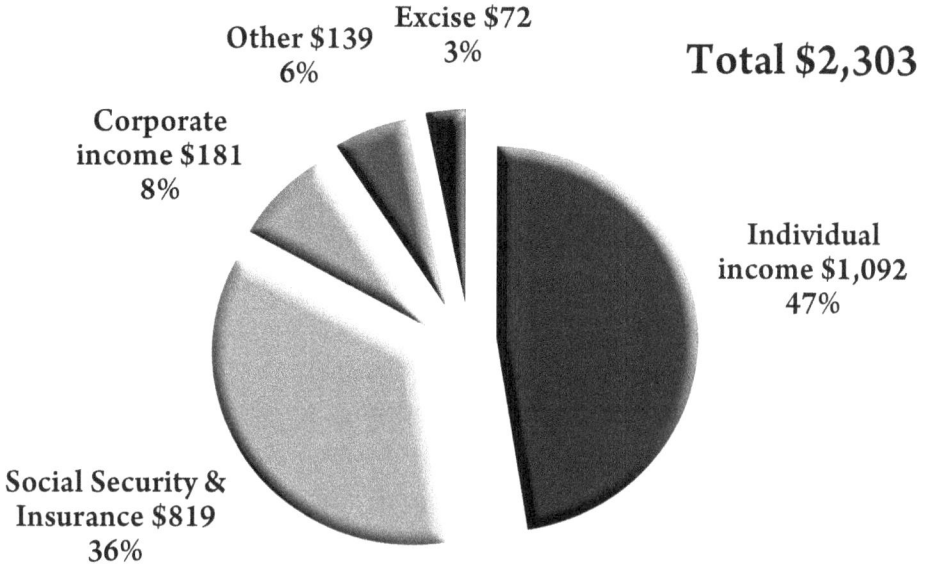

Other $139
6%

Excise $72
3%

Total $2,303

Corporate
income $181
8%

Individual
income $1,092
47%

Social Security &
Insurance $819
36%

U.S. Federal Expenditures, in $Billions (2011)

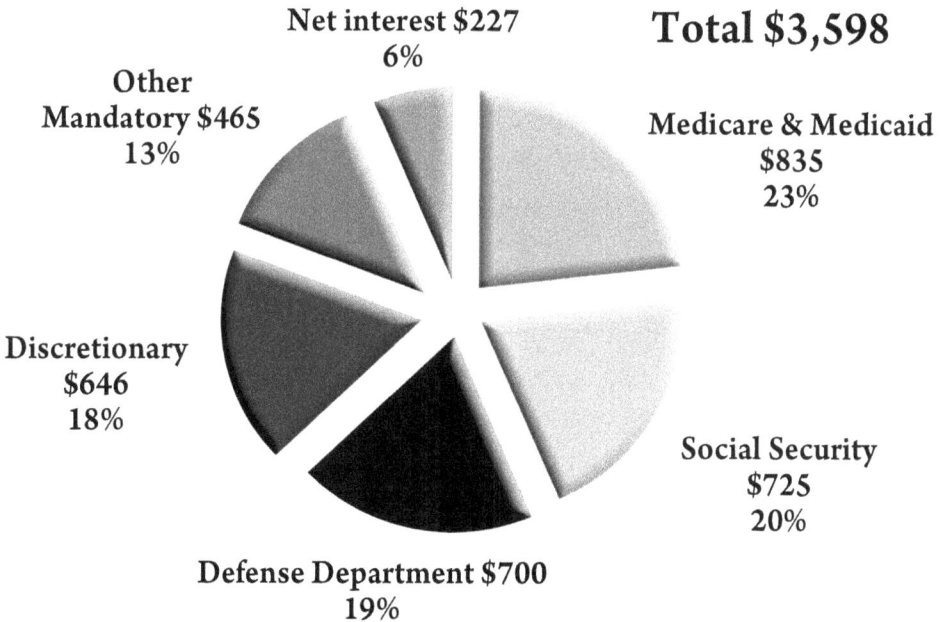

Net interest $227
6%

Total $3,598

Other
Mandatory $465
13%

Medicare & Medicaid
$835
23%

Discretionary
$646
18%

Social Security
$725
20%

Defense Department $700
19%

Source: Congressional Budget Office, Prepared by True Freedom Technologies

intellectual evolutionary transition to a predator free society. Our knowledge of how these manipulation techniques work will help us break these chains of Capitalism. After our minds are free we can create new technically advanced societies and a better future for our species.

You may have noticed something in common with the amount of money our country loses in corporate tax loopholes and the amount of money extracted from our federal budget by the sequester. Some estimates go over $90 billion lost annually in corporate tax loopholes while the budget sequestration is set to extract around $85 billion per year. Just understanding the basics surrounding these two issues provided me a clarifying lesson on how our government works for we the people and what level of capitalistic exploitation seems acceptable among our working-class population.

We could continue for generations dedicating our lives in a futile effort to make Capitalism fair for the working class prey of the world, or we could end our predatory social structure once and for all and usher in a new era of true freedom and prosperity for all people as equals. I have already broken the first chain of Capitalism and made the decision to help others do the same. Now I will dedicate my time toward breaking the second chain of Capitalism by creating technically advanced self-sufficient infrastructures capable of supporting a predator free society. This will allow fellow American citizens and other people around the world to make a clear distinction between both social structures.

The suspension of democracy and the bankruptcy of Detroit Michigan is an excellent example of what Capitalism will do to our entire country as ruling class top predators continue to consume our national wealth, and force the American working class resource into deeper poverty and despair. Our entire country should pay close attention to what happens to Detroit. The level of capitalistic exploitation of the working class resource in Detroit will determine how much the ruling class top predators are in control of our government and laws. Follow the money, who is making profits and who is being made to suffer. Again the irony is our ruling class leaders should know as the education, health and overall prosperity of we the people is systematically destroyed so goes the strength of our country creating a power vacuum for global top predators. Perhaps this is their ultimate objective. Regardless of their motivations, we the people can and should end our predatory social structure long before that and in doing so prevent the suffering and death of millions of our people. It's up to us.

Many Americans have pondered the question, how just a few conservative Republican celebrities are able to provoke such strong passions among their followers when liberal Democrats with equal media exposure seem to struggle at achieving the same level of emotional excitement among their segment of the population. The answer to this question is simply that it is far easier to provoke an emotional reaction than require an objective decision. An emotional reaction may be induced subconsciously provoking a predictable response where an objective decision requires the understanding of factual knowledge before an action is taken.

The process of considering facts works best with out any emotional interference, this may account for what appears to be a lack of enthusiasm among many Democrats. The segment of our population willing to allow their subjective realities to control their lives have always been targeted by predatory humans that fully understand this weakness. Of course the ability to exploit these individuals is guaranteed by law in our capitalistic social structure. And some people are still wondering how things got so bad. Using our intellectual survival trait as a predatory tool to exploit less knowledgeable competitors will also come to its natural end as we make our evolutionary transition to a predator free society.

Even though our political system is designed to force elected officials out of office if they won't do the biding of top predators there are some politicians that truly care more about us little people than the ruling class elite. Because their efforts to make Capitalism fair for us working class prey is one of the most courageous thing an individual can do to provide a higher level of human rights for we the people, they deserve our profound appreciation and highest praise. They are in effect behind enemy lines fighting for our freedoms. It may be a paper battlefield of bureaucratic minefields but these battles can determine whether the job you need to support your family is shipped off to another country just to increase the power and wealth of ruling class top predators.

If you're not familiar with how this battlefield works you may never see the loss of your livelihood coming before it's too late. Know your enemy and the technologies they use as weapons against you. Forcing more Americans into poverty and a higher level of predatory competition poses a far greater threat to our country than a terrorist attack or the war on drugs. Hundreds of thousands of Americans are dying preventable deaths every year to satisfy our predatory need for capitalistic world domination. How much is enough? How many need to die before we learn?

The defeat of Campaign finance reform, the Supreme Court decision of citizens United and voter suppression laws, are all tools to prevent good politicians from holding any position of power that may disrupt the efficient flow of wealth from the working class many to the ruling class few. There is no better way to subvert our democracy and constitutional rights than to allow greater psychological manipulation of the working-class voters by controlling their decision-making process there by securing their exploitation by ruling class top predators. By allowing the use of these intellectual predatory tools while simultaneously defunding our public education needed for us working-class voters to become aware of our exploitation. It's getting easy to see why the rich are continuing to get richer at an accelerated rate while the poor are still willing to accept their preventable suffering and death.

I expect there will be a few of the good politicians more interested in helping accelerate our transition to a predator free society than maintaining our advanced predatory social structure. Some good politicians may still feel it's possible to prevent the destruction of our country by free-market Capitalism and that maybe if they just work a little harder they may be able to re-engineer our predatory social structure to provide a higher quality of life for us working class prey. I believe the futility in their efforts will become even more evident as people become intellectually enlightened as to their systematic exploitation under Capitalism and the control top predators have over our government. The working-class people of the world will never find true freedom and universal prosperity within a predatory social structure that is controlled by the ruling class elite.

At first, all solutions to accelerate our transition to a predator free society must not require any direct help from our political system or government. The first technically advanced Automated Community Infrastructures capable of supporting a predator free society must be created with donations and income generated by the nonprofit organization True Freedom Technologies. The new prototype infrastructures will be online and open to the public with technology displays like programmable weather conditions, robotic chefs and animated Greek Gods. The philosophy behind a predator free society will be available through this book and updated online so people all over the world with Internet access can objectively consider which social structure they would prefer controlling their politics.

I strongly believe once a majority of our population has enough factual knowledge necessary to make an informed decision, they will choose to end our predatory social structure and support a national transition to a predator free society. As support grows our democracy will allow for a peaceful transition to a society that values the human rights of we the people more than our capitalistic domination by ruling class top predators. At this point, our politician will need to adapt to serving the needs of we the people instead of their ruling class masters. Our natural intellectual evolutionary development to a predator free society may have been delayed but it could not be stopped indefinitely. Our species has accelerated our intellectual development, like a child that was isolated all their lives and only allowed to learn a narrow subjective reality, finally leaving their sheltered environment and becoming aware of a whole new world of science, cultures and opportunities they never realized existed before. Once a majority of our population finally makes a collective decision to end our predatory social structure, it will be one of if not the largest paradigm shift in the social evolutionary development of our species.

5. Selling our democracy to the top predators of Capitalism

In the United States of America we have a Constitution intended to protect we the people from systematic exploitation by the ruling class elite. Not allowing the ruling class top predators to have full control over the government and religion used to manipulate the working-class people was, a revolutionary concept for our country, pardon the pun. Even more effective at preventing the working-class people's exploitation was a democracy giving us the right to vote and theoretically have some input over our future social structure. Even though both of these advancements to our intellectual evolution bring us closer to the creation of the predator free society we are still currently living in the most technologically advanced predatory social structure ever created. The level of freedom we Americans experience in our predatory social economic structure is directly proportional to our ability to win our capitalistic competition for survival. The greater our wealth and power is the more politicians, judges and lobbyists we can buy to increase our ability to exploit the working-class resource. That's how free market Capitalism creates super predators so greedy they are willing to let millions of their working-class prey suffer and die to maintain their dominance and control.

You may wonder how the most powerful country in the evolutionary development of our species with a Constitution and democracy intended to protect its working-class population could have evolved into the most efficient and destructive predatory social structure ever created. Sadly, after all the research I did for this book and listening to the leaders of our country for years offer their solutions to our ongoing social and economic crisis, I sometimes wonder why more people aren't asking this question. As long as the majority of our population is intellectually unaware of the source of their exploitation, our suffering and death as a nation and a species will continue as the top predators of Capitalism gain greater control over our government and the laws we are forced to live under. There can be no effective democracy as long as the intellectual predatory manipulation of the voter's decision-making process is legally allowed and socially acceptable.

To be clear not all of the ruling class leaders of our past and present were and still are trying to subvert our democracy or increase their predatory dominance over us working-class prey. We the people would have never won the battles against slavery, women's rights, social security, Medicare, civil rights, equal pay and better health care access for women if all the ruling class leaders controlling our government were more interested in their personal capitalistic success than the suffering and death of their fellow Americans.

The top predators of Capitalism may have lost these battles allowing the working-class people to keep more of the national wealth we generate but they're not done using their power and control of government to subvert our democracy. Their objective is to control all three branches of government and create federal laws to repeal our human rights and transfer more tax revenue from the working-class many to the ruling class few. They know we little people of America and around the world are easier to control when we are uneducated and unaware of our exploitation, while desperately competing against one another for our capitalistic survival. We may be only pawns in their global chess game for capitalistic domination, but we are playing for the future of our entire species.

Working around a Constitution and a democracy intended to protect the American people does present some technical challenges for our top predators. However, operating within a predatory social structure that allows the psychological manipulation of the voter's decision-making process gives them an unfair intellectual advantage over unsuspecting Americans without the knowledge of the process used to deceive them. This book is all about taking away that intellectual advantage thereby shifting the balance of power to the working-class masses so they can simply make an informed decision to end their exploitation process.

We the people of America and around the world have been losing this battle for decades as ruling class top predators use their power and wealth to deceive the public and secure key influential positions in government. Once a ruling class political puppet is installed successfully at the executive level, the exploitation of millions is just a few pen strokes away. Likewise if a ruling class leader sympathetic to the American working class masses is able to attain a position of power, they may be able to allow us to keep more of the national wealth we generate to increase our health, education, infrastructure, productivity and overall quality of life.

If we allow ourselves to think like a top human predator looking for the best way to exploit the working class resources of the world on our way to global domination, America would be the big prize. Consuming 25% of the world's resources and wasting over half of that we are psychologically conditioned and socially engineered to be the most profitable working-class resource for exploitation ever created. All of the greatest empires throughout history could have never imagined the level of power and control over a global working-class resource that Capitalism has created for our modern-day top predators. Since America functions in a free-market predatory social economic structure, as a top predator with millions or even billions my only question would be, how much do I need to invest and what do I get in return

Being a billionaire top predator I would have the wealth and power to make or break most state and federal politicians depending on their willingness to serve my interests over my working-class prey. I can end their political ambitions forcing them back into our predatory competition for survival or I can end their economic struggle giving them top predator social status allowing them and their extended family to live in the lap of luxury for the rest of their lives. All I ask in return is that they pass the laws my lobbyists give them and I will make their dreams come true. Not only do many of our politicians jump at this chance it is often their main reason for becoming a public servant. Remember none of us are at fault for the environmental conditions we are born into or how they manipulate our survival instincts to increase our social status within a predatory social structure. Our focus should be on changing the conditions that create problem, not satisfying our emotional desire to assign blame.

Try to imagine what your daily life would be like if you were born into capitalistic royalty with the social pressures to become a top predator competing for global domination. It's common knowledge among us top predators of Capitalism willing to invest millions of dollars to control our government that US senators cost more than Representatives in the House. Of course this also depends on which committees they sit on and if their position is chairman. I may also make dreams come true for State governors, senators, and representatives on down to local officials depending on their ability to give me favorable access to national resources or more efficient exploitation of the working class people under their control. Or I may require them to deregulate my industries and allow me to determine what level of consumer and environmental protection I want to allow my working-class prey to have. It's all about control and keeping my prey unaware of the process. They cannot learn they have the power to end their exploitation or I will lose all control over them.

Under my capitalistic control the consequences could be devastating for the nation's future health and prosperity, but this is of no concern to me I have million dollar mansions all over the world, I will simply move on to the next working-class resource in other countries using their predatory social structure to exploit their people. Of course as a top predator of free-market Capitalism bent on global domination, world leaders willing to allow the suffering of their people and blatantly transfer trillions of dollars of national wealth to me, is the best capitalistic investment I could make. And the best part is I can make it all perfectly legal and semi-tolerated by the working-class resource that must suffer the consequences and repay the increase in national debt. As a top predator of Capitalism, this would be my American dream.

All of us well educated top predators know how the game is played. Which members of Congress are on what committees, whether or not they are players willing to let unsuspecting Americans suffer and die to increase their personal wealth and power, and how much of a capitalistic investment it will require for them to sell out their country. If any of this seems shocking, it should, even worse it has become a tolerated function of our government.

These symptoms of a predatory social structure can be corrected giving us the knowledge and power to control our future and end our exploitation under Capitalism. But hey, as a top predator of Capitalism I don't want you to know this, so I will pay my political servants to use their positions of power and trust to perpetuate a subjective reality where you feel emotionally satisfied giving your wealth and vote to me and my candidate. It's an ancient trick that's still quite effective as a management tool for any working-class resource socially engineered to make decisions based on their emotional responses to environmental conditions, while in the absence of factual knowledge.

As a top predator I would know the best way to get the largest slice of the American pie (also known as tax revenues and natural resources) is to get as many of my political servants into government as possible. Then my lawyers and lobbyists can write new laws for my politicians to pass creating an infrastructure requiring the little people to pay me for all of their survival necessities. Then I'll spend millions on TV propaganda to deceive we the people by explaining how much I care about them, their health, their children and the environment they must survive in. As a top predator I would want people to know their jobs and ability to survive under Capitalism depends on me now, I can dial up or down their suffering and death to fine tune my control over any working class resource. Their predictable emotional frustration can easily be associated with a known predigest to further capitalize on this manipulation technique.

With my socially engineered society, I can legally intimidate all my employees with losing their ability to survive if they don't vote for whom I want and who will give me better predatory control over their lives. Something like, "I'm not telling you how to vote but if the candidate I don't want wins I will have to layoff every one working at this plant and move all manufacturing job to a more profitable country". You see I can't lose in a capitalistic predatory social structure. At least I'll make sure the little people lose more, so much more that they will fight for my extreme success to ensure their basic survival.

Voting demographics in the U.S. (2008) Presidential election, in Millions

Total U.S. Population	Voting age Population	Votes cast	Democratic Vote	Republican Vote	Independent Vote
304.06	229.95	131.41	69.50	59.95	1.96

100%

Approximately 4.17M or 1.37% ideologically uncommitted Democratic votes

Approximately 3.00M or .99% ideologically uncommitted Republican votes

Approximately 9.13M or 3.00% of the total population that decide elections

75.62%

43.21%

22.85%

19.71%

.64%

Source: U.S. Census Bureau, Prepared by True Freedom Technologies

Another big advantage of having my politicians control government is once I place them in key positions, they can fill all of the non-elected public servant positions possible with people willing to serve my interests over the health and prosperity of their fellow Americans. These non-elected government positions are given the power to subvert our democracy and diminish our constitutional rights for equality and the pursuit of happiness. Many Americans have given up on the pursuit of happiness and would simply settle for a reduced level of exploitation by their ruling class elite. As a top predator I will use my wealth and power to manipulate as many members of the judicial branch of government as possible especially the Supreme Court of the United States.

As a top predator I would also want to control as many election officials in any swing states as possible to prevent the vote of all the people that have become aware of their exploitation and think they can use their democracy to determine their future. Once I have majority control of the judicial branch of government I can determine what level of democracy the people will be allowed to exercise. I can not only save millions of dollars commonly used to psychologically manipulate the decision-making process of voters but also maintain a level of predatory control capable of satisfying my lust for power on the way to world domination. As a top predator it is my divine destiny to rule over my prey, or more accurately my subjective reality and predatory instincts controlling my actions.

One of the things that make buying the American democracy so easy is that around 40% of my working-class prey will not vote or get to decide what level of exploitation I can subject them to in the future. It's like they have no democracy at all and as a top predator that's just the way I like it. I don't need to concern myself with these little people, they will quietly conform to whatever oppressive laws I can get my politicians to pass, and if they don't like that, they can be sent to one of my for-profit jails for breaking some baseless law. I didn't become a top predator by being a fool, or playing fair, so I rigged the game. Are you really surprised? Own the game, make the rules and you can win every time while everyone else loses.

As a top predator I can even make a profit off the least fortunate and economically deprived Americans in this country. If these Americans can't produce enough tax revenue or be willing to work harder to increase my profits their population can be easily reduced by creating new laws limiting their basic survival necessities. It's nothing personal, just good business. Besides if I don't take advantage of this capitalistic opportunity the next top predator in the food chain certainly will. It helps if I don't think of them as real people, as a top predator I've been conditioned to believe they exist to serve my needs. It has always been the divine right of us ruling class elite to manage our working-class peasants, as it is their honor to suffer and die serving their God, King, benevolent ruler or whatever else we top predators can get our prey to believe.

Of the around 60% working-class American people that do want to vote and participate in our democratic process, only about one fifth of them have become aware of their exploitation and who is responsible. Therefore they are no longer susceptible to most forms of deception that we top predators have relied on for thousands of years. They may want to end their predatory exploitation but cannot break the second chain of Capitalism and the infrastructure that we created to make them dependent on us for their survival. Another fifth feel the pain of their exploitation but haven't yet fully identified the source of their suffering and death. They don't feel they can trust us ruling class top predators of Capitalism and that somehow we might be taking advantage of them in ways they don't understand yet.

About another fifth are convinced that their government is the villain but haven't made the connection that we top predators are the proverbial men behind the curtain pulling the levers and the great and powerful Oz is just an illusion. It's an excellent deception where all the frustration of their social competition and managed exploitation is directed at the monolithic illusion of government and away from us top predators that are more often idolized for our capitalistic success than our abuse of power. Our politicians are allowed to use the little people's emotional frustration against them, promising to remove the big bad government from their lives while actually using their positions of bureaucratic power for greater control and creative exploitation.

Over one fifth of voters allow themselves to be completely controlled by a subjective reality where we top predators are idolized for our wealth and power like Gods of Capitalism. This segment of the population has been conditioned for generations to serve us top predators with the highest level of devotion, by simply using the illusion of great rewards, excessive wealth and life after death. Even the exposure to factual knowledge will not alter their subjective belief that we top predators really care more about them than the billions of dollars we are able to exploit from their existence under free-market Capitalism.

Their willingness to deny their intelligence and allow creative forms of induced subjective realities to control their decisions like what to buy, who to vote for or even whether to kill or die for us ruling class elite makes this segment of our population the easiest prey. This segment of working-class people have been willing to tolerate the highest levels of suffering and death for thousands of years as part of a divine subjective reality to serve us God like supper predators. But the best advantage we top predators have over these people is their willingness to self induce their children with the same subjective reality used to exploit their ancestors for thousands of generations. It's a self-replicating form of predatory exploitation that produces a pleasurable emotional response.

And the last fifth of working-class voters are capitalistic dream subjects because they tend to have a higher than average income and can be easily manipulated with greed and the illusion of economic prosperity. Like the practical illusion of winning a lottery they feel the American dream of becoming a top predator is within their grasp if only they work harder and are willing to suffer more than the other working-class prey. They may be too well educated to use an induced subjective reality to convince them into giving up their wealth and survival resources, so a different form of psychological manipulation must be used to ensure their ongoing corporation.

As mid-level predators of Capitalism, some of these voters have already accepted that many of our least fortunate American citizens may need to suffer and die for them to meet their capitalistic goals of becoming an elite ruling class top predator. Their education and knowledge of our political and predatory social structure has made them aware, whatever they may be unwilling to do to accomplish their goals, other mid-level predators with even less compassion and regard for human life, certainly will. Those born into capitalistic royalty rarely denounce their predatory social status based on moral objections. To do so often means becoming one of the little people with no power, no lobbyists or control of government and no easy future for their children.

Free-market Capitalism functioning within a technologically advanced predatory social structure allows us top predators the highest level of control over millions of our working-class prey. Our ability to buy a superior education allows us to use our advanced intelligence to prey on other humans just as our species preys on other life forms for survival. It seemed like the natural way of things and most of the working-class people were willing to accept their social status as prey just as they always had back through time. After all it has been encoded in our genetic memory for millions of years and environmentally reinforced as the only social structure our species has ever known.

working-class people all over the world may just now be reaching a collective level of intellectual enlightenment and political awareness to more fully comprehend their exploitation under Capitalism and their power to end the process. However, we top predators have been aware for generations that this evolutionary transition was inevitable. It was in the end our survival instinct for predatory domination and increased profits that accelerated the intellectual evolution of the working-class people of the world. Now that they have become aware of their exploitation they will unite and use their strength in numbers to peacefully make the natural evolutionary transition to a predator free society. Even us elite ruling class top predators of Capitalism must admit the tipping point in our intellectual evolution is here, this transition could not be prevented any longer. Some of us top predators will miss the good old days, the thrill of the hunt, a chance at world domination and becoming the capitalistic Emperor of human existence. However, what will be the downsizing of the very few, will be the salvation for an entire species. We knew our predatory dominance would not last forever and it was only a mater of time until we lost our intellectual advantage.

Of course I'm not really a top predator of Capitalism, I'm just playing the villain to provide a different perspective. I do wonder how different my perspective would be if I were born into capitalistic royalty and destined to become an elite top predator. If I were conditioned from birth with a subjective reality where becoming an elite capitalistic ruler of the world is portrayed as the epitome of success, how would that affect my perspective on life? How would it affect yours? Understanding the environmental conditions that form our motivations in life will help us control the process and eliminate the need to use our predatory instincts on each other for survival. Before we condemn others for who they have become we should ask ourselves, how different would my perspective be if I had lived their life. Then consider how different their perspective would be if they had lived your life. I guess the real question is, what truly makes us who we are? And what determines how much intellectual control we can exercise to provide a better future for our people. That's the kind of knowledge that has the power to free a species from their predatory existence.

6. How Capitalism creates criminals and corrupts lady justice

As a young man my first experience at parenthood was with a brindle pit bull puppy. At this time in California adult pit bulls had a savage reputation for being out of control mad dog killers. People naturally began to form subjective opinions that this breed of dog was an uncontrollable scourge that needed to be locked up or put down to prevent any serious damage to any people in our otherwise civilized human societies. I tried to raise my little puppy with the love and affection any caring parent would show their furry child. One day after he became a full-grown adult I reluctantly entered him into a dog show not knowing how he would socially interact with so many other dogs and people. Much to my surprise he not only didn't start any trouble but instead won the award for best trick and even went on to claim the highest honor of the entire event, King mutt. He seemed quite satisfied with his performance as he and his Queen mutt posed for pictures and awards. I couldn't be more proud of my furry child, in that he turned out to be such an intelligent and well-mannered example of not only his species but of his particular breed of dog.

At the same time, I was aware that other dogs of his breed were being mentally and physically abused and forced to fight against one another for their survival. After years of abuse some of these dogs escaped or were released onto public streets to socially interact with other dogs and people. As you can imagine their kill or be killed conditioning did not prepare them for social encounters with well-mannered pink pampered poodles or their high-heeled parents wearing the latest in summer fashions. I was fully aware that my well-mannered furry child had the same hardwired killer instincts as other members of his species, but what I didn't know was how much the environmental conditions they were subjected to could alter their adult behavior or their ability to socially interact peacefully with other dogs and people.

This was an important lesson for me and in a way laid the foundation for my interest and desire to understand how environmental influences affect the behavioral actions of any species, but especially us humans. The process needed to altar our hardwired predatory instincts by using the environmental influence of love and compassion to eliminate all forms of crime at its source was starting to become more obvious. If the difference in environmental influences could produce such social extremes within a species of limited intelligence like dogs, just imagine what rapid progress could be made within an intellectually enlightened species like us humans with the ability to objectively comprehend the process. However, like with other subjects in this book finding the solutions to the problems would pale in comparison to the challenge of effectively communicating the concepts to others so the necessary changes can be made.

We know that our hardwired predatory instinct to kill or be killed was necessary to prevent the extinction of our species throughout our species throughout our evolutionary development. We also know that if a less intelligent predatory species like lions all became peace-loving pacifists they would starve to death and become extinct within days. We can now objectively understand that the behavioral actions of any species are a combination of their genetic makeup and the environmental conditions they were subject to, primarily during the early developmental years of their lives. There are also genetic and biological disorders that produce criminal and violent behavior beyond our intellectual control.

As our technical knowledge and understanding of the human body evolved it was discovered there is an area of the brain responsible for moral and social behavior. If this area of the brain is damaged through trauma or tumor growth an individual's ability to determine what is and is not socially acceptable cannot be easily controlled intellectually. We can also be certain from behavioral studies and direct observation that a person with no mental or biological disorders can be altered from one social extreme of showing compassion for others to the opposite extreme of having an absolute disregard for human life. Our hardwired instincts to kill and disregard the suffering and death of others can be environmentally amplified or neutralized for any predatory species, especially us humans.

We may not currently have the technology to medically correct genetic or biological disorders responsible for producing criminal behavior but by reducing environmental contaminants and advancing our research in gene therapy we can greatly minimize this social dysfunction. I would consider any social activity to be dysfunctional when the exchange disregards the suffering and or death of one party while benefiting the other party with greater wealth, power or capitalistic success. What may seem socially dysfunctional to an individual functioning with an objective reality conditioned by a predator free society, may also be considered an acceptable survival activity to someone living in an advanced predatory based society. While working on new technologies to identify and correct genetic or biological disorders and reducing industrial contamination of our water and food, we must recognize the overwhelming contributing factor to our social dysfunctions are environmentally induced by the inherent greed and competitive nature of our predatory social structure.

If we the people truly want to eliminate all forms of social dysfunctions, criminal violence and predatory exploitation for profit, we must correct the root cause of the problem directly. Continuing to deal with the symptoms as if they were the problem is too much of a distraction limiting our progress in finding an ultimate solution. Whatever the environmental conditions are that induce, magnify and perpetuate our preventable suffering and death we need to have the collective courage and determination to change what ever it is, even if it turns out to be an accepted foundational element of our current society. We cannot let our induced subjective realities prevent us from identifying and correcting this fundamental flaw in our intellectual evolutionary development. It's too important to kick down our evolutionary road and hope our descendants can solve the problem. This is why we must collectively break the first chain of Capitalism by using factual knowledge to form an objective reality and then make an informed decision to end our predatory social structure. I know it's just a start, but like the first drops of rain before the storm, they can't control the weather to come but they can help us prepare for evolutionary changes and a smoother transition to a predator free society.

Some people may still be wondering how could the economic structure of Capitalism create the environmental conditions that produce mental instabilities resulting in so many homicides and suicides. If we remove our emotional interference and personal connections to the problem and stand way back to look at the big picture, we can get a more objective perspective of what's really going on and how to correct it. When our minds are caught up in our daily struggle for survival, it can be difficult to find the time to lift our heads high enough out of the fog to get a clear view of our future. These potential perils in our evolutionary development are avoidable but we the people must be united in our determination to create a better future for our children.

The first step to answering any complex question or finding the solution to an intellectually challenging problem, is to gather factual information on the concept, also known as going to school on the subject. Without any education on the subject and factual knowledge to work with, our intellectual survival trait cannot serve its function, thus forcing our decision-making process to rely on our emotional interference, hardwired survival instincts and involuntary reactions to environmental conditions. What good does it do to have the power to control the most advanced survival trait ever known, if we are just going to revert back to a time in our evolutionary past when we had the problem solving skills of a Neanderthal.

The second step is to remove any prejudice or influence from a subjective reality that would interfere with the formation of a valid conclusion or solution to the problem. For individuals functioning with a subjective reality, this second step may need to be accomplished first just to recognize and accept the factual knowledge needed to understand the subject. For many individuals functioning with an objective reality, the answer to this subject's title may already be known. However based on our current intellectual evolutionary progress, the solution to correct this problem has proven to be far more elusive.

For a better understanding of how Capitalism creates criminals and corrupts lady justice we need to go to school on the basic elements of the problem. Like other concepts in this book that have a common connection we need to go back in time to the source of the problem, or perhaps more accurately when it began to create social dysfunctions for our species. For most people Capitalism is just the word that represents a nebulous concept about how our society is supposed to work. As our factual knowledge about Capitalism grows we began to realize it is just a name given to the latest variation of our evolving predatory social structure. The formation of Capitalism as the ultimate achievement of our predatory evolution seems like a highly predictable natural progression of our evolutionary development. This natural progression from our distant evolutionary past, started when our hardwired survival instincts controlled 100% of our decisions and actions. Even at our current state of development we are still attempting to remove our predatory instincts from determining our social constructs, economic systems and moral values.

If we fast-forward our objective reasoning, we realize the real question is how does an advanced predatory social structure that requires intellectual competition for survival affect an individual's ability to control their hardwired instincts/criminal behavior? If we only consider the deaths from violent crimes and low-level predatory activity, the annual loss of American lives would be in the tens of thousands. However, when we add deaths from high-level predatory activity and advanced forms of capitalistic exploitation, the loss of American lives is in the hundreds of thousands per year. The low-level predatory activities and violent crimes are primarily concentrated in and isolated to areas of our country with higher levels of force competition in combination with diminished survival necessities. Where the high-level forms of capitalistic exploitation have been allowed to expand globally, increasing our preventable deaths by millions annually.

The suffering before the death is also magnified with the high-level predatory exploitation by increasing healthcare costs, forcing more families into bankruptcy, desperate acts for survival and leaving us more vulnerable to additional capitalistic opportunists. This is what us working class prey have been conditioned to accept as the American dream. We don't have to settle for this anymore, not now that we know how to fix it.

Another way to look at it is, the much smaller percentage of low-level predatory activities and violent crimes tend to take less time to kill a human prey and only provide lower amounts of profit. While the much larger percentage of capitalistic exploitation by white-collar crimes can be used to fleece a working class population for years before they die, thus providing much higher levels of profit for top predators. If we consider all deaths from predatory exploitation and social dysfunctions to be equally tragic, we must then conclude the economic structure of Capitalism has created the largest criminal network the world has ever known.

Just because Capitalism has become an accepted part of our predatory social structure it does not justify the continued exploitation of millions for profit. If Capitalism were known by any other name, it would still be responsible for the highest number of preventable deaths for the greatest profits given to the fewest people. This begs the question, what should be considered criminal behavior and how can the loss of millions for profit become legally acceptable?

It's important to make a clear distinction between low-level crimes for individuals put in jail for desperate acts of survival and high-level crimes for individuals that don't go to jail but instead get rewarded with billions in profits. It's also important to consider the role model our top predators of Capitalism are creating for our next generation of American citizens. It's far easier for me to excuse and understand why a less educated working class individual at the lowest level of our predatory social structure would commit crimes to survive and support their family, than a well-educated executive who would systematically deceive millions out of their basic survival necessities in the pursuit of excessive wealth and power.

Because all species naturally adapt to their environmental conditions to survive more efficiently, it was becoming abundantly clear how our predatory social structure is creating low-level criminals out of our least fortunate working-class children, and then punishing them by taking away their freedom. While at the same time rewarding our ruling class children for becoming better capitalistic masterminds and the next generation of super predators. This is a terrible design for a social structure, it's not only really bad for 99% of the American working class resource, but it's self-defeating for the 1% ruling class top predators. Our top predators must realize the evolutionary changes taking place for our species and how our forced inequality would reach a breaking point as our intelligence provided optional social structures for consideration.

Even our Lady Justice the symbol of all that is fair and righteous about our country is not immune to the corrupting environmental influence of our predatory social structure. Because our Lady Justice, like the government she stands for consist of and is controlled by individual humans also competing for the capitalistic survival, the corruption of both would be expected. Our Lady Justice's scales and blindfold was intended to represent her impartiality and ability to objectively determine justice without the influence of wealth and power by the individuals in question. Her sword signifies the power of life and death that is held by those making her decisions. But instead, these symbols have proven to signify how the least fortunate of our working-class people without the wealth or popularity to afford the highest paid legal representation lose their freedom, dignity and life, while some ruling class members of our society are allowed to systematically legitimize the suffering and death of millions for profit. How could our Lady Justice have strayed so far from what she stood for?

The individual humans given the power of life and death over others may try to prevent their hardwired instincts, induced subjective realities and emotions from influencing their decisions, but without a good understanding of the challenges they face their intellectual ability to control these involuntary and subconscious reactions will have minimal success. An objective consideration of our past and present court decisions, clearly show the influence of prejudice, bigotry, and greed as well as many other forms of induced subjective realities. We must remember that just because judges wear respectable looking robes, sit behind high wooden benches and are given the power of life and death over others, they are still just people with the same human frailties that are hardwired into all of our genetic memories. These are the individuals that control our Lady Justice and their ability to withstand the corrupting influence of our predatory social structure will determine her impartiality to provide justice for all.

Our juries are one of the cornerstones of our criminal justice system. They generally consist of working-class people that are also making the evolutionary transition of having their decisions fully under the control of hardwired survival instincts and subjective realities to individuals capable of intellectually controlling these involuntary and subconscious influences with the objective consideration of factual knowledge. Many lawyers understand that jurors still make most of their decisions based on their emotional feelings and life experiences than their intellectual comprehension of the facts and evidence. The jury selection process is to determine the individual's emotional vulnerability to these influences so that both sides have an equal opportunity to manipulate their final decisions. Of course the jurors are instructed to not allow these involuntary and subconscious influences from affecting their final decision and if asked most will feel very confident that their decisions were completely based on their intellectual consideration of the facts and the scientific evidence presented.

Our egos and inability to admit our human frailties truly convince us that our emotions and subjective realities have no bearing on our decision-making process, but without a true understanding of this process our intellectual ability to control them will have little success. The well-documented public trial of O.J. Simpson demonstrated how wealth and fame naturally affect our decision-making process to favor our emotions over a mountain of scientific evidence to subvert our legal justice system. To better understand this concept we only need to objectively compare the trial, conviction and execution of Troy Davis as an opposite extreme showing how the difference between freedom and death is too often determined by our emotions triggered by hardwired instincts than they are by our ability to use our intellectual survival trait to consider the facts and evidence.

The inherent corruption of our predatory social structure changes the meaning of the blindfold our Lady Justice wears by instead blinding the people that make her decisions from the blatant inequality clearly visible to so many others not as influenced by power, wealth or subjective realities. Instead of her sword being used as an intimidating weapon to ensure justice for all, it has been turned against the very people it was meant to protect by allowing the suffering and deaths of so many American citizens to increase the power and wealth of a few ruling class top predators of Capitalism.

Our willingness to allow the death penalty to legally kill or legitimize the murder of potentially innocent American citizens is one of the greatest failures of our criminal justice system. Using science and objective factual knowledge to correct the emotional manipulation of jurors and judges, over 100 people that were marked for death by our justice system were found to be innocent, allowing their dignity and freedom to be restored.

One individual was found innocent just two days before they're legitimized murder would have been committed. If this travesty of justice could happen to these innocent Americans it could happen to anyone of us, or our family members. Can you imagine how that must feel, to be locked up day after day just waiting to be executed for a crime you didn't commit? It wouldn't be the facts, truth or justice that condemned you, but instead our species inability to evolve beyond our hardwired instincts controlling matters of life and death for our people. We're better than that now, let us show our progress and set an example to others.

With an estimated one in seven death row inmates being innocent of the crimes they are accused, there seems to be little doubt that of the over 1000 executions committed, our criminal justice system has legitimized the systematic execution of innocent American citizens. And we're supposed to be the good guys, setting a shining example for the world to follow. If only one innocent American citizen was stripped of their constitutional rights, incarcerated for years and then executed, our legal justice system has failed and we the people should demand it be corrected to reflect the human rights and values our country says it stands for. This failure to provide justice for the American people is just one of many symptoms of a corrupting social structure that will fade away as its cause is eliminated and replaced by the environmental conditions of a predator free society.

Ironically some of the same people willing to execute potentially innocent American citizens for the high crime of murdering one individual, justify and admire ruling class capitalist responsible for suffering and death of millions. Whether it be by the legitimized and legal sale of a product or hoarding all the global wealth and resources needed for basic survival necessities, the end result is still increased suffering and death for the least fortunate and weakest of our worlds capitalistic competitors. The subjective belief that the social economic structure of Capitalism is justified in its actions reminds me of a quote by Jean Rostand "Kill one man, and you are a murderer. Kill millions of men, and you are a conqueror. Kill them all, and you are a God." I had to ask myself, how could we be made to callously accept the death of so many while emotionally demanding justice for the death of just one.

Then I remembered it is at the very core of our hardwired predatory instincts encoded in our genetic memory for millions of years during our evolutionary development to accept the death of our many prey to ensure the survival of just one. Our capitalistic social structure has incorporated this inherent lack of compassion for others as another management tool to help condition the working-class resource into accepting their suffering and death as an inevitable part of life. Accepting the suffering of others may be an inevitable part of free-market Capitalism, however, this social dysfunction would not be a natural manifestation within the environmental conditions of a predator free society. If our objective as humans is to use our intelligence to reduce our preventable suffering and death, we must correct the root cause at its source and stop wasting time on the symptoms.

When I was young I truly believed our leaders and government created laws to protect us American citizens allowing us the greatest opportunity for prosperity and ability to help advance our great country. Like a child learning Santa Claus wasn't real, my subjective reality about our government turned objective as the overwhelming factual knowledge broke down my conditioning to deny the horrific truth. The following example is a straight up comparison between two similar drug products widely used by people all over the world for thousands of years. Notice how free-market Capitalism within our predatory social structure manipulates these two drugs, both in the subjective realities it creates around them and how they are used to exploit the American working class resource.

One product is completely legal, the manufacturers give millions of dollars to our government lawmakers, and it is also the number one preventable cause of death in America taking over 400,000 US citizen lives per year. The other product has been made and kept illegal by many of the same government lawmakers yet it has been medically proven to not cause overdose or death. Both products have been around for thousands of years and continue to be used by millions of Americans each year despite our lawmakers attempt to only legitimize the one that is responsible for the deaths of millions, while criminalizing the one that provides medical relief to hundreds of thousands of US citizens. Can you feel your subjective conditioning about free-market Capitalism braking down yet?

When I stood back to look at the big picture I started to realize how much control a subjective reality must have to convince millions their premature suffering and death is acceptable while simultaneously demonizing a relatively harmless drug that has many medical uses to actually relieve pain and suffering. It almost seems too ironic and obvious for anyone not to recognize, yet many of us still have no idea the social systems that are put in place to help facilitate our more efficient exploitation. The more objective my reality gets the more I realize our predatory social structure needs to come to its natural evolutionary end sooner than later. Because all people are naturally becoming more educated about the facts surrounding these two drugs you may already know from this description what they are. The legal drug product is nicotine in tobacco and commonly used by cigarette smokers, and the illegal drug is primarily tetrahydrocannabinol (THC) contained in cannabis and is also commonly smoked or vaporized for recreation.

Knowing how our predatory social structure works to manipulate our legal system, we must always ask ourselves who is profiting the most and who is made to suffer from the laws our legislators create. We working-class taxpayers spend approximately $1 billion per year to incarcerate 750,000 of the estimated 30 million American citizens that recreationally use cannabis. Getting the working class resource to labor and pay for their own exploitation has long been an accepted practice within predatory social structures. Our lawmakers in government have charged US taxpayers over $1 trillion for the war on drugs and arrested over 11 million American citizens for marijuana related crimes. The working class taxpayers are being made to pay for the incarceration and punishment of nonviolent mothers, fathers, sisters and brothers that could be providing productive contributions to their families and our country. Instead they're lives are being used like pawns in a chess game by top predators more interested in increasing their wealth and power than the suffering and death of their fellow Americans. We are just the little people to them.

Now that we know who loses by our lawmakers keeping this drug illegal we need to objectively consider what industries benefit most directly and indirectly from the hundreds of billions of dollars extracted from our working-class people. Because our lawmakers received millions of dollars from corporations to create laws that increase their profits, a close examination of this process would reveal whom they serve. If a drug known to provide the medical relief of pain and suffering were kept illegal this would clearly benefit the pharmaceutical industries that make big profits on their own pain medications. Keep in mind of the around 38,000 drug overdoses in America during 2010 nearly 60% of them around 22,000 involve pharmaceutical drugs. When you compare those numbers with the zero deaths produced by cannabis use, I can see why the pharmaceutical corporations wouldn't want the competition. They certainly wouldn't want an educated free-market to get a chance to choose between these two sources of pain relief.

It seems the tobacco industry would also lose big profits if cannabis became legal for recreational use competing with cigarettes. They are both consumed in a similar manner and can easily be sold side-by-side in retail outlets all over the country placing cannabis in direct competition with tobacco. Even if a consumer decided to switch products the addiction strength of tobacco is known to be similar to that of cocaine giving their customers a little added incentive to remain loyal. Cigarettes may be the purest example of capitalistic perfection represented in a single product. No other product embodies the true spirit and destructive nature of Capitalism more than cigarettes.

This capitalistic masterpiece may be a tough act to follow, but if given true free-market competition with cannabis and non-addicted first time customers, I believe two things would eventually happen. The tobacco industry would lose billions of dollars in profits and millions of lives would be saved all over the world. As an example of our expanding familiarity with these two drug products, the states of Washington and Colorado have legalized cannabis for recreational use, while many laws continue to limit the use of tobacco. We're learning...

We can always count on Capitalism to create a profitable opportunity from an economic crisis. There are millions of unemployed Americans living below the poverty line unable to pay adequate amounts of income taxes to be considered a useful member of the working class resource. The challenge for top predators is how to get the Americans that are too poor to pay federal income taxes, to provide a revenue stream using some form of creative Capitalism. If wealth cannot be directly extracted from the least fortunate Americans then perhaps there's a way to get the contributing middle class taxpayers to pay for them too. The one thing top predator masterminds can count on is that the least fortunate Americans will be forced into desperate acts of survival and low-level crimes to acquire food and shelter. Of course it always helps to control what laws are made and what is considered a crime. Without the wealth and social status possessed by top predators to hire a dream team of lawyers, these individuals committing low-level crime can be quietly added to the largest for-profit incarceration system in the world.

At first all these things I was learning were just confusing and conflicting with everything I was told growing up. Then my objective reality and curiosity about how things really work began to break the control of my subjective conditioning to just accept whatever I was told. It was becoming clear that our country or perhaps more accurately the top predators that control our social structure, value we the people more as a resource for capitalistic exploitation, than fellow Americans all working together to accomplish some national objective. The distinction between the elite ruling class few and the working class many was also becoming more obvious. I knew my first chain of Capitalism was breaking but I wanted to understand the process. I was thinking if I better understood the mechanisms involved, maybe I could help accelerate people's personal transition from a subjective to an objective reality.

In school we learn about the supply and demand aspect of free-market Capitalism. The objective is to find or create a capitalistic opportunity where there is both a very high supply and demand, monopolize the market as much as possible and extract the highest level of profits from all transactions. I was wondering what came first the supply of the largest for-profit prison system in the world or the demand of over 2 million customers needing to be removed from society. Maybe they developed at the same time like the chicken and egg. Or maybe a multibillion-dollar capitalistic opportunity like this takes time to make the political connections to legitimize the process and convince the public to accept it as a necessary part of our predatory social structure. For-profit prisons invest millions of dollars lobbying key organizations and people in government in an effort to increase their customer base.

I can just imagine the smoke-filled back rooms full of top predator masterminds all thinking up new laws they could get past to bring in more customers and increase profits. Turning struggling Americans into criminals by corrupting all three branches of government is nothing personal against the people that lose their freedom, its just a smart business decision for any capitalistic corporation competing for their economic survival. In other words don't blame the corporations, blame the predatory social structure that turned them into self-serving monsters. Or is that the other way around, hum it's that chicken and egg thing again.

To further emphasize how our capitalist predatory social structure corrupts Lady Justice and the individuals paid by American taxpayers to be fair and impartial. One such example is the tragic case of two US judges that received millions of dollars to eliminate free-market competition, help build for-profit prisons and incarcerate young adults, to serve the interests of a wealthy developer and attorney. Of the over 6000 cases 50% were without attorneys and had to rely on the integrity of our American criminal justice system to be fair and impartial. Some children were as young as 10 years old and in less than two minutes were found guilty for harmless acts of teenage rebellion and questioning authority. As prisons are known to be a concentrated form of predatory environmental conditions that promote mental instability. Tragically one child committed suicide after being sentenced and forced to live in these predatory conditions. How many others will continue to be sacrificed at the altar of Capitalism?

Largest prison populations, by Country (2014)

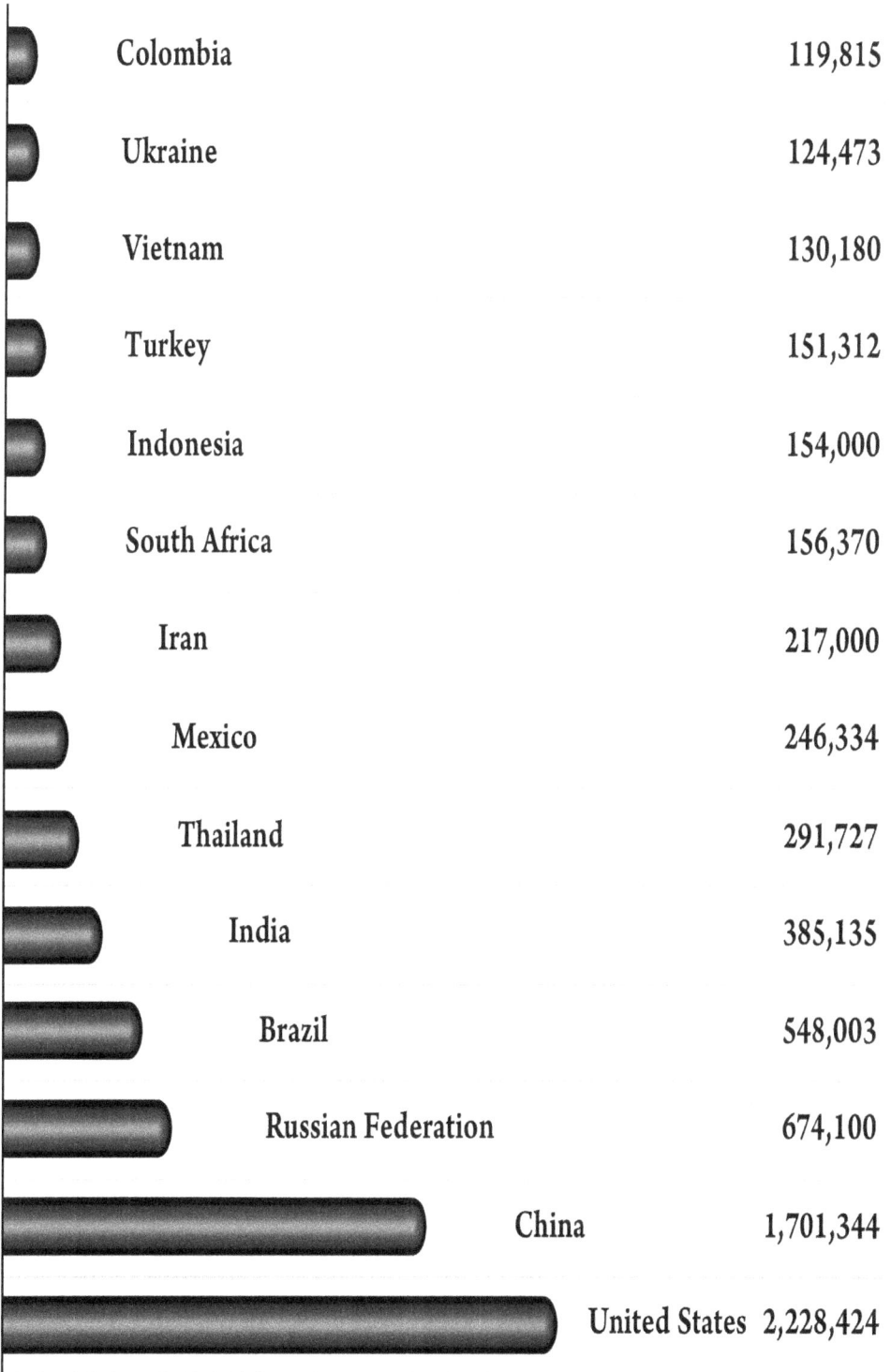

Country	Prison Population
Colombia	119,815
Ukraine	124,473
Vietnam	130,180
Turkey	151,312
Indonesia	154,000
South Africa	156,370
Iran	217,000
Mexico	246,334
Thailand	291,727
India	385,135
Brazil	548,003
Russian Federation	674,100
China	1,701,344
United States	2,228,424

Source: International Center for Prison Studies, Prepared by True Freedom Technologies

Because our capitalistic society promotes profits over the lives of our children we can be certain this is not an isolated incident. When I was young I thought giving judges bribes to subvert justice was something that only happened in third world countries where corruption was the rule and justice was the exception. After competing against other people for years the temptation to use their newfound positions of power becomes too great. It's that power corrupts problem again. Especially when considering most judges understand how our capitalistic social structure allows the ruling class elite to use their power and influence to exploit the working class resource. I guess the best forms of corruption are only available to the top predators wealthy enough to change laws and socially engineer societies.

Even though all gun violence represents a small percentage of the overall preventable suffering and death in our country, I am emotionally and intellectually compelled to speak about the massacre at Sandy Hook elementary school in Newtown Connecticut. Like the rest of our nation I am emotionally disturbed to hear about another gun tragedy especially one that has taken the lives of our most vulnerable and innocent children. To not feel the emotions surrounding this issue would require an individual devoid of all compassion for others, much like the lost souls that commit these tragedies. As easy as it would be to allow my emotions to determine my decisions and actions regarding this subject, I am even more disturbed on an intellectual level with the knowledge that these tragedies will continue to escalate until the fundamental elements that create them are understood and corrected at their source.

It is understandable why our nations emotions are being used to try and enact sensible gun legislation to treat the symptoms of the problem while avoiding the underlying cause. After all we have been conditioned for generations to act on our emotions while simultaneously preventing our intellectual realization of the grave evils of Capitalism and social degradation inherent in all predatory environmental conditions. I refuse to be limited by our social conditioning while determining the underlying cause of these tragic symptoms.

Total civilian guns compared by country, in Millions (2007)

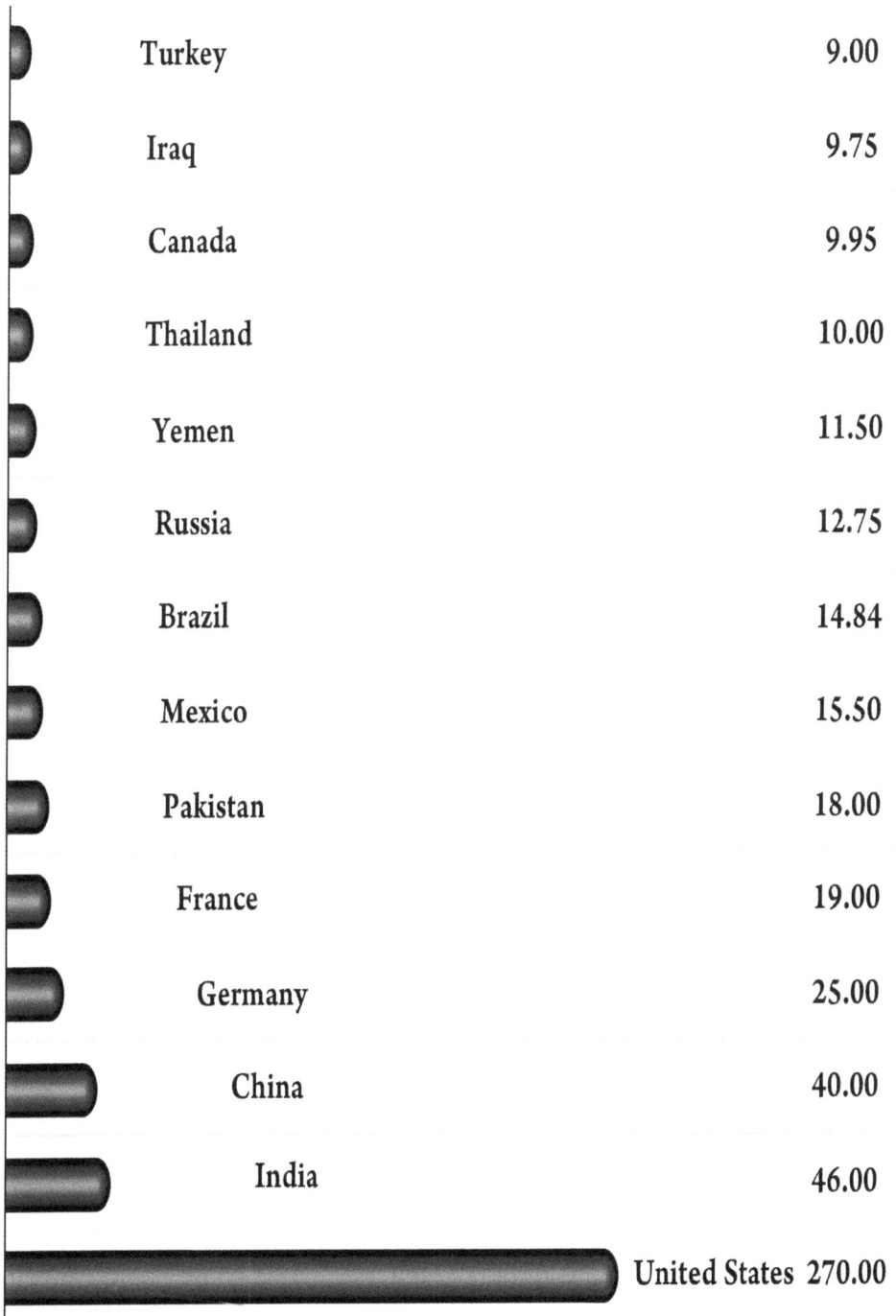

Country	Millions
Turkey	9.00
Iraq	9.75
Canada	9.95
Thailand	10.00
Yemen	11.50
Russia	12.75
Brazil	14.84
Mexico	15.50
Pakistan	18.00
France	19.00
Germany	25.00
China	40.00
India	46.00
United States	270.00

Source: Small Arms Survey, Prepared by True Freedom Technologies

For years now I've been hearing a lot of talk about how we must do whatever is necessary to prevent these tragedies by individuals unable or unwilling to identify the underlying cause and take action. Like the overwhelming majority of Americans, my frustration regarding our leaders inability to provide solutions to our social tragedies has reached intolerable limits compelling me to admit publicly what others whisper about in private. We are creating the very social dysfunctions we claim we want to eliminate. We know how to correct this problem. It's time we replace our leaders comforting words of complacency with meaningful actions that have a real chance at improving our public safety and quality of life.

These gun regulations called for better enforcement of background checks limiting the mentally disturbed, known criminals and straw purchasers that buy weapons for gang violence from receiving guns illegally. After all even with our current background verification system the FBI claims over 100 million checks have been made in the last decade leading to more than 700,000 denials. It seems without these background checks there would be hundreds of thousands of unstable individuals with guns just waiting for that extra push, like finding out the job they needed to support their family just got outsourced to a country with slave labor to increase the profits of some multinational corporation.

With over 99 million background checks coming back okay in the last 10 years, I started to wonder just how many guns the American working class people own. Even though I know we're conditioned to be hyper consumers and our national love affair with guns goes way back, I was still a little surprised to find out that America has the most heavily armed civilian population in the world. Americans own around 270 million firearms out of an estimated 875 million guns worldwide. We only have about 312 million people in our entire country.

If there has only been 99 million background checks verified out of 270 million firearms there must be millions of guns in the hands of individuals that would be and should be denied ownership. I know the sale of these weapons represents large profits for gun manufacturers and their shareholders, but at what cost? Like most forms of capitalistic greed this one will also primarily affect the least fortunate and most desperate members of our society. However, with its inherent unpredictability it has the potential to hurt the very people who profit most. It's like a bad Russian roulette social experiment perpetrated on entire populations just so one industry can maximize their profits. Another symptom of our capitalistic competition for survival has been identified.

Around 30% of the world's firearms are concentrated within the US borders among our civilian population, but this shouldn't be a reason for concern because were mostly responsible gun owners in this country that only dust off our shotguns during pheasant season. Also, in America we are conditioned to feel confident our countries capitalistic social structure will create an atmosphere of peace and harmony among all working class competitors. That subjective reality isn't working to well anymore.

Some people may also feel because we Americans consume 25% of the world's resources the relative abundance of survival necessities would reduce the need for predatory conflicts among our heavily armed civilian population, at least that would seem logical. You may be surprised to know that not only are we the most heavily armed civilian population but we also have the highest gun related murder rate of any other country in the world. As this factual information was helping me form a more objective reality and break my first chain of Capitalism, I was reminded of a quote by Mahatma Gandhi when asked what he thought of Western civilization, he responded, "I think it would be a good idea" I think I finally understand what he meant.

Even though all gun related violence does not even come close to the suffering and death created by legitimized forms of capitalistic exploitation. It does seem to provide a good indication of not only the state of mind created by our society but also our willingness to use our weapons on one another to resolve our predatory conflicts. All predatory social structures are as stressful for the many prey as they are satisfying for the few top predators. It was highly predictable that a hyper competitive and heavily armed capitalistic social structure like America would have a high incidence of mental instability and gun violence among the working class population. This must have been carefully considered and deemed acceptable by many top predators over the years as they socially engineered our society into what we have today.

Back through time it has always been a difficult challenge for the ruling class top predators to manage their working-class resource in a way that keeps them emotionally satisfied with their continued exploitation. I'm not sure our current ruling class top predators have fully consider the changing dynamics of a well educated and heavily armed working-class population that is rapidly becoming aware of their capitalistic exploitation. Depending on what level of capitalistic exploitation the American working-class resource is subjected to in the future, I see the potential for increased mental instability and acts of violence. The good news is we the people have the power to take control of our evolutionary development and make a collective decision to accelerate our transition to a predator free society. Making all the symptoms of our predatory existence and the grave evils of Capitalism fade away.

7. Jobs, jobs, jobs, serving the beast of Capitalism

I consider the American and global jobs crisis from a more fundamental point of view outside the narrow constraints that are provided by our capitalistic conditioning and social economic ideologies. Our primary objective should not be to increase the dependency of a growing working-class population on a social economic structure that values multimillion-dollar salaries for CEOs more than the basic survival necessities of their many employees. Making this advanced predatory economic system more efficient will only lead to greater dependency on the ruling class elite and make more working class people pawns in a chess game of capitalistic conquests.

If our primary objective is to achieve equality and prosperity for all people, our focus should be on creating a social structure that can provide all of the basic and technical survival necessities for our populations so we may reach our greatest potential and contribution to society. I realize our predatory competition against one another was necessary in the past but this was before our intelligence has made us aware of our unnecessary capitalistic exploitation by top predators. Just breaking our first chains of Capitalism and becoming aware of our exploitation will not solve our job crisis this will be done in the next phase of the transition to a predator free society, where the second chain of Capitalism will be broken.

It has taken generations to socially engineer our predatory social structure to make we the people, highly dependent upon our jobs and the corporations that give us the money we need for our capitalistic survival. A predatory infrastructure this well established will take years to convert to predator free societies. However, once started its self-replicating nature will provide for exponential growth. People will no longer need to compete against one another for their basic survival necessities or to get better jobs and social status.

I know manipulating our survival necessities, and controlling the level of the suffering and death among our populations has long been a successful motivational tool for top predators to manage their working-class resource. A major part of making the transition to a predator free society is changing our socially accepted motivational paradigm from fear, greed and the threat of losing survival necessities, to a strong community desire to help others achieve true freedom and prosperity. The motivational paradigm of the predator free communities may quickly evolve into a national objective to eliminate all preventable forms of suffering and death attributed to capitalistic exploitation. The good news is, this isn't one of those things we need permission to do, like asking our ruling class parents in government for the keys to the car. We the people have the power right now to take control of our future and accelerate our intellectual and social evolutionary development.

Instead of being forced to compete against one another to secure our social status and survival necessities, we will be voluntarily cooperating with one another to end the capitalistic exploitation of all people, and help accelerate our species into the next phase of our intellectual evolutionary development. A change this profound will be difficult to adjust to for many older individuals fully under the control of a subjective reality compelling them to continue their exploitation as the only way of life they have ever known. And of course some of the top predators that benefit most from our predatory social structure will also use their power and wealth to prevent our transition.

However, since this transition is a natural and inevitable part of our intellectual evolutionary development we should accelerate the process and prevent the suffering and death of millions of our people. The lives and creative skills we have already lost may have been capable of starting a predator free society hundreds of years ago allowing true freedom and prosperity to be available for all people as equals. Let's correct the mistakes of our past so our descendants will not be faced with the same challenges and regrets.

Just imagine converting the wealth and power generated by a global working-class resource into a force for evolutionary change bringing an end to our predatory past and accelerating our development into a predator free future. Accomplishing this task will be our new motivational paradigm instead of force competition for survival in a desperate attempt to maintain a failed social structure that should have already become a relic of our evolutionary past.

Without the need to compete against one another for survival our new jobs may be diverse in artistic expression and technical skills but they will all have the unified goal of expanding the network of Automated Community Infrastructures allowing more people to make the full transition to the environmental conditions of a predator free society. After the first and second chain of Capitalism are broken and people start living in predator free societies. They will have not only made the commitment to help others, but they will also have the time, creative skills and resources to do so. This will be their new social imperative, mission objective or more commonly referred to as their job.

The transition to a predator free society will change the very definition of what a job is and how they are either used as a divisive tool for predatory exploitation or a unifying force to accelerate the intellectual development of our species. I feel the differences between these two motivational paradigms will become so apparent it will help individuals break the control of their subjective realities and make an informed decision to end our predatory social structure. We already know what kind of job opportunities the predatory social structure of free market Capitalism offers for we the people, it seems the difficult part will be to imagine how much better life would be in a predator free society. I guess that's what this book is for, a chance for me to share my imagination with you. For this book to be successful, readers must not only be able to envision the environmental conditions of a predator free society, but also agree that our evolutionary transition should be a unified objective for our species. Or maybe it will just succeed at advancing the discussion, either way I'm dreaming big, and daring to fail.

Unlike a predator free society where our basic necessities are integrated into the Smart homes and community infrastructures, and where our mission objectives/jobs are not required for survival. An individual living in a predatory social structure is highly dependent upon their jobs for their survival and to continue their capitalistic competition against other Americans. Some top predators want even more control over our survival necessities and use their political assets in government to pass laws allowing them to deny employment based on their religious subjective realities. And you thought there was a separation between church and state. It's not like force competition for survival isn't bad enough, they want to give ruling class employers even greater power to control our livelihood based on voices and visions from Gods, pastors and politicians. When things get this crazy I have to remind myself, at least we got beyond thinking human sacrifices would change the weather. In the big picture, that's progress.

Correcting this fatal flaw that threatens the working-class people's ability to survive is not just the right thing to do to save millions of lives and end our predatory social structure it is increasingly becoming imperative to avoid the natural progression and destructive nature of Capitalism. Keep in mind the grave evils of Capitalism like all predatory social structures will primarily devastate 99% of least fortunate Americans while the ruling class top predators profit from the destruction and watch the show from steel towers adorned with marble and glass or war room bunkers safe underground.

Even though I feel the ultimate solution to the many evil symptoms of Capitalism is a rapid transition to a predator free society, I can't help but to notice two natural progressions of our current predatory social structure, that if not corrected have the potential to create an accelerated extinction event for our species. In a very real sense losing millions of people per year to predatory activities and capitalistic exploitation is like a continuous extinction event for the least fortunate of our global population and fellow job-hunting competitors. I guess it does reduce the competition and keeps the working-class resource more efficient at performing their labor functions. Predatory Capitalism creates its own form of economic survival of the fittest allowing top predators to play God with all us little people. The accelerated extinction that would result from these two natural progressions threaten to destroy the very fabric of our predatory social structure and with it, the fragile infrastructure we were made dependent upon to maintain our capitalistic existence.

Both of these natural progressions are well known among people dedicated to preserving the American standard of living and staying competitive within the global dynamics of our capitalistic evolution. Of course the well educated ruling class top predators will have invested millions to not only understand these natural progressions but more importantly to determine the best way to manipulate their development to make the maximum amount of profit. Because both of these natural progressions are directly related to our intellectual evolutionary development, their continuation is inevitable barring a catastrophic event beyond our species control. One of the most important things we the people of the world have the power to control, is how these two natural progressions develop and whether they are used to reduce suffering and death in a predator free society or as tools for human management and capitalistic oppression of a global working-class resources.

I was just realizing both of these natural progressions that threaten our modern day working-class resource from getting and keeping a job, started thousands of years ago in our evolutionary past. Like our intellectual evolutionary development itself these natural progressions have also been accelerated over the last few centuries. In the true spirit of predatory exploitation any new developing technologies are not directly and freely available to we the people like in a predator free society but instead elaborate mechanisms and bureaucracies are created to extract the maximum amount of profit from the working-class resource. After all using our knowledge and intelligence against others has long been the most efficient and socially accepted tool for predatory survival. It is this need for predatory exploitation and capitalistic dominance that has corrupted these natural progressions and created a fatal deviation in our evolutionary development that must be corrected to minimize the preventable suffering and death of our descendants. The actions we take now will determine the level of destruction our species will continue to suffer in the future.

Many readers of this book may have already gone to school on this subject and have gathered the factual knowledge necessary to become objectively aware of what these two natural progressions are and how to correct their detrimental effects on our society. However, for the Americans that may be working two jobs while trying to support three kids having little time to study up on this aspect of the big picture, I will do my best to explain their dynamics, as I understand them.

The first of these two natural progressions is most commonly referred to as "Globalization". Globalization can and will be very good for our species as we continue to struggle for global equality and prosperity for all people. But for now capitalistic greed has corrupted both natural progressions to benefit the ruling class few at the expense of the working-class many. Let's jump back in time to explore the development of our species globalization process. For most of our social evolution, vast areas of land and water effectively isolated people, cultures and natural resources around the world. Our ancestor's social economic success was primarily a factor of their local natural resources.

When countries and cultures did make contact the stronger of the two would generally plunder, conquer and annex the weaker ones like the European countries did to the American Indians to create the United States. As our species social development became more civilized, peaceful contact and trade between countries and cultures for national resources started to create a natural equilibrium. This process continues today in a global economy where the standard of living and hourly wages naturally seek equilibrium between connected industrialized countries.

A simple way to view the process of global equalization is to imagine several tall glasses of water on a table where each one represents a different country. The level of water in the glasses represent the economic prosperity, standard of living and average hourly wage of the working-class resource in that country. Our intellectual evolutionary development and transportation technology has reached the point where the glasses of water are all being connected allowing a natural equilibrium to take place. Manufacturing jobs from high wage earning countries will flow to the lowest wage earning countries like water running downhill. While this social dynamic effect of global capitalistic domination may help the working-class resource in other countries rise to a higher level of human rights, the nations with the highest levels of water in their glass and above average wages like the United States will experience a relative drop in economic stability and quality of life.

Because we Americans have been conditioned to expect the highest standard of living for so long while consuming 1/4 of the world's resources and casually wasting over half of that, something had to give. Imagine designing the social economic structure of a country to waste over 1/8 of the world's resources knowing that we the people have been conditioned to accept this reality without question. This planed waste of globe resources must represent enough wealth and power to feed entire countries, cure every disease, extend the human life span and build millions of technically advanced predator free community infrastructures all over the world. We need a better social economic system, one that focuses on efficiency and not the best way to exploit the American working-class resource.

Every American job, that pays anything close to a national living wage that can be outsourced, will flow like water to other countries and our predatory competition for survival in the United States will get worse. People will be forced to work harder for less and then conditioned to accept a lower standard of living. Maybe a good patriotic and religious subjective reality by the ruling class elite saying something like, we're all in this together or this is what your God would want you to accept, will do the trick, or maybe not. I think the collective intellectual evolutionary development of our country has come too far to continue allowing these forms of deception, at least for a growing minority of our population.

Just becoming aware of the knowledge in this book will help many people break their first chain of Capitalism and limit their vulnerability to different forms of psychological manipulation commonly used in capitalistic exploitation techniques. Unless all the countries of the world decide to isolate themselves from international trade this natural progression of our evolutionary development will continue. This global equalization of national wages and qualities of life will continue to accelerate as multinational corporations seek the highest profits for their executive salaries and shareholder investments. Because this entire social dynamic dysfunction is a manifestation and symptom of our predatory social structure like all the other grave evils of Capitalism, the best solution is to correct the problem at the source. Eliminating all the symptoms at once is still the best strategic option to accelerate our intellectual evolutionary development into a global predator free society.

The second natural progression is much less talked about and it's future impact on the jobs market for industrialized countries are not as obvious as globalization. This second natural progression is most commonly referred to as "Automation" or the technology of computer-aided manufacturing. New automation technologies are replacing many manufacturing jobs for the production of all products as well as many service industries that use to require a human workforce. While many poorer countries with little education or technology will continue to require forced competition among humans to maintain their social economical structure. The future ramifications of this natural progression are staggering for the working-class resources in industrialized nations that all need jobs for their survival. This fatal flaw of socially engineering 99% of the global population to be dependent upon the 1% of top predators for their jobs, basic survival necessities and the ability to support their families will become more obvious as this natural progression continues.

If we the people had a true democracy where we were allowed to objectively determine our future prosperity we would not have engineered a social structure that makes our survival dependent upon the wealthiest 1% of the capitalistic elite. One of the best ways to tell if a population is under the control of a collective subjective reality is when they are willing to allow their systematic exploitation as part of a government regulation or religious ritual. We don't need to do that anymore. Individuals functioning with an objective reality and the knowledge to make informed decisions would not choose to make their families survival dependent upon a small percentage of ruling class humans controlling their hardwired predatory instincts, emotional whims and lust for capitalistic power. The results would be predictably disastrous for the U.S. jobs market and our relative standard of living.

In an advanced predatory social structure like Capitalism the working-class people will always lose in the long run. It gets back to the efficient management and exploitation of the American working-class resource, it's not something we the people would have made an objective decision to allow. We are simply following the conditioning of our subjective realities and adapting to our predatory social evolution. I suppose even after understanding how much preventable suffering and death our predatory social structure has created for our species throughout our evolutionary development. The millions of years of genetic hardwiring will still be difficult to intellectually control with the application of factual knowledge and objective reasoning. But I know we can do it! In fact, you're doing it right now.

support their families. It seems safe to assume for each one of those million plus people there may be an additional spouse and a couple children heavily dependent upon that income for their capitalistic survival. To have around 4 million of our US citizens lose their means of survival and give up the American automobile industry to other countries would have been another huge unnecessary self-inflicted national wound that would have shown the world the level of control our top predators have over we the people.

During the debate whether to let our auto industry die, and while doing research for this book, I happened to land on the Fox News TV Channel for conservative republicans. There I heard Mike Huckabee, a man that wanted to be president of the United States and who is also a self identified Christian Southern Baptists pastor, referring to the American automobile industry where he had three words to sum up his feelings on the matter. "Let Them Die" he said as the audience erupted with applause and cheers. To see and hear such heartless rhetoric being broadcast on a major TV channel from someone that's a role model. Then hearing the jubilation of the crowd knowing the suffering this would cause their fellow Americans, gave me a new perspective on what's wrong with our country. And this came from religious leader? From what I know about Jesus, let them die would not have been his response to the preventable suffering of millions of children. But then Jesus would have rejected all forms of predatory and capitalistic exploitation. Remember, it is easier for a camel to go through the eye of a needle than for a rich man to enter the kingdom of God. I think he meant the greedy top predators of his time, not wealthy philanthropists using their fortunes to help reduce the suffering and death of others.

There's a happy ending to this story, well over 1 million families and millions of children will not need food stamps or fall into capitalistic poverty. Primarily because one of those bleeding heart liberal progressive Democrats, our president Barack Obama, decided to stick his neck out and risk the political torment from his opponents if his gamble had failed. If the presidential nominee Mitt Romney and other ruling class top Republicans were successful in letting the American automobile industry die it would have helped turned the great recession into a second great depression with global consequences. This symptom of our predatory social structure is a strong example of the tenuous struggle between we the people and our capitalistic elites ability to control our government, and how many jobs we lose. I'm wondering how bad it needs to get before we are inspired to break are induced subjective realities and gain intellectual control over our evolutionary development.

We have inadvertently helped to create the beast of Capitalism, in essence forging our own chains. It may have been a well-established tradition for thousands of years to create societies where people are forced to compete against one another for their jobs, survival necessities and basic human rights, but I've never been big on tradition. It's time we start thinking about the future, rather than clinging to the past. We got work to do.

8. Wars, who suffers and dies, and who makes billions in profits

Wars remind me of the game of chess. Chess is a interesting game of strategy that can not only teach us a lot about wars but also the evolution of our predatory social structures. Known as the game of Kings, chess was played by royalty over 1000 years ago to help develop war strategies to protect and conquer kingdoms. Chess is a board game played by two people each starting out with 16 pieces having different values and capabilities. Each player's 16 pieces represent a kingdom with the King being the most important piece to protect. All other board pieces must sacrifice their lives to protect the King because losing this piece ends the game with the destruction of your kingdom. The next important piece to protect is the Queen, her loss may not end the game but without her protection the King is more vulnerable. Below the king and queen in value are two rooks, bishops and knights all of which have pledged to sacrifice their lives to protect the royal couple. The least valued pieces on the battlefield are the lowly pawns representing the working-class peasants of a kingdom. There are eight pawns forced into battle knowing they will be sacrificed to protect all the more valued members of the kingdom.

It seems whether you're considering the game of chess or real-life it's good to be King, and it really sucks to be a pawn, especially when it comes to wars. It's not that some Kings didn't lead battles from the front like Alexander the great, perhaps following some patriotic or religious subjective reality testing his immortality as the son of a God. As our intellectual survival trait evolved Kings started realizing that they could live longer leading their wars from the rear and fighting their battles more like a game of chess. The more powerful kings may never need to leave the comfort and safety of their castles and win their battles using a pen and wax seal. It is true that many war heroes have gone on to become great leaders, but after achieving ruling class status and or capitalistic royalty they don't go back to the front lines. It's not like we're going to see the president of a modern industrialized country charging into battle on the back of a horse waving a sword, that would be considered crazy nowadays. Although we may see a president land on the back of an aircraft carrier, to create the illusion of a strong military leader.

It's interesting how close the game of chess resembles real life when it comes to how the working-class pawns are used and exploited to serve our modern ruling class Kings of Capitalism. Kings and kingdoms may rise and fall but the ruling class top predators are more like the players that control the board, sacrificing pieces to making the maximum amount of profit and then start looking for the next game to play. I suppose this shouldn't be surprising since the game developed over the need for more advanced attack and defense strategies to keep pace with our intellectual evolutionary development.

Somewhere between sticks in sand and supercomputer simulations the game of chess was a state-of-the-art way of developing predatory survival strategies. But even today we still socially accept the suffering and death of the many working-class pawns to serve the few ruling class rooks of Capitalism, bishops of religion and others that have risen to positions of wealth and power. It's time we working-class pawns came up with a whole new game to play, one that doesn't use us as a resource for exploitation by the ruling class elite, and I just happen to have one in mind that will be a whole lot more fun for we the people to play.

Wars are the most obvious and destructive symptom of our predatory evolution. To find a true root cause of a social dysfunction one must ask, at what point in our evolutionary development did it show up and start causing problems? Because wars seem like an obvious extension of our predatory instincts to dominate a global territory, this problem must have been encoded into our genetic memory long before we acquired and started to develop our intellectual survival trait. Just because we've been genetically hardwired from the beginning to accept our predatory social structure and the inevitable wars it creates, doesn't mean it can't be corrected. In fact we working-class pawns of the world have always had the power to end our socially accepted oppression. However, it seems we are just now becoming aware of how to use that knowledge to peacefully make the transition to a predator free society and finally enter a new era of peace and prosperity for our species. Now that's a game worth playing. Want to play?

For thousands of years the elite ruling class top predators have been playing a global game of chess where the working-class people of the world are the pawns to be sacrificed in their quest for economic domination. This game has gone on long enough, it's time we put an end to the intellectual deceptions that have formed our subjective realities making our predatory existence seem inevitable. Because we gain the power through knowledge and unity, the more we become aware of our systematic exploitation the quicker we can evolve to the next level of our social evolutionary development.

There are many great sources of information detailing with this subject explaining the problem and offering solutions. Some concepts are difficult to imagine using only words in a book. If a picture is worth a 1000 words a functioning predator free Automated Community Infrastructure must be worth trillions. Because I have already broken my first chain of Capitalism my focus is now more on implementing the best comprehensive solution to break the second chain by creating a functioning social system for comparison. However, there are two examples that may be well known to some people but apparently completely unknown to the majority of our populations or we may have already accelerated our transition to a predator free society.

Even though I have become aware of our systematic exploitation by ruling class top predators, learning of this example still blew me away. Fairly recently some of Lyndon B. Johnson's taped presidential conversations were declassified and made available to the public. It seems Pres. Johnson's administration negotiated an end to the Vietnam War in 1968 at the Paris peace talks. The Vietnam War was a highly contentious subject tearing apart our country and bringing it to an end was the number one priority for most American voters.

The then Republican presidential candidate Richard Nixon had built his whole campaign around the belief and induced subjective reality that he was the only leader that could end the Vietnam War. However, the Paris peace talks had a breakthrough providing the proverbial October surprise just before the presidential election. Pres. Johnson announced to the country an end to the Vietnam War was at hand, in essence destroying Nixon's credibility and his ambitions for the presidency of the United States.

What we the people didn't know is that Nixon intentionally sabotaged the peace negotiations to end the Vietnam War in an effort to secure his political and social ambitions. It seems Nixon used one of his servants to deliver a message to the South Vietnamese ambassador, that he and his country would get a much better deal under a Nixon presidential administration. The ambassador already wanting more out of the existing peace negotiations was easily swayed into prolonging the war giving Nixon the strategic advantage he needed to defeat his competitors and go on to become the supreme leader of our country. The arrogant ambitions of one ruling class elite to manipulate the working-class people, just to increase their social status and wealth, was not what blew me away about this historical event.

The most amazing part of this historical event is that Pres. Johnson knew exactly what Nixon was doing but was powerless to take public action against him revealing this act of treason. Something many less influential predators have been put to death for. As it would be foolish for any top predator to not use every technical advantage in their quest for global dominance, our FBI under Pres. Johnson had bugged the South Vietnamese ambassador's phone. Remember that life, politics and wars are all like a game of chess, because in a predatory social structure we are expected to use our intellectual survival trait as a strategic tool to achieve capitalistic success. However, this form of espionage was not only illegal but also really frowned upon in the international community, not to mention very unbecoming of a country with such high moral standards. Pres. Johnson could not admit this deception to the world or expose Nixon for treason. He needed to protect the integrity of our country and the strategic advantage of knowing the thoughts and actions of such a key chess piece and player in our national interests.

Imagine the frustration Pres. Johnson must have felt knowing he had a strategic advantage over Nixon and the ability to stop the suffering and death of thousands of Americans in Vietnam but was prevented for fear of revealing his own deceptions to the world. Pres. Johnson's only solace was in his subjective belief that Nixon didn't have the political support to go on to win the presidential election and benefit from his strategic deception. As we now know Nixon became president, the Vietnam War continued for years longer, and thousands of Americans needlessly lost their lives as pawns in a global chess game among top predators for increased social status and capitalistic domination.

The willingness of the ruling class predators to sacrifice their working-class pawns in wars to increase their social status and wealth has continued for thousands of years. As mentioned throughout this book the only way to end this cycle is for us working-class pawns of the world to unite and change the rules of the game. Or for the ruling class elite to renounce their capitalistic royalty and make the intellectual evolutionary transition to a predator free society. Even more likely and what seems to be taking place is a combination of the two as our entire species becomes more intellectually enlightened and less willing to socially except the inherent suffering and death that has always been a direct result of our competition for survival within a predatory social structure.

Even though I discuss many symptoms of our predatory social structure throughout this book, I would recommend further inquiry and verification from independent nonbiased sources. This will help readers separate the propaganda intended to deceive them from the factual knowledge they need to form an objective reality and make informed decisions. Throughout our predatory evolution Kings didn't need to concern themselves with the working-class pawns suffering and death, their sacrifice was socially expected and even accepted among much of the population, a lot like today. Nowadays with modern democracies our Kings and ruling class leaders must convince us working-class pawns to fight in wars and that our sacrifices will benefit the whole country and not just their social, political or capitalistic ambitions.

We must be convinced it's a shared sacrifice for the greater good of our country something needed to protect our American dream of capitalistic perfection. Sure it's a lot more trouble than sticking a sword and shield in someone's hands and telling them to fight or die, but the stakes are much higher nowadays with billions in profits on the line. A smart capitalist would certainly invest a few hundred million dollars to make billions in profits its just good business and completely acceptable within our predatory social structure. It's not like the smarter ruling class capitalists, their children, or even their grandchildren will suffer and die in these wars because that would defeat the purpose of making billions in profits and securing their bloodline of capitalistic royalty. Still wondering what's wrong with Capitalism?

For a better understanding of the politics surrounding modern day wars please see the MSNBC documentary hubris, selling the Iraq war. Every country in the world that allows their people access to education and factual knowledge are rapidly becoming aware as to what extent their leaders will go to deceive their working-class resource and use us like pawns in a global game of chess. They know the players don't die they just reset the game and count the profits. Perhaps most importantly is how we the people hold our leaders responsible for deceiving us into a war where thousands of American lives were lost and hundreds of thousands of noncombatant families were devastated around the world.

A huge amount of wealth was extracted from the US working-class resource increasing our national debt, leading to the great recession and escalating the economic suffering and death of countless more lives for many years to follow. What kind of message does this send our young Americans when they see this is considered socially acceptable at the highest levels of our ruling class elite? Does it really take something this drastic to break our subjective realities and force a punctuated equilibrium in our intellectual evolutionary development? Let's hope it won't require something worse this lesson came at too high a cost already.

We know who loses our global chess games of war it's always been the working-class pawns that have made the ultimate sacrifice to serve their Gods, Kings, Countries and warlord top predators. But the real question becomes who are the players that move the pieces, the men behind the curtain pulling the levers of power, the ones that benefit most from the suffering and death of so many people? What's their motivation for playing God with so many lives, could it be something as simple as capitalistic greed magnified by the environmental conditions of an advanced predatory social structure? It certainly looks that way. How many millions or billions of dollars does a top predators need to be happy, or is it just about being better than everyone else and becoming the capitalistic king of the world?

It may surprise you to know that we the people of America spent over $690 billion for military expenditures in 2011. To help put that into perspective we spend over five times as much on our military expenditures as the next leading country (China) and more than the next 10 militarized countries spend combine. Or in other words that's enough money to build a small death Star, travel to other solar systems and blow up planets. Imagine what we could do if we beat all those swords into plowshares, or better yet millions of technically advanced self replicating predator free community infrastructures. We the people generate the wealth and power of our country, we must make the collective decision to end our capitalistic exploitation and use our immense resources to accelerate our transition to a predator free society. Our celestial neighbor's may be watching and wondering, what's taking us so long?

Defense Spending compared by country, in $Billions (2012)

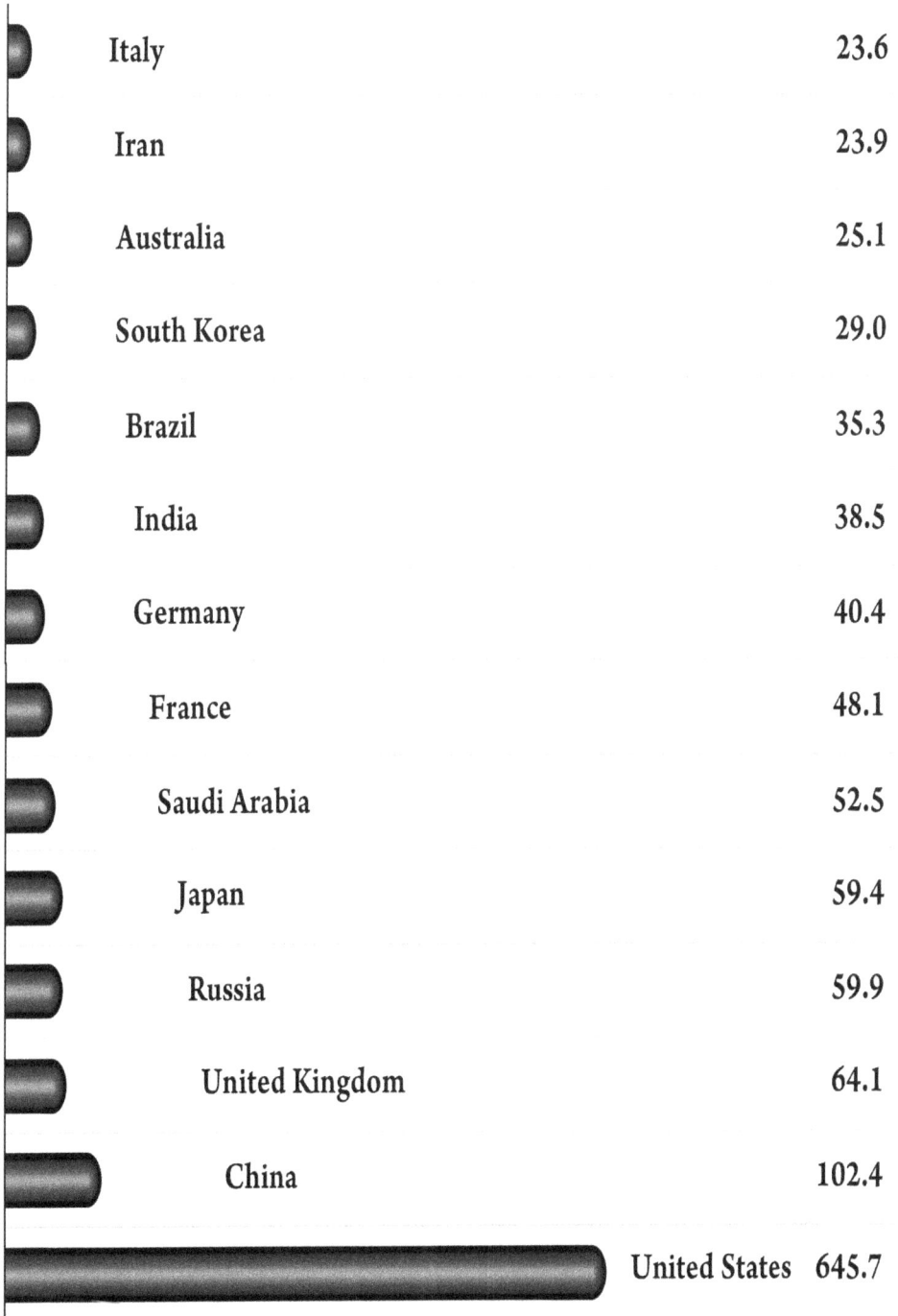

Italy	23.6
Iran	23.9
Australia	25.1
South Korea	29.0
Brazil	35.3
India	38.5
Germany	40.4
France	48.1
Saudi Arabia	52.5
Japan	59.4
Russia	59.9
United Kingdom	64.1
China	102.4
United States	645.7

Source: Center for Arms Control and Non-Proliferation, Prepared by True Freedom Technologies

A for-profit military industry functioning within an advanced predatory social structure is like a self-fulfilling beast of destruction and death. If your corporate and capitalistic survival depends on selling weapons of war, what's the one thing your business needs to stay profitable? We know any self-respecting capitalistic corporation will make whatever business arrangements and investments necessary to increase profits and executive salaries. However, a primary question should be, how far would they go to secure and expand the sale of weapons of war? Has our predatory social structure and capitalistic greed created environmental conditions so bad as to produce individuals and corporations that would initiate and perpetuate the suffering and death of others for profit? Is this what we've become while following our predatory instincts to achieve capitalistic dominance?

Even before we developed our intellectual survival trait, top human predators have exploited the less fortunate masses of our species out of their survival necessities leading to death. After thousands of years, our predatory social structure has adapted and evolved into more advanced and efficient forms of exploitation affecting millions of people around the world and creating billions in profits for an elite few. Trying to make a predatory social system this advanced fare for the prey is a fatal waste of creative skills at a time in our intellectual evolution when we should be ending this phase of our development and establishing predator free societies around the world.

The greater the predatory hostility is between countries the better capitalistic opportunities there will be to sell weapons of war and make billions of dollars in profits for the players of the game. Since wars have become part of free-market Capitalism, they follow the laws of supply and demand. If there is a high demand for a product a smart capitalist will create a business or industry to supply it, likewise if you have a high supply of some product you need to create a demand for it. In an advanced predatory social structure it's easier to induce a demand first through psychological manipulation and then supply a product as the solution to the problem that was created. This way the working-class resource feels their exploitation was of their own free will. Perhaps a patriotic or religious subjective reality will work using a national emergency to trigger an emotional response. Managing a working-class resource can get so complicated and tedious for the ruling class top predators of a technically advanced capitalistic society. However, the top human predators of our world today are rapidly losing their intellectual advantage as their working-class prey and pawns of war become more educated, unified and resolute in ending their exploitation.

Because our weapons of war can be sold to, and used on, the people in other countries, our need to profit from this particular industry creates a lot of destruction, death and resentment among the survivors. Of all the great evils of Capitalism, creating a deep well of global resentment among the people in multiple countries all over the world just so a few top predators can make billions in profits, is one of the worst symptoms of our predatory social structure I've considered. After all, if left unchecked it would continue to promote and eventually initiate a regional or maybe even global war, but then I guess that would be even better for business. It's that self-fulfilling beast again still acting on predatory instincts and unaware it is consuming itself to death.

I know we are the biggest kid on the block with the biggest guns and we have developed a subjective reality that we are so powerful nothing can hurt us anyway, but isn't it kind of stupid to allow this process to continue? It seems our ruling class leaders need to realize this is a global chess game with evolutionary consequences and their not thinking moves ahead. This could be one of the most critical moves of the game, how will we lead, what shining example will we offer the world for its increasingly objective consideration. It makes me wonder if our top predators know and don't care, or if they really don't know. The threats Capitalism poses to all people around the world and the security of our nations extends far beyond the suffering and death created by wars. Capitalism perpetuates and continues to expand the very predatory social structure that must end before we the people can experience true freedom, peace and universal prosperity within a predator free society.

9. Freedom of religion versus Separation of church and state

In the United States of America the first amendment of our Constitution guarantees all citizens the freedom of religion and throughout the civilized world it is considered a basic human right. Our forefathers understood the importance of showing tolerance for the many religions around the world, saying to all immigrants that in this country you can live free from oppression no matter what God you believe in. Our Constitution also recognizes freedom from religion or the right to not believe in any Gods at all. It's interesting that there was so much religious related oppression and intolerance that our forefathers felt it necessary to put it in the first amendment of our Constitution to help prevent this social dysfunction. Creating laws to limit our predatory instincts and violent actions produced by religious subjective realities seemed like a high priority.

This sounds like a modern-day version of a social dysfunction that goes back thousands of years. It starts with a simple conversation about who's God is stronger, and ends with one person killing the other to confirm the power of their God is greater. Later whole wars were fought to eliminate all non-believers, effectively killing their God and any future belief in them. At least we have laws now for people still wanting to act out their religious subjective reality to oppress, exploit or kill others for believing in a different God or none at all. That's real intellectual progress in our social evolution towards a predator free society, especially when compared to other modern day countries that still stone people to death for not submitting to their culturally induced religious subjective reality.

I wondered where did all this religious intolerance come from. Or more to the point why would someone's religious beliefs make them feel justified in oppressing and even killing all those that believe in a different God or no Gods at all. To answer this question and better explain this concept we will need to travel back in time to a point in our intellectual evolutionary development when there were many Gods to love and give thanks to for all the good things in life. And there were Gods to fear, and be concerned about suffering their wrath and destruction for indiscretion or displeasing them in some way. At this point in history, the use of religions as an intellectual predatory tool and the most effective induced subjective reality to ensure compliance among the slaves and working class populations was well known by the top predators. The problem for the uneducated peasant populations is that they had no intellectual awareness of their exploitation process or ways to build predatory defenses to counter the effects of a religious subjective reality that had become a socially accepted standard.

This was a time in our evolution when almost 100% of the human population was absolutely certain that many Gods were real and controlled every aspect of the world around us. Most of the Godlike kings and tyrants of our past would hear voices or have visions giving them the divine right to exploit, torture and massacre populations. One of the problems for the working class peasants is that there were so many Gods to fear and honor with gifts to prevent things like drowning at sea or the loss of crops from lack of rain. The better-educated top predators of our past noticed this strategy was an excellent capitalistic opportunity to exploit other people for profit. In a way this was the birth of free-market Capitalism that promotes the intellectual exploitation of the many to support the lavish lifestyles of the few.

This form of intellectual exploitation had become such a wild success in getting the uneducated masses to give up their wealth, new Gods were coming out of the woodwork and becoming real for the people that believed in them. The better-educated and well-dressed priests representing different Gods were more like wolfs dressed in sheep's clothing. So honored and trusted were these God merchants, their uneducated prey were easily convinced to give up their wealth as an offering to that God. The peasants needed the peace of mind that at least that God would not bring down death and destruction upon their family in the form of a natural disaster or man-made atrocity.

As the peasants traveled down the road there were more Gods and their collectors to please until eventually there was no more valuable possessions, food or drink to give. The next priest they pass warns them of the impending doom his family will suffer unless his God is honored with an offering of wealth. As a form of self-fulfilling prophecy, this priests prediction was correct, but the impending doom that befell this family did not come from the wrath of a God. Instead they died from dehydration, starvation and exposure to the elements as a result of giving their basic survival necessities to top predators that have hundreds of times more than they need. These early priests also may be the first known protection racket, specializing in preventing acts of God.

Like our forefathers, I understand the need to prevent people from allowing their religious subjective reality to turn prejudicial, violent and ultimately genocidal. It would cause civil unrest and disrupt the efficiency of our otherwise harmonious capitalistic exploitation.   However, this too is a symptom of our predatory social structure that will be corrected at the source, rendering the need for a law or constitutional amendment unnecessary. This concept may have been even too revolutionary for our forefathers to objectively consider especially given they did not have the benefit of the greatest intellectual evolutionary acceleration our species has ever known.

Of all the destruction and death that was committed in the name of Gods throughout our evolutionary development including modern-day terrorists and suicide bombers, there is a common denominator that holds true for all of these tragic events. People were acting under the control of their induced religious subjective reality to please a God. Most of these Gods don't exist anymore and really only truly existed as part of a subjective illusion in the minds of those people willing to kill and die for them. I feel if our forefathers fully understood the dangers of induced subjective realities as a tool for predatory exploitation, they may have encouraged our citizens to develop an objective reality eliminating the motivation for our people to use violence in an effort to please some God and satisfy their induced religious beliefs.

I'm for eliminating all forms of oppression and exploitation inherent in our current predatory social structure. However, to allow a sea of conflicting subjective realities to compete for dominance with only a law and the threat of punishment to prevent violent conflicts and civil unrest would seem to be highly ineffective, especially when considering it doesn't even address the source of the problem. Because our forefathers themselves were under the control of the predominant subjective realities of their day, like legitimizing slavery for profit, their visions and solutions for our future were limited. The notion of an ultimate solution eliminating all predatory conflicts at their source by establishing a predator free society seemed beyond the realm of our forefather's objective consideration.

Even today it's not the simplest concept to understand. We must embrace the intellectual progress we have made since the days of legitimized slavery, learn from our mistakes and accelerate the transition to the next phase of our evolutionary development. We will forever be grateful to our forefathers for advancing our social development and providing the constitutional framework necessary to attain true freedom, but to continue reminiscing about the wisdom of our past leaders is preventing us from fully embracing our intellectual progress and enacting modern-day solutions. Now that we've developed the intelligence and technology to solve these problems let's use it and move on with our evolutionary development.

Promoting our citizens freedom to believe in whatever religious subjective reality they want creates a form of free-market predatory competition to determine which domination is most righteous and deserving of the peoples wealth, is very problematic in itself. However, to allow this social dysfunction to permeate our government and determine how our laws are made will provide the lever of power needed to legitimize the exploitation of millions.

Our U.S. Constitution states, "No religious test shall ever be required as a qualification to any office or public trust under the United States". On one hand this limits the possibility of any single religion from dominating our government, creating a theocracy legitimizing the persecution of all other people with a different subjective or objective belief about Gods. On the other hand it allows individuals with any imaginable religious subjective reality to make decisions regarding the future of millions of Americans based on things that aren't real. In other words, we don't want the patience running the asylum. It's bad enough we are forced to compete against one another within an advanced predatory social structure. But to allow the induced subjective realities of our ruling class top predators determine the level of capitalistic exploitation we the people are subjected is beyond crazy. Perhaps the chaos and religious conflicts are used as part of a divide and concur strategy to distract the working-class resource away from the true source of their anguish and despair. It will predictably create more resentment among the growing population of citizens that form objective opinions based on factual knowledge.

Many of our lawmakers in state and federal governments reject well-established cold hard factual science for the warm and fuzzy embrace of a religious subjective reality. While many other politicians have broken their subjective reality but continue to maintain the illusion of a religious belief in the hope that their voters and colleagues will remain emotionally satisfied with their leadership. Many of the working-class Americans that voted for these elected officials in government feel a strong sense of emotional satisfaction knowing their leaders believes in the same God they do. And like all devout religious people under the control of a collective subjective reality, they will follow their Gods perceived wishes without question.

The problem is Gods tend to have a lot of apocalyptic visions for us mere mortals on earth. Also when God's inform their human followers what to do, it often comes in the form of voices in their head or visions in the sky. This alone would be a red flag for a casual observer that has formed an objective reality and present a serous concern about who is controlling our ruling class leaders thoughts and actions. Many modern-day populations have formed an objective reality unwilling to allow our capitalistic leaders to determine our future based on voices and visions from a God. That lame excuse about how our suffering and death is the will of Gods, just doesn't work as well as it used to. This is another example of how our species is rapidly gaining intellectual control over our predatory instincts and subjective realities.

There are many dangers involved for we the people when we allow our ruling class leaders to determine our way of life and level of capitalistic exploitation based on their subjective realities and things that are not real. Any predatory survival instinct triggered by an environmental condition and the involuntary emotional reaction that follows can easily be interpreted as a message from their God. The emotional whims of the ruling class few can easily turn into the suffering and death of the working-class many, just to satisfy voices in their head or an optical illusion in the sky giving them the supreme religious authority to justify atrocities.

No ruling class leader in an intellectually enlightened society should have the legal or constitutional authority to reject factual knowledge and objective reasoning to make their decisions based on the illusion of a subjective reality or what they think their God wants them to do. Between satisfying corporations capitalistic greed for higher profits and some induced subjective reality to please a God. Many of our politicians can't seem to find the time to allocate some of our money back to we the people increasing our level of health, education and basic human rights. They should be listening to the voices of the people, and not the ones in their heads or even the ones supplying them with millions of dollars to maintain their positions of power and control over our lives.

At times I must remind myself we are all still adapting to our predatory social structure whether we're born kings or peasants. It's just the level of predatory and capitalistic opportunities that are different. If I had been born a king or into capitalistic royalty my perspective would be much different all things would seem right as rain, no social injustice to fix in my world. However, as a modern-day peasant or person living below the American poverty line, my perspective and life experiences has finally opened my eyes to our predatory social structure and capitalistic exploitation. This provided the motivation necessary for me to write this book and help accelerate our intellectual evolutionary development to a predator free society.

Once we learn our entire species is making this natural evolutionary transition together, we start to realize it's so much bigger than just our individual social status or how much money we have in our bank accounts. Ending our predatory social structure and all of its symptoms that contribute to our preventable suffering and death will be one of our greatest achievements. It will change everything! Well, almost everything, at least with respect to our social evolution.

Besides the dangers of allowing our ruling class leaders to determine our future based on their religious subjective realities, in a democracy sometimes an induced collective false reality among the people can perpetuate their own preventable suffering and death. Consider the example of a religious sect known as Christian scientists. The title of Christian scientists is an ironic oxymoron since religions have suppress science by use of torture and death for hundreds of years as part of the intellectual isolation needed to maintain the illusion of their subjective realities.

Christian scientists number in the hundreds of thousands and were able to influence members of Congress to allow their religious practice of denying medical care to their children. This practice is now considered a religious freedom protected by our Constitution. If we can cut through the emotional interference of our subjective beliefs and our constitutional right to use them for an insanity defense, it comes down to one thing. Will our society allow the deaths of our children based on things that are not real? Still sacrificing our children at the altar of Gods, how little we have learned over thousands of years. How many must die?

Where is the separation of church and state when it's needed to protect the most vulnerable members of our society too young to decide whether to risk dying for a God or to seek modern medical attention? Conditioning children to perpetuate a subjective reality that rationalizes this form of child abuse is difficult enough to accept, but to know our society allows it because it's considered a religious freedom is really disturbing. It begs the question how far will we let our belief in Gods determine the health and safety of our children or the future prosperity of our species.

Exactly what level of abuse, pain and suffering can a parent inflict upon their children knowing their freedom of religion gives them the right to do so?

I guess our children can feel some comfort that most religions of the world have evolved beyond ritualistic human sacrifice. Since religious people feel their God is the ultimate authority commanding their actions, I'd like to know which Gods are protected under our freedom of religion and U.S. Constitution. Are only the Gods and religions with the greatest wealth, number of believers and influence in government worthy of religious freedom or can anyone start their own personal religion and get away with psychological conditioning and child abuse? This would create a whole new capitalistic opportunity for religious rights lawyers to use the first amendment to demand all cult rituals become socially acceptable under the law. Still wondering why things are so messed up?

Imagine living in a predator free society where there is no need to induce conflicting subjective realities to compete for our capitalistic exploitation and no one wastes time or intellectual energy considering whose God is more powerful or better qualified to determine our future. Many people around the world have finally reached that magical point in our intellectual evolution where we are ready to take control of our future. We're taking the first steps in our evolutionary journey without the parental guidance of Gods. It can be a scary time for any developing species, but we're stronger and smarter now. When we were a younger species we needed more primitive forms of guidance and structure, but now we can start using our advanced intelligence to provide true freedom and prosperity to all people as a universal human right, not a divine luxury only granted by Gods.

One of the more important things we can learn from a religious belief capable of legitimizing tragedies is just how powerful an induced subjective reality can be at controlling our actions. One of the strongest hardwired survival instincts is for self-preservation and the desire to protect our children from harm. If the belief in a subjective reality has the power to defeat a behavioral trait this well encoded in our genetic memory. Then I am certain the application of factual knowledge and objective reasoning will allow our intellectual survival trait to take control of our predatory instincts, effectively breaking our first chain of Capitalism. I would be even more certain of success if the individual started developing an objective reality at an early age within the environmental conditions of a predator free society without the preconditioning of a subjective belief.

Another area where the belief in Gods and subjective realities are given special preference by our government helping to perpetuate the many social dysfunctions that manifest from allowing illusions to masquerade as reality, is when granting tax-exempt status to a nonprofit organization. An objective reader of this book will know, it's not the charitable contributions and activities religious organizations make to help reduce the suffering and death of individuals struggling to maintain their capitalistic competition for survival that is objectionable. This can be done without the belief in Gods or the need to induce a subjective reality. The objection would be in the perpetuation and legitimization of subjective realities for the purpose of transferring wealth from the working class many to the ruling class few, and then redistributing it based on the council of something that is not real.

It's true that some people's intellectual isolation may be so severe that rules on how to be a good human like "Thou shall not kill" may still be necessary to explain, as was the case thousands of years ago. However, to mix sensible rules to try and prevent our predatory instincts from running wild without intellectual control with holy commands like "Thou shall have no other Gods before me" gives this statement credibility where none exists. If an obvious universally accepted statement is written in stone on the same tablet right next to a subjective command to deny the belief in other Gods, it naturally leaves people and government constitutions with the impression that they are both equally as valid and based in reality. A foundational belief built on the illusion of a subjective reality would predictably produce a society with serious structural flaws lacking a universal point of reference based on factual knowledge and rational thought.

One of the things I find most interesting and revealing about the Ten Commandments is, if we assume that Gods or stone carving holy men were smart enough to list these rules in order of priority. It would seem odd that, thou shall not kill, comes in sixth, far less important than the need to prevent the belief in other Gods. Even remembering the Sabbath day and to keep it holy, is listed as a higher priority than killing another human being. But then these rules were made up thousands of years ago when many forms of atrocities were commonplace and socially accepted as inevitable, much like today.

Still wondering what has been preventing our natural evolutionary transition to a predator free society? Whether by creative design from a life form beyond our comprehension or a natural evolutionary process without intelligent oversight, our transition to a predator free society seems inevitable. We only need to understand the barriers that are preventing our transition and our collective power of objective reason will prevail at providing true freedom and prosperity for all people as equals.

The ongoing conflict to provide a separation between church and state, or in other words preventing people from making laws forcing others to submit to their subjective beliefs and religious control, seems to favor freedom of religion. One of the most important benefits allowed for by our government is the 501(c) 3 tax-exempt status for nonprofit organizations. This system is intended to intelligently limit the extraction of wealth from some organizations allowing them to provide humanitarian relief to the least fortunate competitors of our predatory social structure. Allowing these nonprofit organizations to avoid the wealth extraction process design into our social structure is a great privilege and survival advantage that should be given to anyone attempting to make our capitalistic exploitation more tolerable for the ones made to suffer most.

It makes me wonder why we would perpetuate and legitimizes a social structure that justifies the suffering and death of millions, and then hand out Band-Aids to organizations dealing with the predictable consequences? Top predators of Capitalism usually like to profit from creating the problem and providing the solution. But then the fine art of managing a working class resource would recommend providing at least enough hope to maintain the illusion of potential prosperity, or in our case attaining the American dream. And while it's true many people do achieve a quiet secure life in the suburbs, it reminds me of the psychology behind gambling where you need to let some of the players win or all the losers won't have as much fun continuing to play the game.

Two objectives a nonprofit organization may pursue to receive 501(c) 3 tax-exempt status and avoid our national wealth extraction process are, for the "Advancement of religion" and "Advancement of education or science". For our government to suggest that the pursuit of these two objectives are equal by allowing both of them the same tax-exempt privilege not only creates the wrong message for our young citizens to be conditioned with, but it also indicates the level of intellectual progress our country has made towards understanding the difference between them. In all the ways that matter most, the advancement of these pursuits would have an opposite effect on the intellectual evolutionary development of our species.

We must separate the good humanitarian relief many religious people and organizations provide to their community as a way of returning wealth they collected from their believers, from their need to induce their followers with a subjective reality to ensure repeat business. It seems a lot like a miniature theocracy functioning within a capitalistic society subject to the corrupt influence of an advanced predatory social structure. They all collect wealth and survival resources from we the people and return just enough in the most cost effective way to keep us emotionally satisfied with our continued predatory and capitalistic exploitation.

If a religion's objectives were truly focused on humanitarian relief, there would be no need to induce subjective realities. Of the people that can afford to help others, they should do so because of an objective decision to make a positive difference in the world, not to satisfy a subjective belief to receive spiritual rewards and eternal joy after they die. I don't believe we need to use the threat of having our souls burn in hell for all eternity to get people to do the right thing, as long as doing so will not threaten their own survival. The need to induce a subjective reality is not to help the people or to provide humanitarian relief, it's used to increase the wealth and power of corporations and build religious empires. Controlling the minds of large populations all over the world is a powerful tool for manipulating the evolutionary development of a species. This is a power that can corrupt absolutely, especially if our predatory instincts and subjective realities are allowed to control our actions.

It's no wonder religion and Capitalism, or church and state work so well together. They both function like corporations all competing to get the most believers and customers from a shrinking market of consumers outgrowing their need for a comforting subjective reality to give their lives structure and meaning. Our new motivational paradigm to end our species predatory existence and provide true freedom and prosperity for all people as equals should provide all the technical challenges and satisfying accomplishments an individual could possibly want in one lifetime. It may be a little hard to imagine now, but a society without predatory or religious conflicts and the need to compete against one another for our capitalistic survival, will be far more productive and a whole lot more fun to live in.

The concept of separating the powers of church and state is a relatively new development in our intellectual evolution. I guess it shouldn't be surprising we are still working out the bugs. For thousands of years these two forms of predatory exploitation functioned as one almighty power to efficiently extract wealth from the working class resource while maintaining the emotional satisfaction necessary to induce the most popular subjective reality of the day. The Gods and kings of the churches and states may have changed over time, but our evolving predatory social structure always seems to fall into the same pattern, of just a few ruling class elite controlling their many working-class peasants. It was clear an out of the box solution would be needed to break this pattern.

What message does it send our society when they can see our justice system is so influenced by a subjective reality it has witnesses perform the religious ritual of swearing upon a Bible before being expected to render an objective testimony? Are we trying to confuse people or just legitimize a subjective reality with the environmental illusion of objective reason? This may all seem right as rain to an observer under the complete control of their religious subjective reality as long as the ritual, holy book, religion and God is theirs. Imagine how awkward it would be to require a religious ritual based on some other religion, perhaps one that has already become extinct. Many religious rituals involve animal sacrifices, or perhaps the less popular dancing while kissing poisonous snakes. That really would be awkward before a testimony.

I suppose swearing on the Bible was initially intended to provoke the fear of God and the consequences of bearing false witness, even though their honesty may led to their legitimized torture and death. Where's the motivation there? Many of these people were only guilty of things like observing nature and agreeing with new scientific discoveries contrary to the current subjective reality being induced by the church. These unfortunate souls clearly had far more to fear from the emotional whims of those that were given the power of life and death over them than the Gods they were conditioned to believe in. The inability of any system of justice to distinguish between the subjective illusion of things that are not real and the objective consideration of factual knowledge would render it ineffective at performing its basic function. Even worse, it creates a fatal vulnerability allowing the corrupting influences of a predatory social structure to manipulate key individuals willing to take actions on their subjective beliefs.

We should remember even the extinct religions and Gods of the past were real enough for their believers to kill and die for in a failed attempt to perpetuate their subjective beliefs. I know it can be difficult to step back and see the big picture from an historical or evolutionary perspective, but our people are still dying for the same senseless reasons. Only the storylines and central characters of their subjective realities have changed. After thousands of years, how could we allow this to continue as a rational act of a civilized society?

One of the more obvious failures to separate church and state is our United States currency and more than any other symbol in the world it represents what our country truly stand for. Besides our national currency representing the capitalistic spirit of America and the potential to achieve a life of excessive opulence, it also seems to represent a God. It's interesting how money and Gods always seem to be associated with one another. You may have noticed the four little words "In God We Trust" on our United States currency.

Putting these four words on all of our countries currency knowing the working class resources of the world will be visually imprinted with these words and emotionally associate them with all the things money represents, reminds me a little of the subliminal messaging technique used for psychological manipulation. This technique conditioned individuals by flashing word messages so fast that they were only picked up by the subconscious mind and then acted upon by the victim without their knowledge. It seems this form of psychological manipulation for capitalistic exploitation was a little too obvious and once the people found out they were being used like puppets with cash in their pockets, this predatory technique was banned. Of course it would be a far more effective conditioning tool to put a written message or suggestion directly on the face of the national currency of the most financially influential and powerful country in the world. I guess it's not as important how many people get manipulate as long as the subjective reality that they're induced with helps maintain a complacent society willing to accept their capitalistic exploitation as the best quality of life they could hope for.

The first thing I noticed about this message to the people, was the words themselves are artfully constructed to imply solidarity with all religious subjective realities and citizens that trust their God, without showing any favor to a specific religion. Of course like reading a fortune cookie and just knowing it's referring to our life experiences, the predominant religion in our country would rightfully assume that the God they're talking about trusting on our money, must be theirs. And we all know how trustworthy Gods can be, at least when they're not working in mysterious ways, like giving away our nation's wealth to ruling class top predators.

These four words of subjective solidarity must provide the believers in our country and around the world a sense of emotional satisfaction knowing they're capitalistic pursuits are somehow sanctioned by their God. As if to say, our money trusts your God, therefore your God must also trust money, and give his blessing to whatever you need to do to get more of it. And what your God would really appreciate most, is for we the people to faithfully send in your tax revenues to the government, because we can trust our ruling class leaders to follow God's will. This deception has developed despite the fact most religions publicly denounce the pursuit of excessive wealth and power among their followers while privately amassing great wealth presumably to create more giant cathedrals to honor their God and instill a sense of awe in their believers.

It's interesting how easily an induced subjective belief can change from one extreme to the other when highly skilled top predators socially engineer our society to condition their working class resource into more efficient forms of advanced exploitation. The top predators can only maintain the first chain of Capitalism as long as a majority of our populations allow their predatory instincts and subjective beliefs to determine their decisions and actions. They know this process has been under their control for thousands of years so their confidence is high it won't change, at least until we reached that crucial tipping point in our intellectual evolution when we start forming a collective reality objective enough to denounce our predatory past and embrace a predator free future. That time is upon us and we're starting to tip.

Even after we the people started to recover from one of the worst economic extractions of wealth ever inflicted on a working class resource. Our Republican dominated US House of Representatives continues to spend their time and our tax dollars creating and passing a non-binding resolution reaffirming that "In God We Trust" will remain our national motto, instead of providing humanitarian relief or employment opportunities to our citizens reducing the suffering and death in our country. What ever their dysfunction is, their priorities and allegiances are clearly not with the people they took an oath to serve. The deceptions of our ruling class elite in government are becoming increasingly transparent as our knowledge of these manipulation techniques grows among the people. Somewhere between our soft requests for a compassionate society and our lowed demands for basic human rights, we will have our true freedom and prosperity. We have the power to achieve our true freedom and now we are learning how to use it.

It's a little surprising more people aren't concerned that the most influential country in the world is using their currency to promote and help induce a subjective reality to trust a God. This general endorsement of any religious subjective reality and suggestion to trust whatever God you were conditioned to believe in may be popular among politicians playing to an audience. However, it sets a dangerous precedent limiting our future leaders ability to distinguish between a subjective illusion and an objective fact. Making that distinction is the most important asset any leader could have to determine the difference between the increased suffering and death of their people or their ability to achieve true freedom and prosperity for the future of our species.

For our country to promote and induce any subjective reality on all people that handle our currency is a technique and strategy that would effectively delay our intellectual evolution by slowing our ability to form objective opinions and make an informed decision, like how to end our capitalistic exploitation. Or maybe we're just innocently and proudly declaring to the world our willingness to reject the separation between church and state by continuing to allow our subjective beliefs and trust in a God determine the future of our country and the direction in which our species will evolve. Hum, what do you think, is that what you want?

10. Our freedom of speech, the Good, the Bad and the Ugly

Of all the human rights and liberties our forefathers wanted us to have they put our freedom of speech in the First Amendment. Our forefathers knew to silence the working class masses would not be acceptable to we the people causing civil unrest and a breakdown in the social harmony they hoped to produce. We people needed a way to vent our frustrations in a peaceful organized manner that had the potential for a constructive outcome instead of letting the pressure build up to revolutionary levels destroying our infant democracy in its cradle. Most people were use to dealing with many forms of predatory oppression without any form of representation by top predators that only considered them a resource for exploitation.

Our forefathers had the audacity to try and change hundreds, even thousands of years of predatory dominance by the ruling class elite. It is because of their courage so long ago that we the people are now able to publicly voice our opinions and denounce our systematic exploitation by our current ruling class top predators. It's part of our continuing quest for true freedom, equality and prosperity for all, perhaps just as our forefathers intended it to be. It will be our freedom of speech and expression, constitutional right that will be most instrumental in communicating the factual knowledge necessary for all people to make an informed decision to end our predatory exploitation.

Our freedom of speech is a powerful tool we the people can use to build a predator free social structure capable of providing a level of true freedom and technical wonders our forefathers could not have imagined in their wildest dreams. However, like any tool that has the potential for great good it also has the potential for great evil. When any new tool gets introduced into the environmental conditions of an advanced predatory social structure, it will be used in any and every way possible by the ruling class top predators to increase or maintain the capitalistic exploitation of their working class prey. It's only natural that a species conditioned for millions of years to use their intelligence against one another would find the best way to use any new tool to aid in their competition for survival.

In the simplest of terms our freedom of speech gives us the right to publicly communicate all forms of raw knowledge and different concepts for others to consider. Some of that raw knowledge will be genuinely intended to benefit the recipient in some way and given freely without payment required. However, much of that raw knowledge will be intentionally constructed to deceive and manipulate the recipient in some way that will benefit the few top predators at the expense of the many working class prey. On one hand our freedom of speech allows people like me to offer a comprehensive framework to end our predatory social structure and help accelerate our natural evolutionary transition to a predator free society. On the other hand it also allows maniacal ruling class elite top predators of Capitalism to use different forms of psychological manipulation on the working class resource to condition them into feeling emotionally satisfied about giving up their wealth, labor and lives.

It's almost as if our forefathers wanted to create confusion and controversy hoping that the last one standing would somehow have the highest moral standards or provide the fairest social structure to manage we the people. It's similar to how our freedom of religion legitimizes many religious subjective realities and then our forefathers hoped a law separating church and state would help limit the inevitable predatory conflicts for social dominance. Our forefathers must have known our freedom of speech would be used as an instrument of evil as well as good, again legitimizing two extremes adding to the conditions of confusion and controversy. I can't help but to think if our forefathers truly felt the environmental conditions of our predatory social structure dominated by the ruling class elite would somehow take the form of a harmonious society that provides equality and prosperity for we the people, I know they would be sadly disappointed to see what has become of their dream.

I like the philosophical consideration about who gets to determine what is good or evil with regard to our freedom of speech. It's clear our forefathers wanted to leave that decision to the people of their future hoping they would one day gain the knowledge necessary to make the distinction between what is intended to be beneficial for others and what is constructed as a tool for exploitation. If only our forefathers knew the destructive power of induced subjective realities and the influence they would have to subvert the very democracy they hoped to create. And if only they recognized the futility in hoping a predatory social structure would somehow provide equality for the working class prey, I'm sure things would have turned out different back then. In fact we would probably have a Constitution based on a predator free society and already completed our national transition over 100 years ago. We got some catching up to do.

11. Choosing the best social structure for our future

Choosing the best social structure is the most important thing we can do to create an atmosphere of cooperation for the good of the entire community, or one of competition and predatory conflicts for survival. More to the point, our social structure is the environmental conditions that shape the evolutionary development of our species. These environmental conditions will determine whether our species continues towards greater domination by capitalistic super predators, or whether we accelerate our social evolution to a predator free society and the next phase of our intellectual evolutionary development.

This may seem like an easy choice for an individual functioning with an objective reality, but for many people under the control of a subjective reality to accept our predatory existence, deciding which option is best may be difficult. The level of suffering and death created by our capitalistic exploitation is helping people all over the world break their subjective realities, making our choice for social structures a whole lot easier.

Many of us working-class prey have become discouraged that even with our democracy we cannot seem to get our leaders in government to create a social structure that cares more about we the people than the top predators of Capitalism. While it is true that the top predators of Capitalism use their wealth and influence to subvert our democracy and create laws to maintain dominance over their working class resource, it is not true that we the people don't have the power to create the kind of society we want for our future. If for instance we decided to end our exploitation under Capitalism and create a predator free social structure for our nation, we have the power to make that happen. We the people are the wellspring from which power flows. We just need to change the flow of wealth and power back to us, or better yet eliminate the whole wealth extraction process all together.

You may still be wondering as I did, if we the people have the power to end our capitalistic exploitation and accelerate our social and intellectual evolutionary development into a predator free society, why haven't we done it already? I think the short answer is we're just starting to realize we have that power. Our species was simply following our hardwired instincts encoded in our genetic memory to accept the only social structure we have ever known. It all seems so much clearer now. Using our intellectual survival trait to advance our predatory social structures for more efficient exploitation of what has evolved into working-class human prey seems like an understandable natural progression of our evolutionary development.

Now that phase of our intellectual evolutionary development has run its course, our species has finally reached a tipping point where our predatory social structure will no longer be required for survival or considered acceptable for future societies. The working-class people of the world need only become aware of the power they hold to end the predatory evolution of our species. It's not just putting an end to our capitalistic exploitation it's ending a predatory social structure that has dominated our species evolutionary development since the beginning of our existence. Now that's real power.

Once we break our subjective realities and national conditioning to accept our capitalistic exploitation as the best quality of life we can hope for, we will be free to design and create whatever social structure can provide the highest level of prosperity and unification for all people as equals.

During the transition to a predator free society there will be some top predators and many of their most faithful prey unwilling to give up our predatory social structure and evolve to the next phase of our intellectual evolutionary development. For our current ruling class top predators the motivation to continue our predatory society will come down to simple greed and their desire to maintain social superiority, capitalistic royalty and domination over us working-class prey. However, for their most faithful working-class prey under the control of a collective Stockholm syndrome subjective reality, their unwitting motivation will be to defend their continued exploitation by their ruling class leaders with emotional reactions and irrational acts of violence.

For the growing percentage of our population that has already broken their first chain of Capitalism and want to accelerate our intellectual evolution into a predator free society, our challenge will be to determine and create the best social structure for your future. The predator free society that I am offering for consideration in this book is primarily designed to end our predatory social structure and accelerate our transition to the next phase of our intellectual evolutionary development, but in doing so the opportunity to advance the primary areas of security, education, healthcare, production and efficiency was also available. Eliminating all the symptoms of our predatory social structure at its source will in itself create an atmosphere of true freedom, posterity and a spirit of cooperation accelerating our progress in all primary areas. At least that's the plan.

Before we consider the advantages of a technologically advanced predator free society we should understand the different predatory social structures of our past and present to determine what features are worth continuing into the future. How can we fully appreciate our predator free future without a good understanding of our predatory past? We know that before we developed our intellectual survival trait our predatory existence as a species was just as primitive as all the other non-intelligent creatures competing for their evolutionary survival.

As our species intellectual survival trait naturally developed into the most advanced tool for predatory exploitation, our ruling class top predators experimented with many social structures to determine the best way to provide an efficient flow of wealth and labor from they're working class resource. In addition to social structures and laws our ruling class ancestors experimented with inducing subjective realities to create complacency and devotion among their people. An integrated combination of religious rituals and government laws was found to be most effective at managing the working-class resource and getting them to accept their continued exploitation as a fundamental aspect of their social structure.

As we explore some of our past and present predatory social structures we should consider them from the perspective of the ruling class top predators in how they use these two powerful management tools of religious beliefs and government laws to manipulate and control their working-class resource. Also important to consider is how these two powerful forms of social conditioning are used to limit our education or more specifically our awareness of our exploitation and the knowledge that we have the power to end this phase of our evolutionary development. As we learn about these different social structures try to imagine what your life would be like as one of the working-class members of that society or as one of its ruling class elite top predators. It always seem to help the learning process to see things from all perspectives, then look for a common denominator that might be controlling the whole game.

THEOCRACY: is a form of government social structure in which a God or deity is recognized as the supreme civil ruler over an entire population or country. In reality a theocracy is more of a "Hagiocracy" where the social structure, government and laws are created and controlled by holy men, saints or priests. This form of social structure may very well be the first organized form of leadership and control over a population of people. The ancient ruins of Göbekli Tepe showed evidence of a hagiocracy 12, 000 years ago.

The archaeological evidence discovered at these ruins show the earliest signs of holy men or priests forming an elite ruling class of humans to manage and control the rest of the population. It may be difficult to imagine that from these simple beginnings a global empire of capitalistic domination would develop, still using religion and government as instruments of predatory manipulation and control. The planned and organized separation between the haves and have-nots must have begun even earlier in our intellectual evolutionary development, but then time has a way of erasing the existence of the past.

This form of predatory social structure would be great for the ruling class priests presumably getting instructions from some God on the best way to manage and accept offerings from their working-class believers. Even though many Gods have come and gone during the last 12, 000 years of our evolutionary development, there always seems to be holy men willing to collect wealth in their names. Paying your taxes may satisfy the government but the Gods have always seemed to need a lot of money too. It's like it took a few thousand years before we humans started asking the question, why do the Gods need to extract so much wealth from all us poor working-class mortals? Do they need to buy something, and if so where do they shop? I guess we can't be too hard on our ancestors, if you think getting a good education nowadays is difficult just imagine what it must have been like a few thousand years ago. Life must have been like one giant mystery that didn't get much better as we got older.

Besides creating a highly effective predatory social structure a theocracy is at its core based on a religious subjective reality. Conditioning a population with a religious subjective reality may be the oldest and most efficient forms of psychological manipulation ever created by us humans, but it has a fatal flaw. A theocracy requires the intellectual isolation of its working-class believers to maintain the illusion of their subjective reality. Theocracies also commonly humiliate, torture and publicly executed nonbelievers for heresy to control their populations with fear. However now day's larger numbers of better-educated working class believers are breaking their subjective realities with the application of factual knowledge.

Older citizens in a Theocracy may live out their entire lives believing in the God of their subjective conditioning, while younger members of a Theocracy, if given access to factual knowledge and a good Internet connection would begin to ask that all-important curious question, what are the Gods spending all our money on? Making opulent marble temples to display their greatness? Maybe if they let the people keep a little more of their survival resources there would be less suffering and death among their believers. Now that's something to believe in.

OLIGARCHY: is a form of government social structure in which all power is vested in a few persons or families in a dominant class or clique. An oligarchy is similar to a Theocracy or any other predatory social structure in the respect that power is concentrated by the ruling class few to control and exploit the working-class many. However, without some form of subjective reality to induce a sense of emotional satisfaction with their ongoing exploitation the working-class resource of an oligarchy would most likely become dissatisfied with their society and overthrow their ruling class top predators. Although even without the pretense of a religious subjective reality to maintain social stability and oligarchy could retain power with the application of brute force and fear. Even though this form of predatory management is very effective the working-class resources level of education and ability to resist authority must be kept lower than social structures with populations conditioned to accept their exploitation as a privilege or blessing.

DICTATORSHIP: is a social structure where a single ruler exercises absolute power over his working-class people without their consent. A Dictatorship is also very similar to Despotism and an Autocracy where all the people of a country are ruled by a single dictator with absolute power. You know what they say about absolute power corrupting absolutely. It's not just an out of control desire for wealth and power it also corrupts the mind with delusions of grandeur. Dictators can easily become Gods in their minds as their personal subjective realities gain full control over their thoughts and actions. In this type of social structure there is one supreme top predator and they do not share power or the wealth exploited from the working-class resource of their population or country.

A religious or national subjective reality may or may not be used to help maintain social stability among the working-class prey. Inducing one or both of these subjective realities with the very real threat of torture and death make for a very efficient means of controlling the working-class resource and maintaining a dependable workforce for easy exploitation. Like other predatory social structures keeping the working-class resources education and health at a minimum acceptable level will limit the awareness of their exploitation and make them less likely to resist. Considering all the Godlike kings of our predatory past, Dictatorships use to be the predominant social structure. However, as the working-class people of the world became more intellectually evolved this form of social structure was not as easy to maintain.

FASCISM: is a form of government social structure, which is led by a dictator and emphasizes aggressive nationalism and military strength. Fascism places a strong emphasis on the race of individuals to determine their value and it uses severe social and economic regimentation as a form of control. This social structure also uses violence to forcibly suppress any criticism or opposition to the dictator's autocratic control of the working-class resource. As complicated as Fascism can get it seems to have the same basic elements of the more primitive forms of dictatorial rule except the leaders may command more sophisticated resources and destructive power. I suppose any smalltime racists warlord dictator oppressing a population to extract wealth and power would be considered a fascist if they also forcibly suppressed opposition to their predatory domination.

Where a Theocracy primarily uses a religious subjective reality, Fascism emphasizes a national or patriotic subjective reality to condition its population into accepting their predatory social structure. Both social structures successfully induce a sense of emotional satisfaction with the systematic exploitation of their working-class resource and the self-righteous disregard for anyone that doesn't accept their subjective reality. Again, both of these forms of conditioning have been around for thousands of years.

To believe in the wrong God, King or dictatorial top predator was known to get whole families and villages tortured and executed as an example to others. It could also serve as a good excuse to plunder and enslave an opposing population. No wonder talking about religion and politics can still provoke involuntary emotional reactions limiting our ability for intellectual and rational thought. Our genetic memory has been encoded over thousands of years to trigger a survival instinct producing subconscious reactions to these environmental conditions. The artificial selection and elimination from the human gene pool of all individuals unwilling to submit to predatory subjective realities, has also shaped our tolerance for social exploitation.

PLUTOCRACY: is a social structure where the government is controlled by a wealthy class and they exercise power and influence by virtue of their wealth. You may be wondering as I did, how is this different from Capitalism? I suppose Capitalism allows more opportunities for potential top predators to ascend into economic royalty where a Plutocracy does not. A Plutocracy and Capitalism share the same basic social structure but with a few notable differences. Capitalism creates the illusion of shared prosperity and requires elaborate psychological deceptions to get their working-class resource to comply with their exploitation, where a Plutocracy without a democracy doesn't have to care as much about what the little people think. In reality Capitalism seems to be an advanced form of Plutocracy that required a higher level of intellectual manipulation to maintain our predatory social structure and keep pace with the evolutionary development of our species.

A Plutocracy is generally considered really bad for the working-class resource, which begs the question why were we the people willing to accept Capitalism as the best social structure when we knew it would have the same drawbacks. Maybe we weren't given a choice and we were conditioned from birth to believe all red-blooded Americans must fully embrace Capitalism. To not embrace Capitalism would be considered unpatriotic, not a team player, one of "Them", but not one of "Us".

Not being a team player and embracing Capitalism may get you labeled a national traitor and sympathizer of the social structure held by some hostile country. We may not stone people to death like they still do in other countries for not submitting to their religious or national subjective realities, but to be rejected by our family and community could severely limit our ability to compete for our capitalistic survival. Now that America has become the champions of Capitalism, we must learn from our mistakes, correct the problem and set a new precedent for the world to consider.

CAPITALISM: by its most fundamental definition is an economic system where wealthier private individuals own the means by which a country survives rather than a government elected by or representative of the people. The wealthiest private individuals control all the products and services that allow a country and its working-class people to be healthy, productive and prosperous. Or when these survival necessities are withheld, their working-class populations will quickly experience increased levels of suffering and death. This allows for an excellent control mechanism for the wealthy private individuals of this social structure to efficiently manage their working-class resource.

I don't know if I can emphasize this enough, but this is a terrible social system for the working-class people and an unbelievably sweet capitalistic opportunity for global exploitation by the wealthiest ruling class individuals in the world. A social economic structure designed to concentrate wealth and power among the few giving them full control over we the people's basic survival necessities is a strategic nightmare for the working-class populations of the world. This social system makes us catastrophically vulnerable on multiple levels, most notably from the predatory instincts and emotional whims of ruling class private individuals deciding the fate of millions based on their profit potential.

Remember, using our intellectual survival trait to achieve predatory success over others has long been the accepted social standard for our species. This strategy has been very successful for decades allowing trillions of dollars to be extracted from the global working-class resource.

This artificially assisted natural cycle of our intellectual evolutionary development is finally coming to an end as our global population is becoming aware of their capitalistic exploitation and starting to demand equality.

COMMUNISM: is a social structure where a government owns all the means by which a country survives rather than wealthy private individuals. The working-class individuals of this social structure are not allowed any private ownership of survival necessities placing their fate in full control of whoever runs the government. A communistic government does not require the approval or representation of the people and maybe completely totalitarian with an absolute disregard for the suffering and death of its population. Once the ruling class communists become corrupted by power and greed they predictably become unable to control their predatory instincts. This social structure would closely resemble fascism in the respect that all political opposition and cultural diversity is forcibly suppressed or eliminated.

Some form of national or patriotic subjective reality may be induced among the population to help reduce the need for more costly government correction techniques to maintain the efficient exploitation of the working-class resource. Inducing a religious subjective reality would not be advisable within a communistic social structure unless it was a single religion sharing the exact same nationalistic objectives. Allowing for hope and the possibility of salvation would only distract the workforce from their labor objectives and may initiate a revolutionary uprising. This would be an example of bad management of the working-class resource by their ruling class elite top predators.

SOCIALISM: is a social structure like Communism, in the respect that it also places the ownership of industries in the control of a government rather than wealthy private individuals like Capitalism. The real question with Socialism, Communism, Capitalism or any social structure becomes, who gets to control the government. Both Communism and Capitalism fail at controlling their government well enough to provide social equality for their people, but do excel at their ability to exploit their working-class resource. As both of these societies function within our overall predatory social structure the exploitation of the working-class resource would be expected.

The social structures of Communism and Capitalism remind me of Goldilocks comparing extremes until she found a compromise between the two. Some of the aspects of Socialism may provide that compromise and be worth considering for a predator free society. For example, Socialism allows for the production and distribution of goods and services to be directly proportional to the economic demands and human needs of its working-class population. Instead of being driven by greed and predatory dominance as allowed for under Capitalism and Communism.

It's interesting that the efficiency of this system to provide products and service on demand to meet the needs of the community seemed so obvious it was already part of my proposed predator free social structure before I knew its association with Socialism. Communism, Fascism and Socialism were all names I remember being conditioned to have a negative emotional response with and were clearly the anti-American enemy of Capitalism. I needed to break my national subjective reality to objectively consider if all of these social structures should be considered the same, and if any of them have redeeming qualities. Of these three social structures it seems Communism can be the most oppressive to its people where fascism could create the illusion of a rational civilized society for those of the correct race and national spirit. Socialism on the other hand allows for a variety of structural variations some of which offer greater opportunities for equality and prosperity of the working-class resource.

Even the United States, as the global champion of Capitalism, has incorporated and recognizes Socialism as the most efficient system for providing human rights and social equality for its citizens. I guess our democracy does work sometimes to make our predatory exploitation more acceptable despite the control our ruling class top predators have over our government. This battle still goes on today, to determine whether we will allow our elite capitalists to hoard the wealth created by the American working-class resource or to allow socialistic programs like Social Security and Medicare reduce the suffering and death of our people. Only in a predatory social structure would this still be a topic for debate.

I suppose we should be thankful there is even a debate and ruling class capitalists have not been successful yet at eliminating or privatizing all socialistic programs giving them more control and domination over us working-class prey. If they could just prevent our education and more people from becoming aware of our capitalistic exploitation they could retain control of government for years even generations. And when trying to prevent our intellectual enlightenment began to fail, they started focusing on subverting our democracy with voter suppression techniques and making it legal for the wealthy elite to have greater control over our political system, government and laws. The top predators of Capitalism know our education and democracy will play a key role in ending our predatory social structure. They will identify themselves with their actions by trying to prevent the intellectual evolutionary development of our people and our ability to choose a better future for our species.

After the discovery process to find the root cause or primary factor responsible for the most preventable suffering and death throughout our evolutionary development was complete, it became self-evident a new social economic structure would be needed to replace Capitalism. Designing a new predator free social structure will provide challenges and opportunities. One challenge will be to create a system flexible enough to allow for a peaceful evolutionary transition from the predatory social structures of our past and present to the predator free societies of our future. Both social structures must have a symbiotic relationship that is mutually beneficial during the transition. One of the greatest opportunities in designing a new predator free society is we can use the latest in technologies, evolutionary knowledge and creative skills to offer better solutions.

They'll be no need to incorporate planned obsolescence or socially engineer transportation and housing systems to waste over half our energy to increase profits for top predators. The wealth generated by the citizens of a predator free society will be directly reinvested back into the community to accomplish our mission objectives without any ruling class top predators deciding how much we the people get to keep. The hundreds of billions of dollars lost annually to capitalistic corruption and predatory greed will eventually be used to accelerate and expand a network of predator free communities relieving the suffering and death of millions of our least fortunate citizens.

One major challenge is to design an advanced technical infrastructure self-sufficient enough to remove we the people's dependency upon the top predators for any of our basic survival necessities. Once this management tool to manipulate the working-class resource is eliminated the ruling class elite will lose their predatory power and control over our future, effectively breaking the second chain of Capitalism. Another challenge is to create a social and technical infrastructure capable of not only sustainability but also self-replication of the community network. The predator free society must also have a new motivational objective to replace our predatory competition for survival. This new motivational paradigm will focus on cooperation with others to expand the network of smart home community infrastructures allowing more people to make the transition to a predator free society and have an opportunity to experience the true freedom and prosperity our intellectual evolutionary development has finally provided.

One major opportunity in designing a new predator free society is that we the people can choose what aspects of the known social structures we like and may want to incorporate and which ones must be rejected as systems for exploitation. Because most of the predatory social structures of our past were specifically designed for efficient exploitation of the working-class resource and to increase the wealth and power of its ruling class elite there are few moral or administrative qualities worth incorporating into an advanced predator free society. Of all the advanced social structures I have objectively considered, only Socialism has the flexibility capable of providing a level of equality and prosperity necessary to achieve a predator free society.

It seems Einstein and other progressive thinkers in our past had also come to this conclusion, but our species collective intellectual evolutionary development had not reached a point where this was possible. However, things are different now and the working-class people of the world are not only becoming aware of our predatory social structures, but they're starting to demand their equality and an end to our systematic exploitation under Capitalism. Again, once the working-class people of the world make this collective decision to end our predatory existence, there will be nothing the top predators can do to stop our evolutionary transition. Our species quest for true freedom and universal prosperity will become a reality.

12. A win-win and win solution for the people

What are the national and economic advantages of moving an average four-person family from capitalistic poverty and forced predatory competition into the environmental conditions of a predator free social structure? Even from a capitalistic point of view to make a one-time investment of approximately $250,000 worth of predator free infrastructure for each four to six person family unit would provide the ultimate return if our national objective were to create the healthiest, happiest and most productive population in the world. The investment versus return would seem to be unparalleled win considering the exponential growth and self-replicating nature of the predator free social system. Each new family can use their skills to help expand the network of Automated Community Infrastructures allowing even more people to end their capitalistic competition for survival. As this investment multiplies it would naturally start a chain of events resulting in the first known species to break the control of their hardwired predatory survival instincts. How is that for a return on an investment? What's that worth?

As of January 2013 the US population is just over 315 million. Out of that population just over 48 million of us are living in poverty. Even though poverty in the United States is like living in royalty when compared to many other countries, it should not be considered a reason to accept our capitalistic exploitation or considered an act of kindness used to induce a collective Stockholm syndrome. Moving a family living in capitalistic poverty to a predator free infrastructure provides a win-win and win solution for most of our social economic problems and social dysfunctions by correcting them at their source.

The first win is for our current predatory social structure and national budget by taking a family unit with a negative revenue flow and little opportunities for future prosperity and giving them the environmental conditions necessary to become a highly efficient and productive member of a predator free society. After some orientation time new predator free family members will be maintaining, designing and creating automated production systems to provide a specific infrastructure necessity not only for the community members but many products will also be sold to the general public.

It will be a lot like running a family business at home with a connected production studio/storefront and garden domes functioning like a living grocery store. But instead of competing against others for their capitalistic survival, the entire social and technical infrastructure of a predator free society is designed to help people achieve their greatest potential. Many of the TFT (True Freedom Technologies) products produced by family members will have technically advanced utility value, artistic appeal and even entertainment qualities. These products will be offered for sale to the general public to enhance their quality of life and provide a revenue source for an expanding predator free community network.

The second win is for the families living in capitalistic poverty, they will see immediate relief from their exploitation and the stress of predatory competition. All of the physical and mental degradation that is inherent in forced competitions for survival will begin to heal in environmental conditions where cooperation and compassion for others becomes the new social paradigm. Living under the control of a subjective reality can provide top predators a way to exploit their working class prey for generations. However, living in a predator free society while developing an objective reality will remove the need and desire for all forms of predatory behavior for profit or social status. The technical solution of a predator free infrastructure is designed to provide these environmental conditions into our species future.

A new predator free family will be some of the first members of our species to deliberately break our hardwired predatory instincts and subjective realities allowing better intellectual control over our decisions and actions. They will be some of the first people to achieve true freedom from our predatory past and become pioneers as we make one of the most wondrous transitions in the intellectual evolutionary development of our species. I am looking forward to becoming one of those pioneers and having the opportunity to offer social and technical solutions for the most efficient and peaceful transition to a predator free society.

The third win is for the predator free society itself, because every new family unit increases the community's ability to expand its network infrastructure and it adds to our creative diversity and collective intelligence. And with the environmental conditions of a social structure that emphasizes the pursuit of knowledge and technology to be used for the benefit of all people, just imagine what we could accomplish. Even in our wildest imaginations we may not be able to comprehend the future opportunities that will be possible once our intellectual evolutionary development is accelerated by the predator free environmental conditions.

It's true that top predators of Capitalism will not be able to continue their predatory domination and systematic exploitation of their working class resource but that small inconvenience for the very few will allow an evolutionary leap for our entire species. I feel many successful capitalists are uncomfortable being forced to compete in a predatory social structure that makes them compromise their ethical and moral values just to stay ahead of the competition. It may be part of our capitalistic conditioning, but we should not be using our intelligence as a predatory tool to exploit entire populations for our individual accumulation of wealth and power.

The ultimate win would be for the evolutionary development of our entire species. To finally break the evolutionary barrier between a life form still following there hardwired instincts for predatory domination, to an enlighten species capable of using factual knowledge and rational thought to control their actions and guide their future. Once we turn that evolutionary corner and experience the true freedom and prosperity of a predator free social structure, we'll only look back to wonder, what took us so long.

Part 3 - Our predatory past versus our predator free future

1. Security

There are six social economic areas that will show high levels of improvement once the burden of predatory competition is removed as a survival necessity. The subject of security is the best place to start because it deals with more immediate threats to our survival and with out it the other five areas for improvement would be meaningless. From the most primitive predatory social structures to the most intellectually challenging capitalistic competitions for global domination, our primary imperative is security or more to the point staying alive during our pursuit of happiness. More than any other survival necessity, our security requires a secure and dependable shelter.

Of course we still need clean water, nutritious food, etc. but without a secure base of operations and a way to know what we create will last our social behavior starts to resemble that of our hunter-gatherer ancestors. Like going from job to job and house to house as the waterholes and food resources dry up and we need to look for the next capitalistic corporation to sustain our existence.

When it comes to security there are two primary levels to consider. Our personal and more immediate security deals with things like getting to work or the grocery stores without being concerned about crime or predatory attacks by some of our more desperate American competitors. Or knowing our children will be safe walking back and forth from their homes and public schools. Or even knowing our families will be safe in our homes from natural disasters that frequently destroy so many lives and cost billions of dollars in personal property and national infrastructure damage.

Then there is our national and world security dealing with our war industries and their need to make profits over allowing peace. And there is our global climate change that has the very real possibility of initiating a mass extinction event for our species making all other matters of discussion irrelevant. We don't want to get caught carefully arranging the deck chairs on the Titanic without taking the time to look up and see the icebergs in our path. Whether it be icebergs, meteors or global climate change brought on by the youthful indiscretions of a developing intellectual species, the sooner we look up and see what's coming the better our chances will be at avoiding an accelerated extinction event.

Climate change is not only a threat to our national security but it also threatens the evolutionary development of every species on this planet. When scientific theory is repeatedly validated by observation it becomes an accepted fact among individuals functioning with an objective reality to form their decisions. Attempts to induce a subjective reality where climate change is not real will lose their effectiveness, as more lives and infrastructure is lost from increased storm activity, rising sea levels, wildfires and drought. The increased suffering and death of the working-class population in combination with an accelerated interest in factual knowledge about this subject will break the control of this subjective reality allowing valid decisions to be made and more effective solutions to be found.

We should not allow more lives and infrastructure to be lost denying climate change and the destructive force of Mother Nature. Mother nature always reminded me of the big bad wolf that huffs and puffs, and blows whole communities away. Lucky for us we are like the little pigs from the future building base isolated reinforced concrete infrastructures safely tucked away under the ground where even the big bad wolf would not threaten the structural integrity of our homes, or even prevent community activities. Although I'm afraid he'll continue to find many surface structures made of sticks and brick to blow away and crumble to the ground.

To use national resources rebuilding infrastructure in the path of certain destruction creates a system of planned obsolescence. Having a national infrastructure strategy that intentionally repeats the cycle of destruction and creation by rebuilding homes and businesses in the path of certain natural disaster, defines the condition of insanity. At some point we're going to have to accept the loss of land and infrastructure from rising sea levels and increased natural disaster events. Building new homes and businesses below or anywhere near sea level is to not learn from our mistakes. And to allow the cycle of destruction to continue would indicate some combination of incompetence, insanity or corruption at the highest levels. Natural disasters may be a good way to unite and distract us working class people from the exploitation of our capitalistic social structure, but that doesn't help prevent us from losing more lives and property costing our nation billions of dollars in disaster relief.

We may have been able to stop polluting our atmosphere with the lead we put in our gasoline and reduce the hydro fluorocarbons known to eliminate our ozone in the atmosphere allowing ultraviolet radiation to destroy life on earth. However limiting our CO_2 emissions to help minimize adverse global climate changes, will be much more difficult. The top predators of Capitalism have invested too much money creating an infrastructure dependent upon fossil fuels and control of key government officials willing to allow the continued exploitation of the global working-class resource for profit. For the political assets of top predatory capitalists to suddenly care more about our future global climate conditions more than the millions of dollars they could receive next week is highly unlikely. I guess it's up to us little people to take control of our future.

It seems once again we cannot expect a universally beneficial solution to come from a social economic structure dominated by the top predators of Capitalism. The solution to climate change must start with we the people demanding that our preventable deaths and global security take priority over the top predators capitalistic desire for economic domination of the world. People living in countries with free speech must share the factual knowledge necessary to help others make an informed decision to first minimize and eventually reverse the damage done to our global environment.

Like with the transition to a predator free society, a critical mass of intellectual enlightenment will cause a tipping point where the exploitation and destruction of our global environment will not be considered socially acceptable anymore, not even for profit. Then we can use our democracies and strength in numbers to peacefully but resolutely request that all the symptoms of our predatory social structure come to their natural evolutionary end, helping to save our global environment and our descendants from extinction level events. I hope we can count on our ruling class leaders support after all it's their world too. And it's not like we have another planet to move to. Whole empires may rise and fall throughout our evolutionary development, but we only have one planet to screw up. Our species must quickly learn to live in peace or die in ignorance from our inability to intellectually evolve beyond our predatory instincts.

More than any other thing, our security relies on a dependable source of basic survival necessities like shelter, water, food etc. Knowing our survival necessities can be taken away at any time without notice because of a corporate decision to increase profits keeps millions of Americans in a stressful state of perpetual uncertainty about their future. This has become the accepted standard of life within our predatory social structure contributing to the high incidence of mental instability and suicides.

Removing our dependency upon top predators is one of the primary objectives of a predator free society and to prevent ruling class capitalists from using we the people as a resource for exploitation. This necessary process to achieving true freedom and an advanced level of security is referred to in this book as breaking the second chain of Capitalism.

Our current social structure leaves we the people extremely vulnerable to many avoidable security risks in order to maintain our efficient exploitation. The security vulnerabilities within our current social system and infrastructure that contribute to our preventable suffering and death fall into two primary categories consisting of natural and man-made disasters. All technical infrastructure designs capable of supporting a predator free society must not only break the second chain of Capitalism but also completely defeat or minimize the fatal and destructive effects of all the natural and man-made disasters we are currently vulnerable to. Most of the technical infrastructure advancements proposed in this book seem like obvious common sense improvements when greed and the need for capitalistic exploitation are removed from the equation and only what's best for we the people remains as an objective.

The notion of providing personal security to individuals in a predatory social structure is a lot like trying to make Capitalism fairer for us working-class prey. This is not to say that our level of capitalistic exploitation cannot be managed by ruling class top predators in such a way as to decrease or increase the suffering and death experienced by the working-class resource. However, to consider any relief in our managed exploitation, as an act of kindness, would be to fall under the control of a collective Stockholm syndrome with the potential desire to emotionally or even violently defend our ruling class oppressors.

Our level of security in an advanced predatory social economic structure like Capitalism is directly related to our ability to accumulate wealth and power. It's not like we all get our own personal Secret Service or access to stealth strike drones to eliminate potential threats like political or religious rivals... things could never get that bad... could they? Any notion or feeling of security among the working-class resource in a predatory society is likely part of our environmental or national conditioning to accept our induced subjective reality and believe that our current social structure is the best we can hope for.

Our hardwired instinct to attain security for ourselves and families, or perhaps more accurately secure shelter and survival necessities, provides another psychological manipulation tool that can be legitimately used on the working-class resource to increase profits. When we perceive our personal security to be threatened it triggers a subconscious and involuntary chain reaction, where our survival instinct of self-preservation produces a negative emotional response. This negative emotional response can then be associated with a person, race, ideology, religion, social structure or whatever helps the currently accepted subjective realities get the working-class resource to enthusiastically comply with their systematic exploitation.

We must admit from a strategic point of view, it was a very smart move to socially engineer a society to keep us working-class people highly dependent upon our ruling class elite top predators of Capitalism for our security and ability to provide basic survival necessities for our families. The best-educated top predators throughout our evolutionary development have realized the power this lever of social manipulation gives them and when used wisely can help keep the working-class prey blissfully unaware of their exploitation.

We must also recognize even though some individuals and countries will want to make the transition to a predator free society there will continue to be predatory attacks from others that must be defended against. If we concentrate our technical skills and resources more on defensive measures to secure our country's safety and human rights, as opposed to allowing top predators to make big profits on offensive weapons of war, our goal to promote a predator free society would be better served.

If our country can't lead by setting a good example, we don't deserve to be followed. Leading our species into this evolutionary transition will be a great honor and opportunity for any country. Or perhaps instead of any one country taking the lead, a unified and resolute multinational movement among freethinking individuals will begin predator free societies in all corners of the world. This would allow for the maximum acceleration of its self-replicating social system and network of community infrastructures.

I wonder, now that we the people have allowed our security to become dependent upon our ruling class capitalists lust for power and profit, what will we do to correct this mess? I'm hoping the majority of people that become aware of their exploitation will feel like me and want to end this phase of our evolutionary development. I'm looking forward to dedicating my creative skills to this task and all the technical challenges that lie ahead knowing the advanced level of security and peace of mind will help accelerate our transition to a predator free society.

2. Education

Our education is the most important of the six social economic areas that will show wondrous advancements once we the people are allowed to adapt to the environmental conditions of a predator free society. It can be difficult to express the magnitude of importance that education holds for the evolutionary development of our species. In the simplest terms, our education could mean the difference between the extinction of our species or breaking the control of our predatory instincts and subjective realities to create peaceful societies into the future.

These are the extremes of course but now that our species has developed the intelligence and technology to create either future why not provide our people with the highest quality of life possible. This shouldn't be a difficult decision to make. Is there something preventing the natural intellectual evolutionary development of our species from enjoying the true freedom and prosperity that our technology can provide right now? Could there be some invisible force so powerful it could control our evolutionary progress and the subsequent fate of most life on our planet? Yeah, and to control this force is to determine the destiny of our species.

With most subjects of importance that need to be understood well, it always seems to help to step back, and try to look at the big picture. Even this first step can be difficult as most of our intellectual energy is consumed and intentionally diverted to our daily routines of social competition and

United States education costs

Compared to 6 of the top 14 highest GDP producing countries with as good or better academic results

National wealth spent on education for one year

Per Citizen — In $Dollars   Total — In $Billions

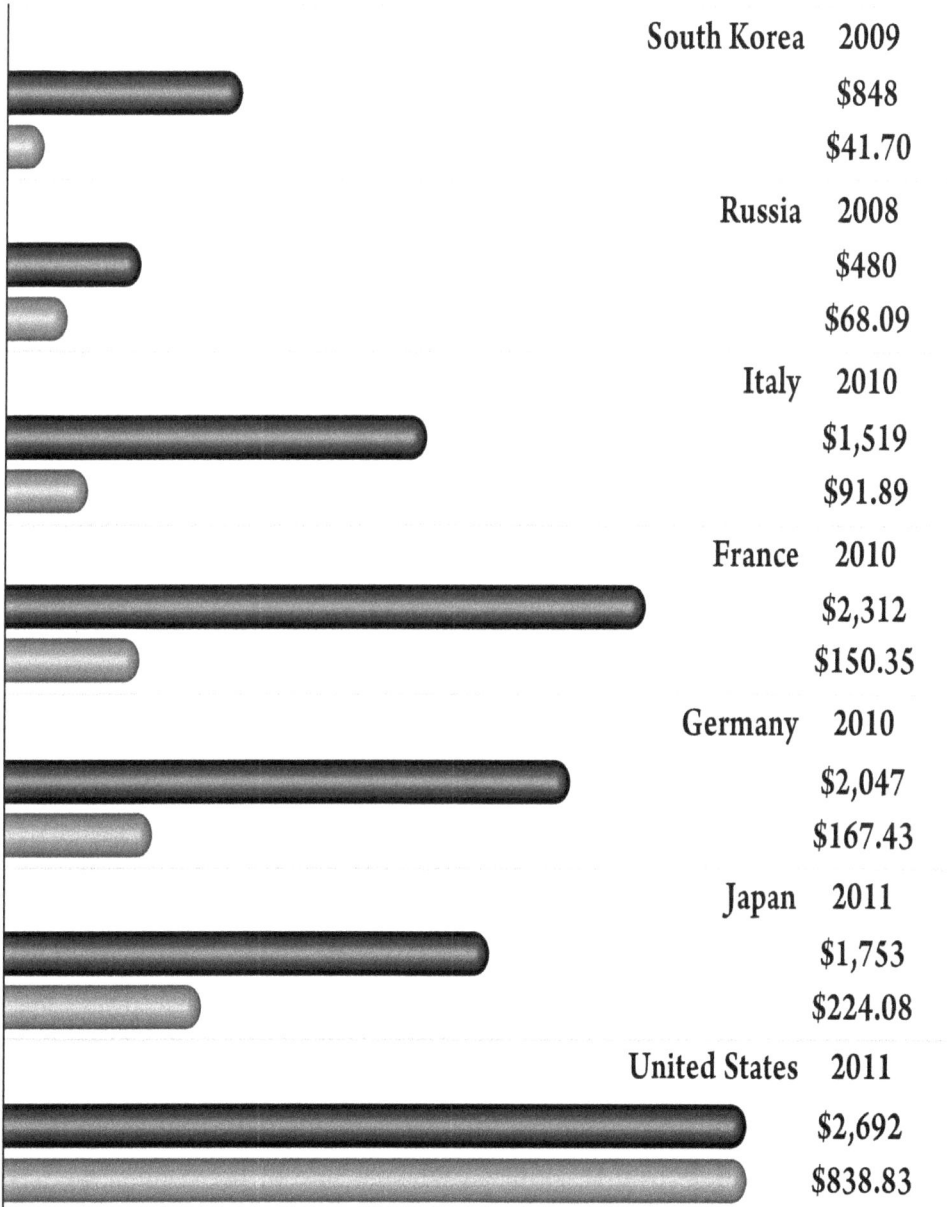

	Per Citizen	Total
South Korea 2009	$848	$41.70
Russia 2008	$480	$68.09
Italy 2010	$1,519	$91.89
France 2010	$2,312	$150.35
Germany 2010	$2,047	$167.43
Japan 2011	$1,753	$224.08
United States 2011	$2,692	$838.83

Source: The CIA World factbook, The World Bank, Prepared by True Freedom Technologies

capitalistic survival.   However, during the quiet moments of our lives when our minds are free, our knowledge and imagination can become one allowing glimpses into possible futures. It is then our ability to perceive the big picture becomes much clearer. Once that big picture becomes clearer to more people revealing a path to a predator free future. It will accelerate our evolutionary transition marking the beginning of a new and wondrous era for our species. At least this is what my glimpses into the future have shown me.

If education is the delivery truck, then factual knowledge and intellectual skills are the packages we hope to receive. One of the biggest problems surviving in a predatory social structure is we are expected to use our intelligence against one another as a competitive tool for survival. This accepted social behavior promotes all kinds of wildly imaginative forms of deception that gets packaged into some subjective reality and induced into an unsuspecting working class population as a technique for capitalistic exploitation. Our most trusted sources of knowledge or in some cases only means of education may not be providing us with factual information. I guess this has become less of a shocker to many people.

The level of deception in our society is so high and ubiquitous we've become desensitized to its social integration helping to increase our complacency about our overall capitalistic exploitation. The good news is our sources of factual knowledge that promote the formation of objective realities and rational thought, are starting to overpower all the organizations, institutions and individuals attempting to induce subjective beliefs as part of a predatory technique to extract wealth, labor and resources from we the people.

There is a quiet war being fought where the side that always loses is unaware of the conflict. This war is over the control of our intellectual evolutionary development, and whether we the people receive the level of education necessary to become aware of our capitalistic exploitation, is right in the middle of this conflict. On one side of the conflict we have ruling class top predators throughout government and the private sector that are fully aware of the concepts in this book. They understand the accelerated education of the working class people will break our subjective realities to serve Gods and governments, leading to the end of all forms of predatory exploitation.

Our current top predators strategy would be to delay our transition to a predator free society for as long as possible to increase profits and maintain a dominant social status. Among the better-educated top predators it must be known this is a war they cannot win in the long run. Holding back the intellectual evolutionary development of a species may even produce an undesirable rebound effect where a smoother transition would be preferred.

On the other side of this conflict we have ruling class leaders in government and many individuals throughout the private sector fighting to expand education for the American people as a human right and not a privilege for our more successful capitalistic competitors. Also on this side of the conflict are we the people, otherwise known as the American working class resource that deserve to have the best quality education in the world provided to us as a human right, especially when our tax dollars more than pay for the privilege.

Our education like many of the rights and privileges we pay for, as American citizens will be willingly forfeited by a percentage of our population under the control of subjective realities induced by the very top predators their condition trust implicitly. As mentioned throughout this book, these kinds of deceptions and various forms of psychological manipulation to exploit the working class resource would be expected in an advanced predatory social structure like free-market Capitalism. The real surprise isn't that it happens, it's that our intellectual evolutionary development as a species hasn't reached a level where we have already rejected our predatory social structure. I know it's easier to just fall in line and follow our environmental conditioning or give control of our lives to some primary character in a subjective storyline, but our people will continue to suffer and die until we learn this most critical of lessons for any developing intellectual species.

An education system capable of delivering factual knowledge and teaching technical skills without the need to induce subjective realities or the physical and emotional distractions of competitions for survival should be our ultimate goal. Like all the areas of our society that contribute to our preventable suffering and death, the greatest barriers to providing an effective education system are also symptoms of our predatory social structure that will be corrected at their source during our evolutionary transition.

When I first started considering ways to improve our education system, I thought the only acceptable solutions would need to provide capitalistic success for predatory competition. An in the box solution, for an in the box problem. As time went on I began to realize how futile this effort would be. When between observing the frustration of others and becoming aware of our evolutionary transition to a predator free society, it all started to feel like a distraction to treat the symptoms when we really needed to concentrate on eliminating the cause.

It is a strategic management technique used by top predators to redirect the working class people's emotional frustrations away from the cause of their exploitation and on to the symptoms of our predatory competition for survival. These diversionary techniques severely limit our ability to educate our young people and directly interfere with the natural intellectual evolutionary development of our species. This piece of the fact puzzle helped me clear up my big picture and broaden my perspective on life, while simultaneously increasing my problem-solving capabilities.

Without access to factual knowledge our intellectual survival trait cannot formulate effective predatory defense strategies leaving us completely vulnerable to induce subjective realities and all forms of capitalistic exploitation. The billions of dollars invested over decades to socially engineer our society for increasingly efficient means of capitalistic exploitation of the working class resource, would indicate this is no accident or honest mistake by our ruling class leaders. But instead, a well orchestrated strategy to limit our education and maintain predatory dominance. This strategy has been effective at keeping we the people unaware of our predatory exploitation and preventable suffering and death until the recent acceleration in our intellectual development.

Our sources of education are still replete with false knowledge attempting some form of predatory exploitation. However, our advanced communication technologies are starting to break down the barriers of intellectual isolation and conditioned intolerance for the racial and cultural differences in others. People all over the world are starting to realize were pretty much the same in all the ways that matter most. What truly separates us is the nature of our environmental conditioning or more accurately the specific subjective realities we were induced with throughout our lives that create the diversity in our cultural and religious beliefs. We must remove all forms of conditioned intolerance and intellectual competition for survival from our educational environments, thereby eliminating the biggest problem at its source before it is passed on to others and further damages our society with its corrupting influence.

In order for our current education system to be successful it must prepare our young adults for competition within our advanced predatory social structure. When I compare the education system within a predator free society with how Capitalism conditions our young adults to intellectually compete against one another for their survival, it seems like Dark Age mentality to me. It's no wonder we're having trouble making our education system work when our objective is to create more technically advanced predators to compete against one another for the capitalistic domination of the world. What could go wrong with a social construct like that? The best equality we can hope to receive from an education system under capitalistic control is a result where 50% of we the people are winners and the other 50% are losers of our social economic competition for survival. Sure there are different levels of survival for us to determine where the line between winners and losers would be, but is this really the game we want to keep playing? Isn't it time we changed the rules.

As the transition to a predator free society will create a paradigm shift in our social motivations, our entire concept and approach towards education will also undergo big changes. Just as we must currently prepare our young adults for capitalistic competition to ensure their individual survival, in a predator free society children will need to learn how to communicate and cooperate with one another to increase the survival potential of the entire community.

The technical infrastructure of a predator free society is designed to automate the production of most basic necessities for the community removing the need for predatory or capitalistic competition for survival. This would result in a social structure where 100% of the people are winners from birth, compared to Capitalism where over 90% of the people are designed to fail as working class prey, during their pursuit of happiness. Once we have created a predator free social structure where 100% of our citizens can feel secure about their basic survival necessities, we can concentrate on accelerating our intellectual evolutionary development as a unified species, and not well-dressed predators still following our hardwired instincts for social domination. We're better than that now.

In true capitalistic form all our basic survival necessities and requirements for social competition provide an opportunity to exploit the working class resource. Because increased knowledge and intellectual skills are the most important survival tools to use against other competitors, convincing us working-class prey to pay for our education and capitalistic training was an easy sell. After all it is true that competitors with multi-thousand dollar degrees and associated debt from well-known universities get the best jobs, social status and survival luxuries.

Even among lesser competitions in life we expect to pay top dollar for the latest technologies, anything that can give us an edge and increase our chances of winning the game. Of course we're going to want every advantage while competing in the most complex game ever played and be willing to give up our wealth for the chance our children will have more capitalistic success than we did and be able to afford a higher quality American dream.

If our future American working class resource, otherwise known as our sons and daughters, were being unnecessarily burdened with over $1 trillion in tuition debt before entering our free-market capitalistic competition for survival, then some form of systematic exploitation must be suspected. Then when we Americans learn our state and federal legislators have pushed up the student loan interest rate to 6.8% for our kids or 7.9% for us parents, we begin to ask more questions. And then when we finally find out our ruling class top predators have such a strong control of our government, they take loans from our federal tax dollars at the interest rates of 0.75%, the puzzle pieces begin to fall in place and the big picture gets clearer. It is at this point that our subjective beliefs begin to lose their control and the reality of our capitalistic exploitation begins to sink in.

Over years of objective observation an individual may even begin to wonder how these levels of blatant exploitation did not already lead to the intellectual enlightenment of a large enough majority of the population to end our predatory social structure. Or at least get us a lot closer to that goal than we are now.

It's nice to know that even within an advanced predatory social structure like Capitalism there are a growing number of leaders in government determined to minimize our exploitation as working class prey. And to help prevent our ruling class top predators from having greater management control over our freedoms and future prosperity. My new favorite senator Elizabeth Warren from Massachusetts decided to make a stand for the young people in our country conforming to our social standard of acquiring large educational debt.

Like peeling back the stranglehold top predators have on the throat of government one finger at a time, this champion for we the people had the audacity to present a bill suggesting that the interest rate on federal loans should be the same for students as it is for our elite financial institutions. On one hand we have the future leaders of our country being exploited even before they enter our capitalistic workforce. And on the other hand we have the same financial institutions that helped crash our economy, create the great recession and then they got billions of our dollars taxpayers wealth, while continuing to hand out multimillion dollar bonuses. All Americans need to be educated how a capitalistic government works to make an informed decision to end this exploitation process.

That's the beauty of having capitalistic control of a government where the top predators can legitimately exploit trillions of dollars from their working class resource while limiting their public education and the realization of their systematic exploitation. It's no wonder this lever of social manipulation has been so effective at keeping us little people accepting our patriotic subjective realities. Like the notion of shared sacrifice and all Americans working together for a common goal or even that most of our ruling class leaders care more about we the people than the capitalistic opportunities their positions of power and influence will allow them.

At some point you may begin to wonder how could a country of, by and for the people become so corrupt we can't even borrow back our own money at the same interest rate given to the elite top predators. I suppose if I were an evil ruling class capitalistic mastermind of social engineering I would be quite satisfied with my creation knowing my long-term investments paid off so well. However, being one of the little people I have a different perspective.

Sometime after I learned the power of education, but before my son was born, I took an interest in early childhood education and developmental psychology. I wanted to learn the mystery behind knowledge and intelligence, where did they come from, why do some people seem to have more of them than others and perhaps most importantly, are they things you must be born with or do we acquire them during our lives. To truly understand I first needed to know the difference between knowledge and intelligence.

If using our knowledge and intelligence to solve a problem was like building a house. Our knowledge would be the stacks of materials ready to use, and our intelligence would be the best way to use those assets to create a more secure home. If we were cooking a gourmet meal our knowledge would be like all the ingredients and our intelligence is how to turn those raw materials into a culinary masterpiece. When our sources of knowledge are corrupted by the overwhelming influence of our predatory social structure, it would be similar to building a house from rotten wood or baking a cake with moldy flour. Even worse when this corrupt knowledge becomes socially legitimized and culturally accepted as factually real, we can live out our entire lives unaware our decisions and actions are being manipulated for profit.

If we rule out our genetic memory, that produces reactionary behavioral traits to certain environmental conditions to be an act of intelligence or a source of knowledge, we can safely assume that both are acquired after conception. Even though our knowledge is definitely acquired after birth our intelligence or ability to use that information in creative and constructive ways may be more or less enhanced by our genetic makeup. This underscores the importance of eliminating industrial environmental contaminations known to produce genetic disorders depriving countless children of the equal opportunity they deserve to acquire the knowledge and intelligence they will need to compete for their capitalistic survival. If top predators were running a capitalistic corporation that created baby brains as a product for profit, I think their quality control would be much better than if they considered our children a resource for future exploitation.

There are always exceptions within our biological development that seem to enhance human creativity and the desire to acquire more intellectual skills. However, without knowledge even these gifted individuals would have never had the opportunity to use their intelligence to advance the evolutionary development of our species. Just imagine how many potential Archimedes, Galileo's or Einstein's all over the world have been deprived of the knowledge they needed to help advance the collective intellectual development of our species or reduce the suffering and death among our people.

Over the last couple thousand years of our evolving predatory social structures, many of these gifted individuals may have been killed for the money in their pockets or the clothes on their backs. Or perhaps they died in some petty war before they had a chance to acquire the knowledge they would have later used to save thousands even millions of lives. Now we will never know what might have been. The best we can do now is to learn from our mistakes and make the necessary corrections to our intellectual evolutionary development, defeating this social dysfunction at its source.

I would like to fast forward beyond the many years of predatory devastation for our species, to a time when our true freedom and prosperity within a predator free society has already been established. In a predator free social structure we can simply define our educational objectives without consideration for profit or capitalistic success. For example, we could provide the knowledge and intellectual skills necessary to form objective realities and break the predatory conditioning of subjective beliefs. Or say for instance we want to create a society where 100% of the functioning adult population has a level of knowledge and intellectual skills capable of designing and prototyping advanced automated technologies and products. We can do that.

They say the best place to start is at the beginning. So we will start at the beginning of a human life. It seems our overall educational objectives are to accelerate the personal intellectual development of our children in the areas of technology, the arts and social enlightenment. Even though most of these advanced educational goals will naturally manifest as a result of adapting to the environmental conditions of a predator free social structure, the first logical step is a full in-depth analysis of the system to improve.

If we look at things from the perspective of a design engineer, a preliminary analysis would suggest we have a biological subsystem (our brains) contained with in a larger mobile support system (our bodies). It seems one of our biggest problems so far is not realizing we're trying to improve a biological subsystem without truly considering if it's support system has the necessary environmental conditions to function at optimal capacity. It's like clipping a bird's wing feathers knowing it must fly to survive. We should take care of the obvious stuff first. This is another symptom of the root cause and example how we are creating the problems we should be correcting.

We need to expand our perspective to encompass the entire support system and its environmental conditions, or in other words stand back and look at the big picture. Its no wonder were having so much trouble trying to improve the efficiency of an integrated biological subsystem, when the primary support system must suffer the environmental conditions and detrimental effects of our predatory social structure. It's all becoming much clearer to me now, I only hope these concepts make sense to other people too. It's a learning process... but then that's what makes our evolutionary journey through life so interesting.

Beyond the inherent advantages the environmental conditions a predator free society will have on accelerating the learning process, there are many other areas of technology to explore specifically to increase our capacity to assimilate knowledge and develop advanced creative skills. Somewhere during my parental research I learned about a technique in developmental psychology that was known to increase the neural network of a child's brain if used primarily between birth and one year of age, and then losing its effectiveness beyond that point. Lucky for me I had a ready and willing test subject with a little brain just raring to go. Isn't that one of the best things about being a parent, we can perform brain-altering experiments on your children. Don't worry he turned out fine accept for that third ear on his neck. I probably shouldn't have tried genetic manipulations, but the good news is he has excellent hearing now.

After hearing about this technique and understanding what seemed to be an effective process to increase the neural network of a baby's brain during critical stages of their development. I figured why not give it a try, and I think my son gave me a thumbs-up, although it's a little hard to tell with newborns. We agreed to tell his mom later, if things turned out well. After all what more could a parent do to prepare their child for intellectual competition within a predatory social structure, than to provide them with the highest level of knowledge and creative skills possible.

As it turns out this technique is something parents might do inadvertently while they're playing with their babies. However, without knowing the actual process the beneficial effects cannot be maximized. It should also be known that an increased neural network does not necessarily guarantee more advanced intellectual skills and creativity although, it does offer a greater capacity for these things. Other environmental conditions throughout their life's can greatly influence whether that neural network continues to grow at a decelerated rate or diminishes from lack of use. The use it or lose it concept seems to be in play here.

This technique to increase the neural network and intellectual capacity of a developing child's brain is so effective because it manipulates and enhances our natural hardwired survival traits to adapt to whatever environmental conditions we are born into. For example if a baby from our time were to be born in the future he or she would naturally adapt to the advanced technologies and philosophical beliefs of a predator free society, where if that same baby were to be born in the past they would adapt to even more primitive forms predatory conflicts than we have today.

Now that we can see and understand the learning curve for the intellectual evolutionary development of our species, let's take control of that process and accelerate our transition. We can do this and our education is the key, because without becoming intellectually aware that a problem exists, there's nothing to fix and our predatory social structure would continue indefinitely. But we're not going to let that happen.

There are three primary components to this neural network expansion technique; the first one utilizes our visual and audio knowledge inputs to the brain, otherwise known as our baby's eyes and ears.

The second component functions like knowledge glue helping to better imprint our memory engrams with information that can be used later by our intellectual problem-solving skills. The third component may have provided the inspiration for one of the primary concepts in this book, and it simply suggests that you provide your developing baby's brain with intellectually stimulating environmental conditions. The first and second component of this technique are used during active conditioning or interactive lessons and the third component is more for their rest time when mom and dad are away and their baby is quietly taking in their environmental conditions while making neural connections in their brains.

Even before clear visual and audio recognition is possible a baby's brain will start to make neural associations with the sounds they are hearing and the emotions they are feeling. Once their vision clears up and they can recognize faces, patterns and shapes our baby's brains will be ready for the neural network expansion process, otherwise known as their first lesson. This technique only requires the simplest of tools because at this stage of their development less can be more. Simple black-and-white flashcards with bold numbers and letters on the front and on the back is a color image like an apple for the letter A. or a boat for the letter B. etc.

The flashcards are like the props for the lesson but the parent is the true performer that makes the magic happen. Without any other visual or audio distractions in the room a single parent can show black-and-white flashcards while reciting the number or letter satisfying the first component for this technique by providing direct audiovisual input to the baby's brain. It may not look like there's a lot going on but your baby's brain is creating neural associations between what they hear and what they see, and by the time they can speak, they may already have something to say.

The second component of this technique is provided by the parent's performance in presenting the black-and-white flashcards like they are the most exciting and interesting things they have ever seen. It was found that our memory engrams are better imprint when accompanied by an emotional response, which makes sense from an evolutionary perspective.

Your baby's attention should shift back and forth between your face of excitement and the black-and-white flashcard.   Keep your audio reinforcement as simple and clean as the black-and-white flashcard. They shouldn't hear any other recognizable words to confuse the association with that letter or number.

It's also important to enunciate the word clearly and correctly to build a more accurate recognition and association with that letter or number. When a baby sees their parent excited it triggers their developing brain to respond as if this is something important they need to remember to increase their chances of survival. Perhaps the neural network expansion process is a result of that evolutionary need to survive. The lesson durations will be pretty short at first getting longer as the months go by. But as soon as your performance to make black-and-white flashcards seem exciting loses your baby's attention, the lesson is over. This component of the technique gives parents a chance to work on their theatrical skills and may provide some memorable moments to look back on. Get your cameras ready.

Think of your baby's lessons like workouts at the gym. You may work your muscles hard for a short time, but it's all the off time with good nourishment and rest when they really grow.   Providing intellectually stimulating environmental conditions seems like an obvious technique if you want to create a smarter child or a population of more intelligent people. Yet many children even in the most powerful countries in the world go without adequate amounts of this component. At first your baby's educational décor should be simple, bold and concise like their visual audio lessons. Larger black-and-white letters and numbers around the room to gaze at while they're falling asleep or waking up will help reinforce what they have learned during their lessons.

As our baby's brains grow and their ability to comprehend more complex information increases, the intellectual environmental conditions must stay a few steps ahead of their current level of development. Like how the environmental conditions of lifting more weight at the gym makes our muscles bigger. It tricks our developing brains into thinking we need to be smarter in order to survive more efficiently. It would be a natural biological manifestation while adapting to intellectually stimulating environmental conditions. In other words our brains naturally want to develop much higher levels of intelligence if given the basic requirements to do so.

Even though I only had one test subject to experiment on and a larger control group would be necessary to make any scientific conclusions. Our son's kindergarten teacher came to us one day to tell us how intellectually advanced our son was and that he should be tested for a special program set up for gifted children. Of course it's natural for all parents to feel their children are brilliant, but to have their kindergarten teacher point it out and recommend them for a special class was pretty gratifying. It was starting to look like this technique was effective. He ended up being accepted and continued these classes into high school.

My son was eventually tested and found to be in the top 3% of all children in Washington State, prompting a letter suggesting he take a different test to accurately assess his academic skill level. We even got an offer from John Hopkins University to enter him in a special genius program where other kids like him from around the country could learn together. Sadly our economic status did not allow us to move across the United States and take advantage of this generous offer. Knowing how the smallest of things can make such a big difference in a person's intellectual development, I sometimes wonder how something this profound could have altered the course of our lives. Our future leaders neural networks need all the help they can get, because we will have some pretty interesting challenges ahead in creating the first technically advanced predator free society for our children.

If we again consider solving our educational challenges from the logical perspective of an engineer, we may realize that our biological subsystem brains have evolved the natural ability to acquire and retain large amounts of knowledge, much like a computer. An individual that has been deprived of factual knowledge and intellectual stimulation is like a computer without any software, they both have amazing potential that could be realized if only given the chance. It would be impossible to calculate the amount of intellectual breakthroughs and humanitarian achievements our species would have made if providing an education and prosperity to we the people were as much of a national priority as the more efficient exploitation of the American working class resource.

The more extensive our knowledge base is the better chance our intellectual survival trait will have at creating the best solutions. I can understand how our knowledge and intelligence work together to perform problem-solving skills, but where does creativity and imagination come from. Why do some people seem to have more of them than others and is it something that can be learned and developed like an intellectual skill? I had a hard time acquiring knowledge growing up because of some dyslexic problem limiting my ability to develop intellectual skill, but I was artistically creative and did have a wild imagination so you can imagine the amount of satisfaction I felt when I heard this quote from Albert Einstein when he stated "Imagination is more important than knowledge. For knowledge is limited, whereas imagination embraces the entire world, stimulating progress, giving birth to evolution. It is, strictly speaking, a real factor in scientific research".

Our imaginations are only limited by the boundaries of our biology and knowledge of what may exist. For example we may try to imagine what lies beyond the limits of our known universe but on an evolutionary scale it would be similar to a whale imagining what swimming in space would be like. Our imagination seems to be a factor of our developing intelligence forming abstract connections based on our accumulated knowledge. We know that accumulated knowledge and intellectual skills can be developed by anyone but what causes those abstract connections to form flashes of inspiration and those proverbial Eureka moments? Still working on that, but I do know a way to severely limit an individual's or apopulation's ability to formulate Eureka moments, and with that knowledge perhaps we can work backwards to find an answer.

I would consider our collaboration of knowledge and intelligence culminating in a Eureka moment to be one of our higher cognitive brain functions. Considering this to be true, these higher cognitive functions can be severely limited by manipulating the environmental conditions of the subject. Stressful environmental conditions like predatory competitions for survival altar our brain chemistry in such a way as to bring out our primitive hardwired instincts overriding our intellectual survival trait's ability for rational thought, creative imagination or any other higher cognitive functions.

An objective consideration of the factual knowledge would suggest if we find an environmental condition that is known to have severe detrimental effects on our higher cognitive functions limiting our ability for creative out-of-the-box thinking and imaginary visions for the future. To limit and eventually reverse this process should have the opposite effect. This environmental condition may not be as easy to recognize or eliminate as lead paint contamination but its detrimental effects on the intellectual development of our species is immensely more profound.

A logical conclusion would seem to be once the environmental conditions that force our brain chemistry into more primitive states of intellectual evolution are eliminated by the transition to a predator free society. Not only will increased knowledge and intelligence be a natural manifestation but also our imaginations will be set free to extend far beyond the boundaries of our current social reality.

It makes sense that the greater the evolutionary leap is in our social structure the more difficult it will be to imagine for the majority of our population. However, the boundary line and transition between our predatory past and predator free future is no ordinary leap in our intellectual evolutionary development. After all this is the first time an intellectual species has reached a level of social development and intellectual enlightenment capable of sustaining a technically advanced predator free society. So it's no wonder why it may take a little time to get used to and imagine what life would be like in those new environmental conditions.

There are three primary ways to solve this problem and help others find the factual knowledge necessary to form an objective opinion about ending our predatory social structure. And help all people to imagine the quality and structure of life within a predator free society. This book should serve as an introduction to the predator free philosophy and proposed technical solutions. The next phase will aid the imagination by offering 3-D models, video presentations and philosophical explanations on the TFT (True Freedom Technologies) website. These two information sources will help fill in the missing pieces of your fact puzzle, so we the people can stand back and get a better view of the big picture. The last phase will both astonish and inspire the imagination of all that tour or visit the first fully functional, technically advanced, Automated Community Infrastructure.

If we truly wanted to create a society of intellectually advanced and socially enlightened individuals we could simply make it a national objective to use currently available technologies and resources to accomplish that task. However, if the objective of our ruling class leaders that manage our predatory social structure was to maintain a working-class resource with a level of intellectual skills just high enough to perform their labor tasks, but not quite enough to become aware of their systematic exploitation, then they would continue to defund our public education system. Allowing our ruling class top predators of Capitalism to control this process is the number one barrier to educating all of our people around the world. And more to the point it is preventing our natural intellectual evolutionary development to a predator free society.

The solution is to take the control of this process away from the top predators by breaking both chains of Capitalism allowing we the people to determine the best way to accelerate our intellectual development. Once our bodies and minds are free from the predatory competition for survival that has dominated our species development since the beginning of our existence, the whole concept of education will make an evolutionary transition as our social motivations change from hostile conflicts to peaceful collaborations, from individual greed and the pursuit of excessive wealth to compassion for others and a desire to support the entire community as a whole.

3. Healthcare

Having a healthy body and mind is not only necessary to maximize our intellectual potential but it is the foundation for everything we do in life. Living without the security of dependable basic survival necessities and the healthcare needed to keep our bodies and minds functioning correctly, are the two areas that have the greatest potential for improvement. And they also provide the most efficient levers of power for top predators to manipulate and manage us working class prey.

Consider for a moment our healthcare crisis through the eyes of a ruling class top predator of Capitalism with the primary objective of exploiting the working class resource to extract the maximum amount of profit. They would know from their class in predatory strategies for capitalistic masterminds that the wealthiest working class resource on this planet has a large baby boomer population with an increasing demand for medical services and products.

They will have also learned this increased demand to buy medical services and products will be magnified many times by our predatory social standards that value excessive profits for the wealthy few over the health and prosperity of our entire nation. Our top predators will also know the psychology of an aging population willing to spend the last of their life savings to enjoy the American dream for as long as they can afford it.

One of the most important considerations for ruling class top predators when managing their working class resource, is to determine what level of capitalistic exploitation a population under their control will tolerate before breaking their subjective realities and demanding an end to their systematic oppression. Remember the goal of this capitalistic competition is to acquire the largest percentage of the immense tax revenues extracted from we the people specifically allocated to create an adequate health care system to supply our country's needs.

There are several social economic indicators well known to top predators that help determine the psychological temperament of the public. Or in other words what level of suffering and death the American working class resource will tolerate, so they may adjust their levers of power keeping our exploitation at acceptable levels. This Goldilocks zone is the most difficult management skill our ruling class top predators needed to master throughout our evolutionary development.

The top predators carefully consider the number of American citizens that become aware of these social indicators because their ability to deceive and dominate the public depends upon a large percentage of our population not realizing they're being exploited. It is the smaller percentage of our population that is aware of these social indicators and their ability to disrupt the flow of wealth from the working class many to the ruling class few that concern the top predators most. One known indicator that can be used to determine our willingness to accept our legitimized social exploitation is that around 45,000 American citizens die from lack of healthcare every year even more than the annual 42,000 deaths from auto accidents in our country.

To help put this in perspective it would be equivalent to around 90 fully loaded jumbo jets crashing or 15 - 9/11 terrorist attacks every year. You may wonder, if the same number of innocent American lives were lost in each event, what would make one of them a horrible tragedy demanding immediate action and the reallocation of national wealth to correct while the other event is allowed to continue ever year like an accepted function of our capitalistic society. I wanted to believe our country valued every American's life equally without preference for their economic status, genetic origins or ethnic backgrounds. However, an objective comparison of these tragic events has helped to bring my big picture into better focus. Revealing our healthcare crisis to be one of many preventable symptoms of our predatory social structure, that will be corrected at the source as we make our evolutionary transition to a predator free society.

To allow tens of thousands of our least fortunate American citizens unable to adequately compete for their capitalistic survival die every year from lack of health care is bad enough. However, when the general population starts experiencing over 60% of their bankruptcies from a medical cause, then this social indicator would suggest bad management by our top predators. Or perhaps an arrogant sense of overconfidence that we the people will not break the control of our subjective realities even with the higher levels of suffering and death. I think of the tremendous stress and suffering this would cause families knowing they may lose their basic survival necessities because they were unable pay for the health care they needed to continue their pursuit of happiness. It seems our health and prosperity really do depend on how well we compete against other Americans.

I suspect the treat of these medical bankruptcies forced many American citizens into becoming one of the 45,000 that die from lack of healthcare every year. Forcing a population into poverty and poor health within a predatory social structure increases mental instability, limits intellectual growth and promotes primitive acts of violence. This may be good business for the incarceration industry but it is a predictable and preventable tragedy for our country.

If we allow our capitalistic conditioning to form an opinion based on predigest and predatory instincts, it becomes easy to think that this kind of tragedy may only happen to people that don't work hard enough or aren't willing to make the necessary sacrifices to be successful in our society. We tell ourselves something like that could never happen to me, because I have a dependable job and my employer cares more about us laborers than the excess profits they could make outsourcing to an economically depressed country. It can be hard to break through that subjective reality until someone in our family or we personally experience this form of tragedy, and sadly this is occurring at an increasing rate in America. Many of the nearly 50 million Americans living in poverty must choose between getting the health care they need and losing their basic survival necessities from a medical bankruptcy.

This is the choice millions of Americans are forced to make while competing for their capitalistic survival. I feel the level of preventable suffering and death created by this symptom alone will become so unacceptable among Americans it will help accelerate the transition to a predator free society. Between the top predators poor management of their working class resource to prevent the awareness of our capitalistic exploitation and the accelerated intellectual evolutionary development of our species, things are about to change.

You may have wondered as did, why the people in the wealthiest democratic country in the world, can't simply vote to allocate enough of our national wealth to take care of our citizen's entire healthcare needs? Again, it's not that we don't have the national wealth to provide quality healthcare for all American citizens as we have been conditioned to believe. In America we the people pay the highest healthcare costs per person in the world yet our overall health system performance comes in 38th behind some countries most of us have never even heard of. What's up with that?

This social economic indicator should be a giant red flag for any objective observer considering how to repair or replace our healthcare system. When we consider over $800 billion per year of our extracted wealth is allocated to increasing we the people's health and longevity yet by the time that money reaches the American working class resource we only receive a disgraceful 38th in overall efficiency compared to other countries. In free-market capitalistic terms, this is a really bad investment for us working class prey and a super sweet opportunity for exploitation by the ruling class elite top predators that control our extracted wealth. In true capitalistic fashion, maybe we should just eliminate the middleman and save the billions of dollars they take for their cut. Problem solved.

I will give our ruling class top predators the benefit of the doubt that they may not have identified our predatory social structure as the root cause to the many symptoms that contribute to our preventable suffering and death. Or that our entire wealth extraction process is unnecessary once our environmental conditions don't require the exploitation of the working

United States healthcare costs
Compared to 6 of the top 17 highest GDP producing countries (2012)

Their World Health Organization 2000 report ranking in overall Healthcare performance, is included for perspective

Per Citizen ⬤ In $Dollars   Total ⬤ In $Billions

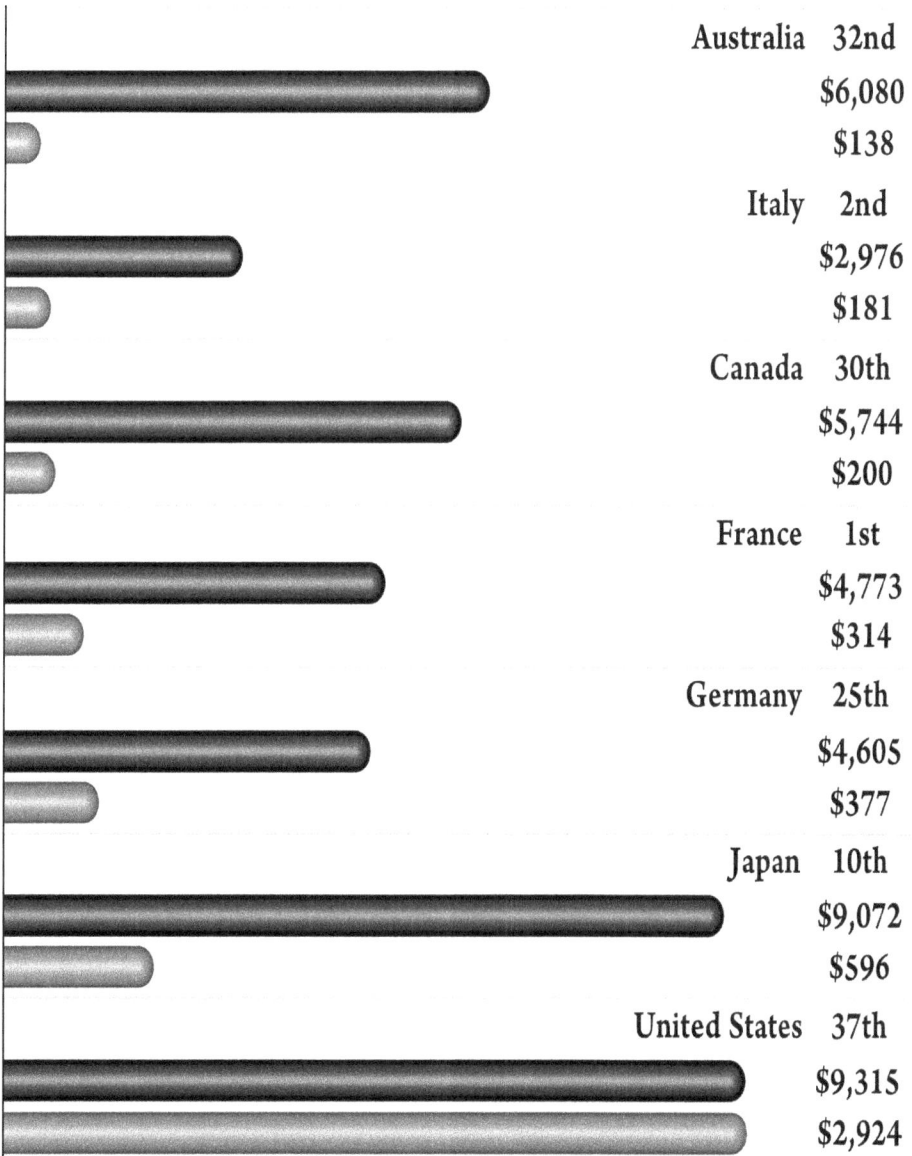

Australia	32nd
	$6,080
	$138
Italy	2nd
	$2,976
	$181
Canada	30th
	$5,744
	$200
France	1st
	$4,773
	$314
Germany	25th
	$4,605
	$377
Japan	10th
	$9,072
	$596
United States	37th
	$9,315
	$2,924

Source: The World Health Organization, The World Health Report 2000, page 152,
(http://www.who.int/whr/2000/en/whr00_en.pdf), The World Bank,
Prepared by True Freedom Technologies

class resource to be an accepted social standard. It's not that they would happily give up their predatory domination or social status as capitalistic royalty, but they may consider helping our evolutionary transition and being on the right side of history.

The one thing I'm sure our ruling class leaders are aware of is that 37 other countries in the world were more efficient at providing healthcare for their citizens. Another thing I'm sure of is our top predators do not want we the people to realize this discrepancy is not the result of sheer incompetence and lack of collective intellectual skills by our entire nation for decades. But instead was a carefully engineered social system to transfer vast amounts of wealth from the working class many to the ruling class few.

Our international healthcare rating of 38th in the world is more than an insult to our ingenuity as a nation but it also provides the top predators a way of measuring the level of capitalistic exploitation the American working class resource will tolerate without breaking our subjective realities to serve Gods and governments, or more accurately the ruling class elite that represent them. Many of our self-proclaimed fiscally conservative leaders in government are fighting hard to maintain a system that wastes billions of our tax dollars, and we pay their salaries and healthcare so they can continue to serve their predatory masters.

A CEO running a multinational corporation would never get away with wasting billions of shareholders dollars, through the floor job performance and the ongoing preventable deaths of thousands of their employees. Yet when it comes to we the people suffering under a Capitalistic government, all of these things somehow become socially acceptable. I guess it depends on the effectiveness of our social conditioning and the value our country places on the 45,000 American citizens that are left to suffer and die every year.

The health and prosperity of our entire species is too important for us not to eliminate this threat at its source. We must free all people from the burden of predatory competition for their survival and accelerate our transition to the next phase of our intellectual evolutionary development. Again, it's not like we don't have the technology, resources or collective intellectual skills as a nation to accelerate our evolutionary transition leading to our true salvation within a predator free society. It seem a simple process of elimination also points to the symptom of Capitalistic greed and the root cause of a predatory social structure.

As I started to objectively consider how to advance our healthcare system one of the first things that dawned on me was doctors would find it very difficult to stay true to one of the most foundational elements of medical ethics. This basic element of ethics that states "First, do no harm" would be difficult to maintain when practicing their medical profession within a predatory social economic structure that forces all competitors to value profits for wealthy investors over the long-term health and prosperity of the patients. Like Capitalism itself, I certainly wouldn't want to make this system more efficient at exploiting the working class resource and transferring national wealth to the ruling class elite.

I started to realize implementing any solution attempting to provide a higher quality of health and human rights for we the people within a predatory society would be a lesson in futility that would need to endure violent opposition from mediocre minds. At best it may provide a level of evolutionary social progress equivalent to a snail's race. Even though Social Security, Medicare and Obamacare has made great progress towards increasing the health and human rights of we the people, reducing the suffering and death of millions of American citizens, including those that were successfully conditioned to reject their own social equality. It demonstrates the level of progress possible while functioning from within the narrow confines of a political construct socially engineered by capitalistic masterminds. That's just not good enough anymore and when compared to the level of true freedom and prosperity possible within the environmental conditions of a predator free society, it appears to be barbaric in contrast.

Because our species has spent our entire existence adapting to increasingly more sophisticated predatory social structures, it can be difficult to imagine what a healthcare system would be like within the environmental conditions of a predator free society. As with all the other symptoms created by forced competition for survival, our healthcare system will also make a wondrous transition. By reversing our motivational imperative from the individual accumulation of wealth and power, to providing complete healthcare services to all people as a human right, it will provide a foundation to build on. Once the burden and barriers of predatory competition are removed we can concentrate all of our collective intellectual skills in an effort to provide a universal solution to benefit the entire community, country and planet. In this way not only will our ability to solve complex problems increase many fold but also any solutions found by an individual or group within the network can be sent out to all communities as an update to increase their health care system efficiency.

Like education the healthcare of a community is so important one of the eight divisions planned for a predator free society will be dedicated to this task. This means, of the eight primary families living in a single Automated Community Infrastructure, one of them will be designated to provide healthcare. The skills of at least one experienced healer will be needed to monitor the health of the people within their community as well as offer checkups for public visitors. Without the need to consider the best way to maximize profits for the ruling class elite, new healthcare technologies can be developed and delivered with much greater efficiency. Services can be delivered directly to the people who need them most, while minimizing our preventable suffering and death, which should be our primary objective anyway. A technically advanced predator free society will not only attempt to utilize all currently available technologies to accomplish our tasks. But also all community members will be given the environmental conditions necessary to innovate beyond what is currently considered the state-of-the-art in their area of interest. I'm looking forward to working with new community members and offering them some advanced projects to fire up their imagination and help get things started.

If we consider correcting our social healthcare dysfunctions from the perspective of an engineer, the more basic elements of the problem and the corresponding solution may become more apparent. I find it helpful to shed any predetermined notion of failure by others and just concentrate on the basic elements of the problem. It's a little like tuning out all the static on a radio until pure notes can be heard leading to the identification of the song title, artist's name, instruments being played etc. Once we can hear and or see the basic elements of the problem better, we can then apply our intellectual survival trait and objective reasoning to that factual knowledge forming new solutions.

If our environmental conditions are free from distracting influences and our Biosystems are functioning at high efficiency, then abstract connections between seemingly unrelated bits of knowledge can take place spontaneously forming creative solutions. Of course a subjective reality can prevent this entire process from taking place especially with any subject that would help break the exploitation process allowing us to gain objective control over our lives.

At the most basic level we have the full lifecycle of a human Biosystem to consider with hardwired survival necessities preinstalled in our genetic memory. These preinstalled survival necessities need to be satisfied by the Biosystems environmental conditions. Or that system will first complain by sending distress messages to the brain and then if ignored for too long will cause damage requiring healthcare services. The logical solution would be to prevent this chain of events by supplying the environmental conditions needed by the Biosystem allowing it to perform at optimal efficiency and have a higher quality of life. Then the problem quickly becomes how do we create the environmental conditions that can provide our survival necessities as a human right and not a privilege to compete for. Breaking the second change of Capitalism and the formation of a predator free society will solve this problem with the creation of the first technically advanced smart infrastructures design specifically to accomplish this task.

There are so many logical preventative measures to increase the health and longevity of an individual human Biosystem or an entire interactive bio-community of people. I started to realize if the negative social influences of our capitalistic exploitation within a predatory social structure could create an epidemic of obesity, tobacco deaths, industrial contamination related birth defects etc. then I am certain the opposite must also be true were a higher level of health and longevity should be a natural manifestation of adapting to the positive environmental conditions within a predator free society.

For example one of our favorite survival necessities to satisfy is our need for food. However, we need more than just the cheapest, sweetest, least nutritional food products possible that can make the highest profits for top predators. It seems our evolving technology has provided a solution to this problem that can be easily integrated into a predator free community infrastructure offering a wide variety of cuisines and nutritional requirements as an on-demand system capable of continuous operations, subject to available food resources and a sufficient energy supply.

Because a secure supply of nutritional food is a requirement to remove our dependency on top predators and finally break our second chain of Capitalism, bio domes needed to be integrated within the community infrastructure providing convenient access to this survival necessity. Having convenient access to a wide variety of nutritional foods is such a critical survival necessity to maintain optimal health one of the eight divisions of the predator free society in this book is dedicated to supplying this requirement.

The on-demand technical solutions will be integrated within each community infrastructure and even though they would prefer the title, masters of culinary expressions we will mostly refer to them as our robotic chef's, or just Chef for short. The Chef will remember the culinary preferences and nutritional requirements for each community member and when combined with the automated delivery system it becomes like a high-tech room service where nutritious food just shows up enticing us to eat healthy meals. Now if we only had robotic personal trainers... we'll work on them later.

At first the level of medical services and products offered to the community and public will be limited but as resources grow and the network of predator free infrastructures expands I feel certain radically advanced new technologies will emerge. Even now our advancing technologies are blurring the lines between our mortal past and present and a future approaching and eventually achieving different forms of immortality. The very concept of healthcare will change once our intellectual evolutionary development has reached a level of technology when all of our required body maintenance is automatically detected and repaired without the need to interfere with our primary activities. Using emerging technologies we will be able to upgrade many of our Biosystems to a higher level of durability and dependability providing failsafe redundancy on critical systems that could terminate our lives.

At the most extreme fundamental level, the things that make us truly unique are the neural patterns in our brains created from our life's experiences, our knowledge of the world around us and every creative skill we have ever developed is all contained within this one vulnerable bio control system. We may be genetically hardwired and socially conditioned to associate our outward appearance to who we are, but when it really comes down to it, if we were able to transplant our brains into different technically advanced bioengineered hybrid bodies we would continue to be the same people, just look different on the outside. Something like, getting a new car to drive around.

Of course our brains are not plug-and-play components that have a biotech interface capable of monitoring and supplying all of the sensory inputs and outputs needed to keep us happy, at least not yet. However, this does seem like a logical milestone during our natural evolutionary progression towards the ultimate goal of immortality. Prompting a philosophical discussion on what a society would be like if all its people could choose to live indefinitely or grow old and die a natural death.

Because we are literally a set of unique neural patterns in a Bio control system that is our brain, we know exactly what area needs to be objectively considered to preserve the essence of who we are. Limiting the natural cellular degradation process that occurs in our brains would seem like an ineffective approach, as long as the environmental and biological conditions that create them are not removed first. If high-energy radiation from our Sun and space degrades our genetic blueprint for new cellular growth over time then minimizing our exposure with some form of shielding would in theory extend our lives. One of the many advantages of placing a technically advanced community infrastructure belowground is that all the people working, sleeping or just having fun within it will be shielded from harmful surface radiation during that portion of their lives.

While functioning within our predatory social structure, our quality of national healthcare and level of human rights will never rise above what is necessary to ensure our efficient output as a working-class resource. If we the people truly want quality healthcare we must break both chains of Capitalism, to gain better control of our decision-making process and then use our national wealth, technology and creative skills to create a society designed to supply the needs of the people and not the predatory desires of our ruling class elite. Our descendants will look back at this phase of our intellectual evolutionary development and know this was the point in time when our species made an informed collective decision to reject our predatory past and embrace a predator free future. Now all we need to do is make it happen.

4. Production

We naturally feel a sense of pride and purpose when we get to use our knowledge and intellectual skills to help improve the quality of life for our family, friends and community. In fact I'm hoping this desire will help people break their capitalistic conditioning for predatory conflicts and consider a new motivational paradigm for survival. Throughout our entire evolutionary development our motivation to stay productive was directly related to our hardwired instinct for survival within primitive predatory social structures. In other words, you work or you die.

In a predator free society where all forms of capitalistic exploitation and intellectual competition for survival are removed, our only motivation to stay as productive as possible will be our desire to help others experience the same level of true freedom and prosperity enjoyed by members. Knowing that our fellow Americans and other people around the world are still suffering in working-class poverty and being systematically exploited by top human predators is motivation enough for me.

Even within a managed predatory social structure like Capitalism, ruling class top predators must allow their working class resource enough education and healthcare to maximize their labor output and the amount of wealth that can be extracted. It's a little like keeping the goose that lays the golden eggs productive. They don't want to be bothered with the goose or its quality of life they just want to keep those golden eggs rolling into their bank accounts. From a strategic point of view it's foolish for top predators to make their working class resource suffer from lack of basic human rights and survival necessities. It will increase the awareness of our exploitation and minimize our long-term profit potential. But then I guess the American working class resource is still the wealthiest population in the world most willing to allow our capitalistic exploitation as an acceptable social function of our society.

Clearly a balance must be struck between the amount of wealth that can be extracted from a working class resource's production capability or GDP (gross domestic product) and the percentage of the population that must suffer and die to effectively manage our predatory social structure. However, as globalization equalizes capitalistic economies around the world and the American working class resource is made to work harder for less, this will also help accelerate public awareness and the desire for true freedom and prosperity within a predator free society.

Before we developed more advanced automated technologies, our production capability was directly related to our ability to perform manual labor. If a ruling class predator wanted to maximize the production of a product the only way to accomplish this was to increase the manual labor output of their working class resource requiring the inconvenience of payments sufficient enough to keep most of their workforce alive. Acquiring working-class prey willing to allow their exploitation for profit was not only easy it was and still is the accepted standard for survival in our predatory social structure. Now that we have created a global capitalistic infrastructure making the working-class resources of the world dependent upon their ability to provide manual labor to their ruling class top predators, what happens to us human prey when were not needed anymore and the production of most products and services become automated? Will our level of capitalistic exploitation increase along with the suffering and death of our least fortunate working class citizens? Yes, and it's already begun.

Perhaps it's not bad management skills after all that our ruling class top predators are willing to allow the suffering and death of so many of us working-class prey, if automated technologies can increase their production output while replacing the pesky human element that's always complaining about health care and workers rights. Top predators won't have to worry about robotic production equipment trying to form unions or crying out for a living wage capable of surviving our capitalistic pursuit of happiness. The big dilemma for top predators is robots don't make good consumers.

With the correct application of intellectual skills we can get a robot or automated production equipment to do just about anything. However, creating a society of robotic consumers is not to my knowledge an interest being pursued. Unless of course you expand that definition to include an engineered society with biological units willing to perform their labor function and accept their social status as one of the cogs in a global machine designed for capitalistic exploitation. I was just realizing it's probably easier to psychologically condition a diverse working-class resource with a unifying subjective reality that considers their capitalistic exploitation to be an accepted social ritual than it would be to program a society of robotic citizens to perform consumer functions.

Our automation technology will continue to advance at an accelerated rate increasing profits for primarily our wealthy elite, while at the same time the working-class resource will lose the jobs they need for basic survival necessities. Because this entire mess is a predictable and avoidable symptom of forced intellectual competition within a predatory social structure, any solution should eliminate the source of the problem first and then repair the residual damage. Our current strategy of treating the symptoms as if they are the cause while seemingly oblivious to the primary factor responsible will continue to fail at an increasing rate as our populations grow.

Assuming our objective is to advance our production capability in both quantity and level of technical sophistication, we must first create the environmental conditions to allow this to happen naturally. Trying to force intellectual creativity and a higher production rate out of a society with the incentive of greed and the threat of losing survival necessities may have been acceptable for our predatory past but not for our predator free future. The first advantage we will have in achieving our advanced production goals will be our new environmental conditions, like the other five social economic areas targeted for improvement. Because they're all so closely integrated an improvement to one will benefit the others so you can imagine how correcting all the symptoms of our predatory social structure at their source will provide a tremendous advantage for attaining our production goals and overall progress towards a predator free future.

Once our minds are free of predatory conflicts for survival and the control of subjective realities to serve Gods and governments, we can then continue our evolutionary journey into a predator free future full of technical wonders and a whole new appreciation for life. Our newly formed objective realities unburdened by our predatory past will quickly discover that the same automated technology primarily benefiting the wealthy few, can instead be used to relieve the suffering and death of the working-class many. Say for example under our current predatory social structure one automated production machine could replace 100 labor jobs each supporting a family of four. The initial investment is high for the corporation but eliminating those hundred jobs provides a tremendous savings to quickly pay off the automated production systems creating big profits for those wealthy enough to exploit this capitalistic opportunity.

On the other hand advanced automated maintenance and manufacturing technology is pre-integrated into the smart home community infrastructure of a predator free society as a kind of perk intellectual species should get once they cross the evolutionary boundary of this critical social transition. So for example that same automated system used to eliminate we the people's ability to survive our capitalistic competition will be designed, manufactured, installed and maintained by one or more of those hundred individuals that would have lost their jobs, and instead of all the benefits going to just a fortunate few it will increase the quality of life for an entire extended community.

Of the six social economic areas targeted for improvements, the predator free society proposed in this book focuses primarily on education and production. Our ability to produce advanced automated technologies, products and services will provide the tools necessary to build the future and our education will provide the wisdom to guide us through this critical evolutionary transition into a new era of true freedom and prosperity for our species. It will be our education that breaks the first chain of Capitalism and our advanced production capabilities that will allow us to break the second. I am really looking forward to helping make this future a reality as soon as possible by creating the first technically advanced prototype ACI (Automated Community Infrastructure) capable of supporting a predator free society. One of the greatest things about ending our predatory social structure is all that national wealth, resources and intellectual skills that was getting sucked up by top predators can now be used to provide true freedom and prosperity to we the people and accelerate the network expansion of predator free ACIs.

There are eight primary divisions with production potential within the social structure of the predator free society proposed in this book. Competitions between divisions, teams or individuals for best designs, highest levels of production, sales to the general public or most contribution to the society may take place, just not ones where our survival or social status hangs in the balance. Friendly short-term competitions preferably among teams to design and prototype different combinations of technologies to be used in some new advanced product service may be fun.

Something newer members can do to develop their knowledge and creative skills. But at the first sign any competition starts to limit our overall progress towards accomplishing our mission statement of ending our predatory social structure, we will simply have to find another way to have our fun and there will be plenty of interesting options to choose from.

If a community member living within a functioning predator free infrastructure could sum up their daily activities in three words they would be, learning, teaching and enjoying life. For me these three things are so closely related they have almost merged into one. One of the greatest advantages of using advanced automation technologies within a predator free society is that we can remain highly productive while were learning, teaching, enjoying life or even sleeping.

While learning how an automated system works an apprentice will also be productive by running diagnostics checkups and doing maintenance on community infrastructure components. As this apprentice goes about their day learning and being productive they will likely have one or more younger members of the community in training with them forming a little team that goes on repair missions. These repair missions will be like technical mysteries to solve turning they're learning and teaching lessons into a kind of game. Remember, when lessons are company with an emotional response they are better retained by our memories. This scenario would place our apprentice in the position of learning and teaching at the same time, and if they appreciate the challenge, responsibility and sense of accomplishment, then we can add enjoying life satisfying all three objectives.

Starting a production process will often begin with individuals having a Eureka moment much like it does within our predatory social structure. However, the differences between the two environmental conditions begin to appear right away. The first notable difference would be the more relaxed intellectually stimulating environmental conditions of a predator free society would naturally increase our ability to have flashes of inspiration leading to the development of advanced automation technologies and production systems.

This social system not only allows everyone to reach their highest creative potential but it maximizes the amount of intellectual skills a given population can offer to solve any problems affecting the entire community, country or world. We need to consider the big picture and how much weaker we are when we allow ourselves to become divided over petty differences in appearance or culture, and how much stronger we will become once our objectives are unified and a predator free existence for all intellectual life becomes the new accepted social standard.

The next difference is after the Eureka moment occurs. In our current social structure the knowledge, concept or intellectual property must become a trade secret until some form of patent protection can be paid for to help prevent predatory attacks and capitalistic exploitation. We the people are allowing our predatory social structure to suppress our intellectual evolutionary development as a species because we must hoard knowledge and technical discoveries to maximize their profit potential for the wealthiest few among us. It has become clear this social dysfunction has interfered with the natural intellectual development of our species. Unless of course one feels the interference, and even Capitalism itself was part of that natural development. The obvious effects of artificial selection during thousands of years of our evolutionary development should settle that point.

If that same Eureka moment occurred within a predator free society, that concept could immediately be shared with and validated by others initiating the first stages of the production process and starting a team selection of other community members known to be interested in that subject. Because predator free societies must function as islands within a larger predatory social structure, advanced concepts and technical discoveries must remain as trade secrets to outside capitalistic opportunists and freely available to community team members developing a project. The same precautions corporations currently use to prevent predatory attacks on intellectual property must also be used to protect a predator free society and their ability to complete their mission statement. Even if the selected team does not live in the same community infrastructure they may get together with a videoconference to consider the Eureka concept and brainstorming. This chain of events so far could happen in less than a day or even during a few hours depending on the subject complexity and team availability.

Once the team considers the concept worth pursuing and developing into a product or service, a team member can first create some 2-D computer drawings to scale, transforming the nebulous organic analogue process of human creativity into a digital representation of high definition vibrant colors allowing others to literally visualize our imaginations taking form. After getting the 2-D update some team members may have suggestions and want to show their modification advantages. Once all 2-D modifications are agreed upon the leader or other team member can create a full 3-D virtual model of the product, or service function. The virtual 3-D model update is then sent out to all team members for their virtual inspection and any modification suggestions.

At this stage of the prototype production process different design variations are tested against one another in a virtual 3-D environment. A team member can show their modification advantages in a 3-D simulation including virtual sensors recording test data into charts for a more effective presentation and comparison with the real world data collected later from a full scale-working prototype. Each production project that makes it to a full scale-working prototype will allow us to calibrate our virtual sensors and the accuracy of our 3-D design and simulation environment with their real-world counterparts.

The 3-D simulation environment for prototype development is designed to naturally adapt to the manufacturing needs of the community much like how we humans learn from our environmental conditions and adapt accordingly to function more efficiently. After virtual 3-D modifications are made and agreed upon by team members, 3-D parts are printed out and assembled into a small-scale working model. The time it takes to reach this stage of the process could take as little as hours or as long as months depending on the complexity of the finished product, like how many subsystems need to be integrated.

The products created within a predator free society would range from the relatively simple production of a one-piece single material item like a ceramic plate or a drinking glass to coordinating the highly complex subsystem integration of a multipurpose aircraft with advanced transformation technologies. The environmental conditions of the predator free society should provide creative challenges for people at every level of their personal development. After extensive testing and refinements of the scaled-down model, the team agrees to start constructing a full-scale prototype.

A project team may want to divide larger projects into smaller bite-size pieces by giving each team member their own subsystem to focus on. Each team member's progress will update in real time to a virtual 3-D model being assembled in cyberspace, like Gods creating a new life form. Even more interesting is the product this team could be working on may be a smart tree created to produce and store electricity, biofuels, hydrogen gas etc. like their organic counterparts produce fruit and food energy for us humans. So in a way they are creating an artificial life form and becoming techno-Gods to a whole new product line of developing species.

I know they don't have real brains like us humans and they're not even self-aware yet. But I'm already feeling a sense of parental pride knowing how our new line of developing species will someday help usher in a higher level of integration between the organic and technical life forms of the world. They will become the exotic hybrid life forms of the future that produce and store the different kinds of energy we need to create, maintain and expand a network of technically advanced ACIs. By creating our own artificial life forms that integrate symbiotic systems between the organic and technical, it may even provide a foundation for our own evolutionary fusion of our slow-moving biology and our rapid developing technologies.

As the individual team members finish their subsystems that's when things start to get interesting as the integration of components in the real world hopefully fit together as smoothly as they did with the virtual 3-D model. Even though components are cast, machined, fabricated or printed to exactly match the dimensions of that 3-D model part, some fine-tuning may be necessary to produce the required precision for that system. If earlier 3-D and scale model testing was extensive enough there should be no need for large design corrections or return to an earlier stage of product development.

We would rather not invest in potentially expensive materials like carbon fiber composites to create a full-scale prototype without a high level of confidence it will meet or exceed expectations. Because the virtual design environment of the model simulator has been closely calibrated to match the real world, the subsystems of the finished product should fit together like the pieces of a finely machined 3-D puzzle, which is basically what it is. Full-scale tests are conducted on all subsystem functions and their ability to integrate with others until the whole team is satisfied this product can begin limited production. This will provide new systems to incorporate into an ACI and possibly sell to the public creating an additional revenue source.

When any product becomes popular enough to sell to the public, the team leader for that project and the head of that division will subcontract out its manufacturing to different companies throughout the United States. This benefits both social structures during the transition. Entire subsystems may be manufactured by different companies and sent to a predator free community infrastructure for final assembly, testing and sale to the customer. The multi-function design of an ACI also allows for demonstrations and display models for each division and some of the key products they produce. Customers may visit the ACI and explore advanced products from all eight different divisions of a predator free society while enjoying its relaxed sunlit atmosphere and perhaps a bite to eat prepared by the integrated robotic chef's of the Food Tree Café and restaurant. It will be an intellectually stimulating environment of wonder and excitement certain to spark the imagination and leave a lasting impression of new knowledge.

Some of the eight divisions of the proposed social economic structure might have their own offshoot businesses that operate under their control, and like all the other revenue sources for the society, their income would be considered a donation to the parent nonprofit organization TFT (True Freedom Technologies). By creating a self-replicating system that converts American families from working-class poverty and capitalistic oppression into a life of true freedom and prosperity. Our government allows nonprofit organizations like TFT to avoid the wealth extraction process experienced by for-profit private corporations.

In return our country will have less of our people needlessly suffering and dying from a lack of basic human rights and survival necessities. Our governments policies and actions towards its citizens often seem contradictory, what one hand giveth the other hand taketh away. I guess it's all part of the evil mastermind training for top predators on how to best manage a working-class resource without them becoming aware of their exploitation. I'd like to leave all that behind us, and concentrate on our predator free future.

What started as an idea for a new product or service would be quickly developed and distributed among the network of ACIs so all the people could rapidly benefit from this single flash of inspiration. It will be interesting to observe how the new structural environment of a predator free society will accelerate our intellectual evolutionary development and our ability to rapidly produce and distribute new products. Even though logic would suggest a predictable outcome, the creation of the first technically advanced ACI with the integration of a new predator free social economic structure is still untested and a kind of evolutionary experiment.

The design and production process of creating an entire predator free society with an advanced technical infrastructure can be considered from the same perspective as our fictitious product example except far more complex with many more subsystems to integrate. A project like this will need a much larger team to develop the many subsystems simultaneously so the first prototype ACI can go online sooner and families can begin integrating and adapting to their new predator free social structure and environmental conditions.

I was just realizing one of the primary intellectual considerations and creative pursuits of a predator free society will be to create advanced symbiotic relationships between biological and technical systems as with the new artificial life form product line developed in the Smart Tree division. However, what's interesting is the integration of the first technically advanced ACI and a predator free social structure of multiple family units will be like the ultimate symbiotic relationship between the organic and technical or the analog and digital worlds. A goal for all products especially the most complex, is to balance its artistic appreciation or aesthetic value with its utility usefulness in solving some problem.

Creating ACIs and integrating the first predator free families will be very much like testing an incredibly advanced product that must achieve its utility goal of breaking both chains of Capitalism. And must provide true freedom and prosperity for we the people while also creating an artistic ambience and the relaxed environmental conditions that accelerate our intellectual evolutionary development. How hard could that be? We may be technically part of the experiment but as long as we the people are in control of the process and our objective is unified, the end result will be predictable. We will achieve a predator free existence as a predictable stage in our intellectual evolutionary development, but we the people now have the opportunity to control the timeline of this process allowing for a peaceful transition and millions of lives can be saved.

When I try to project my consciousness into the future of a predator free society I visualize what would seem to be an ultimate plateau in the evolution of our production technologies. We should keep in mind our consideration of ultimate technologies will always be directly relative to our overall intellectual evolutionary development, just as the Godlike mystical events of the past have become grade school science projects, our advanced technologies today will seem like child's play in the future. However, if we just fully utilize our currently available technologies and unleash the intellectual skills and creative potential in our country alone, our advanced production possibilities begin to expand exponentially. If we move past our need to maintain a society of planned obsolescence and socially engineered predatory exploitation of the working-class resource, it starts to become apparent we have many options to solve our inefficient production technologies. And the need to force people into wasting precious time and intellectual skills on performing an automated labor task just to pay for their basic survival necessities will become a thing of our past.

It will be one of the design challenges of a predator free society to create the ultimate in futuristic production systems using the technologies that are currently available today. Many of these systems have already been designed and are ready for 3D modeling and virtual prototyping. However, if we fast-forward the evolution of our production technologies it's clear the ultimate objective is a total automation system or what is referred to as a "lights out factory" so-called because a factory where only machines are required to produce the product would not need the lights us biological units would need to perform a similar labor function.

Imagine designing a machine where raw materials go in one side and high precision technically advanced prototypes and finished products come out the other side. I think I'll need to make a scaled-down test model with a clear plexiglass front so each stage of the process can be seen performing its function. I could present this scaled-down model to the rest of the team for their suggestions, modifications and ultimately their approval on a full-scale application. As with many other products developed within a predator free society the scaled-down model can also be used as one of the educational demonstration displays placed throughout the ACI. It occurs to me that maybe we should break the first chain of Capitalism and our subjective realities that make killing other people seem socially acceptable, before we make machines so sophisticated they could create almost anything we can imagine. Perhaps not all products should be offered to the general public, at least not yet.

5. Efficiency

When trying to improve a system or a primary aspect of our society like efficiency, I assume other well-intended individuals have been actively trying to solve the problem and remove the barriers preventing our progress. However, the very first thing I started to notice is that in a free market predatory social structure, we can't assume there are well intended logical individuals trying to solve any problem unless there are profits to be made. Again, it was also clear a lack of collective national skills or incompetence were not to blame. Instead I found it is quite the contrary, our social structure was carefully engineered for generations to perform its function exactly as designed. It seems improving our national efficiency had just become more complicated.

At first I was expecting our inefficiency problems to be more of a technical challenge to identify and correct. Then I learned it was a small part of a larger system created to legitimately exploit the working-class people of our country, I started to realize a whole new strategy would be needed to accomplish this task. After realizing how legitimized and socially acceptable our exploitation had become, the sensible thing would be to give up such a futile task and just allow my capitalistic conditioning to take control of my ambitions. However, just as I needed to give up and grow out of my subjective belief in Santa Claus as a child. I must now as an adult intellectually evolve beyond my capitalistic conditioning and induced subjective realities to serve Gods, governments and ultimately our ruling class elite. If we cannot evolve beyond this point, the problems we work to solve may only be illusions intended to distract us and prevent the ultimate solution from being discovered and put into action.

While considering the dynamics of our national inefficiency problems and the connection between every other key social economic area targeted for improvements in this book. I had a eureka moment realizing first the larger the problem is the greater the relief will be once it's solved and that if the social dysfunctions were linked to a common source then perhaps all of them could be corrected at the same time.

Eliminating the problem at its source would be the most efficient strategy to correct all the symptoms contributing to our preventable suffering and death. That's not to say correcting the cause at its source will be easy or quick. However, a good self-replicating predator free society can expand exponentially and if given access to our tax dollars the process can be accelerated even more. One thing is certain it will be truly wonders. This intellectual and social transition in the evolutionary development of our species will be similar to that of a blooming flower just beginning to show its true beauty, humanity and creative potential for all to see. Then maybe we'll find out who's watching.

There are so many examples how our advanced predatory social structure limits our efficiency as individuals, nations and as an evolving intellectual species. Or perhaps more accurately, how it is specifically designed to waste vast amounts of energy and then get we the people to pay the top predators for all our survival necessities and tools for capitalistic competition. It's not so much for the products we have been socially engineered to consume, but more so their expert management skills and psychological manipulation techniques to get us working class prey to accept our exploitation as just another day in our pursuit of happiness.

Now that's a work of capitalistic perfection on the grandest of scales. It's no wonder our education as individuals and our intellectual evolutionary development as a species needs to be suppressed, the top predators of our world today must be aware this is the key to ending their predatory domination and allowing true freedom and prosperity to flourish throughout our global community.

The knowledge of our evolutionary transition will grow among the people, like a deep reservoir of hope and creative solutions building up behind a dam of deteriorating deceptions and antiquated subjective beliefs. The natural progression of this process seems to be leading to an epic event similar to having a dam collapse as opposed to the controlled release of water to avoid a potentially tragic punctuated equilibrium in the evolutionary development of our species. This can and should be avoided to decrease the level of suffering and death of our least fortunate competitors until the transition to the environmental conditions of a predator free society is complete.

As a child in school I remember learning that our country wastes more energy than most other countries use altogether, as if it were an admirable quality and symbol of our power to exploit global resources. It can be difficult to imagine why any country would socially engineer its society to unnecessarily waste vast amounts of energy, until we realize who's paying for it and who's laughing all the way the bank, day after day and year after year for generations. As a matter of common sense and national pride it would seem all Americans would agree to allow our greatest minds using the latest technologies to determine the most efficient ways to save and produce the energy we need for our people's health and prosperity.

After all isn't it our national objective to reduce our dependency on other countries, pay down our enormous debts to them and advance our infrastructure to become totally energy independent and self-sufficient? From a scientific or engineering point of view it's a straightforward objective to make a system or process more efficient. We are the most technologically advanced country in the world, so we have to ask ourselves how can our ruling class leaders have created a system to waste over 50% of the American peoples combined foreign and domestic energy, when we could be creating a society designed to produce a surplus?

To help put into perspective the impact one capitalistic superpower willing to waste vast amounts of energy to exploit their working-class resource and serve their ruling class elite can make on the world. Consider for a moment that our United States of America consumes around 25% of the world's energy or basic human survival resources even though we only comprise around 4.5% of our planet's population. This fact alone should be enough to embarrass any self-respecting country into radically expanding their green industries as a matter of national pride, especially a one that hopes to project an example of leadership for the world to follow. It's not like the growing intellectual community of the world doesn't recognize the

the irony between the freedoms we say we stand for and the level of capitalistic exploitation we are willing to subject our own people to. Talk about mixed messages... we the people of America can fix that and create a country that represents our predator free future and not our predatory instincts to dominate and control the more vulnerable parts of our world.

At our current level of managed exploitation we the people have been conditioned to accept a socially engineered infrastructure that wastes over 50% of the money we give our ruling class top predators for our national energy needs. Then if we also consider that our capitalistic conditioning or induced patriotic subjective reality justifies the consumption of 25% of the world's energy the conclusion would be 12.5% or 1/8 of our entire planet's life saving energy is being wasted by design to satisfy the predatory desires of capitalistic royalty. How can this be considered rational or an example of justice for all? I hope this exploitation process is as unacceptably crazy to other people as it is for me, or it may continue until a more catastrophic implosion and demise of Capitalism takes place.

From the perspective of a casual observer functioning with an objective reality, our national policy toward the efficient use of global resources would appear to show a complete disconnect between the haves and the have-nots of the world. Our justice for all, motto that we hold so dear wasn't supposed to be just for the ruling class elite to use as another subjective belief to manage we the people. However, once subjected to the evil influences of Capitalism and our overall predatory social structure our fate as working-class prey was sealed. As a concept worth reiterating in this book, we the people and the working class prey throughout history have always had the power in numbers to end our predatory oppression and take control of our intellectual evolutionary development but we just lacked the knowledge necessary to make the transition, until now.

Our willingness as a people to allow our predatory social structure to determine our intellectual evolutionary development is the single most damaging factor preventing our efforts to achieve maximum national efficiency. It was clear right from the start any efforts to improve our

Estimated United States Energy use in 2012: - 95.1 Quads

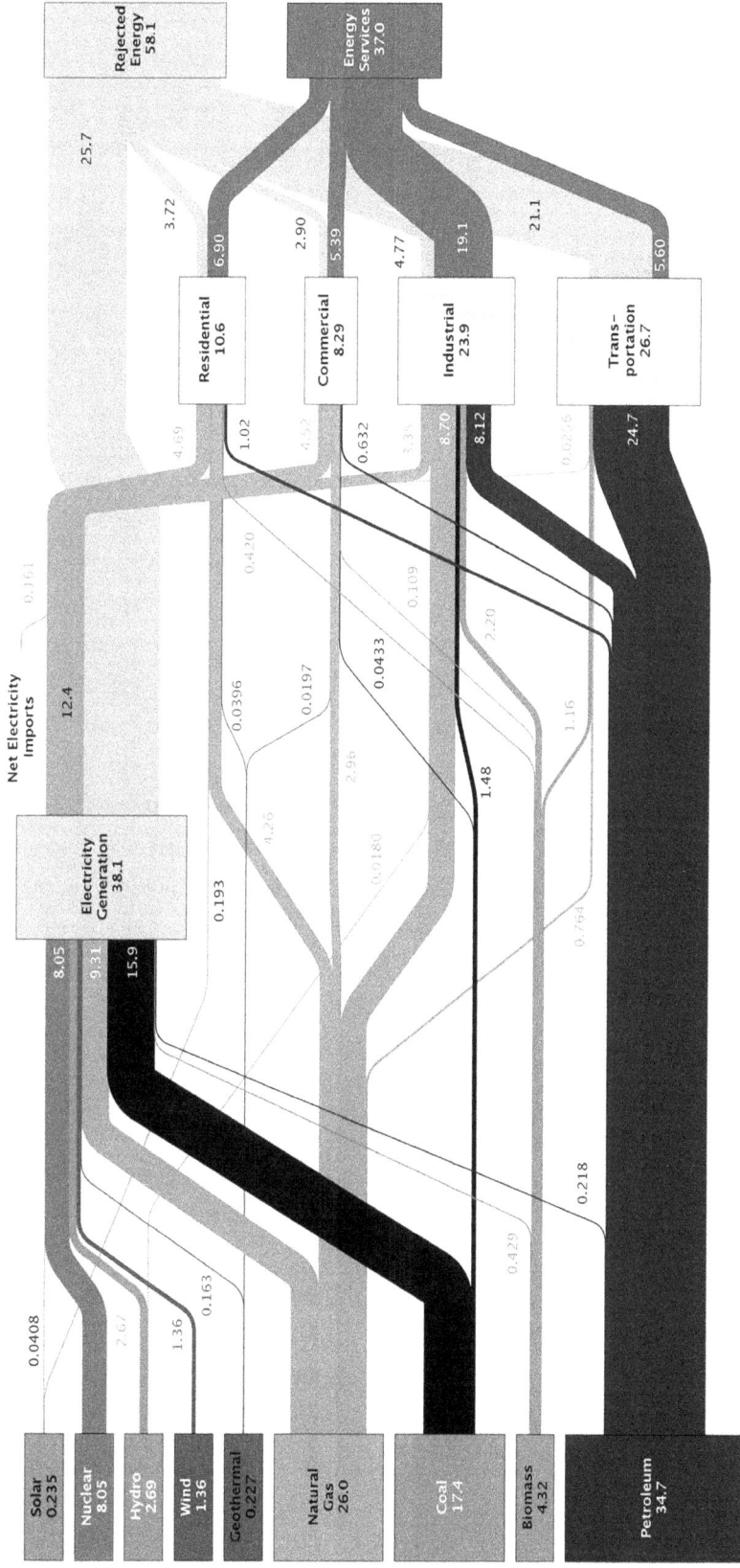

Source: Lawrence Livermore National laboratory, see full size charts and more details at - https://flowcharts.llnl.gov

personal or national efficiency must begin from outside the corrupt influences of capitalistic greed and predatory competition for survival. The idea to create an advanced self-sustaining, multi-function community infrastructure was born. In reality this seems like the only plausible solution and even better it provided a fresh start and opportunity to design a social structure from scratch using the most advanced materials, technologies and creative skills that can be assembled to achieve the highest level of efficiency possible.

I see attempts to make our predatory social structure and free-market Capitalism fairer for us working class prey, similar to trying to rebuild a dilapidated home with no roof one board a day, while our family members continue to die from exposure. When removing the debris of our predatory past and clearing the way for a clean new construction of a safe and secure predator free future would be far more cost-effective allowing us to truly achieve our maximum efficiency goals

Some of the key benefits to living in a predator free society and advanced ACI is our ability to be extremely efficient. Or more accurately to produce, store, conserve and consume energy in a manner that provides the least amount of waste. The efficiency benefits of a predator free society are evident in both its social structure and the technical design of the ACI. If we approach our national inefficiency problem logically and determine where the greatest loss of energy is coming from in our current social structure we will have an excellent starting point for our design challenge. The first thing we notice is most of the energy being wasted in America is for our residential, commercial and industrial electrical needs and our consumer, commuter and industrial transportation systems.

Now that we have identified the targets to analyze for improvements we can compare different solutions for efficiency. It's also important to objectively consider, of the 1/8 worlds energy that we are socially engineered and conditioned to waste, the vast majority of it is fossil fuel. It's become a necessity we must buy from top predators to survive while contaminating our biosphere and increasing climate change creating more droughts, firestorms, hurricanes, tornadoes, destruction of our coastal cities and communities. All of this destruction that contributes to our preventable suffering and death is an insult to the creative ingenuity of our country, yet were forced to accept this level of exploitation to satisfy the capitalistic greed of our current top predators. This is why it is so imperative we end our predator evolution as soon as possible.

Even though our primary design objective is to create a technically advanced community infrastructure capable of supporting a predator free society. As it turns out, by ending all of the dysfunctional symptoms inherent in our predatory competition for survival, many other advantages start to become more apparent. A technically advanced predator free infrastructure is specifically designed to eliminate the socially engineered inefficiencies that allow for the transfer of billions of dollars from the working class many to the ruling class few. The two areas of our society that have been engineered to waste the largest percentage of our national energy are addressed directly, and almost entirely eliminated by the ACI technical design and the social economic structure of a predator free society. Like receiving a psychic premonition from the future readers of this book, I can almost hear the words of healthy skepticism "that's too good to be true", perhaps in the past before the acceleration of our technical and intellectual evolution, but things are different now.

As we objectively consider the extremes between our current advanced predatory social structure that gives our ruling class elite full strategic control over their working-class resource. And a fully transformed predator free nation where all of our people live in smart homes within a network of ACIs, the awesome advantages we will enjoy start to become even more apparent. It's also important to consider that by targeting the inefficiencies in America that waste 1/8 of the world's energy first, is like a fireman directing his water at the base of the main flame, then dealing with the smaller hot spots to finish the job. A predator free societies efficiency objective for our nation is to create a network of ACIs all individually capable of producing, storing and distributing 110% of their energy needs. This would not only remove our dependency upon top predators for our survival necessities and practically eliminate the depletion of the 25% of the world's resources we now consume, but also allow that excess 10% energy to help expand the predator free network in other countries.

Because each ACI is designed for the automated production of all the components necessary for reproduction, it kind of resembles the properties of a single living cell in our bodies. And just like those cells contain a DNA blueprint and the ability for self-replication so too will our network of predator free ACIs. With larger multicellular life forms cells can group together to create specialties subsystems like the organs in our bodies. In larger networks of ACIs some may group together and specialize in processing and distribution of local resource throughout the predator free society, while still retaining the ability for self-replication.

In so many ways it seems we're still trying to technically emulate the efficiency, splendor and beauty of nature and perhaps it's biological or evolutionary adaptation to the changing environmental conditions of our planet. Many aspects of the ACI network expansion will incorporate the efficiency of organic systems and the benefit of millions of years of evolutionary adaptation. Like a new transportation system based partially on the circulatory system of the human body only with redundant hearts that can be added on as needed for network expansion. That's the kind of improvement we may be giving our own bodies as our biology and technology merge in the future

Another overall strategic advantage of the predator free social structure is its primary function of self-replication and expansion not only provides for exponential growth, again like organic systems, but also as this need diminishes their advanced automated production systems can be easily reprogrammed for future tasks. As ACIs designed to last hundreds of years begin replacing our fragile residential surface structures constructed for planned obsolescence, our country will continue to gain strength in all six social economic areas targeted for improvements. By converting the least fortunate capitalistic competitors in our current predatory social structure into highly productive members of a technically advanced predator free society, it will not only relieve the pressure on our social welfare system and give Americans an opportunity at true freedom and prosperity but also provide an excellent example for others to objectively compare, further accelerating our transition process.

Another example of how the transition to a predator free society will boost the overall efficiency of our country is, as the need for local network expansion becomes less of a demand the percentage of products produced for sale to the general public can increase, providing higher revenues to purchase more building materials and resources imported from outside the community. Because most of the energy created and consumed by a predator free society is primarily allocated with accomplishing our mission statement and network expansion. The extra 10% will slowly rise to nearly 100% as more Americans make the transition and less people need assistance. The new members will also become part of the solution by increasing our capacity to expand the ACI network.

The demand for products sold to the public will also decrease, as more of the general population won't be required to purchase their survival necessities. Likewise as the predator free society grows more of our rare commodities will be produced within the extended community network. The revenue produced by sales to the public will be reduced dramatically and eventually replaced by an exchange system based on the TER (Total Energy Requirement) to produce the item. A TER exchange or TERE will be networked directly into all smart homes and provide a more scientific means of accurately assessing the energy requirements to produce various items. This will allow for a universally accepted and quantifiable means of fair trade across a wide spectrum of dissimilar materials and resources. The automated exchange of items can take place in an advanced delivery system functioning much like the circulatory structures in our body that can deliver specialized cells throughout its extended network.

After identifying the areas of our society that are socially engineered to consume 25% of our world's survival resources and then waste half of that, our technical and social economic design challenge can focus on eliminating this threat to we the people's pursuit of happiness and true freedom. Most of the energy our social structure is designed to consume and waste falls into two categories that need to be considered and solved separately yet integrated in the end to produce maximum efficiency. It's like working on two complicated subsystems that need to function well together so the larger system we call our society, can provide us humans with the highest quality of life possible. The first and most wasteful category is for the production and distribution of our electrical demands for the residential, commercial and industrial segments of our country.

Imagine for a moment you are a member of a technologically advanced society that uses design challenges as a form of intellectual entertainment like playing a game of chess or doing crossword puzzles. When you are presented with a design challenge to improve the efficiency of a subsystem that wastes more than two thirds of the energy it consumes. The first thing that would cross your mind is that your instructor was playing a joke on you because no system in the future would be allowed to continue functioning at that level of efficiency, that would be ridiculous, but then there are no top predators at this time to exploit the process.

More advanced students would be comparing the difference between 96% and 99% efficiencies to determine the winner of their design challenges. To add a level of complexity to this design challenge any technical or social economic solutions must not require the direct assistance of our government or any ruling class top predators, at least until we the people can unite and respectfully request our national wealth and resources be used to expand our new predator free society. However, on the other hand we can and should unite all the people with like minds to use our combined wealth and resources to not only design solutions but also create functioning examples for the world to see.

Our current energy conversion technologies and their efficiency ratings are becoming better known, allowing for more accurate design challenge solutions. For instance one of the best green technologies using concentrated sunlight to heat a Stirling engine connected to a generator can convert solar energy into electricity at around 31% efficiency. I found it to be an interesting coincidence that our national conversion efficiency rate using the primary combined resources of coal, natural gas, nuclear and Hydro for electrical generation is almost the same as this new developing green technology. However, the big difference is one makes us dependent on top predators for our survival and the other helps us break our second chain of Capitalism by using free energy that falls from the sky.

Because our current social structure has taken generations to socially engineer, reversing this process while making the transition to a predator free society, will also take time. The billions of dollars we are currently giving to our ruling class top predators for the fossil fuels we need to maintain our capitalistic existence will slowly but surely become unnecessary and obsolete as the free and abundant domestically available energy from the sun and wind becomes the accepted social standard. Our objective should be to create highly efficient self-contained ACIs within stable countries to serve as an example to compare with whatever existing level of capitalistic exploitation has become the accepted standard. Once the very first prototype ACI has become fully operational for a few months, many of its inefficiencies will have been identified and corrected. Improvements will be incorporated into new ACIs as they are being constructed.

Creating an energy solution that provides distributed generation of abundantly available free solar and wind energy goes a long way towards eliminating the first of the two wealth extraction techniques used by capitalistic top predators. This will also eliminate the need for an extremely costly and fragile electrical distribution network that is highly vulnerable to destruction from seasonal storm damage and natural disaster devastation. A distributed generation system will maximize our efficiency and the built-in redundancy will greatly increase reliability.

Because the electrical demands of our residential surface structures are primarily needed to counteract the seasonal temperature changes and maintain comfortable living conditions. The subsurface smart homes in the ACI will almost entirely eliminate this waste of energy by maintaining a more consistent temperature that is naturally raised and regulated by the internal biological and automated production activity. If cooling is needed we can generate more electricity as heat energy is allowed to escape into the external ground environment. If heating is needed thermal reservoirs can circulate hot water into radiators to warm the extremely well insulated subsurface smart homes and community infrastructure.

The second area of our advanced predatory social structure that allows top predators of Capitalism to extract billions of dollars from the working-class resources around the world is our transportation system. This system has been designed to consume and waste almost exclusively petroleum fossil fuel energy. Making the modern industrialized working-class resources of the world fully dependent upon the top predators for their survival necessities and requiring them to accept the health hazards of environmental contamination to continue their capitalistic existence. About 75% of the energy used for our nation's transportation is lost giving this subsystem a 25% efficiency rating at converting its fossil fuel into usable energy, but we the people are still made to pay 100% to continue our capitalistic competition for survival.

Some people may still be under the impression that our current transportation system is the most efficient and advanced possible using available technologies and that even the collective intelligence and creative skills of the United States could not design anything better. To design a transportation system to achieve higher than 25% energy efficiency is not rocket surgery and our country does have the highest number of Nobel laureates in the world, so we got smart people. I guess those men behind the curtain controlling the levers of power that manipulate our predatory existence, have done a good job convincing us to be content with this level of capitalistic exploitation. However, that's all about to change.

Before we begin this design challenge on how to improve a subsystem that rejects 75% of the energy it consumes, we should first realize the tremendous advantage we will have by removing the burdensome mandate of trying to create a system that effectively transfers wealth from the working class resource to the ruling class top predators. Then we will be free to focus on what should have been our primary objective all along, to use advanced technologies and creative skills to achieve the most efficient transportation system possible.

One of the most tantalizing aspects of our pre-design challenge considerations, is that because we the people are made to pay billions of dollars for the 75% energy loss in our current transportation system, any efficiency improvements we can make will provide a substantial savings for our country. Then we will get to decide the best way to spend this new multibillion-dollar windfall. Buying additional resources needed to create a more efficient transportation system, or perhaps paying back the national debt incurred during the dark ages of Capitalism when top predators exploited our county's wealth and resources. Finding technical and social improvements for a subsystem this corrupt and inefficient has its advantages, like after it has been corrected all of those life-saving resources can be returned to the American working class people. These resources will not only reduce our own suffering and death, but also create a power base of knowledge and creativity capable of leading the world into the next phase of our intellectual evolutionary development.

For this subsystem design challenge we need to step back and consider the entire system requirements and objectives. Our first design objective is to find a way to satisfy the same social function to our society as our current transportation system provides, but without the need to consume any form of energy at all if possible and from there only allow what's necessary to perform the task. It's more of a strategic improvement for the entire system as opposed to a technical advancement of a single subsystem. The first thing I learned was 65% of our transportation energy is directly consumed and wasted by the working class resource itself, as a requirement of our capitalistic competition for survival. While about 20% goes to our heavier transportation requirements like trains, ships, tractor-trailers etc. and around 15% going to our air traffic. Of that 65% transportation energy we the people are conditioned to consume and waste, the majority is required first for our commutes to work and home and then our recreation, family, business and shopping activities.

If I were a ruling class mastermind of social engineering, I would want to create a society to consume and waste the maximum amount of my product by spreading out the People's transportation needs like their job location, churches, children's education, healthcare, food source, etc. anything that will make them drive farther and more often. Then I would want to multiply this socially integrated wealth extraction technique, but in order to do that I would need to allow a majority of my working-class prey just enough of a living wage to pay for this survival necessity and expand my customer base. Of course a carefully constructed subjective reality is always effective on that segment of the population most willing to accept their exploitation and make decisions based on their emotional feelings, instead of factual knowledge. This wealth extraction technique has become amazingly successful over generations and surprising accepted among the exploited populations of the world.

Once we realize how the game is played and that we the people have the power to change the rules allowing our true freedom and prosperity to win out over the top predators desires for global domination. We can begin this design challenge with a better knowledge base to help our intellectual survival trait make the abstract neural connections we call flashes of inspiration or Eureka moments. Another advantage of knowing how our top predators maximize the exploitation potential of us working class prey, is that we can first explore the logical approach of reversing the process by making our daily social activities more centralized turning what used to be a commute to work wasting fuel and precious time from our lives, into a healthy walk around a climate controlled community infrastructure. I'm already starting to like the way this solution is shaping up. If we can correct and eliminate the need to consume and waste these billions of dollars worth of foreign oil and instead create a social structure and lifestyle that promotes health and longevity, just imagine the fuel savings and efficiency advantage we may enjoy by making our other daily activities locally accessible too.

It was all starting to make sense, if we could design and create super secure technically advanced infrastructures that could not only eliminate our need to commute to work but also to our schools, grocery stores as well as many recreational and shopping activities, we could save over 50% of our national transportation costs right from the start. I'm feeling more efficient just thinking about. It may be difficult to imagine how an ACI in combination with a predator free society can provide this level of advanced efficiency, production, education, nutritious food generation, preventive health care, entertaining animatronic displays and recreational activities all locally. However, once the first prototype ACI is complete and fully functional it can be observed directly. Scheduled tours, bed-and-breakfast guests, customers to the integrated food tree Café/restaurant, videos and 3-D simulations on the TFT website (truefreedomtechnologies.org) will all provide opportunities for the public to better understand the technical functions of an ACI and the philosophy of a predator free society.

It is perhaps the most under appreciated and misunderstood efficiency advantage of all the features a Smart ACI provides, is its ability to protect it's advanced technologies and all the people that work at, live in and visit the facility. One of the technical design criteria was to create an infrastructure capable of lasting 1000 years with little to no maintenance and the ability to update the interior decor and keep current with the trends of the future. This may be one of those long-term criterions we won't get to find out about in one lifetime. However, we already have the technology to satisfy this criterion and I'm sure if we apply some of the knowledge we have learned since the Romans created the pantheon we can accomplish this task. The inconvenience and additional cost of placing ACIs belowground is far outweighed by their ability to survive all forms of surface disasters, remain intact for hundreds of years and provide a high level of security, efficiency and peace of mind for the members of our future predator free societies.

Even though the advanced efficiency of a predator free society would save our country hundreds of billions of dollars, it's still only one of many symptoms of our overall predatory social structure that will be corrected at the source as we make our evolutionary transition to the next phase of our intellectual development. As the need to serve top predators, Gods and governments becomes part of our evolutionary past a growing desire to eliminate wars, hunger, poverty, despair, suffering and death will begin to take priority in our predator free future.

6. Quality of Life

Our quality of life is far more than just a social economic area in desperate need of improvement it is the primary indicator and measure of how well we're doing solving all the other symptoms of our predatory society. The primary problem is our social system is not designed to increase the quality of life for its working-class resource, but instead to maintain their existence for continued exploitation. Predatory social structures by nature are never good for the prey and they always seem to favor the top predators of the species. Especially when that species starts using their intelligence as a competitive tool for survival.

Because the other five primary areas targeted for improvement are all major symptoms of our predatory social structure that collectively tear down our quality of life, correcting all of these social dysfunctions at their source will have an equal and opposite effect. Removing these burdens will increase our quality of life like bringing water to a barren landscape just waiting to bloom into a thriving community of technical wonders and social equality.

Transitional growing pains adapting to a predator free society are to be expected, after all we have been genetically encoded and environmentally conditioned to accept our predatory competition for survival since our life form began developing. And we will be the first species that we know of to make an evolutionary transition like this. However, once and objective comparison between social structures is made the advantages start to become apparent. By ending our need to intellectually and physically compete against one another for our basic survival necessities it will allow the deep wounds of our predatory past to heal. Once this transition begins to build momentum, our quality of life will be greatly enhanced primarily for the people within the predator free society, but also their surrounding communities.

When I consider advancing any technical system or correcting some induced social dysfunction of our society, I first try to find the basic elements of the subject to see if there may be a more fundamental solution for eliminating the problem. I started to wonder what is it that we people really need to have a healthy, happy and productive quality of life. The first thing that dawned on me is that our actual quality of life in material terms is far less relevant than the perception of our social status in comparison with other capitalistic competitors. The expression "keeping up with the Joneses" comes to mind.

Like so many other things in our predatory society, our quality of life is relative to the observer and the social standards they have become accustomed to throughout the environmental conditioning of their lives. In other words providing what we need to have a high quality of life in an advanced society is not what concerns me, it's dealing with the capitalistic desires of what we've been conditioned to want in order to feel emotionally satisfied with our social status that could be a problem. We humans still have such a hard time distinguishing the difference between what we want and what we need. It's a lot like basing our decisions and actions on a false subjective reality about how we want things to be, as opposed to accepting the way they really are and then finding a logical solution.

Even if the second chain of Capitalism was broken first by removing our dependency upon the top predators for our survival and providing a high quality of life to all people as a human right. The residual effects of our capitalistic conditioning would continue to inspire predatory acts of deception and possibly violence in an attempt to hoard basic resources. A strange subconscious and involuntary desire to take advantage of other people will continue to rear its ugly head as generations of capitalistic conditioning dissipate and fade away into our primitive past. Just like the socially accepted practice of human sacrifice, which at that time seemed like a perfectly rational way of pleasing the Gods to prevent our mortal destruction.

The rising tide of our evolutionary transition to a predator free society will eventually lift all of our people out of poverty like millions of little boats floating on a shining sea of hope and prosperity. Because our quality of life is directly affected by all the social dysfunctions inherent in our current predatory social structure this one of our six social areas targeted for advancement should show the highest levels of improvement first, as all the other symptoms are eliminated simultaneously.

When considering the advanced technologies available and the national wealth of creative skills at our disposal, we the people do not need to consider our managed exploitation an acceptable quality of life or social standard for our future. Accepting our fate as working class prey is part of our capitalistic conditioning that must be broken before we will be completely free of the first chain of Capitalism, in fact the lingering effects may continue to shackle our minds even after we adapt to our new predator free environment conditions.

On a physical level our bodies will begin to heal in the nurturing environmental conditions of a predator free society. Some members will still hear the call of the wild and experience a seemingly unexplained desire for predatory aggression and the associated emotional response. However, now we know how to recognize the process and avoid any detrimental effects. That's not to say we can't have a wildly good time while still accomplishing the primary mission of our parent nonprofit organization, True Freedom Technologies. Achieving the highest quality of life possible is our goal but not just for the fortunate few, any solution must allow for universal prosperity for all people as equals.

Part 4: Breaking the second chain of Capitalism

0. Designing an advanced Automated Community Infrastructure

Even after we break the first chain of Capitalism and our minds are free from the induced subjective realities that make our managed exploitation seem like an acceptable way of life. And after we have better intellectual control over our hardwired predatory instincts and make an informed decision to advance our social structure to a predator free society. We will still need to break the second chain of Capitalism by providing a technical solution that allows all of our basic survival necessities to be available at the smart home and community level.

Without creating an ACI (Automated Community Infrastructure) and social system that integrates our basic necessities as a human right instead of a privilege for the more fortunate capitalistic competitors, our predatory struggle for survival could continue indefinitely. Because this design challenge is almost entirely technical with an almost singular objective it allows us to focus all of our creative skills like multiple laser beams all hitting the same target. Nothing can stop us from solving this design challenge and creating the opportunity for more people to end their capitalistic competition for survival. Our intellectual evolutionary development has come too far as a species to allow our continued predatory exploitation. That's not to say this design challenge will be easy... But then, what fun would that be.

Before we begin our technical design challenge a little background on what aspects of our social economic structure need correcting and why is a good place to start. Gathering important knowledge and technologies that can help us accomplish our design challenge is like learning about new building materials and tools available to create a modern architectural masterpiece. That's when things start to get interesting as we get to use our intellectual survival trait to find the best way to arrange those new assets into the most efficient and effective solution.

It has been known by ruling class top predators for thousands of years that one of the best ways to manipulate their working-class populations is to control their basic survival necessities. They simply create a social infrastructure whereby their working-class resource is dependent upon them for their water, food, shelter, etc. Our primary design objective is to create a technical infrastructure allowing us to remove our dependency upon top predators and return control of our basic survival necessities to we the people. Yeah... it is a big job, but remember at first we only need to create the seeds not the entire forest. The self-replicating nature of a predator free society along with its exponential growth capabilities should naturally expand the network of ACIs.

Those of us willing to dream big and dare to fail while braving the violent opposition from mediocre minds will realize, this could be the mother of all design challenges with the greatest rewards for the future of our species. By designing and prototyping the first ACI capable of supporting a predator free society, we will be building a kind of primordial seed with a DNA type blueprint capable of self-replication much like its smaller organic counterpart. Contained within these seeds will be all the knowledge necessary for self-replication to be used at a time when enough energy and building materials are available to create a new ACI, again like the organic process of cellular reproduction.

It's a wise technical designer that considers the processes of nature, after eons of trial and error only the most efficient bio systems for survival remain available for our observation and education. The more Biosystems we observe to understand what made them so successful, the more bits of knowledge we have for our intelligence to work with, greatly increasing our potential to have flashes of inspiration and those Eureka moments.

For example how a tiny little garden spider could build what must be one of the most elaborate feats of architecture, using building materials created from their own bodies all without the benefit of a college degree in advanced engineering. Imagine trying to rope off an entire community in less than a day using a specific pattern to increase the strength of your net making it capable of catching the equivalent of a VW bug. Then you can begin to appreciate the skill level of these little non-intelligent arachnids.

While researching an unrelated subject on intelligence, I learned about ancestral or perhaps better known as genetic memory. Or in other words, it's the kind of memory we're born with and not acquired after birth. At first I thought this genetic memory was only to aid in the most basic of survival functions until I remembered our garden spider friend and their ability to build complex web patterns. In a kind of Eureka moment I realized spiders don't teach their young how to build webs. Therefore, it seemed logical that the genetic memory of all creatures must have the capacity to store far more complex bits of knowledge, and like our garden spider, they may provide extraordinary survival advantages. What if we humans were born with the genetic knowledge capable of conceptualizing advanced technologies to aid in our survival it could save a lot of study time and tuition fees, sounds like a future challenge to me.

We know the primary objective for this design challenge is to provide a technical solution to eliminate our dependency upon the ruling class elite, thus allowing for the predatory existence of our species to come to its natural end. This technical solution cannot be a temporary fix easily dismantled by top predators determine to use their power, wealth and influence to regain control of their working-class resource. In order for we the people to retain our true freedom and prosperity while continuing to expand the predator free society, all prospective solutions for this design challenge must satisfy a strict set of criteria to be considered a viable option.

The first criterion may be the most difficult to satisfy for our design challenge and the most important to the viability and sustainability of our new predator free society. I like to start with the biggest problems first, somehow it seems to make the smaller ones easier to accomplish or maybe just more fun knowing the harder stuff is out of the way. This first criterion also deals with the largest components that need to be created for the network expansion of ACIs. These components are the reinforced concrete arch segments and domes that comprise a technically advanced ACI.

As a jewelry designer, I often wondered how long my works of art might survive if cared for. The chains I made of precious metal could last thousands of years and continue to provide a sense of emotional satisfaction and art appreciation for generations into the future. I think over the years I've gotten used to this standard and feel it should be applied to all products if possible, but especially to those that directly relate to any of our survival necessities. The first criterion for this challenge is to design an advanced community infrastructure capable of surviving 1000 years with the lowest maintenance possible. The second criterion is the design must utilize rapid construction technologies with a high degree of automation to create the reinforced concrete modular components that comprise an ACI.

Satisfying the first criterion came down to two options. First option, create a structure that could withstand every form of natural and man-made disaster, the increasingly violent seasonal storms, the annual thermal cycling from winter to summer and predatory attacks from other humans for a period of 1000 years. Or the other option, the infrastructure can be placed below ground level. As much as I would like to avoid the energy loss and cost of placing ACIs below ground level, the first option could not satisfy the criterion without excessive amounts of reinforced concrete construction materials. Also there was the consideration of extensive repair and cleanup after a disaster event has passed. Reducing the threat of predatory attacks from other humans would require far more resources to provide security for a surface ACI than a subsurface one.

The energy savings of placing an ACI below ground level alone would have been convincing enough even without all the other security benefits it provides. Eliminating the primary source of energy consumption for a single family home multiplied thought an entire ACI provides a tremendous advantage for us to incorporate into our design challenge. No heating or cooling costs from seasonal changes, just one constant temperature with programmable controls. Another technical advantage of a subsurface infrastructure, there would be no exterior maintenance allowing that additional savings in time and money to be used on aesthetic considerations within the interior of the individual smart homes and community surroundings.

A less considered but substantial benefit is all of the surface land that would have been occupied by wooden residential structures designed to waste huge amounts of energy, can now be used for the power and light trees, algae bio domes, gardens, orchards, beautiful landscaping and artistic displays. It really didn't take long before the advantages of a subsurface ACI became overwhelming evident it was the only option that could satisfy the first criterion to create a predator free community infrastructure capable of withstanding the destructive forces of time.

Because an advanced predator free society attempts to takes full advantage of all emerging automation technologies, it would only seem natural that a rapid construction systems specifically designed to create infrastructure components would be an integral part of this overall design challenge. In some cases a compromise may be needed between automated systems sophisticated enough to produce complicated shapes, and systems designed to make simple infrastructure shapes easier to automate. As it turns out the infrastructure shapes that provide the highest level of structural integrity are also the simplest to re-create for automated rapid construction systems. Lucky for us satisfying this second criterion will be far less difficult and after objectively considering the overwhelming advantages of a subsurface infrastructure, I feel like this design challenge is getting off to a great start.

There are eight specialized divisions that comprise the social economic structure of the predator free society proposed in this book. One of these divisions will specialize in the construction of infrastructure components, their automated functions and eventually designing new systems for the community. Now that we know our basic survival necessity of shelter will be secure we will have a much higher level of confidence that all the technologies and products we integrate into the infrastructures may continue to provide utility and aesthetic value. The era of planned obsolescence for residential surface structures designed to waste and extract wealth from the working class resource, will come to an end.

The next criterion that must be satisfied for this design challenge is energy independence. Even though the highly efficient nature of a technically advanced ACI will only require a fraction of the electricity consumed and wasted by surface structures. Our expanded use of automated public services and product manufacturing will require a reliable means of creating, storing and distributing energy. This criterion will be satisfied by the "Smart Trees", which are a line of products that are designed to produce, store and distribute different forms of energy needed for the community's electrical and transportation requirements. The Smart Trees will use primarily sunlight and water like their organic counterparts. I figure if Mother Nature only needs sunlight, water and a few nutrient elements to work her magic. We intelligent humans should be able to come up with some new semi-artificial life forms capable of producing a variety of our energy requirements. The product line of Smart Trees will be so diverse and their need for the community is so vital, that one of the eight divisions within a predator free society will be dedicated towards accomplishing this task.

Another criterion for this design challenge will also be vital to the success of a predator free society to provide its community members with the highest quality of life possible. The infrastructure of a predator free society must incorporate systems to provide all of the beverage and food requirements for community members and guests. Because clean water and nutritious food are basic survival necessities that need to be supplied at the Smart home and community level, one of the divisions of the predator free society will be given this task. This division will be called the "Food Tree" and most of it's basic functions will be automated as soon as feasible until such time, student guests and predator free members in training may be needed to assist in these tasks. The Food Tree is more than just a division within a predator free society it symbolizes a kind of "Tree of life" and its ability to provide nourishment and greater opportunities for health, happiness and prosperity for all people fortunate enough to have one serving their community.

So far our design challenge to create a technically advanced infrastructure capable of supporting a predator free society will satisfy all the criteria relating to our most important basic survival necessities of secure shelter, clean air and water as well as a source for nutritious food all provided at the Smart home and community level. Once community members acclimate to their new predator free environmental conditions without the need to compete against others for their capitalistic survival, we can begin the work of our mission statement, to expand the network of ACIs bringing true freedom and prosperity to our extended family of fellow humans. It will be necessary to secure the needs of the community members first creating a strong base of operations like building a solid foundation for a home before the main construction begins.

The last criterion that must be satisfied to complete this design challenge is self-replication. This last criterion cannot be solved by technical means alone or completely automated, at least not yet. It will require an integrated predator free social system with members dedicated to accomplishing their mission statement of offering true freedom and prosperity to others by expanding the network of ACIs. Even though this is an unknown element that cannot be fully predicted, it seems many individuals are reaching a level of awareness where continuing their capitalistic struggle for survival is no longer an acceptable life style.

The paradigm shift in our social motivations from predatory competition for survival to predator free cooperation to help others break their bonds of capitalistic oppression, may take a little time to get used to. Once we fully understand the magnitude of this evolutionary accomplishment and realized were breaking the control of hardwired predatory instincts that have dominated our thoughts and actions since the beginning of our existence, a few transitional growing pains that may take months or even years to resolve will seem more than acceptable.

Even though this first prototype ACI design may be a good start, it will no doubt go the way of the Ford model T. as new technologies and creative skills become available. We could call this design challenge solution ACI 1.0. Maybe we can come up with a better name later, but it's really what this technical system does that makes it so cool. It creates the environmental conditions of a predator free society that will be capable of ending our predatory evolution by eliminating the primary factor responsible at it source. We will naturally adapt to this new social structure as all the symptoms of our predatory past fade away.

Even with the technical advantages an advanced ACI can provide by satisfying all of our basic survival necessities at the Smart home and community level, it will be the dedication of we the people to offer true freedom and prosperity to others that will truly accelerate this evolution transition. Just as the environmental conditions of an advanced predatory social structure like Capitalism promotes competition and greed leading to mass exploitation of us working class people. The environmental conditions of a predator free society will produce the exact opposite effect by promoting cooperation and compassion uniting an entire community to free all of our people struggling to maintain their capitalistic competition for survival. As our automated construction technology improves and the socially integrated exponential expansion of the predator free society kicks in, creating a better future for our people should get a lot easier.

The really good news is ACIs are built to last for many generations freeing our minds and bodies from the predatory competitions that have wasted so much of our lives. Now that our basic survival necessities and many luxuries are provided for, we can concentrate on the important things in life, like spending more time with our children, providing them an advanced education in philosophy, science and technology. And then we can use our new skills to help others end their capitalistic existence and make the evolutionary transition to a predator free future.

Finally we can create structures using common sense designs and advanced technologies specifically to benefit we the people and remove our dependency upon top predators. This will eliminate our capitalistic exploitation and the wealth extraction process that has dominated our social existence for thousands of years. It keeps coming back to we the people and our ability to make an objective decision to end our predatory existence and take control of our evolutionary development. How soon will we realize the future of our species hangs in the balance?

1. TFT - Education

Education is one of the eight specialized divisions that comprise the social economic structure of the predator free society offered for consideration in this book. Like all of the divisions in a predator free society there will be a primary family with at least one member that specializes in that subject. Other members of the primary family can assist as secondary helpers in their own division or any other within their community. This will allow greater flexibility for individuals to contribute their creative skills and help accomplish the mission statement of our parent nonprofit organization, TFT (True Freedom Technologies). Many options will be available to choose from and conveniently accessible within their community infrastructure.

When the initial families are selected for new ACIs, a balance must be made to ensure a sufficient number of primary, secondary and student individuals to perform the functions within all eight divisions. Their knowledge and skill levels will determine their positions. Until all the bugs get worked out, and certainly during the initial setup of the first prototype ACI, a higher number of paid assets from outside the community will be needed to get things started.

The responsibilities of an educational primary within a predator free society are first and foremost the education of the youngest members within their community infrastructure. Even though at a very early age they may begin an apprenticeship into one or more of the specialized divisions. The educational primary will provide them with generalize knowledge to better prepare them for any subject or area of interest they may choose. In this way the educational process within a predator free society will be similar to our current system of education allowing for an easier transition for the primary and secondary individuals responsible for this task.

One of the advantages of having so many subjects of interest conveniently located within an ACI is that field trips to explore different technologies will only require a healthy walk around the community infrastructure without the extra expense, loss of time, fuel consumption and pollution produced by diesel buses burning fossil fuels. Of coarse some field trips outside the community will also be arranged to help facilitate the educational process and show the contrast between a predator free society and our current capitalistic social structure. Hopefully by then we can arrange for some form of hybrid electric/biofuel transportation.

Each of the eight primary family Smart homes will have an attached production dome that will also have access to the central courtyard or the inter-ring of the current ACI 1.0 design. This will allow easy access for members and guest interested in learning about that subject. The children's parents will be performing most of their mission activities/jobs within the community infrastructure providing additional convenience and peace of mind for all members of the family. Even though most of the primary family's attached domes are oriented towards automated production of technical and artistic products, the educational dome will be constructed more like a classroom to create the advanced minds of our future.

Knowing that our ability to provide an advanced education for the children today, directly determines the future success of our species. I wondered why would any social structure even a predatory one, be so foolish to transfer the national wealth we need to accomplish this task to some of the most fortunate ruling class individuals in the world. That is until I learned how Capitalism works. Some of our leaders even want to abolish the Department of Education for the entire United States of America, devastating our country's ability to survive our capitalistic competition against other nations in the world and leaving we the people completely vulnerable to intellectual manipulation and capitalistic exploitation by top predators. They may want this social dysfunction to continue but that lever of control and power will soon change hands. Perhaps more than any other reason this is why we must take control of our intellectual evolutionary development and accelerate our transition to a predator free society.

All the members of a predator free society will learn how to form an objective reality and not allow their hardwired predatory instincts or induced subjective realities control their decisions and actions. Even though the belief in subjective realities is encouraged throughout our existing predatory social structure to make we the people more susceptible to all forms of capitalistic exploitation, this form of psychological manipulation will not be allowed within a predator free society. Because the use of induced subjective realities has been socially acceptable for thousands of years as the most efficient tool for mass exploitation of a working-class resource, many individuals have fallen prey to this form of psychological conditioning. Breaking our subjective beliefs to serve Gods, governments and the top predators that represent them, will be an important function of the education division helping to free our minds of the elaborate illusions of our predatory past.

The primaries of a predator free society should have already attained a level of awareness where their thoughts and actions are not controlled by subjective beliefs, voices in their heads, visions in the sky or some form of non-corporeal supernatural entities like angels, demons and Gods. All the primary individuals in a predator free society must form objective reality where their decisions and actions are based on factual knowledge. This is especially true for the educational primary more so than the others because they will be considered one of the most knowledgeable leaders in the community helping other people form an objective reality and break the control of their subjective beliefs. This task will be quite natural and easy to accomplish for the youngest members of a predator free society, as they will simply adapt to their new environmental conditions. However, many older individuals especially outside the community will find it very difficult to break decades of subjective conditioning.

Once all the other negative factors of our predatory social structure that degrade any attempts at an adequate education for our children have been eliminated by the environmental conditions of a predator free society. An educational primary can focus all of his or her creative skills to accomplishing the task of advancing the personal intellectual evolution of their community members. When I think of the best way to accomplish this task the design engineer in me considers the necessity of providing a growing Biosystem what it needs to perform at peak efficiency. On the other hand the artist in me looks at a child's developing brain like a work of art in progress on its way to becoming a beautiful masterpiece of factual knowledge and intellectual skills. Not just any work of art, but one capable of solving the most complex problems that threaten our species future health and pursuit of happiness. Now that's a beautiful mind.

Just imagine an advanced civilization where everyone naturally develops these beautiful minds working at peak efficiency by simply adapt to the intellectually stimulating environmental conditions of a predator free society. An educational primary must fully understand these concepts in order to become an integral part of those environmental conditions and more effectively help individuals of all ages discard the mental residue of our primitive predatory past and embrace the wonder and joy of our technically advanced predator free future.

Because a predator free society integrates advanced education more directly into its social structure every community member over the age of five naturally becomes an assistant for the educational primary helping him or her complete their task. You may wonder how a five-year-old could help an advanced intellectual community? Depending on the five year old they may not have a lot to offer the six, seven and eight year olds that were also educated within the environmental conditions of a predator free society, but for children of these ages living outside the community with limited education opportunities their skills may seem advanced in comparison. Because the assimilation and dissemination of factual knowledge is one of the most fundamental objectives of a predator free society all individuals will be required to share what they have learned with others as well as learn new skills themselves from within the diverse community.

Our five-year-old child may start to develop their mentoring skills by sharing the knowledge they have gained from older members of the community, and then showing the four and three year olds what they have learned. The process may begin with the simplest of tasks at an early age accelerating their ability to share more advanced skills as they grow. Instead of developing advanced predatory skills for capitalistic exploitation of our less fortunate fellow Americans, our five-year-old child will be free to develop intellectual skills based on compassion and cooperation with others intended to benefit the entire global community. This extreme difference in environmental conditions will produce either, capitalistic super predators willing to sacrifice millions of working class prey to achieve their economic domination of the world. Or we can create an advanced benevolent society determined to unite our species and reduce the preventable suffering and death of all our people as equals. It's really our choice.

Even before the education process begins we must ensure the healthy environmental conditions for our baby's developing brain in preparation for the intellectually stimulating surroundings of a predator free society and the many advanced technical skills, philosophical concepts and artistic creations that will become part of their daily lives. In order to accomplish this task we must first ensure the physical and mental health of our baby's parents. After all how can our mothers create healthy baby brains if their environmental conditions do not provide adequate nutrition, prenatal care or even the peace of mind that comes from not having to compete against others for their survival?

A capitalistic corporation that makes cars would give far more quality control considerations to producing their product than our society devotes towards making sure our babies brains are prepared to assimilate information, or to use that knowledge to form abstract solutions to complex problems. Again, this is not an act of incompetence by the entire intellectual community of our country for decades, but instead the manifestation of a well engineer predatory social structure designed to manage we the people. After thousands of years of predatory social structures, many generations of capitalistic exploitation and all the damage done to the intellectual evolutionary development of our species, there is a simple solution for correcting these social dysfunctions. Redesign our society... and I just happen to have one in mind.

I didn't fully realize until later, it's not just technically advanced products that a predator free society will produce, but it will also quite literally create advanced human beings. Starting with parents making the transition from our current predatory social structure their child would be a first generation member of a predator free society and our first baby brain product. We shouldn't expect all first generation members to be geniuses right from the start; after all, most product lines have some glitches at first. But when we're dealing with the most complicated biosystem known in combination with accelerating the intellectual evolutionary development of our species, it may take a little time to get our geniuses factory up to peak efficiency.

Our developing baby brains will begin their education before they're born or at least they can start their audio recognition for familiar sounds like their parents voices, people's names, words, letters, numbers etc. They may have to wait to start building their visual recognition until after they're born, but neural patterns will begin to form from the sounds they are exposed to. A study to determine how much audio recognition a babies developing brain can process may provide an advanced challenge project for members in the educational division of a predator free society.

The more we understand about the natural processes used to accelerate or decelerate the evolutionary development of our intellectual survival trait, the better we can simply assist the ones that work and diminish the ones preventing our progress. Of course this logical approach can only take place in a predator free social structure that values the health and prosperity of its citizens more than their exploitation potential as a working-class resource. For example, it's known that poverty, forced competition for survival, lack of basic survival necessities increased physical and mental health disorders are all things that prevent our children's developing minds from reaching their full potential. It is because we are required to use our intellectual skills as a competitive tool against other Americans, that the less fortunate children of our country are intentionally put at a disadvantage, perpetuating their social status as working-class prey.

Once we the people unite and make a collective decision to end our predatory social structure, our entire country can begin its accelerated transition to a predator free society. All of our nations wealth and resources that is currently being exploited by our top predators can be used to break both chains of Capitalism and provide true freedom and prosperity for all Americans. Now that would be a monumental accomplishment we all could be proud of, something to inspire national pride and prove to the world, this is what America stands for. It's the kind of thing peace loving people in every country would respect and follow once we find the courage to break our subjective realities and lead the world into the next phase of our intellectual evolutionary development. Sure it's a big job, but we the people truly do have the power to accelerate this evolutionary transition, and lead our species into a predator free future. I think our future is counting on us, and we can't let it down.

2. TFT - Infrastructure

A TFT (True Freedom Technologies) ACI (Automated Community Infrastructure) designed to support a predator free society can be considered the ultimate creation we offer to the public. This ultimate creation unlike the other products, will not be for sale, but instead offered to Americans living in capitalistic poverty interested in helping provide true freedom and prosperity to other people still in need. Instead of top predators raising the level of capitalistic exploitation on the members of our current society, those of us with enough strength and wealth will share both to help initiate the self replicating nature of a predator free society and allow it to reach its full exponential growth capabilities.

This technical solution gives us Americans the power to, save each other from our capitalistic oppression, reduce our dependency on top predators for our basic survival necessities and it allows we the people to take control of our social evolutionary development. But best of all, it reduces suffering and death by accelerating the demise of our predatory evolution and the beginning of our predator free future. It's a good start.

Even before the first prototype ACI is constructed a few arches and domes will be created on the surface to evaluate different rapid construction technologies and to run structural tests on the finished products. The most efficient automated construction system will be used to create the first prototype ACI, allowing community members in the infrastructure division to have a finished working model to live in and study.

The infrastructure "Primary" (the head of that division) will need to become thoroughly familiar with the semi-automated rapid construction technologies used to create the individual components of the first prototype ACI. The individual arch sections that make up the circular courtyards as well as the various sized domes that comprise an ACI, will be standardized where possible for construction efficiency.

Creating the structural components of an ACI will be the responsibility of the TFT infrastructure primary, secondary individuals living in the community, visiting students in training and when necessary subcontracted assets from the outside community. As with all eight divisions of the predator free society proposed in this book, the individual designated as the infrastructure primary will live with their other family members in a residential dome between the inner and outer circular courtyards. Like the other primary family residential domes, a production dome connected to the inner courtyard will provide easy access for all community members as well as visitors interested in the technology of that division. The primary families production domes will be a lot like having a storefront for a family business with community and public access from the inner courtyard. Scale models of some division systems will be on display for the education of both members and visitors.

While designing the ACI proposed in this book it became apparent a Goldilocks size would be needed with respect to the number of permanent and visiting residence as well as the amount of space and resources each unit would require to complete. On one hand, it would be nice to create smaller ACI with a faster completion rate, requiring less resources and it could help build confidence among the members knowing they can accomplish our primary objective and mission statement. On the other hand, the smaller the ACI the less permanent residence there will be to provide a healthy level of social diversity.

Even though ACIs are designed to replicate and expand outward from one another providing easy access to other communities and the outside world, it seems important to have enough of a permanent and visiting population to provide a rich diversity of people and interests. The many technical and artistic variations designed into the eight divisions of a predator free society will offer a wondrous set of interests for individuals within the community. The main integrated attractions include; educational tours of the infrastructure, Beach Dome, bed and breakfasts facilities, the Food Tree café, as well as the Center Dome offering nightlife activities. These attractions can adapt to the needs of the community and should provide enough diversity to keep life interesting.

Even though the design of an ACI may conform to available terrain, the first prototype will be more standardized and require a semi-level 500 foot square plot of land with a high-level of sunny days per year, a minimal amount of annual rainfall and preferably room to expand into a multi-community network. The ACI and predator free society has a set of specifications that could be used for comparison with our capitalistic social structure, similar to picking the best computer to buy. Instead of choosing between which infrastructure design is more efficient at delivering a higher quality of life for its predator free citizens, our first comparison must be with our current social structure and the ever-increasing levels of capitalistic exploitation we the people are forced to endure. An objective consideration of the facts should allow for a quicker decision as to which social structure and environmental conditions we would like our children to adapt to.

This design challenge will be to create the most efficient technically advanced community infrastructure within a 500-foot square section of land. The primary criterion remains structural sustainability for around 1000 years using materials and construction technologies capable of accomplishing this task. The interior design, decor and ambience created within the infrastructure's spaces will only be limited by our ever-expanding imagination and future considerations of function and beauty. The important thing is that the infrastructure will continue to perform its function of supplying shelter, freshwater, nutritious food and energy enough to maintain the automated systems within the community. It must also allow for the creation of advanced products for community members, as well as for sale to the public, and have the ability to self-replicate for network expansion. In order to create the environmental conditions of a predator free society, all of these basic survival necessities must be provided by the ACI as a human right to all people not just a privilege for our more fortunate capitalistic competitors.

The specifications for TFTs first 500-foot square ACI 1.0 are as follows:

Production;
8 - 50-foot diameter production domes corresponding to each of the eight divisions of the predator free social economic structure. The interior may be arranged with a single level high ceiling or incorporate a second-level where appropriate. These production domes are under the control of the division primaries and will be modified to best achieve their objectives to serve the community. Designing and prototyping new products in their divisions, coordinating activities and training secondary assistance, will all be part of their mission objective as one of the eight primaries living in a predator free society.

Residential;
8 - 50-foot diameter two-level residential domes, capacity 4 to 6 family members = 32 min to 48 max per community.
8 - 40-foot diameter two-level residential domes, capacity 3 to 4 family members = 24 min to 32 max per community.

True Freedom Technologies 500' Square (ACI - 1.0)

Residential   Agricultural   Personal transport

Production   Recreation   Mini electric car

Aquaculture   Beach   Full size electric car

Utility   Multipurpose   7' to 10' dia. Trees

High resolution, color, Automated Community Infrastructure (1.0) can be seen at
https://www.truefreedomtechnologies.org/hi_res_aci.html, Please see True Freedom Technologies website at
https://www.truefreedomtechnologies.org/home.php for more information.

8 - 24-foot diameter single -level residential studio domes, capacity a single student or a couple = 8 min to 16 max per community.

Multipurpose utility;

4 - 50-foot diameter one or two-level multipurpose utility domes with direct access to the inner courtyard.

4 - 45-foot diameter single level multipurpose utility domes on each entry/exit to the inner courtyard. These domes will be used for small transportation docking and security.

12 - 24-foot diameter one or two-level multipurpose utility domes with direct access to the outer courtyard.

20 - 17-foot diameter single level multipurpose utility domes

24 - 12-foot diameter single level multipurpose utility domes

40 - 10-foot diameter single level multipurpose utility domes.

Aquaculture;

8 - 50-foot diameter two-level Aquaculture domes, with an 8 level garden to equal around 10,000 square feet minus the center column and walkways equals approximately 8000 square feet of small plant garden space per dome. Collectively the 8 aquaculture domes will provide a capacity of approximately 64,000 square feet of secure small plant growing space for the community fueled by natural sunlight from the surface and nutrients from the shrimp and tilapia incorporated into the flooring system of each unit.

Community and limited public access areas;

1 - 500-foot diameter outer courtyard ring approximately 50 foot wide.

1 - 200-foot diameter inner courtyard ring approximate 75 foot wide.

Recreation, beach and product testing;

1 - 80-foot diameter recreational dome with year around beach, natural sunlight, whirlpool and sauna. This recreational dome will also be used for testing amphibious and underwater products.

True Freedom Technologies basic 50-foot diameter, two level dome

Designed to resist or prevent damage from all forms of natural and man made disasters for several hundred years

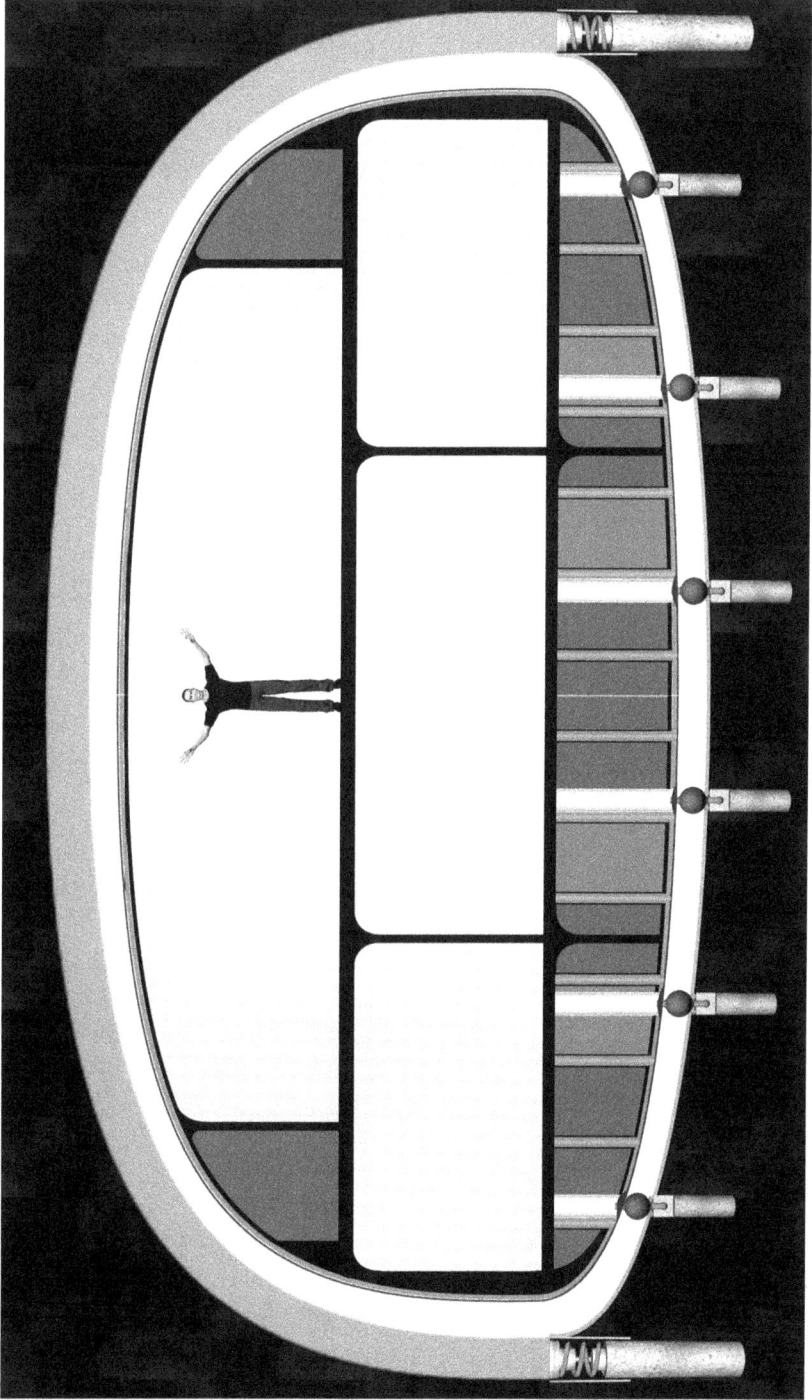

Large-scale multipurpose Production and product testing;

2 - 80-foot diameter large-scale production and product testing domes will be used primarily for infrastructure components and large transportation products using advanced transformation technologies. The flooring system in these domes can be designed to adapt to different production and community needs.

Agricultural;

1 - 80-foot diameter Agricultural dome for primarily Dairy goats and chickens. This dome can adapt to the changing agricultural needs and desires of the community.

Recreation/entertainment;

1 - 50-foot diameter single level recreation and entertainment dome at the center of the ACI. This recreational dome may be referred to as the "Center Dome" and will be used for nightlife activities including music, dancing etc.

Standard amenities not shown on the ACI 1.0 diagram;

1 - Robotic master of culinary art and at least two automated Sous Chefs will be on duty 24 hours a day to serve the community members and visitors. These robotic chefs will also be part of the educational entertainment for public guests to the Food Tree Café.

1 - 45' and possibly the connected 40' diameter multipurpose utility domes will be used for a flower garden oriented towards beauty and ambience as opposed to the aquaculture domes designed for output efficiency.

Residential extras;

16 - 30'x15' half dome retractable extensions for patios, garage, storage etc. connected to the 50-foot diameter dome residences. These retractable half domes will be located within the outer courtyard.

Multipurpose utility extras;

8 - 30'x15' half dome retractable extensions for community utilities, extra storage, overnight guests etc. also located within the outer courtyard.

Temporary residential;

8 - 30'x15' half dome retractable extensions for bed and breakfasts guests. These retractable half domes can accommodate 2 to 4 guests and will be located within the outer courtyard.

Aquaculture extras;

156 - 7' to 10' diameter. Fruit and ornamental Trees securely located within the outer and inner courtyard. An undetermined number of automated fish farms may be installed in the flooring system of the inner and outer courtyards. Koi Ponds, waterfalls, small ornamental bushes and flower gardens will also be placed throughout both courtyards.

Power and Light, Smart Trees;

174 - 20' diameter Smart Trees will collect and concentrate natural sunlight for subsurface expansion throughout the ACI 1.0 as well as heat up a solar energy storage system to run heat engines and generate electric power.

Power and Fuel, Smart Trees;

8 - 50-foot diameter Smart Trees using hybrid biotech "Lifeform" technology that can transform into a dome like shape suitable for temporary shelter against the heat of the day or the cold of the night. These hybrid Smart Trees may only produce enough electric power to automate their systems because their primary purpose is the production and storage of biodiesel and ethanol fuels. Additional permanent and mobile Power and Fuel Smart Trees may be installed or deployed as needed.

When new communities are finished, the most senior secondary and their family will have the opportunity to become the primary in the newly completed ACIs. As ACIs are completed the original infrastructure primaries will advise the new ones as the network of communities expands outward. At first their commute to the job site will be within walking distance. However, as the ACI network expands a bicycle or an electric transport may be required. More experienced infrastructure primaries may travel to new startup communities where their expertise will be most needed. All community members will learn secondary skills in case their primary skill cannot be used or are temporarily not required. An experienced infrastructure primary may eventually transition their skills to another division within their ACI helping to create the advanced products sold to the public and used to furnish new communities. In this way older infrastructure primary can still provide many valuable contributions towards achieving our mission statement, while giving them the option to stay closer to home and spend more time with their families.

3. TFT - Healthcare

Like education, healthcare is one of the six social economic areas targeted for improvement as well as one of the eight divisions in the predator free society proposed in this book. The environmental conditions of a predatory social structure and the corrupt influence of Capitalism has allowed both our education and healthcare to be used as management tools to better manipulate we the people and keep the efficient flow of national wealth from the working class many to the ruling class few. Knowing the immense damage that results from depriving a working-class resource the adequate healthcare they need to lead happy and productive lives, additional resources will be allocated in an attempt to repair generations of capitalistic exploitation. The induced epidemic of obesity, diabetes, cancer, heart disease etc. will take generations to repair and these will be the consequences we must suffer for allowing our predatory social structure to reach such high levels of mass exploitation. We must take control of our future and end this process as soon as possible.

I realize many people still feel that if they just worked hard enough for their entire lives maybe they can make our advanced predatory social structure fairer for us working class prey, like continuing to treat the symptoms of a fatal disease with band-aids. Lucky for us we know how to reverse the effects of this disease and bring the patient to full health before things get worse. Many well-intended people are determined to make a difference and perhaps they feel this is the only option they have to lessen the preventable suffering and death of the less fortunate competitors. Before I realized that all of our symptoms have a root cause that must be corrected at the source, I considered designing medical devices to help save the lives of people that could afford advanced healthcare, and following my conditioning to become a good Capitalist, but that didn't feel right. I wanted to use my creative skills to improve the health of all people regardless of their social status, capitalistic success or predatory prowess. We needed a solution where compassionate caring people all over the world determined to help others improve their healthcare are given the chance to maximize their creative skills without the corrupting influence of a predatory social structure.

Just imagine what we the people could accomplish if providing healthcare and prosperity for our country was as important as ensuring the efficient exploitation of the working-class population. Instead of having to be concerned about extracting the maximum amount of wealth from the working-class resource and keeping us on the edge of survival, we can concentrate all of our collective creative skills towards providing an advanced healthcare system for all our people as a basic human right not a privilege to compete for. I think people in our country and all over the world are tired of playing our predatory game for survival, and the endless lessons in futility trying to make life fairer for the designated prey.

Eliminating the source that continues to perpetuate our preventable suffering and death is the only viable solution to providing advanced Universal healthcare to the least fortunate members of our society. Millions of healthier people will then have the opportunity to make great contributions to our entire species. We humans can't afford to lose any creative skills that may help advance our intellectual evolutionary development and save our species from any further preventable destruction.

In the beginning, all individuals living within the first ACI will need to acclimate to their new environmental conditions. It may feel a little like moving into a futuristic technical school that emphasizes the automated production of advanced products and services. Adapting to the new motivational social standard and philosophical beliefs of a predator free society will also have an impact a member's physical and mental health. Its more that just a big change, its an evolutionary transition. Preparation cases will be available to lessen any concerns about what to expect.

Like the other divisions of the predator free society there will be one individual for each community infrastructure designated as the healthcare primary. The individual designated as the senior secondary healthcare provider, will assist the primary and will also live in a permanent residence within the ACI with their family, but instead will occupy one of the two level 40-foot diameter residential domes connected to the outer courtyard. There will also be several assistance living within the ACI that may have healthcare as a secondary interest or be in training for a more advanced position in that division. As the ACI network grows there will be other healthcare primaries available to share their expertise with less experienced members interested in expanding their knowledge and brainstorming on better ways to keep our community healthy and prosperous.

The healthcare primary will have a connected 50-foot diameter production dome that can be configured to have one or two levels depending on efficiency and preference. The healthcare production dome may include a room for the design and prototyping of advanced diagnostic and/or medical devices, but in general it will be configured to accept individuals for the treatment of minor accidents and preventative checkups in an attempt to eliminate health-care problems before they start. Until more advanced surgical procedures can be performed within the predator free community, a group healthcare plan must be secured for members needing more extensive medical treatments.

Our healthcare strategy for increased efficiency within a predator free society will be based on one of my favorite proverbs. I learned it was

Benjamin Franklin who said, "An ounce of prevention is worth a pound of cure". The immense power and meaning these words hold, has been lost over the years, as the need for capitalistic success by top predators became more of a national priority than following a commonsense suggestion made by one of our forefathers. One of the best ways to prevent a health related crisis or emergency is to monitor our Bio-systems so any potentially dangerous irregularities will automatically notify the community member and their designated healthcare provider so it may be corrected before becoming more serious.

As the healthcare primary becomes more comfortable with their position in a predator free society, and during the times when their medical services are not required, they may initiate a design challenge. The nature of the design challenge may span the entire range of healthcare needs with an overall objective of increasing the efficiency of the entire Biosystem we call our bodies. It seems like a good place to start would be the number one subsystem responsible for the most deaths, like our circulatory system and heart. Luckily the younger members of the predator free society can take well-known commonsense precautionary measures eliminating the capitalistic exploitation and induced environmental conditions that promote heart disease and death for profit.

After a strong and healthy base of operations can be established for a predator free society, efforts must be taken to offer free health care to the general public and help correct the damage done in the name of free-market Capitalism. Hundreds of thousands of Americans are lost every year and the global spread of Capitalism is resulting in the degradation and demise of millions of our people all over the world. Until our evolutionary transition to a predator free society is complete our objective must be to find the most efficient way to minimize our preventable suffering and death. While also, educating the public as to the necessity of eliminating the source of the problem instead of continuing to treat the symptoms.

Life-saving medical procedures are becoming more technically complex, and even though the capitalistic competitors of America are willing to give up their entire life savings, sell their homes and go bankrupt for operations costing hundreds of thousands of dollars. This can be accomplished for far less once the primary objective of exploiting the working-class resource is replaced with a genuine desire to value human life over personal profit. Only then can our people begin to heal from a predatory competition that has dominated our evolutionary development since the beginning of our existence.

4. TFT - Transportation

The transportation division within the predator free social economic structure proposed in this book may offer the greatest revenue potential to help support the community and our mission statement. Where education and healthcare tend to concentrate more on keeping the community members functioning at peak efficiency with less emphasis on revenue, the transportation division will focus more on creating advanced products for sale to the general public. At first the focus will be supplying the community's transportation needs specifically the automated systems that help the ACI perform its functions. Those functions entail the transportation of materials, people, food etc. around the ACI. For example manufacturing materials and personal goods will need to have an automated transportation system to shuttle things from a surface structure where shipments are received, to the subsurface productions domes or residence. Non-electric vehicles that emit carbon monoxide and other airborne toxins cannot operate within the subsurface environment. In some cases these vehicles can be shuttled electrically to belowground residence, but mostly they'll be parked on the surface requiring additional transportation to reach any location within the subsurface areas of the ACI.

An automated transportation system must deliver fresh produce from the high-efficiency aquaculture domes, the subsurface orchard and micro-gardens located within the outer courtyard as well as the extended surface gardens to the Food Tree production dome. Where processing can take place, providing the robotic chefs what they need to supply the community and visitors with a nutritional variety of culinary masterpieces. A joint design challenge between the Automated Systems and Transportation divisions may improve upon the mobile systems that deliver prepared meals anywhere within the ACI as well as perform the functions of a waiter for the visitors to the Food Tree Café.

At first newer members to a predator free society will require vehicles manufactured outside the community for personal, recreational and TFT business use. As the community transportation needs are met this division may begin to concentrate on creating commercial vehicles for sale to the public. These vehicles will have many advanced features pushing the envelope on technologies currently considered to be state-of-the-art. One of these features is the ability to recharge its own power storage systems. This future also makes the vehicle a mobile electric generator for remote areas.

Another feature integrated into these advanced vehicles is the ability to transform into a small office studio with bathroom, shower, and mini kitchen for convenience and comfort when traveling for recreation, research or TFT business activity. An advanced transportation system by TFT will integrate the ability to perform the first two features on land or water increasing its utility value as a multipurpose platform. A two or four seat vehicle in its compact configuration with the solar collector and studio expansion retracted may extend hydrofoils as an option for faster nautical speeds. These multipurpose transportation systems as well as many other advanced products have been pre-designed at TFT to help accelerate the production process.

Just because TFT transportation systems offer advanced utility functions doesn't mean they can't be aesthetically pleasing. Like most products created inside a predator free society one of the greatest design challenges is to merge advanced utility value with exceptional beauty. This may be easier to do for some products than others. For example a two-seat sports car would allow for more artistic appeal compared to larger vehicles designed primarily for utility value.

The larger vehicle platforms can be designed to expand and provide a wide variety of uses like a mobile construction office for new ACIs including power generators and room for a four person crew with bathroom, shower and kitchen.

As education is another human right that must be denied to maintain control over the working class resource. Mobile learning centers can be used to provide the factual information needed to help American citizens break their subjective realities and take objective control of their decisions and actions. Our objective will not be to create more advanced capitalistic predators to compete against one another, but instead explaining how they may break their chains of Capitalism and achieve true freedom and prosperity. The larger transportation platforms may also be used for family vacations as recreational vehicles and some may be equipped with an amphibious option transforming them into houseboats, again extending their utility value for different applications.

An advance transportation system from TFT does not have to be limited to land and water. Creating a multipurpose craft capable of transportation through the air, on land or water that is also street legal for highway use has long been an ultimate design challenge. A technically complex transportation system of this nature is a perfect design challenge for a predator free society encouraging a good working relationship between the different divisions needed to prototype this advanced product.

Smaller high bypass Turbofan jet engines burning algae biofuel can be more easily integrated into a two or four passenger aircraft design. Many design variations are possible to create a multi-craft capable of vertical takeoffs and landings from land or water and transforming down to a size capable of fitting inside a tractor-trailer.

With the jet engines turned off and using only electric drive much like an advanced hybrid car, this multi-craft can easily move around inside the subsurface environment of an ACI like the more conventional zero admission electric vehicles.

Creating advanced vehicles of this nature not only presents a great design challenge for a predator free society but also provides environmental conditions with a high level of intellectual stimulation. Once these environmental conditions have also eliminated the need for predatory competition and provide our basic survival necessities as a human right, our intellectual evolutionary development will accelerate giving us greater control over our hardwired instincts and subjective realities.

Advanced transportation products by TFT will not only provide a revenue stream to accomplish our mission statement but also greatly accelerate our objective to educate all people about our evolutionary transition to true freedom and prosperity. The advanced products by TFT are designed to blow minds and draw attention to the philosophy of a predator free society. It also seems that the segment of our population most interested in advanced technical products with futuristic appeal would also be most likely to appreciate and understand the need for our species to end the ways of our predatory past and accelerate our transition to a predator free future.

The transportation primary and secondary assistants, like other members of a predator free society, may start their technical training at whatever level is most comfortable for that individual. More technical details on advanced products and automated production systems will be released as patents and predatory protections can be secured allowing individuals to learn more about the different divisions within an ACI and their various functions. Like the other divisions, there will be one primary and one senior secondary individual responsible for transportation activities. Their family members may assist as secondaries in their division or any other within the ACI. The transportation division will use one of the 80-foot production domes for the fabrication and assembly of larger products. One or more of the utility domes will be equipped with large-scale 3-D printers and other automated manufacturing systems creating parts for the various transportation products. The primary 50-foot production dome will be used for the designing and prototyping of new transportation products as well as the automated manufacturing of small parts and subsystem assemblies.

Longer distance transportation systems to connect ACI clusters to each other may have higher speeds for moving people, materials and products. The main power for the primary propulsion system must be distributed, locally generated and redundant with an additional backup energy source in each individual transportation unit. Each transportation unit will have enough power to reach the next exit where the electric vehicle it carries can continue on its own energy. The power systems and transportation infrastructure must also avoid destruction from all forms of natural and man-made disasters to meet the 1000-year ACI design criterion.

The power and fuel Smart Trees designed to support the needs of an ACI, may be distributed along a linear line of travel and integrated into this design challenge to provide energy for the primary propulsion systems. At some point in the future automated TBM (tunnel boring machines) will need to be employed to expand an advanced transportation network connecting ACIs across the nation and eventually around the world. Larger projects like an automated high-speed transportation system designed to function with renewable energy sources will be an excellent opportunity for multiple divisions to integrate their creative skills to benefit not only our entire current community but also future generations.

Only after we decide to end our predatory evolution, can we begin to build an advanced transportation system designed to serve the needs of we the people. Then we can eliminate one of the greatest wealth extracting tools top predators have ever socially engineered to exploit a working-class resource. Keep in mind to deny our capitalistic exploitation and to consider it an acceptable social structure, is a natural manifestation of adapting to our predatory environmental conditions. But we don't have to let that control us anymore, not now that we have the intellectual ability to make an objective decision to end the process.

You may have wondered as I did, if we currently have the technologies and intellectual skills to create a national transportation system capable of eliminating most of the around 32,000 highway deaths in America each year, why don't we do it? What could be more important than protecting the lives of American citizens? Once I learned enough to realize our nation has the technical and intellectual expertise to eliminate the suffering and death of we the people, yet something else was considered a priority. That's when I really had to find out what our country found more important than protecting its American citizens.

5. TFT - Smart Trees

The first question people may have is, what makes a tree smart? Starting when they're just little seedlings they are shown love and affection within intellectually stimulating environmental conditions. Just kidding, that may work on us humans but that's not how these TFT trees get smart. An ST (Smart Tree) is designed with technical features that allow them to sense and adapt to changing environmental conditions. Once an environmental condition is detected like rain or the sun moving through the sky, an ST will respond according to their hardwired programming and or their installed software. If this technical sequence leading to a programmed response sounds familiar, it should because it closely mirrors how our own bodies function as well.

For example when we detect raindrops from the sky we instinctively take cover, the solar STs will also retract to protect them selves while others may deploy to collect water or harness wind power. While we humans sense and adjust to our environmental conditions by moving into or out of direct sunlight, STs may follow the sun through the sky to maximize their power collection, much like their organic counterparts. Our ability to learn new technical skills is also very similar to a ST getting a software update allowing them to perform their functions more efficiently. The big difference being we humans are programmed by our hardwired survival instincts encoded in our genetic memory and the conditioning of our subjective realities, while our new synthetic life forms like STs are designed to provide universal utilities for all people as a human right. Following this analogy, an induced subjective reality will have the same destructive results on a developing human brain as downloading a software virus would have on our new synthetic life forms. Especially if that virus designed to transfer wealth and power from the working class many to the ruling class few.

Once we understand the similarities and differences between the evolution of our own Biosystems and the synthetic life forms we create it becomes easier to contemplate our entire existence being a controlled experiment by an advanced race of beings. I feel pretty certain about one thing, if they are keeping track of our intellectual and social development, were about to blow their minds. Or maybe they're wondering what's taking us so long to reject our predatory programming compared to other developing species following a parallel track of intellectual development. Something to think about…

I consider the wondrous variety of trees and plants on this planet a little like Mother Nature's artistic ability to provide beauty and utility value within multiple forms of life. In a way our organic trees and plants already perform some of the functions I hope our STs will provide by converting sunlight, rain and other elements into the energy needed to expand a living network of ACIs. After millions of years of evolutionary trial and error, and unable to drill for fossil fuels, our organic trees and plants survive on their ability to utilize free and abundant resources primarily sunlight and water to sustain a peaceful existence and prevent their extinction. It's interesting and a little sad that non-intelligent trees are using a better survival strategy than us humans. Aren't we supposed to be the smart ones?

Imagine what would have happened if plants developed intelligence and a predatory capitalistic society where the bigger top predator trees could make all the smaller plants compete against one another and pay for the sunlight and water they needed to survive. Even without intelligence trees and plants follow their natural hardwired instincts to hoard and consume as much sunlight and water as possible to grow larger regardless of the many smaller plants below them struggling to survive. Are we humans just mindlessly following our instincts too, is this why so many of our people had to suffer and die? I wonder what the exact date will be in the future when our species finally says enough. I hope it's soon.

Learning from Mother Nature, STs will primarily utilize the radiant energy from the sun to provide the power and light needs for the community. It is for this reason that ACIs will need to be constructed in sunnier areas to maximize the amount of energy that can be collected and minimize the number of STs needed to support an individual community. The STs are not only designed to supply the power and light needs of community infrastructures but they are also intended to be a signature product line of TFT. This unique product line may be as diverse as their organic counterparts and only limited by our rapidly advancing technologies, expanding imaginations and creative skills. Some ST designs may look organic or even alien in appearance with a high degree of artistic appeal and or entertainment value while providing less of a utility function. While other ST designs may have a more technical appearance and higher utility value. In addition to the design challenge to merge artistic and utility value there is a third element to consider, the integration of living Biosystems.

Incorporating living Biosystems into a ST design or any other TFT product creates another balance to consider as to what level of artificial versus organic contribution our new hybrid lifeforms will use. At first it seems the addition of Biosystems will provide more of a utility advantage than artistic appeal. However, if the Biosystems can be displayed in a way that provides educational and entertainment value, then the artistic appeal could be high. For example, a small-scale aquaculture system may be incorporated in larger STs showing how the automation functions work.

Incorporating bioluminescent microorganisms into ST designs and throughout the interior of an ACI will provide many creative opportunities for night lighting and special effects. Also because our STs are designed to sense and respond to environmental conditions all night lighting and special effects can be made interactive, like walking on beach sand during a red tide and seeing a mysterious glow radiating outward from each footstep. It's a beautiful phenomenon that can be duplicated in a controlled environment and used for artistic expressions.

Like their organic counterparts, the ST product line will be offered in a wide range of sizes and shapes. STs will fall into different categories according to their size and function. One of, if not the most important design will be the PLST (Power and Light Smart Tree). At full bloom or fully deployed these PLSTs can have large diameters, but one around 20 feet will allow for easier placement in-between individual subsurface domes as well as the inner and outer courtyards. The primary function of the PLSTs is to collect, concentrate and re-expand full spectrum radiant energy from the surface to the subsurface environment of an ACI. Incorporating a system to secure full spectrum natural sunlight for the ACIs provides many advantages for a controlled subsurface environment.

Full spectrum artificial lighting may also be incorporated into ACIs as a backup source of radiant energy for people and plants. However, the abundant and free energy from our Sun will provide lighting during the day without draining power or fuel reserves. In the highly unlikely event radiant energy from the sun is blocked for months back up fuel reserves can be designed to maintain a living subsurface environment long after surface life has died. Even though this would be considered a low probability high-impact event such as a super volcano eruption or large meteor strike, ACIs that are designed to last 1000 years must take these things into consideration. Under these extreme circumstances the survival of a predator free society would be determined by the nature and magnitude of the natural disaster, months or years of total darkness and back up fuel reserves to power the full spectrum artificial lighting systems.

The secondary function of the PLSTs is to provide electric power for the residential, recreational and automated production needs for a community infrastructure. 20-foot diameter PLSTs will concentrate radiant energy like a giant magnifying glass down to around a 3-inch diameter beam of light. This highly concentrated beam of light will heat up an extremely well insulated high temperature solar energy storage system using molten salts. The heat from this thermal storage system can then be used to generate electricity using Stirling engines, steam turbines, thermoelectric generators etc.

Different technologies will be virtually prototype for efficiency however, a new Stirling engine design, in combination with thermoelectric generators seems to show promise so far. Other technologies such as Solid Oxide Fuel Cells may be integrated into the design allowing for many interesting possibilities for increased efficiency, flexibility and utility value. As more designs and products are prototyped and patented, technical specifications will be released on the TFT website.

Another Smart Tree design is a PFST (Power and Fuel Smart Tree). Fully deployed PFSTs may have a diameter of up to 60 feet and installed in any full sun area where space permits. The PFSTs are a hybrid design that incorporates living Biosystems for the production of fuel. Because all of the automated subsystems of PFST need to be scaled down, smaller lifeforms like algae, yeast, baby shrimp etc. are a good size to work with and integrate into new designs. PFSTs technologies are designed to produce and store the products of oxygen, hydrogen, biodiesel, ethanol, electric power, heat and pure H_2O steam or liquid.

In addition to the products it produces it can also be made portable for on-site placement or permanently installed with the ability to retract into the ground avoiding any damage from surface devastation events. When fully deployed the dome canopy of a PFST will also provide temporary shelter and a more temperature-controlled atmosphere for work or recreation. The PFSTs control functions, diagnostic displays and fuel storage levels, etc. will all be available through wireless remote for easy access, as well as accessed manually on-site. As with the entire ST product line, this advanced hybrid species will be used not only throughout the predator free communities but also sold to the general public to help reduce their dependency upon top predators and to increase revenues for an expanding network of ACIs.

Some STs will be designed to utilize the wind to generate their power especially for remote areas that tend to have much more wind than radiant energy from the sun. These trees will be designated as PWST (Power and Wind Smart Tree) and must also be capable of accomplishing the self-preservation criterion. Designs using vertical axis generators seem like they may be easier to integrate the self-preservation criterion compared to the more conventional horizontal axis wind generators. PWSTs may have other integrated systems like photovoltaic cells to convert radiant energy from the sun into electric power. If weather conditions turn dark and windy this form of ST may be the best way to generate and store energy.

Of all the Smart things these trees can do there is one thing that matters most above all the rest, the ability to sense danger and protect them selves from destruction. Sometimes I wonder what it would be like to be a living tree with the intelligence to comprehend the death and destruction left after a wildfire, tornado or hurricane. What would I be thinking watching the devastation getting closer and closer, I'd probably be thinking I wish I had legs instead of roots so I could take cover and protect myself until the disaster has passed. If were going to play techno tree Gods and create new synthetic life forms, we want our works of art and their utility value to be capable of withstanding the most severe surface disasters that commonly destroy their organic counterparts. Until our new life forms are capable of self-replication and preservation they need to rely on us to design in a good survival characteristic.

The larger STs that are permanently installed will retract into the ground with a removable reinforced concrete cap to protect them against the harshest surface devastation events. The larger STs that are made mobile and towed behind an electric vehicle must take cover inside an ACI to prevent their destruction from surface disasters. In addition to the larger permanently installed and mobile STs, there will be a smaller product line referred to as SP (Smart Plant). The big difference between STs and SPs besides their size is the larger trees are either permanently installed or mobile and the SPs are in pots. All of the SPs functioning within ACIs will be protected from surface disasters and operate on natural sunlight beaming in from the PLSTs.

Even the smallest SP should have the ability to convert sunlight into enough stored energy it can perform its artistic, utility and entertainment functions. Larger designs may also store enough energy to recharge smart phones or power tablets and laptops. Some SPs may also be designed to dispense hot and cold beverages like a limited miniature version of the Food Tree concept. Indoor SPs will need to get a few hours of full sunlight per day through a window to provide self-powered nighttime entertainment and or utility functions. However an AC power option can be used for areas with too little light or for extended use like at a social gathering.

I was working on some advanced animatronic techniques for a human face at the same time I was thinking of some cool SP designs to try. And in one of those eureka moments it dawned on me that I could combine both of these technical interests into a single SP product. The idea for the "Face Plant" was born. A Face Plant is a natural to alien looking synthetic life form that is designed to be more of an entertaining work of art than a utility system. The face plant product line is an excellent example of an item that uses elements from different TFT divisions within a predator free society.

These products could be easily made in the Smart Tree, Advanced Arts or even Automated Systems divisions or perhaps a collaboration between all three, encouraging more cooperation to benefit the entire community. One of the things I like most about the face plant product line is that it offers designers the ability to express and merge their artistic and technical skills using four primary elements.

Of the four elements that comprise this product the first is the pot base and it should appear like any number of commonly accepted designs to enhance the illusion that it may be a living plant. Also the pot base should be considered a supporting element to enhance the main subject and not detract from it. The pot base doesn't tend to leave much room for artistic expression. However, what the pot base lacks in artistic expression it makes up in utility value. Needing to be the heaviest element for stability and offering an inconspicuous volume of space this would be where most of the utilities like water tanks, batteries and control systems would go. The SP's round base can also be designed to serve as one of the rotational axis for solar tracking increasing the efficiency of any solar collector or photovoltaic systems.

The real artistic flexibility for the face plant product line is with the other three elements of branches leaves and the face. For creative inspiration we only need to observe the diversity of organic plant life and floral structures to re-create similar synthetic works of art. An array of leaves will most likely be the main solar collector although the branches and even the pot can be used as thermal electric generators. The broader leaf designs have more surface area to collect solar energy and can make tracking the sun easier. Also the SPs don't have the requirement of retracting into their pot in order to protect themselves from seasonal storms or natural and man-made disasters like their larger outdoor siblings the ST. However, a SP can be designed to grow taller and change shape as part of an entertainment program or as a response to sensory inputs detecting someone's presence.

The face of the plant is the central element and main focus for people's attention much like a large flower would be in the center of one of their organic counterparts. Floral, plant, and human characteristics can be integrated and artistically express in a wide variety of ways. What appears like an exotic flower from a distance transforms into a face as someone approaches. A background lowlight mode can be designed in to a system conserving power until a passive infrared proximity sensor detects the presence of a visitor. The flower face can slowly reveal itself the closer someone gets by moving its leaves and or petals. The face's eyes can be designed to open depending on the visitor's proximity. For example wait until an unsuspecting visitor makes a close inspection to a sleeping flower face and then have the eyes opened suddenly, providing some entertainment value. At least I think the kids would love it.

You probably didn't expect to hear about animatronic faces in a section about Smart trees, but a really brilliant tree should be able to interact with us and one of the very first things we see and can relate to in life are faces. The artistic possibilities with this primary element are more than just all the genetic diversity, ethnic and cultural variations on this planet but may also include how we imagine what extraterrestrial life forms might look like if they have faces and plant bodies. Clear and translucent RTV (Room Temperature Vulcanizing) silicone rubbers are flexible and strong enough to be used as skin on an animatronic face capable of moderate to complex expressions. Clear and translucent materials allow for LED lighting special effects and more options for artistic expressions.

Most Face Plants will have simple leaf, pedal and facial expression movements as a response to a sensory input much like we humans do to our environmental conditions. Even though the face plants are not intended to use more complicated micro controller based animatronics they can serve as an introductory platform to more advanced lifeform projects. SPs are small convenient products to design, prototype and test for the younger members of the community to learn on. Younger and new members to a predator free community can have fun designing the artistic and entertainment aspects of their synthetic life form while also learning about more advanced materials and technologies. ST and Plant displays of different designs, materials and technologies will be available throughout ACIs creating an intellectually stimulating environment for members and visitors to enjoy. The community will evaluate new smart plant designs to decide which ones will be developed and included into the product line offered to the public.

New ST and SP designs are converted into an automated manufacturing file that can be sent out to other ACIs equipped with standardized production systems. In this way any technical improvements or new artistic expressions made by one member, can be rapidly shared to benefit an entire network of ACIs. Even if that network is global and benefits an entire species. Newly discovered philosophical concepts to help eliminate preventable suffering and death or to accelerate our intellectual evolutionary transition to a predator free society may also be transmitted throughout an extended community, like a knowledge update for our minds keeping our objective reality current.

The individual designated as the Smart Tree primary within the social economic structure of a predator free society, like the other division heads, will live in one of the eight 50 foot diameter two level residential domes located between the inner and outer courtyards of the current ACI design. The 50-foot primary domes have room for five other family members that can provide secondary assistance within their own division or any of the other seven conveniently accessible inside their ACI. Division primaries that are single or with smaller families may live in another residential dome closer to their needs.

The Smart Tree division primary's main responsibility is to coordinate the semi-automated production of STs and SPs made for new communities and sale to the public. A Smart Tree primary will consider design improvements from other community members. The more promising designs will be virtually prototype by secondary assistance working in the Smart Tree division. Scaled-down and eventually full-size models can be prototyped and tested in the Smart Tree 50 foot diameter production dome, 80-foot diameter multipurpose dome and on the surface.

The materials and technologies available to design and create STs is growing rapidly but the real challenge is how to combine them in new ways to significantly advance and merge their artistic, entertainment and utility value into beautiful synthetic life forms. This design challenge will also be a good opportunity to merge our accumulated technical knowledge and creative skills with our imaginations allowing out-of-the-box abstract solutions to spontaneously emerge as flashes of inspiration and full on Eureka moments.

Oh what a wonderful world awaits us, and we're so close to making that evolutionary transition beyond the insanity of our predatory past and present into a future where all people may live free of capitalistic exploitation and use their intellectual skills to benefit the many rather than serve the few. The development of Smart Trees and Plants as emerging synthetic life forms will help accelerate our species transition to a predator free society by eventually eliminating our dependency upon top predators for our basic survival necessities and energy needs, eventually breaking the second chain Capitalism for all people.

6. TFT - Automated Systems

The TFT Automated Systems division will be the most diverse and technically challenging within a predator free society. Because this division uses advanced automation technologies to provide community services as a human right and the product production systems for an ACI, this division primary and secondaries will be called upon for many design challenges. Other TFT divisions may require a special component designed and possibly made by Automated Systems for integration into a new product. For example the TFT Transportation division may require an automated subsystem to more efficiently guide materials and room service delivery robots around the community infrastructure. Or for instance the TFT Food Tree division may require assistance to increase the efficiency for a new robotic chef design. Automated Systems will be the go to division for the most technically complex design challenges a predator free society may encounter. This is the division for individuals that really like a good technical challenge, a chance to turn our wildest imaginations into advanced products and best of all the opportunity to use our creative skills to help others make the transition from capitalistic poverty to true freedom and prosperity.

All the members of a predator free society may provide secondary assistance in the Automated Systems division to learn new technologies and teach others what they already know. Depending on the community's current production needs this division may require the highest number of secondary assistance to accomplish our overall mission objectives. To make the task easier for the individual designated as the Automated Systems primary not all subsystems need to be created from scratch. Many commercially available off-the-shelf OEM (Original Equipment Manufacture) products and subsystems may provide a more cost-effective option. These OEM subsystems are specially designed for integration into new products and buying them from the outside community will help alleviate the jobs crisis and reduce capitalistic poverty during the transition process to a predator free society. Especially if less capitalistic companies that care about the health and human rights of their employees are given the contract.

One of the primary objectives of the Automated Systems division is to design and create standardized programmable manufacturing systems. The standardized systems must be capable of accepting the same automated manufacturing file format to create exact copies. This will provide a tremendous boost in efficiency and quality control while increasing customer satisfaction and conserving costs. It's amazing how eliminating the burden of predatory competition and the need for capitalistic exploitation of a working-class resource makes designing a social structure to benefit we the people so much easier. At nearly the speed of light a manufacturing file containing exact instructions on the automated production of a new TFT product or synthetic lifeform is sent out to a global network of ACIs allowing others around the world to instantly benefit from the creative inspiration of a single individual. The more we learn about the advantages of a predator free society, the easier it will be to see how this transition will accelerate the intellectual evolutionary development of our species.

The automated production of these products may require several standardized machines each creating different specialized parts in the most efficient way possible. Especially for products like the more advanced amphibian lifeforms from the Transportation division or an interactive Face Plant may need different manufacturing systems to create and assemble their parts. For example some parts are easier to fabricate from sheet, wire, tubing etc. while others need to be cast and or machined. The design and material of the part will determine the most efficient and cost effective standardized automation system to use. More complicated products containing multiple subsystems and hundreds of parts will group files according to their manufacturing process. After a new file is released into the network of ACIs they are downloaded directly to the machines responsible for producing their parts with notifications to the division primaries that they have a new product that can be made and what materials are needed to make the part.

CNC (Computer Numerical Control) machines will be used to create automated production systems small enough to fit on a desktop for high precision parts and products all the way to something the size of a house for the production of architectural and infrastructure components. Once a manufacturing system has CNC precision we can program the exact position of a multipurpose tool base. This tool base is a lot like a print head in a desktop printer but instead of putting ink on paper it may control a CO_2 laser, plasma cutter, a rotary machining spindle etc. Many CNC machines will only need two axes an X. and a Y. to perform things like two-dimensional cutting procedures on sheet materials, while more advanced systems will require multiple axes for three-dimensional parts and product construction. A 3-D printer uses an X and Y-axis CNC to print an additive material in layers while using a Z. axis to adjust the model's position for each new layer applied.

Developing advanced 3-D printer technologies to increase production efficiency and offer commercial products to the general public will be a main objective for the Automated Systems division. Many advanced 3-D printer designs have been under development at TFT for years in preparation for the first ACI construction. I believe this technology has far greater potential for the automated manufacturing of advanced products than currently accepted.

At least two standardized 3-D printer machines will be online and functioning for the first Automated Systems primary and secondaries to study and learn how to operate. Standardized 3-D Manufacturing files for different parts and products will be preinstalled in each unit. Including a file for the parts, materials and different machines needed to re-create the 3-D printer itself. Members working in Automated Systems will naturally notice inefficiency along the way and are encouraged to make suggestions to improve a current process or eventually design entirely new standardized machines.

Until we develop an advanced 3-D printer or manufacturing process that can grow all the dissimilar materials found in a complicated product like an electric car, we will still need to automate the assembly of individual parts. The automated assembly of parts into a finished product has long been a technical challenge for many manufacturing industries. Under Capitalism our accelerated automated assembly technology will continue to benefit the wealthy few while leaving the working-class many with obsolete labor skills and no jobs to support their family.

In a predator free society not only would our automated assembly technology and intellectual development be accelerated with our new environmental conditions but all the profit and social advantages will benefit the entire community and help others to break their chains of Capitalism as well. After an objective consideration of this social strategy the overwhelming advantages for the 99.9 % of our species should become increasingly obvious as our collective subjective realities to accept our capitalistic exploitation is replaced with a unified determination to provide a better future for all our people as equals.

If all the individual parts are lined up and fed into an automated manufacturing system it can be programmed to assemble complicated products. Many advanced products will continue to have a semi-automated manufacturing process requiring some human assembly or assistance. This will provide a good opportunity for the younger and less experienced members of a predator free society to become more familiar with how these technical products work. Even though most of the ACI's functions are designed to have easy automated maintenance by replacing plug-in modular systems, the malfunctioning units still need to be analyzed for why they failed and repaired so they may be put back into service.

Again, this process will provide a good learning opportunity for secondaries working in the Automated Systems division giving them the knowledge they need to make better recommendations on design improvements. Each malfunctioning unit will provide a technical mystery to solve some may be rather obvious while others will offer a much greater challenge. An intellectually stimulating environment of this kind will make knowledge of advanced technologies and a good philosophical understanding of human nature, commonplace among the members of the predator free community. Most of the activities will also be a learning, teaching and socially interactive experience increasing the quality of life for all community members, while accelerating their personal intellectual evolution and development.

Besides the CNC and 3-D printer products offered to the general public by the Automated Systems division, a product line of modular components allowing individual inventors to customize and create their own machines will also be made available creating additional revenue to help expand the network of ACIs. These modular components will consist of precision linear and rotary motion tables, advanced smart motors and controllers with sensory feedback, power backup systems and integrated software with an intuitive graphical user interface.

After the custom CNC system is created it may consist of two or more axes with some combination of linear and rotary precision motion control. The business end of the machine will need a head attachment to a universal mounting plate. A wide range of head attachment should be made available to satisfy any customers automated production needs. A primary objective with this product line is to provide affordable automated manufacturing, allowing we the people to benefit from advancing technologies and to help eliminate the need to depend upon top predators to maintain our existence.

One of the most interesting design challenges in a predator free society is to create realistic looking synthetic people with fluid body motions like we humans have. This design challenge would require the Advanced Arts division creating the illusion of a human exterior with skin, and fat layers while the Automated Systems division would create the programmable framework using something like bones and muscles to provide motion. Some designs may attempt an exact synthetic reproduction of the organic form while others may have a more technical or artistic appearance. The synthetic people that need to move around and navigate through a community infrastructure will need a base with wheels to stand on or integrated as part of the main body from the waist down.

Realistic looking animatronic people will provide an excellent opportunity for members of a predator free society to show off their advanced technical and creative skills to the rest of the world. At first, this design challenge will have more educational, entertainment and artistic value for the predator free community as opposed to providing a commercial product that can be sold to the general public to increase revenues. However, as animatronic people become more realistic and capable of replacing many of our current manufacturing and service jobs these synthetic lifeforms may become one of the signature products created by TFT.

As with the other divisions in a predator free society, the Automated Systems primary and senior secondary will both have permanent residence along with their families living in 50 and 40-foot diameter two level domes. All community members wanting to contribute their secondary skills to the Automated Systems division will have easy access to its 50-foot diameter production dome as well as other utility structures using CNC systems. All primary and senior secondary family members may provide assistance in the Automated Systems division or any of the others within their ACI.

To provide the greatest opportunity for individuals to expand their minds, members of a predator free society will be encouraged to explore each division as a secondary interest to their primary contribution activities.

This reminds me of the phrase "try it you might like it". A world of diverse interests and opportunities will be available at the community level for family members to explore increasing their overall knowledge base and ability to make more objective decisions regarding multiple subjects.

7. TFT - Advanced Arts

The TFT Advanced Arts division will be the place where community members can express their most creative skills in a wide variety of artistic mediums. Many of the art forms created in this division will be handmade, however, common household items like ceramics and glassware may need to be reproduced thousands of times. For items that need to be reproduced many times a programmable standardized automated production system should be created and available within each community infrastructure. Like other advanced products designed, prototyped and produced in a predator free society, newly created art forms by a single individual can be made into standardized files, and sent throughout the ACI network.

Community members can use an Internet browser to view all available art forms created in mediums like wood, metal, ceramics and glass. Selected items can be downloaded to their local communities where a standardized automation production system needed to re-create that work of art will accept the file. Depending on whether this automated system is in use or needed by the Advanced Arts division and with the primaries consent a member may replicate and even customize their selected work of art for an on-demand production.

Like the other divisions that make up the social economic structure of a predator free society the Advanced Arts divisions primary objective is to supply the community's needs first including the expanding network of new members. After that is accomplished the majority of production can focus on product lines sold to the public. The increased production of these product lines will provide additional revenue and accelerate the construction of new ACIs. Imagine getting the satisfaction from creating a beautiful work of art that others may enjoy for many generations with the additional reward of knowing what you are doing will allow even more people to end their predatory competition for survival and make the evolutionary transition to a predator free society.

The Advanced Arts division seems like one of the most rewording ways to make a contribution and help speed up the process especially for the younger members of our new society. After Education the Advanced Arts division will provide an introduction for younger members to explore the integration of beauty and technology that will become part of their daily lives as they adapt to their new environmental conditions.

A fully independent and self-reliant society must eventually produce not only all of its basic survival necessities like food and water but also many common household, personal and technical consumer products as well. For example the Advanced Arts divisions will create many forms of glassware from drinking glasses and stained glass windows to laser and prismatic optics. Glass is such an important medium for any technically advanced society that standardized systems must be created to automate the production of products made by this material.

This is also true for the medium of ceramics that will provide a wide range of artistic expression and utility functions like dinner plates and custom tiles to fuel cell electrodes and stainless steel casting molds. Because the mediums of glass and ceramics both require a high-temperature heat source they may share a similar or possibly the same automated production system. Either way the automated system should be programmable for customization and standardized to allow exact reproductions in every ACI throughout an extended network.

Creating an ambience of beauty and technical wonder for each ACI will be the responsibility of the Advanced Arts division. Other divisions like Infrastructure and Automated Systems may help with the technical wonders, but Advanced Arts should design the landscaping and decor for the surface and subsurface levels. The Advanced Arts primary and secondaries will have many elements to incorporate in their environmental designs. The real challenge may be how to use these elements in a way that shows off their full beauty and splendor.

Besides stained glass, prismatic displays and custom ceramic tiles, the element of stone mosaics will make a beautiful edition for walls and floors. Mosaics made from pieces of different colored stones not only have the ability to last over a 1000 years but also designing an automated system to reproduce custom patterns created on a computer should be a relatively simple task. A similar automation system can be used to cut and arrange stained glass or glaze a custom pattern on ceramic tiles. Other artistic elements in an ACI may include, waterfalls, Koi ponds, Smart Plants, sculptures, fruit trees, educational and entertainment displays.

Wood may be too biodegradable and temporary to use as a structural element in surface structures like residential homes. However, fine woodwork in the form of house furnishings can retain their beauty and function for hundreds of years especially when protected by the security of an ACI. As a teenager I worked in the finest exotic hardwoods making beautiful little boxes with silver inlays and set gems. My favorite trick was to disguise the pushbutton lid release as one of the inlays to add a little entertainment to the artistic and utility value. My main interest was to find the highest quality exotic hardwoods to work with. However, being young with little knowledge of the world I was unaware some of these species may be harvested into extinction to supply the demand of woodworkers like me. Many of the countries these exotic hardwoods come from have people competing in a primitive predatory social structure. These people are desperately trying to survive, so the extinction of a tree species would be one of their last concerns. It doesn't have to be this way, we don't have to choose between the extinction of another species and providing basic survival necessities for us people, at least not after we end our predatory social structure and make the transition to a predator free society.

It may be getting more difficult to find hardwood materials sustainable enough that it will not endanger a species from becoming extinct.

However, among the ones that are, a wide variety of wood products can be made. Besides being a fun medium to work with by hand it is also an excellent material for the automated production of parts. A standardized automation system can be programmed for intricate carvings on a matching dining room set or an armoire for the bedroom, coffee tables, cabinet work, mirror and picture frames even elaborate jewelry boxes with multiple drawers are among the many products that can be made. Wood also makes a very affordable medium for the budding artists to develop their skills. Unlike the medium of clay or even glass, wood is a material that if you cut too much off you can't just add more back on, forcing us to be a little more careful when creating these works of art.

A high precision programmable production system will not only be capable of creating technical parts, but also many creative forms of functional and non-functional jewelry products. At first community members will practice many techniques by hand to get a better feel of how the materials will react when used together. Of course very unique original works of art will continue to be made by hand and possibly sold through the many fine jewelry galleries around our country or even the world. However, many jewelry products like cast rings and pendants with set gems or stone inlays lend themselves very nicely to an automated production process.

Making copper enameling and cloisonné products is an excellent introductory medium for younger artists to develop their fine motor skills and creative potential, I'm sure it helped me. Silversmithing skills can be developed creating advanced products like a locket pendant with pushbutton catch and my old favorite custom handmade chains and clasps. Working in this area of the Advanced Arts division should provide many interesting challenges for community members. I am looking forward to teaching these skills to other community members.

One of the most interesting and challenging areas of the Advanced Arts division is creating flexible exteriors for synthetic life form products. These lifelike exteriors may have an alien appearance or attempt an exact reproduction of an existing organic life form. For example a Face Plant may have familiar looking leaves with an exotic looking face instead of a central flower. A design challenge to create the most entertaining desktop lifeform with a programmable response to environmental conditions should provide some interesting results and possibly a new product line to help generate revenue for the community.

The interest in robotic pets, humanoids, dinosaurs and exotic lifeforms seems to be growing as our species technology and creative skills accelerate. The ultimate goal of these pursuits would seem to be the creation of new synthetic life forms so realistic that their authenticity would be difficult to determine by an average observer. The Automated Systems and Advanced Arts division will need to work together to accomplish this goal and create products this challenging.

The command structure of the Advanced Arts division will also consist of a primary individual for each community infrastructure responsible for coordinating all activities under their control. The Advanced Arts primary will be assisted by a senior secondary also living in a permanent residence within the community infrastructure. Primary individuals and their families may live in one of the two level 50 foot diameter residential domes while the senior secondary and their family will reside in one of the two level 40 foot diameter domes. All family members of a predator free society can contribute to the community by helping in any or all divisions in their ACI.

Family members will have easy access to the knowledge and new skills each TFT division can offer. Many of the technologies in different divisions will begin to overlap creating a more objective perspective on how all things work. The same accumulated factual knowledge used to allow technical breakthroughs can also be beneficial in stoking the imagination and forging masterful works of art with new forms of beauty and wonder our species has yet to experience.

All of the performing arts including music, dance, theatre, cinematography, etc. will also be coordinated by the Advanced Arts division.

These art forms may not only provide large income potential to expand a predator free society but also help educate others as to how important making this social transition will be for our species intellectual evolutionary development. Finding areas that provide, beauty, entertainment and a revenue stream for the community while also offering a positive education source to build objective realities, is a force multiplying activity that allows the most efficient use of energy.

The challenge here will be how to create compelling and dramatic works of art while also conveying the message that we the people truly do have the power to end our predatory social structure as soon as we gain intellectual control over our hardwired survival instincts and induced subjective realities. Or at least convey a message of compassion and prosperity for all people as equals.

Many extraordinarily talented artists have expressed a message of equality and a need for social justice for years helping to prepare our species for the evolutionary transition to a predator free society. Now that a solution capable of ending our nightmarish predatory past and present is available, we can shift our energies from explaining the many detrimental effects of capitalistic exploitation, to creating the predator free environmental conditions necessary for this evolutionary transition to take place. That's when the true magic and technical wonders of our predator free future will become more obvious.

8. TFT - Food Tree

The Food Tree is more than a division within the TFT nonprofit organization and an integral part of the social economic structure of the predator free society offered for consideration in this book. The Food Tree started as a concept to provide a semi automated technical system capable of surviving most natural and man-made disasters to offer beverages and food relief to survivors. Like organic trees the Food Tree's output will be limited by its size, available sunlight and water. However, unlike their natural counterparts they are designed for continuous production of a wide variety of items throughout the year. Some items can be stockpiled for emergencies, but the Food Tree design is more of a continuous output system to produce balanced nutritious meals to be consumed fresh directly after harvest. This continuous food production system will require a community of people to consume its output and maintain its non-automated functions. The food production byproducts will also provide tasty treats for dairy goats, chickens, fish etc. helping to create a more self-sufficient community.

The primary responsibilities of the TFT Food Tree division is to coordinate the harvests from all aquaculture and agriculture domes, subsurface and above ground orchards, dairy goat, chickens, fish farms, extended surface gardens as well as any additional supplies that need to be imported from outside the community. The combined output of a single ACI is designed to exceed the food requirements of all the permanent residence and visiting guests. The additional output not needed by residential members of the community, will be offered commercially to the public through the Food Tree Café. This will provide an additional revenue source for an expanding predator free society. A continuous production Food Tree system designed to provide meals for an established community and restaurant customers will inherently produce an excess of nutritious perishable food items form time to time. That excess can be used to help feed our least fortunate Americans competitors outside the community still struggling in capitalistic poverty.

Originally the Food Tree concept was a design challenge to create a synthetic life form to securely automate the production of different food items like oranges and onions with the ability to dispense the end product at the end of branches much like their organic counterparts. As novel and interesting as this life form would be it started to seem more efficient to create a system where people could select from a list of items on their smartphone or tablet and have the items ready at a specialized tree branch capable of drive-through pickup service or automated delivery within the community infrastructure.

Even more efficient would be to offer freshly prepared on-demand healthy appetizers, a variety of beverages, nutritious gourmet entrées and desserts taking the Food Tree concept to its logical conclusion. One design challenge would be how to deliver complete meals through specialized branches for disaster relief, while another would be how to bring culinary works of art on custom ceramic plates to a romantic dinner setting for two. The same Food Tree can be designed to provide both services with the help of robotic chefs, waiters and the dedicated members of a predator free society working in this division.

The most recent Food Tree design presented an interesting challenge to create a semi-automated system to convert free radiant energy from the sun and water from the sky into prepared meals while also capable of protecting itself against natural or man-made disasters. Sometimes even the wildest figments of our imagination may have technical solutions that can turn them into reality. Its times like this when it helps to remember, all of our greatest accomplishments as a species were literally unimaginable at one time. We may not be quite ready for energy to matter conversion like a Star Trek replicator, but if a Food Tree system can convert sunlight and water into a programmable selection of freshly prepared nutritious meals and beverages, I'd be happy with that as a baseline to improve upon. Even though the meals prepared by the robotic chef will be made to order, as needed, the actual Food Tree process to create this end product will have started months in advance.

The Food Tree process starts by collecting full spectrum radiant energy from the sun and water from the environment just like their organic counterparts. Instead of using organic leaves to collect sunlight for photosynthesis we will use an array of power and light Smart Trees to provide the solar and electric energy needed to maintain an automated Food Tree system. The surface structures and landscaping above an ACI is designed to collect rainwater while subsurface systems are designed to filter, purify, store and supply this survival necessity to people, animals and plants.

An array of Smart trees will concentrate their collected light into high output 50-foot diameter aquaculture domes securely located in the subsurface level of the ACI. These two level aquaculture domes will have multiple garden layers using an aeroponic system where water and nutrients are metered and delivered to the plants roots. Even though the aquaculture domes can handle something the size of dwarf fruit trees, their most efficient for growing plants less than 2 feet tall. Other Smart trees will be arranged to direct natural sunlight into the outer ring courtyard of the subsurface infrastructure allowing for a variety of larger fruit trees to be grown. Surface gardens and orchards may also contribute to the available resources used by the Food Tree system and this TFT division of a predator free society.

One of the biggest advantages of creating a subsurface growing environment is that we humans become Mother Nature with the ability to control how plants change to their artificial seasons. Controlling these artificial seasons can allow for several smaller harvests per year. No longer do we need to be restricted to one large crop per year, making things more difficult to manage, distribute and store, often leading to unnecessary waste or rationing if crop devastation occurs. If taken to its logical extreme, creating artificial seasons can produce a continuous output system where harvests can be made on a daily basis. The entire lifecycle of different plant species from seedling to harvest must exist at all stages of its development at the same time. During the same time a plant is harvested and removed from the system a new seedling will be introduced to continue the growing cycle. In this way a controlled and continuous output of fresh food supplies can be delivered to the robotic chefs for their preparation of nutritious treats, hors d'oeuvres and entrées.

The aquaculture domes are specifically designed to automate the process of growing small fruit and vegetable plants as well as shrimp and fish. A semi to completely closed system should be used where the plant life grown can feed the shrimp and fish while their waste byproduct can provide the fertilizing nutrients needed for an aquaculture garden. The automated harvesting of dissimilar small fruit and vegetable plants as well as introducing a new seedling into the continuous output system, will provide many design challenges to keep life interesting.

Another technical challenge is how to automate the processing of freshly harvested food items and making them available for the robotic chefs on-demand output of gourmet meals. Many of these systems will be prototyped and tested before the first ACI is made. However, until a totally automated system can be created, some processes of the Food Tree division will be manual. These harvesting and maintenance activities should provide an excellent opportunity for community members to socially interact and brainstorm on technical solutions capable of automating their processing tasks.

In addition to coordinating the harvest of fruits, vegetables, shrimp and fish the Food Tree division will also be responsible for an 80 foot diameter agricultural dome with the capacity to process at minimum a small herd of dairy goats and a flock of chickens enough to supply dairy products and eggs for the permanent residents and guests of a single ACI. Even though this agricultural dome should be designed for continuous use, goats and chickens will have easy access to areas on the surface during the day, but may take shelter at night or during destructive surface conditions. Automating the process of collecting milk and eggs does present a different design challenge compared to harvesting plant life.

Plants are much less temperamental and stay in one place during harvest where animals need to be tricked, convinced or condition into cooperating with an automated process. This process would be similar to how Capitalism has convinced the working class resources of the world to accept their exploitation as a commonplace social, religious or national ritual.

I guess if our human top predators can convince our own species to passively comply with the exploitation of their wealth and labor, we should be able to find a way to convince goats and chickens to happily give up their milk and eggs.

The Food Tree division of a predator free society will not only be responsible for providing a variety of nutritious treats, hors d'oeuvres and entrées for the permanent residents but also bed and breakfast guests as well as public visitors to the ACIs integrated café and restaurant. The Food Tree will be located primarily in the enter courtyard ring of the subsurface level. However, temporary surface structures will also deploy to merge with the existing landscape elements providing a pleasant ambience and unique dining experience. In addition to the revenue the Food Tree Café can generate, a wide variety of nutritional products can be created within this division for sale to the general public.

If a nutritional product is determined to be commercially viable for sale to the general public it can be subcontracted out to a private company for higher volume production. A transaction of this nature would create a quadruple win scenario starting with the customers having another nutritional food product to choose from, the private company and hopefully their employees will benefit from the extra business, community members will gain another revenue source and last but not least, the additional income will allow more ACIs to be created and the opportunity for more people to end their predatory existence. Now that's a good solution.

Perhaps more than other divisions, the Food Tree may require subdivisions to better organize and execute the different tasks it performs for the community. The social economic evolution of the first predator free society should reveal which divisions will require more assistance and the need for subdivisions. Even though the individual designated as primary will be responsible for all activities in their division, they may prefer to delegate the control of subdivisions to the senior secondary or other secondaries that are qualified for the task. This form of expansion within each division will allow individual members the opportunity to create whole new concepts that may benefit the community and help accelerate our transition to a global predator free society.

The individual that is most influential in the development of a new beneficial concept would logically have the opportunity to be in control of any subdivision that may need to be created for their project. These individuals would most likely be the team leader of the design challenge to develop that line of products. The more senior and experienced team members will tend to offer their technical expertise while the younger members will provide more assistance for the less automated tasks.

As with the other divisions in a predator free economic structure the Food Tree primary and their family will also live in a 50-foot diameter two level residential dome within their ACI giving them easy access to all of the systems under their control. Primaries with smaller families or ones that are single may live in other residential dome equal to number of individuals in that family. The responsibilities of the first primaries will be as challenging as they are rewarding however, to make things a little easier all of the systems in each division will be prototyped and tested before the first ACI is created. How the systems function in each division, a full technical description of the required activities and the philosophical beliefs of a predator free society will all be made available on the TFT website allowing potential primaries and secondaries to become more familiar with what their new lives would be like.

As the transition to a predator free society accelerates, what was once extraordinary among our species will become commonplace and great knowledge can be used as a tool to benefit the many instead of serving the few. It's gratifying to know that the working class prey of our species will unite to gain control of our evolutionary development and finally end our predatory social structure. And the best part is we the people have the ability to help accelerate this process starting right here and now, no one can take this power from us. We may be convinced not to exercise this power or be unaware that it exists, but those barriers will soon fall.

Part 5: The TFT Social Economic Structure

1. The TFT Mission Statement

It is customary for new nonprofit organizations to present a concise description, mission and vision statement to characterize the benefits they hope to provide to our society. Nonprofit organizations generally provide some form of humanitarian relief to the least fortunate competitors struggling to survive various levels of predatory social structures from the primitive forms common in undeveloped countries to the most sophisticated forms of global capitalistic exploitation.

Many of these organizations concentrate on providing emergency relief to prevent the immediate suffering and death of exploited people, in effect treating the symptoms while allowing the cause to escalate for generations as our populations grow. The notion of creating a comprehensive framework for a social economic structure capable of correcting all of the symptoms by eliminating the cause at is source, seems to be a somewhat new approach. The objective isn't to put all the other charitable organizations out of business, but instead make them obsolete as our entire species makes the transition to a predator free society eliminating the need for capitalistic exploitation of the working class resource.

The TFT Description;

True Freedom Technologies, is a nonprofit organization specifically designed to create a technically advanced self replicating social economic system capable of supporting a predator free society. The primary objective of TFT is to reduce preventable suffering and death by eliminating the root cause at its source. TFT offers for consideration a social system and technical solution capable of providing advanced security, education, healthcare, production, efficiency and quality of life for working class people living in poverty.

The TFT Mission Statement;

"To help accelerate our natural transition to a predator free society and the next phase of our intellectual evolutionary development"

The TFT Vision Statement;

"To end the predatory evolution of our species and the need to compete against one another for our survival"

I like the way it's called a "Mission" statement. What started out as a simple intellectual challenge to answer a question, transformed into a mission to save the world. Perhaps more than other nonprofits the mission analogy seems well suited for an organization attempting to end global exploitation and accelerate a natural evolutionary transition for our species. TFTs mission is to create a movement powerful enough to finally bring an end to the predatory evolution of the human species, while ushering in the next phase of our intellectual evolutionary development.

Your mission, should you choose to accept it, is to acquire more factual knowledge about the information in this book from independent nonbiased sources capable of verifying facts. Try to avoid sources of known propaganda to manipulate your decision-making process into accepting our capitalistic exploitation. As our factual knowledge grows the control of these predatory manipulation techniques will diminish allowing for objective realities to form. Forming an objective reality is like getting a pair of prescription glasses for our mind, bringing into focus many details of life previously unseen by our subjective reality.

We will need a strong body and mind for this mission, so nutritious meals and exercise will be part of our training routine. Some may feel a mission of this magnitude may appear to be, dare I say, impossible. However, we can take comfort knowing that this transition of our intellectual evolution is inevitable barring an unforeseen catastrophic event. Our mission is not so much to initiate the transition, as it is to accelerate an existing process. That's not to say our mission won't be challenging, we're going to need all the new technologies and creative skills we can get.

We'll know our mission objectives are be satisfied when a rapidly growing minority of our population breaks their first chain of Capitalism and begins to request our national wealth and resources be used to help break the second chain. Once individuals become aware of their systematic exploitation under Capitalism and compare the social economic structure of a predator free society, our mission will get a lot easier. This is truly one of those missions, where failure is not an option. Every human being on this planet and all of our future descendants are counting on us to save the intellectual evolutionary development of our species from evil capitalistic masterminds bent on global domination. Now that's a mission. Who's in?

2. The Golden Rule

Of all the religious and philosophical phrases I have heard the golden rule is my favorite. There has been many variations of this rule throughout our history but I like this one best "Do unto others as you would have them do unto you" it's so simple and to the point. It seems if people could honor just this one rule it would solve all the worlds conflicts and social dysfunctions while creating an atmosphere of harmony and trust within a society.

Sadly in a predatory social structure that forces us to compete against one another for our survival the Golden rule becomes "Do unto others before they do unto you". Even if we tried to force compliance with the golden rule using laws and the threat of punishment, our competition for survival would still trigger our self-preservation instinct and override our intellectual desire for social harmony.

I started to realize it's not that the wisdom of the golden rule wasn't known for thousands of years, but something more fundamental was keeping it from being used in practice. I also asked myself who would benefit most from a social structure that used the golden rule to guide our moral objectives and who would prefer to disregard it. The very essence of the golden rule stands for equality and compassion for others. This of course would favor the working-class masses and prevent the ruling class top predators from exploiting the people under their control.

Again and again the root cause has revealed itself to be our capitalistic social structure reinforcing our predatory instincts with forced competition for survival. For individuals to practice the golden rule within an advanced predatory social structure like Capitalism would be similar to putting pacifists on a battlefield. It's no wonder the golden rule never caught on. Throughout our evolutionary development the individuals capable of rising above their predatory instincts to offer compassion to others, would quickly be deceived out of their possessions and sometimes their lives, only to be replaced by more efficient and ruthless competitors. Continue this process for thousands of years and starts to become clear how things got so bad?

The best part about having a root cause for so many problems is that once it is corrected all of its many symptoms also fade away. The golden rule could not only be sustained in the environmental conditions of the predator free social structure but it would naturally become common practice in a society that values equality and compassion for others as a primary moral objective. Once the need to compete against one another for our survival is removed the primary objective will be to expand the predator free infrastructure network allowing others to experience the same level of equality and prosperity. As a version of the golden rule our society's motto could be, "Give unto others the true freedom and prosperity that was given unto you". This reminds me of the expression, Sell a man a fish and you keep him dependent on you for his daily survival, teach a man to operate an automated fish farm in an advanced ACI and he helps feed and an entire community for a lifetime, or something like that...

The essence of the golden rule will become part of the predator free philosophy learned and taught among the members of the community.

New predator free community members must agree to treat others with the same level of respect and compassion they themselves would wish to be treated with. Our social competition for survival has a way of diminishing our self-respect and the level of compassion we hope to receive from other competitors, however, this too will change as new standards in human rights are achieved.

Even though intellectual deceptions will not be needed for survival within a predator free society, the transition may still be difficult for many people formally under the control of a subjective reality to serve Gods and or governments. Depending on the intensity and duration of the subjective reality conditioning our brains can become so altered as to readily accept things that are not true, while emotionally rejecting the very factual knowledge necessary to correct this barrier to intellectual growth and a better understanding of the world around us.

Even a law as pure and simple as the golden rule could never survive a free-for-all predatory society where inducing subjective realities for profit has become a standard tool for manipulating a working-class resource. When ruling class top predators are allowed to limit a population's education and induced them with any subjective reality that best facilitates their efficient exploitation, the meaning of the golden rule could be completely reversed or just lose its relevance while we adapt to our predatory social structure. In fact any society that denies reality and logic would be unable to maintain even the simplest of laws when its people are conditioned to believe in things that are not real. Even horrific acts of violence become justified as a glorified accomplishment satisfying their induced subjective realities. The good news is once we understand the mechanisms behind this destructive form of psychological conditioning we can reverse its effects for the younger members of our society and prevent its corrupting influence for the future ones.

We must redefine what should be considered right and wrong in our society based on factual knowledge of the subject and the actual harm it does to others. We cannot allow our induced moral standards from religious beliefs or corporate propaganda campaigns determine what is right and wrong. For example the social ritual of the working class many transferring their wealth to the ruling class few in the form of a tithe to religious leaders or tax to a government controlled by corporate capitalists. This basic carrot and stick form of psychological manipulation has worked quite well on a majority of our population unable or unwilling to receive the factual knowledge necessary to break their environmental and social conditioning. When someone breaks their conditioning and stand up for equality, there labeled troublemakers, often stopped by laws and violence, then use as an example to discourage others. However, history has proven this is not always successful at killing the message or ideas they believed in, as with the life and death of Jesus. Who, as I understand was the original source and inspiration for the golden rule.

Have you ever felt like our social system is rigged against us? And even when we the people do everything we're told we still seem to just barely get by. The carrot and stick technique may have been the most effective tools to manage a working-class population for thousands of years during our predatory evolutionary development. However, all forms of psychological deception for power and profit will not be needed or allowed in a predator free society. The golden rule will naturally become the new social standard, and besides being so strategically sound and logical, it just feels right.

3. All for One and One for All

You may have become familiar with the phrase "All for One and One for All" by watching old Three Musketeers movies as I did. During my childhood these words always seem to hold some great power and hidden meaning that I couldn't quite understand. Like most young people just wanting to make sense of our world I tried to relate these noble words with the capitalistic society around me where greed and deception are the social standards for survival. Of course there are always exceptions especially for those so secure in their social status that helping others does not threaten their own survival. However, for the average working class citizen, giving assistance to another competitor seems counterproductive towards winning the game. After all, the very stranger you help today to become a better competitor may be the same person that gets the job you were counting on to bring your family out of poverty. Once you have realized your good deed did not go unpunished, an important survival lesson will have been learned and we will naturally adapt to our predatory social structure.

After all we have been genetically encoded and environmentally conditioned for our entire existence to accept the suffering and death of less fortunate competitors, so it shouldn't seem surprising when we show such disregard for others. Like Capitalism itself, we humans are responsible for creating this problem or at least making it a lot worse. This also means we hold the solution and the power to correct the problem as well. It's just a matter of how long it will take for we the people to realize we have the power to end our predatory exploitation and act on our convictions.

Like so many other words of wisdom throughout history the power hidden in the phrase, all for one and one for all, could never truly be realized in a predatory social structure. It's true that a capitalistic country will predictably unite in times of war giving the working-class resource a sense of satisfaction knowing hundreds of billions of our tax payers dollars are being diverted to private corporations. However, when the economic drain on our country increases poverty among our least fortunate competitors while war industry lobbyists and executives receive multimillion-dollar bonuses for a job well done. We can only consider Capitalism an "All for One" system, not a "One for All" society.

After standing back and looking at the big picture, I'm often amazed that we the people could allow our society that stands for freedom, equality and opportunity for all, to systematically exploit the very citizens it should be protecting. If the wealth extraction process is gradual enough, the working-class resource can be conditioned to tolerate the additional suffering and death within the community. Increasing profits for those wealthy enough to afford the investments in government and media propaganda campaign to induce the most effective subjective reality. Life as a top human predator has become quite complicated in modern days demanding the use of equally sophisticated countermeasures by us working class prey to break this evolutionary cycle and finally achieve true freedom and social equality for all people.

Expressing the true spirit behind the words of this section's title may not be possible in our current predatory social structure. Fortunately for us, this philosophy will become a natural manifestation in the environmental conditions of a predator free society. At first predator free citizens following the TFT mission statement will be living more of the "one for all" as opposed to the "all for one" part of this statement.

The one for all, part of this statement could also represent the few standing up for the many. The first predator free ACI may be few in people but with the powerful ability of self-replication they will expand the network allowing many other families to end their capitalistic competition for survival. As new ACIs start to self-replicate with exponential growth, then the few helping the many will eventually shift to the many helping the few. There is another way for the many of our country to help the few in a predator free society with our mission. By using our democracy and convincing our ruling class leaders in government to allocate some of our tax revenues back to we the people so we may accelerate this evolutionary transition as a more unified nation.

The members of a predator free society will have the flexibility to adapt and concentrate all of their physical and mental energy on an individual problem relating to a single person giving true meaning to the, all for one, part of the section's title. When it comes to problem solving, thousands of heads are better than one. Solving a difficult problem may only take one flash of inspiration from a single person in a much larger network. Hopefully eliminating any scenario where someone must unnecessarily suffer or die just because the person or people that held the solution were simply unaware of the pending crisis, or that they could have saved a life.

The social economic structure of a predator free society also puts into practice the, one for all, philosophy by allowing any extraordinary accomplishments by a single community member to be rapidly shared throughout the entire extended community network. The predator free environmental conditions not only allow for the few to help the many but it also provides them with the knowledge and resources to accomplish the task. It will become their new job or mission objective while exploring and enjoying their journey through life. Our capitalistic conditioning to allow the ruling class few to exploit the working class many will eventually fade away as another symptom of our predatory social structure becomes part of our evolutionary past.

4. Learning - Teaching - and Enjoying Life

In an advanced predator free social structure most daily activities would fall into one of three categories, learning, teaching and enjoying life. By integrating learning and teaching into a society as a right and civic duty, not a privilege for better competitors, and by emphasizing their importance by making them a primary social objective, the intellectual evolutionary development of our species will accelerate significantly. Enjoying life should not be considered a luxury for the more fortunate capitalistic competitors, but instead a fundamental right and primary objective for all community members to achieve.

It's not just that we want everyone to be happy, it's also that happier people are healthier, more creative, productive, and have less social aggression. After generations of adapting to our predatory social structure we have been conditioned with a narrow perspective of what freedom and enjoying life means. Many commonsense social corrections will be made to eliminate the barriers our predatory past and present have imposed upon we the people preventing us from reaching our true potential, not just as individuals or even countries but as a species. Just imagine how much better things will be once the transition is complete.

For many people like me, the social objectives of learning, teaching and enjoying life can be done at the same time. For example one of the things I enjoy most about life is learning new things that may be used to help solve some future problem. I also enjoy teaching and helping others to develop their knowledge base allowing them to make more informed decisions. The environmental conditions of a predator free society will also allow others to more fully enjoy the art of learning and sharing factual knowledge once the need for predatory competition has been eliminated.

Almost everyone has the capacity to learn and teach. Most of the learning and teaching activities will probably take place during the setup procedures for automated production operations. A society that is structured to accomplish multiple social objectives during a single activity will be far more efficient at achieving its goals. Because a technologically advanced predator free society will emphasize an energy independent infrastructure and the automated production of products and services, most of the learning and teaching would involve designing, creating and maintaining these systems.

Learning by example with hands-on training is the best way to develop advanced technical and artistic skills. The individuals designated as primaries and senior secondary in a predator free social structure will likely be the most experienced and knowledgeable people in the community. Knowledge will tend to flow from them into the minds of all other members. More knowledgeable secondaries will then share their knowledge with less experienced members and they in turn will do the same. In this way all community members will become students and teachers as the collective intellectual development of the predator free society begins to accelerate.

It is known that we humans experience better mental health when exposed to intellectually stimulating environmental conditions, at least when there not required as part of a predatory competition for survival. If we objectively consider the opposite extreme of intellectual isolation and sensory deprivation it becomes easier to see the advantages of an education rich environment. Keeping our brains active will enhance our quality of life, expand our creativity and increase our ability to contribute to the entire community.

When a new skill or concept is learned it can be taught to or shared with others during casual social interactions, organized online computer classrooms, hands-on demonstrations or during production operations. The ambiance or atmosphere of the community will be much like that of a school that makes advanced products with educational displays for all the members and visitors to experience and enjoy. The intellectually stimulating environment of an advanced predator free infrastructure and a society that incorporates learning and teaching as a primary social objective should provide great assistance to the educational primaries, as they accomplish their mission to increase the knowledge and creative skills of the community.

The ability to accept new factual knowledge and effectively transmit or communicate that information to others is itself one of the skills that will be learned while adapting to a predator free social structure. Breaking our conditioning to hoard knowledge for profit and use our intelligence to compete against one another will be difficult at first. I know breaking thousands of years of conditioning to accept our exploitation as working class prey may seem daunting at first, some people may feel it can't be done, why even try, we should just accept our fate. After all we're talking about changing human nature, the very essence of who we are as a species. Knowing the enemy, we already have a comprehensive solution that will only get better, besides the greater the challenge the greater the reward. Part of becoming an intelligent species is taking control of our evolutionary development. However, it's what we do with our newfound power that will truly define our success.

5. Designing an advanced predator free social economic structure

After we break our first chain of Capitalism by gaining control over our induced subjective realities and hardwired survival instincts. And after we break the second chain by creating more ACIs capable of supporting a predator free society, we will still need a social economic structure with the ability to maintain equality and prosperity for all community members. There will be many considerations in designing an advanced predator free social economic structure. However, we will have a tremendous advantage right from the beginning by eliminating the social objective of mass exploitation of the working class resource. We will be free to use all of our creative skills to design a social system where all of our people can benefit equally from emerging technologies and in the process end the growing tensions and violence created by class warfare and the escalation of our predatory evolution.

It is becoming better known that capitalistic globalization by top predators has been reducing wages and available jobs for the working class resources in wealthier nations like the United States by legitimizing slave labor conditions in other countries. We know that this practice has increased the wealth and power of the top 1% of the most fortunate competitors while decreasing the basic survival necessities for the 99% of our population designated as working-class prey. We also know that our current predatory social system is responsible for accelerating the preventable suffering and death of our people by producing the environmental conditions of despair, apathy and forced competition for survival.

When I evaluate a social economic structure this corrupt and flawed I realized once these areas are corrected all of the wealth and resources that were extracted from the American working class resource can then be used to reduce our preventable suffering and death. Just as globalization is leveling the playing field for the working class resources of the world, the transition to a predator free society will bring equality to all people eliminating the need and desire for class warfare during our pursuit of happiness.

All social economic system designs for our new predator free society must accomplish a set of criteria to be considered a viable option. First and foremost, it must be capable of ending our predatory competition for survival. We can no longer force the people of the world to compete against one another to serve the interests of the ruling class few. Breaking both chains of Capitalism will create the predator free environmental conditions necessary to correct the root cause of our preventable suffering and death at its source. For a new system to accomplish this first criterion would be to minimize and eventually eliminate nearly every social dysfunction that has plagued our societies throughout our evolutionary development. As monumental as this accomplishment will be there are two other major considerations and criterions to satisfy.

Because our new predator free society must exist and expand from within our current predatory social structure we'll need a system solution capable of providing a smooth transition, preferably one that would benefit both populations during the process. The nonprofit organization TFT (True Freedom Technologies) will provide a kind of bridge between both social structures allowing an exchange of survival necessities, construction materials and products. The members of a predator free society will have similar responsibilities as employees of a for-profit corporation with specialized divisions working together to accomplish a primary objective. While the corporate structures can be similar, their primary objectives are quite different. For profit corporations use the working class people as a resource to increase the power and wealth of the most fortunate few, while nonprofit organizations reinvest their income to benefit the least successful competitors still living in capitalistic poverty, hoping to receive basic human rights like clean water, nutritious food, shelter, education and healthcare.

The third criterion for our new social structure is the ability to self-replicate providing the opportunity for more families living in capitalistic poverty to make the transition to a predator free society. Because the citizens of our new social structure will no longer be required to compete against one another for their capitalistic survival they may focus all of their intellectual and creative skills towards providing true freedom and prosperity to others by expanding the network of ACIs. Accomplishing this criterion will produce exponential growth as each new ACI and their new predator free citizens have the ability for continues reproduction allowing many families to end their capitalistic existence. This criterion is critical to the rapid acceleration of our species overall transition from primitive predatory creatures to enlightened beings capable of understanding and controlling our own intellectual evolutionary development.

A typical day for a member of a predator free society will be similar in many respects to one in our current social structure. A family may or may not have breakfast together then the adult members would prepare for their primary and secondary activities within the ACI while the children get ready for their day of learning, teaching and enjoying life within the education division. Parents may walk their children to the education dome before they begin their daily activities primarily located within their own ACI or perhaps another one being created nearby.

The eight individuals in a community infrastructure designated as primaries and their senior secondaries will be organizing and overseeing the activities in their division. All community members will learn multiple secondary disciplines to provide a little spice of life keeping things interesting. We wouldn't want our members contributing activities to become too repetitive, after all that's what the automated manufacturing and service systems are for. Besides, new environmental conditions and unexpected experiences can spark the imagination resulting in more Eureka moments. We'd like to encourage that.

All community members that are not primaries will be designated as secondaries. These individuals will have a primary interest in one of the eight divisions but will also provide secondary assistance in any of the others divisions located within their ACI. A member of a predator free society with a secondary designation may contribute their creative skills to several different divisions throughout their day. Much like going to different classes in a school however instead of just learning new skills members will also be contributing to the success of the entire community and accomplishing our mission to bring true freedom and prosperity to others. Secondary members will also attend and sometimes teach technical demonstrations on the use of new automated systems or advanced products to be used by the community or sold to the public.

Another advanced feature of a predator free society is that the need to extract wealth from the working class masses in the form of taxes will be removed as a social economic objective. A member of a predator free society traveling outside the community making commercial purchases will still pay taxes on those items but all of their basic survival necessities and many luxuries within their ACI will not require any form of payment. Our parent nonprofit organization TFT will have many tax exemptions, however, it will still be required to pay other forms of wealth extraction until a more complete national transition to a predator free society has taken place. Until then the eight divisions of a predator free society will offer technically advanced products and services for sale to the general public providing a revenue stream to pay for any associated taxes and other expenses the entire community may encounter.

As I was designing the predator free society and technical solution offered for consideration in this book, I found myself disagreeing with some very prominent historical figures, in particular two of the forefathers of our Constitution. James Madison said, "The power of taxing people and their property is essential to the very existence of government." I think this may depend on our definition of government and the role it should play in its citizen's lives. Especially whether it should extract wealth from the working class many to serve the ruling class few.

Benjamin Franklin said, "The only things certain in life are death and taxes." As much as I admire Benjamin Franklin, I think I'm going to have to prove him wrong on this one. We must remember things were different back then and I believe if Benjamin Franklin were alive today he would instantly understand the logic and wisdom of creating a predator free society and we would be reading his books on how to create one.

When it comes to taxes and the way predatory Capitalism extracts wealth from the working class many to serve the ruling class few, an infamous yet startlingly truthful quote by one of our countries more successful capitalistic competitors summed up the actions and sentiments of many of our wealthy elite. Referring to the ruling class elite, Leona Helmsley known for her tyrannical behavior was quoted saying "We don't pay taxes. Only the little people pay taxes". Spoken like a true top predator proudly proclaiming their dominance over the working class resource as if we were unable to comprehending our capitalistic exploitation. Then again this was back when many Americans were conditioned to believe in trickle-down economics and that if we the people allow the most fortunate predatory capitalists to extract our wealth they would practice compassionate conservatism and this would certainly end poverty in America, income inequality and create prosperity for our nation. Yeah right, that deception is not working too well for them anymore, especially after the great recession. We're rapidly becoming too smart as a people for this subjective reality to continue as an effective tool for social engineering and psychological manipulation of the American working class resource.

Something else our forefathers could not have envisioned that should become a commonplace function in a technologically advanced predator free society. A "real-time democracy" where all community members are directly involved with local changes in their own ACI, global issues involving the entire predator free movement as well as the activities of our parent nonprofit organization TFT. Real-time voting will be made available through the smart home computers or the TFT website. Trying to tamper with someone's vote would be equivalent to breaking the security on a bank's website and changing the amounts in an account. If a capitalistic mastermind of computer hacking were to change votes it would be quickly detected, corrected and re-verified by the individuals that cast them.

Countermeasures will also be deployed to trace the origin of the security breach making any attempts at voter tampering less likely and ultimately pointless. All adult members of a predator free society will discuss community issues during social activities giving them the knowledge necessary to form an objective opinion. As part of our philosophy no issues will be decided based on subjective beliefs or anything else that does not exist in reality. All issues involving the future survival of the predator free society must be made based on factual knowledge and objective reasoning without any emotional interference triggered by hardwired instincts encoded in our genetic memory.

All members of a predator free society will have full equal rights regardless of sex, race, nationality or ethnic background. There are some things we don't get to choose in life, like our genetic makeup therefore these attributes should not be used to degrade or enhance our ability to survive. Where we are born and the kind of environmental conditioning we are subjected to are also things outside of our realm of control. The more fortunate people of our world should try to understand how different their lives would be if they were born into a tribal family located in some remote region of Africa. How would they perceive life growing up in those environmental conditions? These things outside of our control will no longer be used as tools to induce prejudicial subjective realities in an attempt to divide, manipulate and distract we the people from becoming aware of our capitalistic exploitation, and uniting our species.

Eliminating the social conditioning of our predatory past and gaining better intellectual control over our hardwired instincts, will of course be much easier in theory than practice. Even small lifestyle changes to break a genetic addiction to food can be difficult so one can imagine the level of resistance we may encounter removing our predatory instincts from our social structure. As a species we should be patient and expect a slow but gradual global transition, but as an individual I want to see immediate results something tangible our children could start to benefit from right away. We may not be able to change our predatory past but we can certainly learn from our mistakes to create a better future for our species.

6. The new American dream

Our American dream is a subjective concept most people associate with basic freedoms, human rights and the ability to make a lot of money. This subjective concept has changed throughout our evolutionary development to mean different things starting with the earliest, more primitive predatory social structures where the least fortunate of the working class people were considered subhuman property to use and discard like any other resource. The dream for freedom back then would be to live a life without the need to serve some top predator and their insatiable desire for power and wealth. Actually, that part sounds a lot like modern day Capitalism only with different characters, titles and outfits. Even though slavery is still widespread in our modern civilized societies as yet another symptom or manifestation of our predatory social structure, at least we have created laws to discourage its legitimate use for profit. That's progress, but its still treating a symptom not correcting the cause.

Having a life not considered the property of some ruling class elite, was the first level of freedom we humans dreamed about for thousands of years. The second level of freedom we humans dreamed about achieving is the right to live a life without the absolute rule from dictators, kings or governments controlled by the wealthiest top predators. It seems some top predators that control different governments around the world were over exploiting their working-class resources by taxing them into excessive levels of suffering and death.

There was no need to condition the working-class resource with a trickle-down economics theory the most powerful top predators just took what they wanted knowing there was nothing we little people could do about it. Creating a democracy where the working-class resource has representation in government was supposed to provide that second level of freedom to ensure we the people could never be exploited or manipulated again by ruling class top predators. The first level of freedom took our species thousands of years to achieve so it's not surprising were having so much trouble trying to accomplish the second. The attempt to provide a second level of freedom for our people is in its early stages. On an evolutionary scale, our intellectual and social development is like a toddler still learning how to walk. We want to stand tall and provide a basic level of human rights to all people, but we're not quite coordinated and strong enough to keep from falling back to ground and to a more primitive stage in our development.

The great news is there's a third level of freedom and our species is about to make a giant evolutionary leap forward turning the first two achievements into obsolete relics of our predatory past. Our current level of freedom is still directly proportional to our social status and wealth, as is typical of predatory based societies. Achieving a functioning second level of freedom for the working-class resource of America could be prevented indefinitely in a capitalistic society that values profits for the wealthy elite over the basic survival necessities for its least fortunate citizens.

It has become abundantly clear trying to make Capitalism fair for the working-class prey will continue to be a lesson in futility as long as our ruling class top predators are more interested in global domination than the health and prosperity of all us little people. In a society where wealth and power manipulate the laws its working-class citizens must live by, the level of freedom experienced by the population will be determined by the emotional whims and predatory ambitions of their capitalistic elite. It's no wonder we're having so much trouble achieving our second level of freedom. Luckily our third level of freedom will originate from we the people not requiring the permission of our ruling class elite and this evolutionary transition cannot be stopped by their control of government.

The subjective realities that have allowed the ruling class few to systematically exploit the working class many, can no longer be maintained as more people become aware of how this psychological manipulation technique has severely limited our progress towards achieving every level of freedom. As we break the first chain of Capitalism a third level of freedom will spontaneously occur and accelerate, as the need for predatory competitions between people and countries becomes a tragic phase of our evolutionary past. Achieving this third level of freedom is far more significant than the first two because it eliminates the primary factor responsible for our preventable suffering and death at its source.

Achieving our third level of freedom will be directly proportional to our intellectual evolutionary transition to a predator free society. This third level, referred to in this book as true freedom, can only occur in the environmental conditions of a predator free social structure void of competitions for survival. Both chains of Capitalism must be broken to provide true freedom of mind and body, and then we'll get a chance to see the level of compassion and creative skills our species is really capable of.

Our hardwired instincts and social conditioning can make it difficult to imagine a life without predatory conflicts, but as our picture puzzle acquires new piece of factual knowledge the path to true freedom will become easier to see. As our understanding of this evolutionary transition grows and more people reject their capitalistic exploitation our definition of the American dream will also need to change to reflect our new ambitions and motivations.

Once the working-class masses realize that we have the power to end our predatory existence, we will have a new goal to achieve, a new standard for the American dream. Not just a dream for the more fortunate capitalistic competitors but instead something all people may benefit from. I feel with power and wisdom comes responsibility and an inherent obligation to help others less fortunate. We the people of America have one of the greatest opportunities our species has ever encountered during our entire evolutionary development.

To be the first country to accelerate our transition to a predator free society will be an extraordinary accomplishment. Now that's the kind of healthy competition our nations should be conducting. Can I play? Our people have been dreaming of freedom and prosperity for thousands of years all leading up to this moment in time when our species is finally capable of understanding and accelerating this transition. The American dream, or at least the desire for true freedom and prosperity is so universal among all people around the world, we may need to rename it "The Human Dream". And we the people of America can help make that dream come true.

7. Communicating our need for true freedom

Communicating our need for true freedom will be a crucial first step to accelerating our evolutionary transition to a predator free society. A multi-pronged communications strategy is needed to educate the general public as to the primary differences between our past and current predatory social economic structures and non-predatory based society. This will allow more people to make an informed decision as to which environmental conditions they would prefer for their family and the future of our species. This book will provide the first prong in our communication strategy and others will follow as needed.

The TFT website will provide a second prong offering a wide variety of multimedia information about the philosophical beliefs of a predator free society and the need to provide true freedom to all people as a human right and not a privilege to compete for. A third prong and possibly the most effective way to communicate our message of true freedom, is by creating a wide variety of advanced technical products for sale to the public. Nothing seems to grab the attention of the general public like advanced technologies and new products doing things no one has ever seen before. Even people condition by Capitalism to not care about other competitors or saving our species future are fascinated by new technologies. A fourth prong can focus on audio and visual musical recordings as well as cinematic presentations and documentaries providing information and entertainment with each work of art. Interactive multimedia DVDs and applications for smart phones and tablets could be considered a fifth prong.

All prongs of this communication strategy can help provide information about a predator free society to an international community allowing people all over the world to consider their options. During the process of actively promoting this communication strategy a sixth prong of unpredictable nature should begin to develop. If the desire to end our predatory past and make the transition to a predator free future is strong enough among all people around the world then our advanced communication technologies and social networks should naturally accelerate the process through what use to be called, word of mouth.

It's difficult to express the magnitude of our evolutionary transition. This would be the first time any species has taken control of their intellectual evolutionary development by using recently developed global communication technologies. I guess that could explain why our transition to a predator free society didn't happen generations ago. Now it's up to us to make sure our future generations won't be struggling to understand why our people are still suffering and dying needlessly, while at the same time our global wealth and survival resources are mysteriously finding their way to the most fortunate few of our species.

Before we attempt to communicate to others the importance of our evolutionary transition to a predator free society, we must first accept that not all people will understand or agree this change is necessary. Any form of change can be difficult for creatures of habit like us humans so it's understandable how an evolutionary transition of this magnitude will take some getting use to. Even though we inherently know a big out-of-the-box solution will be necessary to correct our global inequality, many people will still resist change once presented with the option. The effects of the collective Stockholm syndrome will become more evident at this time. The people most likely to resist change will fall into certain demographic groups. For example our more successful capitalistic competitors that benefit most from our current predatory social structure may prefer to keep things just the way they are for as long as possible. After all it took our top predators generations to socially engineer our global societies into a masterpiece of capitalistic exploitation.

Many individuals fully under the control of a subjective reality to serve the ruling class individuals representing Gods and governments will emotionally and possibly violently reject any factual knowledge contrary to their conditioning. Communicating the practical advantages of ending our predatory exploitation will be far easier when talking to the younger members of families induced with subjective realities, as they have not been fully conditioned to reject factual knowledge yet.

When we communicate our need for true freedom to others and help them see the factual differences between our predatory past and predator free future, we're actually helping them break their first chain of Capitalism. Once more individuals break their first chain of Capitalism, the level of respectful requests to accelerate our transition to a national predator free society will increase in frequency and intensity. Our humble requests for true freedom, equality and prosperity for all people as equals will not need to turn into demands for justice. Once our social options are better known, we the people can simply make a collective decision to accelerate our intellectual evolutionary development. Even, though we have been suffering through the tragic symptoms of a predatory social structure for thousands of years. We should take comfort in the knowledge that we, the working class resources of the world have the ultimate power to end this phase of our intellectual evolution, and it all starts with our ability to communicate the importance of this transition to others.

8. TFT website, truefreedomtechnologies.org

The TFT website will be our magic window to the world. This website will provide information on all eight divisions of the nonprofit organization TFT and the philosophical beliefs of a predator free society. Progress reports towards designing and prototyping of the first technically advanced ACI (Automated Community Infrastructure) will also be posted on the TFT website. This magic window will allow visitors the option of choosing which questions about the predator free society philosophy and technologies they would like answered in short videos or perhaps a more extensive webcast.

The website will be the place to order this book in as many variations and languages our resources will allow, other promotional products like shirts, mugs and hats may also be available. There will be an effort to provide this website in different languages allowing our evolutionary transition to begin accelerating in other countries around the world. The advanced technical and artistic products designed and created by a predator free society may also be browsed and bought online as these items become available.

Sending words and images through the air, magic windows showing glimpses of our creative minds, these things that could have only been the work of Gods in the past, has now become commonplace among us mere mortals, at least the ones that can afford computers and smartphones. It's easy to take our advanced communication technologies for granted nowadays, but sometimes I can actually remember there was a time before computers and the Internet. It's hard to overstate the advantages of having access to a global communications network and how it will help accelerate our evolutionary transition to a predator free society.

Any predator free society attempted in the past could have easily been stopped at the local level by destroying factual knowledge, replacing it with a subjective reality and limiting the education of the working class resource thereby ensuring their continued exploitation. Even though defunding public education is still used as an effective management tool by ruling class top predators to prevent the intellectual enlightenment of their working class resource. Our communication technologies are finally allowing us to break the subjective realities that have controlled our thoughts and actions for thousands of years. This will truly be the most wondrous transition for the evolution of our species and the TFT website is intended to chronicle and facilitate this process.

Information on the economic structure of the TFT nonprofit organization will be available on this website showing how it is designed to break the second chain of Capitalism for the members of a predator free society. Each of the eight specialized divisions within the TFT social economic structure will have dedicated web pages showing things like the daily activities of a community member working in that area, 3-D models of new product designs, prototype testing videos etc. to offer website visitors a better understanding of what the environmental conditions of a truly free society would be like. Because all eight divisions are conveniently located within the ACI a walk-through presentation video showing a typical public tour will also be offered online for visitors all over the world to objectively consider and compare with the predatory social structures of our past and present. The TFT website will offer online training videos to help prepare new members making the transition to a predator free society. Once a new ACI is ready to move into new community members must be matched with their primary division interests to create a balanced and complementary set of creative skills.

The skill levels of the first predator free members must be high enough to ensure its initial success. However, after the self-replication process begins to expand the network of ACIs this will become less significant. The TFT website will post a set of criteria for prospective members to become familiar with. An online enrollment system will be made available as a pre-selection process to create a group of individuals and families to choose from. It is an objective of TFT to help individuals and families most devastated by our capitalistic social structure first and then work our way up to the more successful competitors. Allowing the Americans living in capitalistic poverty to make the transition first will reduce our national welfare costs while creating a technically advanced workforce with a unified objective to offer true freedom and prosperity to other people in need. The TFT website will help facilitate this transition while providing progress and information updates.

The publication of this book will initiate and announce the beginning of TFT and the predator free movement to accelerate the intellectual evolutionary development of our species. We can consider this process to be phase 1. Using book sales for an initial income and other tax-exempt donations, we hope the website will announce the beginning of phase 2, consisting of a small possibly mobile research and development system. Many of the primary components integrated into the first ACI can be virtually prototyped and tested at this time. Smaller components can be prototyped as a finished product and tested for production.

Different automated construction technologies will be tested to create reinforced concrete domes and archways. After these surface structures are tested for use in a subsurface ACI they can be made into additional design studios and office space. After many of the ACI components have been completed and certified for installation, the TFT website will post the beginning of phase 3 consisting of a larger R&D facility located in the southwest United States. This facility will serve as a proto-ACI just large enough to test and supply larger infrastructure components and create the systems necessary to furnish the first ACI 1.0. The location of this facility must also allow for the creation of adjoining 500-foot square ACIs.

Once the subsurface infrastructure components of the proto-community have been tested, the TFT website will hopefully announce the beginning of phase 4, the construction of the first technically advanced prototype ACI 1.0. After the proto-community has created the first functioning ACI it will then provide assistance during the first replication process. The first ACI will then assist the second with their initial replication process while simultaneously starting their next ACI.

If all goes well the self-replication process designed into the predator free society will begin the exponential expansion of technically advanced ACIs while the proto-community will remain as the primary research and development facility for TFT. Any discoveries made by R&D to improve the prototype ACI or its modular subsystems will be made available for download into standardized manufacturing systems located within each community. Each of the eight TFT divisions will receive regular updates with things like new product suggestions and system efficiency improvements. The TFT website will serve a dual function, to inform the public of their social structure options and provide members of a predator free society secure online access to their community services. Any sensitive design challenge projects involving new products or matters regarding the security systems of an ACI may use more secure means of transportation not accessible online or available to the public.

One day in the not-too-distant future, the TFT website would really like to report the beginning of phase 5, where we the people have used our democracy to convince our leaders in government that some of the national wealth we generate should be allocated towards ending our predatory social structure and helping our citizens make the transition from capitalistic poverty to a predator free society. I know… it seems like an impossible task, after all our top predators spent generations securing their dominance within our capitalistic society, what in the world would make them give up the social inequity they worked so hard to achieve? The simple answer to this question is, we the people.

However, a more complicated explanation would be that the development of our intellectual evolution has finally reached the point where our predatory social structure is no longer acceptable, at least for the 99% of our species designated as working class prey. Nothing can stop the will of the people once they realize their salvation is at hand and the solutions to achieving it is within their realm of control. Just us mere mortals will have achieved what all the imaginary Gods of the past and present could not, true freedom and prosperity for our people. From such humble beginnings, great things can be achieved.

Conclusion

There is always so much more to say, especially for a subject of this complexity, but at some point I guess an author must be satisfied with good enough for now. I'm sure right after publishing I will think of improvements to the solutions offered for consideration in this book. Like the course of our predatory evolution itself, the solutions to correct our social dysfunctions must also adapt to eliminate this threat from destroying any future prosperity for the working class majority of our species. The good news is our species natural evolutionary transition from non-intelligent creatures functioning purely on hardwired instincts, to enlightened human beings capable of using our intellectual survival trait to provide true freedom and prosperity for all people, is accelerating. Our mission as members of a predator free society or any individuals wanting to help create one for the future of our species is to further accelerate this transition process thereby reducing the preventable suffering and death of millions of people unable to compete for their capitalistic survival.

It has occurred to me that the information in this book could be used by top predators to better manipulate us working-class prey, and how knowledge is more often used to exploit the uninformed masses rather than unifying an evolving species into breaking their hardwired predatory instincts and subjective realities. I guess you could say it would be my worst nightmare to have this knowledge be used for evil and strengthening the chokehold our capitalistic masters have on our minds and bodies instead of accelerating our transition to a predator free social structure. In the past not only could this knowledge not reach the working-class masses but if released would only be read and understood by the well-educated top predators and then extinguished before any chance social equality could be achieved. But things are different now.

The natural progression of our intellectual development would indicate that a large enough minority of our global populations will understand this knowledge and agree this is the time for our species to make the transition to a predator free society. Our top predators have quite naturally ruled our species since the beginning of our existence. However, now that we have gained intelligence we don't have to do that anymore, we can finally end the root cause of our preventable suffering and death by eliminating predatory conflicts as the social standard for survival. Knowing all this I'm still counting on we the people and other educated working-class resources around the world to make an objective decision based on factual knowledge to end their capitalistic exploitation.

I must also sadly acknowledge millions of our people needing true salvation of mind more than body, will be unable to break the psychological conditioning of their subjective realities and thus will continue their predatory exploitation as the only form of existence they have ever known. This test to determine the intellectual progress of our species may be the first of its kind especially when considering the predatory exploitation of millions of our people could be avoided based on the results. Knowing the consequences this could have for our species the suspense has become intense.

It has been known for many years that knowledge would be the power to end our predatory existence. And that knowledge is simply this; our species has outgrown the need to continue our predatory social structure, we the people do not need to compete against one another for our survival any more. The least fortunate many do not need to serve the most fortunate few. We do not need to remain dependent upon the top predators of our species for our basic survival necessities. And that we the people are the true strength of our countries, we are the wellspring from which power and wealth flows from the working class many to the ruling class few. Of all the knowledge our capitalistic masters don't want us to know, the most important thing is simply that we little people possess the greatest power of all, the ability to end the predatory social structure that has dominated our species development since the beginning of our existence

I realized the difficulty involved trying to change a social standard hardwired into our genetic memory, something that we have been environmentally conditioned to accept from birth. However, through a better understanding of the processes involved we will gain control of our intellectual evolutionary development and eventually achieve true freedom and prosperity for all people as equals. The power to achieve this amazing task is within us. It's something that can never be taken away only suppressed by inducing subjective realities and masterful works of social engineering designed to condition us into accepting our systematic exploitation as the best quality of life we could hope for.

I also realize these forms of psychological manipulation and predatory control over a working-class population, have been enormously successful at suppressing the intellectual development of our species for thousands of years. But should we let little things like this weaken our resolve towards accomplishing our ultimate goal of social equality and universal prosperity for the future of our species, I don't think so. Our deliberate and controlled evolutionary transition to a predator free society will mark the birth of a new enlightened species with emerging possibilities still beyond our ability to imagine. These are the things I see for our future. "You may say I'm a dreamer, but I'm not the only one", and like John Lennon said, "I hope someday you'll join us and the world will live as one".

Authors Bio

Marco D'Anna is the author of Breaking the Chains of Capitalism, An Evolutionary Journey to True Freedom and founder of the nonprofit organization True Freedom Technologies. Both of these projects are part of a larger plan of action to help inform the general public about the importance of ending our predatory evolution and to offer an alternative to capitalism. After a discovery process identified the primary factor responsible for the most preventable suffering and death throughout the evolutionary development of our species, it became apparent that an integrated social and technical solution would be required to correct the problem at its source.

By creating the first technically advanced automated community infrastructure capable of supporting a predator free society, Marco hopes to show the social economic advantages of cooperation for the benefit of all people as equals, over forced competition among the many to serve the most fortunate few. Over the last few years Marco has pre-designed many of the automated manufacturing, maintenance, infrastructure, transportation and energy systems needed to support community members and their mission objective to help others still competing for their survival under capitalism. Marco has dedicated all book sales to help True Freedom Technologies accomplish its mission objectives.

Glossary

ACI (Automated Community Infrastructure): is a subsurface infrastructure designed to support a predator free society, survive all forms of natural and man-made disasters and provide basic survival necessities for all permanent and visiting residents for hundreds of years.

Artificial selection: is a process by which humans control the evolutionary development of a plant or animal species to allow only individuals with desirable traits to reproduce.

Biological evolutionary development: is a process using mostly natural selection where by some genetic attributes provide survival advantages to changing environmental conditions. These attributes allow some members of the species to survive long enough to reproduce, and pass on that survival trait to their young, while others without the attribute die before they reproduce.

Capitalistic exploitation: is a form of exploitation that utilizes the free-market system and superior intellectual skills as predatory tools to take advantage of less fortunate working-class people forced to compete against one another for their survival.

Factual knowledge: is information that can be verified with things that exist in reality, something scientifically repeatable and empirical in nature.

First chain of Capitalism: is a metaphorical reference to the psychological conditioning inherent in a predatory social structure to accept our Capitalistic exploitation with emotional satisfaction and national pride.

Genetic memory: (Also known as Ancestral memory), is a form of memory encoded in our genetic makeup that exists at birth and not learned by environmental experiences. It provides us with behavioral instincts and fast involuntary responses to environmental conditions that may threaten our survival.

Hardwired survival instincts: are behavioral survival traits encoded in our genetic memory that aid in our competition for survival.

Human predators: are members of the human species that uses their superior size, strength, speed or intelligence against others as a predatory tool for survival.

Intellectual evolutionary development: is a process where by lifeforms progressively adapt to their changing environmental conditions using an intellectual survival trait. The adaptation knowledge is generally enhanced and passed down from one generation to the next. This process gives us the ability to understand and end the predatory evolution of our species.

Jerusalem syndrome: is a psychological phenomenon whereby people of faith loose their sense of reality when visiting the holy city of Jerusalem.

Objective reality: is a reality whereby an individual will require factual knowledge to make decisions and take actions in their life.

Predator Free Society: is a social structure where all survival necessities are provided by advanced technologies as a human right and competitions against others for personal gain are replaced with cooperation to increase the quality of life for all people as equals.

Predatory social structure: is a social structure whereby superior size, strength, speed or intelligence, wealth and power are used to provide a predatory advantage against other life forms also competing for their survival. It creates the environmental conditions that perpetuate our predatory evolution and the root cause of our preventable suffering and death.

Punctuated equilibrium: is the belief that after log periods of time rapid evolutionary changes can take place as a species is forced or allowed to adapt to new environmental conditions.

Psychological conditioning: is the act of altering an individual or an entire populations decision making process by manipulating their environmental conditions. Used as a management tool to control a working class resource and socially legitimize their systematic exploitation.

Ruling class elite: is the wealthiest and most powerful top 1% of our populations that often socially engineer our societies for more efficient capitalistic exploitation of the working-class resource.

Second chain of Capitalism: is a metaphorical reference to the social economic engineering of our societies to keep the working-class resource dependent upon the ruling class top predators for our basic survival necessities.

Social dysfunction: is any social activity or ritual that allows and or legitimizes the exploitation of others for profit and power. The socially accepted standard of using our intellectual skills to compete against each other for our survival would be considered a structural social dysfunction. Allowing our predatory instincts and subjective beliefs determine our social evolution, is a fundamental dysfunction responsible for the greatest preventable suffering and death throughout our existence.

Subjective belief: is a slight to extreme belief in things that are not factually valid and or do not exist in reality. Subjective beliefs are induced as a tool for manipulating the working-class many into serving the ruling class few.

Subjective reality: is a reality where by an individual will not require factual knowledge to make decisions and take actions in their life. People under the control of an induced subjective reality may commit atrocities following their belief in things that are not real.

Index

E

F

G

H

M

Q

R

S

T

W

Z